# Delhi &
# Northwest India

Vanessa Betts & Victoria McCulloch

# Credits

**Footprint credits**
**Editor**: Stephanie Rebello
**Production and layout**: Emma Bryers
**Maps**: Kevin Feeney

**Publisher**: Patrick Dawson
**Managing Editor**: Felicity Laughton
**Advertising**: Elizabeth Taylor
**Sales and marketing**: Kirsty Holmes

**Photography credits**
**Front cover**: Mikadun/Shutterstock
**Back cover**: Dmitry Rukhlenko/Dreamstime

Printed in Great Britain by Alphaset,
Surbiton, Surrey

Every effort has been made to ensure that
the facts in this guidebook are accurate.
However, travellers should still obtain advice
from consulates, airlines, etc, about travel
and visa requirements before travelling.
The authors and publishers cannot accept
responsibility for any loss, injury or
inconvenience however caused.

**Publishing information**
Footprint *Focus Delhi & Northwest India*
1st edition
© Footprint Handbooks Ltd
February 2014

ISBN: 978 1 909268 75 3
CIP DATA: A catalogue record for this book
is available from the British Library

® Footprint Handbooks and the Footprint
mark are a registered trademark of
Footprint Handbooks Ltd

Published by Footprint
6 Riverside Court
Lower Bristol Road
Bath BA2 3DZ, UK
T +44 (0)1225 469141
F +44 (0)1225 469461
footprinttravelguides.com

Distributed in the USA by Globe Pequot
Press, Guilford, Connecticut

# Contents

**5 Introduction**
4 *Map: Delhi and Northwest India*

**6 Planning your trip**
6 Best time to visit Delhi and Northwest India
6 Getting to Delhi and Northwest India
7 Transport in Delhi and Northwest India
12 Where to stay in Delhi and Northwest India
13 Food and drink in Delhi and Northwest India
15 Festivals in Delhi and Northwest India
17 Essentials A-Z

**23 Delhi**
27 **Places in Delhi**
28 *Map: Old Delhi*
34 *Map: New Delhi*
38 *Map: Connaught Place*

**59 North from Delhi**
60 **Chandigarh and around**
61 *Map: Chandigarh*
67 **Amritsar and around**
68 *Map: Amritsar*
71 *Map: Golden Temple*
76 **Southern Himachal**
76 *Map: Shimla*
78 *Map: Shimla Mall and The Ridge*
87 **Kinnaur and Spiti**
88 *Map: Kinnaur and Spiti*
100 **Kullu Valley**
102 *Map: Kullu Valley treks*
105 *Map: Manali*
116 **Lahaul and the Manali–Leh road**
117 *Map: Manali to Leh*
122 **Northern Himachal**
123 *Map: Dharamshala*
125 *Map: McLeodganj*
129 *Map: Dalhousie*
143 **Trekking in Himachal**

**149 Jammu and Kashmir**
150 **Kashmir Valley**
152 *Map: Srinagar*
160 *Map: Ladakh and Zanskar*
171 **Ladakh**
173 *Map: Leh Orientation*
174 *Map: Leh centre*

**197 Footnotes**
198 Index

Capped by the mightiest mountain range on earth, the northwest region of India encompasses the most dramatic and beautiful terrain in all the country. Many travellers come to experience the great outdoors, whether trekking, skiing, rafting, climbing, or some seriously challenging biking. But the region is equally rich in cultural heritage, with Buddhism the dominant religion in mellow Ladakh, and pockets of Tibetan refugees scattered throughout the Himalayan foothills. The Kashmir Valley is another experience entirely, with remarkable tiered mosques and sufi shrines covered in colourfully painted papier mâché. A visit to the sublime Golden Temple at Amritsar – the holiest place of the Sikhs – further enriches a journey to or from the hills.

Perhaps the most striking landscapes are Ladakh's high-altitude plateaux and Spiti's narrow gorges – contrasting desert dust with sharp blue skies and snowy peaks, and where monasteries perch by ribboned rivers. The apple orchards and pine-clad hills of Himachal Pradesh and the lotus-fringed lakes of Kashmir are a verdant antidote to these harsh terrains.

The delightful houseboats in Srinagar hark back to the colonial era, and staying aboard for couple of nights is a highlight of any visit to the northwest. Relics of the Raj can also be seen in Himachal Pradesh, especially in quaint Dalhousie and Mussoorie or the capital, Shimla, where churches, clubs and promenades now throng with Indian tourists escaping Delhi's heat.

But be sure to leave some time for the plains – to discover the unique architecture of Chandigarh and the inspiring Mughal monuments and ancient cities of Delhi. And the road from Leh, either via Manali or Srinagar, might leave you in need of a rooftop beer in Hauz Khas or high tea at the Imperial Hotel.

# Planning your trip

## Best time to visit Delhi and Northwest India

The best time to visit Delhi, the Punjab and Himachal Pradesh is from October to May. It is intensely hot on the plains in June and then humidity builds up as the monsoon approaches. The monsoon season lasts from between two and three months, from July to September, with the east seeing the strongest and longest rains in the Himalayan foothills. If you are travelling in Himachal Pradesh and Kashmir during the monsoon you need to be prepared for extended periods of torrential rain and disruption to travel. Ladakh, however, being beyond the monsoon line, is almost always visited only in the summer season (May-September) when there are clear skies and the road is open. Hot summers are followed by much cooler winters, and even in Delhi the temperatures can plummet to near freezing in January. Some of the region's great festivals such as **Diwali** take place in the autumn and winter.

## Getting to Delhi and Northwest India

### Air

Most international flights arrive in Delhi or Mumbai. Some carriers permit 'open-jaw' travel, arriving in, and departing from, different cities in India. Some (eg **Air India**, **Jet Airways** or **British Airways**) have convenient non-stop flights from Europe, eg from London to Delhi, takes only nine hours.

You can fly to numerous destinations across India with **Jet Airways**, **Indigo** or **Spicejet**. The prices are very competitive if domestic flights are booked in conjunction with **Jet** on the international legs.

**From Europe** The UK remains the cheapest place in Europe for flights to India. From mainland Europe, major European flag carriers including **KLM** and **Lufthansa** fly to Delhi from their respective hub airports. In most cases the cheapest flights are with Middle Eastern or Central Asian airlines, transiting via airports in the Gulf. Several airlines from the Middle East (eg **Emirates**, **Gulf Air**, **Qatar Airways** and **Oman Air**) offer good discounts to Indian regional capitals from London, but fly via their hub cities, adding to the journey time. Consolidators in the UK can quote some competitive fares, such as www.skyscanner. net, www.ebookers.com, or **North South Travel** ⓘ *www.northsouthtravel.co.uk (profits to charity)*. In 2013 the cheapest return flights from Delhi to London started at around £500, but leapt to £900+ as you approached the high season of Christmas, New Year and Easter.

**From North America** From the east coast, several airlines including **Air India**, **Jet Airways**, **Continental** and **Delta** fly direct from New York to Delhi. **American** flies from Chicago. Discounted tickets on **British Airways**, **KLM**, **Lufthansa**, **Gulf Air** and **Kuwait Airways** are sold through agents although they will invariably fly via their country's capital cities. **Air India** flies from Los Angeles to Delhi and **Air Canada** operates from Vancouver. **Air Brokers International** ⓘ *www.airbrokers.com*, is competitive and reputable. **STA** ⓘ *www.statravel.co.uk*, has offices in many US cities, Toronto and Ontario. Student fares are also available from **Travel Cuts** ⓘ *www.travelcuts.com*, in Canada.

## Don't miss...

1 Qawwali singing at Nizamuddin's Tomb, Delhi, page 40.
2 The Heritage Walk around Qutb Minar and Mehrauli with Surekha Narain, Delhi, page 55.
3 Morning prayer at the Golden Temple, Amritsar, page 69.
4 A dip at the hot springs in Vashisht Temple, page 106.
5 Walking the Kora in Mcleodganj, page 124.
6 Sleeping on a houseboat in Srinagar, page 163.
7 The ancient murals of Alchi Monastery, page 180.
8 Nubra Valley's remote and friendly villages, page 183.

Numbers relate to the map on page 4.

**From Australasia** Qantas, Singapore Airlines, Thai Airways, Malaysian Airlines, Cathay Pacific and **Air India** are the principal airlines connecting the continents, although Qantas is the only one that flies direct, with services from Sydney to Mumbai. Singapore Airlines, with subsidiary Silk Air, offers the most flexibility. Low-cost carriers including **Air Asia** (via Kuala Lumpur), **Scoot** and **Tiger Airways** (Singapore) offer a similar choice of arrival airports at substantial savings. **STA** and **Flight Centre** offer discounted tickets from their branches in major cities in Australia and New Zealand.

**Airport information** The formalities on arrival in India have been streamlined during the last few years and the facilities at the international airports have greatly improved. However, arrival can still be a slow process and you may well find that there are delays of over an hour at immigration. When departing, note that you'll need to have a printout of your itinerary to get into the airport, and the security guards will only let you into the terminal within three hours of your flight.

    **Departure tax and passenger fees** Rs 500 is payable for all international departures other than those to neighbouring SAARC countries, when the tax is Rs 250. This is normally included in your international ticket; check when buying. Some airports have also begun charging a Passenger Service Fee or User Development Fee to each departing passenger. This is normally included in international tickets, but some domestic airlines have been reluctant to incorporate the charge. Keep some spare cash in rupees in case you need to pay the fee on arriving at the terminal.

## Transport in Delhi and Northwest India

### Air

India has a comprehensive network linking the major cities of the different states. Deregulation of the airline industry has had a transformative effect on travel within India, with a host of low-budget private carriers offering sometimes unbelievably cheap fares on an ever-expanding network of routes in a bid to woo the train-travelling middle class. Booking a couple of weeks in advance, you can expect to fly between Delhi and Leh for around US$100 one way including taxes, with three months' notice and flying with a no-frills airline can reduce the price to US$40.

The best way to get an idea of the current routes, carriers and fares is to use a third-party booking website such as **www.cleartrip.com**, **www.makemytrip.co.in**, **www.travelocity.com**, or **www.yatra.com**, although some of these refuse foreign credit cards. Tickets booked on these sites are typically issued as an email ticket or an SMS text message, though they must be converted to a paper ticket at the relevant carrier's airport offices before you will be allowed into the terminal. **Makemytrip.com** and **Travelocity.com** both accept international credit cards.

## Rail

Trains can still be the cheapest and most comfortable means of travelling long distances saving you hotel expenses on overnight journeys. It gives access to booking station Retiring Rooms, which can be useful from time to time. Above all, you have an ideal opportunity to meet local travellers and catch a glimpse of life on the ground. See also **www.indianrail.gov.in** and **www.erail.in**.

**High-speed trains** There are several air-conditioned 'high-speed' **Shatabdi** (or 'Century') **Express** for day travel, and **Rajdhani Express** ('Capital City') for overnight journeys. These cover large sections of the network but due to high demand you need to book them well in advance (up to 90 days). Meals and drinks are usually included.

**Classes A/c First Class**, available only on main routes, is very comfortable with two- or four-berth carpeted sleeper compartments with washbasin. As with all a/c sleeper accommodation, bedding is included, and the windows are tinted to the point of being almost impossible to see through. **A/c Sleeper**, two- and three-tier configurations (known as 2AC and 3AC), are clean and comfortable and popular with middle-class families; these are the safest carriages for women travelling alone. **A/c Executive Class**, with wide reclining seats, are available on many Shatabdi trains at double the price of the ordinary **a/c Chair Car** which are equally comfortable. **First Class (non-a/c)** is gradually being phased out, and is now restricted to a handful of routes in the south, but the run-down old carriages still provide a pleasant experience if you like open windows. **Second Class (non-a/c)**, two- and three-tier (commonly called **Sleeper**), provides exceptionally cheap and atmospheric travel, with basic padded vinyl seats and open windows that allow the sights and sounds of India (not to mention dust, insects and flecks of spittle expelled by passengers up front) to drift into the carriage. On long journeys Sleeper can be crowded and uncomfortable, and toilet facilities can be unpleasant; it is nearly always better to use the Indian-style squat loos rather than the Western-style ones as they are better maintained. At the bottom rung is **Unreserved Second Class**, with hard wooden benches. You can travel long distances for a trivial amount of money, but unreserved carriages are often ridiculously crowded, and getting off at your station may involve a battle of will and strength against the hordes trying to shove their way on.

**Internet services** Much information is available online at www.railtourismindia.com, www.indianrail.gov.in and www.trainenquiry.com, where you can check timetables (which change frequently), numbers, seat availability and even the running status of your train. E-tickets can be bought and printed at www.irctc.in, although the credit card process can be complicated, and at time of writing does not accept credit cards issued outside India. The best option is to use a third-party agent, such as www.makemytrip.com or www.cleartrip.com. An alternative is to seek a local agent who can sell e-tickets, and can save hours of hassle; simply present the printout to the ticket collector.

**Note** All train numbers now have five digits; in most cases, adding a '1' to the start of an old four-figure number will produce the new number. Otherwise, try your luck with the 'train number enquiry' search at www.indianrail.gov.in/inet_trnno_enq.html.

**Tickets and reservations** It is now possible to reserve tickets for virtually any train on the network from one of the 1000 computerized reservation centres across India. It is always best to book as far in advance as possible (usually up to 60 days). To reserve a seat on a particular train, note down the train's name, number and departure time and fill in a reservation form while you line up at the ticket window; you can use one form for up to four passengers. At busy stations the wait can take an hour or more. You can save a lot of time and effort by asking a travel agent to get your tickets for a fee of Rs 50-100. If the class you want is full, ask if special 'quotas' are available under any of **Indian Rail**'s special quotas. **Foreign Tourist Quota** (FTQ) reserves a small number of tickets on popular routes for overseas travellers; you need your passport and either an exchange certificate or ATM receipt to book tickets under FTQ. The other useful special quota is **Tatkal**, which releases a last-minute pool of tickets at 1000 on the day before the train departs. If the quota system can't help you, consider buying a 'wait list' ticket, as seats often become available close to the train's departure time; phone the station on the day of departure to check your ticket's status. If you don't have a reservation for a particular train but carry an **Indrail Pass**, you may get one by arriving three hours early. Be wary of touts at the station offering tickets, hotels or exchange.

**Timetables** Regional timetables are available cheaply from station bookstalls; the monthly *Indian Bradshaw* is sold in principal stations. The handy *Trains at a Glance* (Rs 30) lists popular trains likely to be used by most foreign travellers and is available at stalls at Indian railway stations and in the UK from **SDEL**.

## Road

Road travel is sometimes the only choice for reaching many of the places of outstanding interest, particularly national parks or isolated tourist sites. For the uninitiated, travel by road can also be a worrying experience because of the apparent absence of conventional traffic regulations. Vehicles drive on the left – in theory. Routes around the major cities are usually crowded with lorry traffic, especially at night, and the main roads are often poor and slow. There are a few motorway-style expressways, but most main roads are single track.

**Bus** Buses now reach virtually every part of India, offering a cheap, if often uncomfortable, means of visiting places off the rail network. Very few villages are now more than 2-3 km from a bus stop. Services are run by the State Corporation from the State Bus Stand (and private companies, which often have offices nearby). The private companies allow advance reservations, including e-tickets (check www.redbus.in and www.viaworld.in) and, although tickets prices are a little higher, they have fewer stops and are a bit more comfortable. If you travel on a 'sleeper' bus, choose a lower berth near the front of the bus as the upper berths are almost always really uncomfortable on bumpy roads.

**Bus categories** Though comfortable for sightseeing trips, apart from the very best 'sleeper coaches' even **air-conditioned luxury coaches** can be very uncomfortable for really long journeys. Often the air conditioning is very cold so wrap up. **Express buses** run over long distances (frequently overnight) and are often called 'video coaches. They can be an appalling experience unless you appreciate loud film music blasting through the night.

Ear plugs and eye masks may ease the pain. They rarely average more than 45 kph. **Local buses** are often very crowded, quite bumpy, slow and usually poorly maintained. However, over short distances, they can be a very cheap, friendly and easy way of getting about. Even where signboards are not in English someone will usually give you directions. Many larger towns have **minibus** services which charge a little more than the buses and pick up and drop passengers on request. Again very crowded, and with restricted headroom, they are the fastest way of getting about many of the larger towns.

**Bus travel tips** Some towns have different bus stations for different destinations. Booking on major long-distance routes is now computerized. Book in advance where possible and avoid the back of the bus where it can be very bumpy. If your destination is only served by a local bus you may do better to take the Express bus and 'persuade' the driver, with a tip in advance, to stop where you want to get off. You will have to pay the full fare to the first stop beyond your destination but you will get there faster and more comfortably.

**Car** A car provides a chance to travel off the beaten track, and gives unrivalled opportunities for seeing something of India's great variety of villages and small towns. Until recently, the most widely used hire car was the Hindustan Ambassador. However, except for the newest model, they are often very unreliable, and although they still have their devotees, many find them uncomfortable for long journeys. Ambassadors are gradually giving way to more efficient (and boring) Tata and Toyota models with mod-cons like optional air conditioning – and seat belts. A handful of international agencies offer self-drive car hire (Avis, Sixt), but India's majestically anarchic traffic culture is not for the faint-hearted.

**Car hire** Hiring a car and driver is the most comfortable and efficient way to cover short to medium distances, and although prices have increased sharply in recent years car travel in India is still a bargain by Western standards. A car shared by three or four can be very good value. Even if you're travelling on a modest budget a day's car hire can help take the sting out of an arduous journey, allowing you to go sightseeing along the way without looking for somewhere to stash your bags. Local drivers often know their way around an area much better than drivers from other states, so where possible it is a good idea to get a local driver who speaks the state language, in addition to being able to communicate with you. The best way to guarantee a driver who speaks good English is to book in advance with a professional travel agency, either in India or in your home country. You can, if you choose, arrange car hire informally by asking around at taxi stands, but don't expect your driver to speak anything more than rudimentary English.

On pre-arranged overnight trips the fee you pay will normally include fuel and interstate taxes – check before you pay – and a wage for the driver. Drivers are responsible for their expenses, including meals (and the pervasive servant-master culture in India means that most will choose to sit separately from you at meal times). Some tourist hotels provide rooms for drivers, but they often choose to sleep in the car overnight to save money. In some areas drivers also seek to increase their earnings by taking you to hotels and shops where they earn a handsome commission; these are generally hugely overpriced and poor alternatives to the hotels recommended in this book, so don't be afraid to say no and insist on your choice of accommodation. If you feel inclined, a tip at the end of the tour of Rs 100 per day is perfectly acceptable. Be sure to check carefully the mileage at the beginning and end of the trip.

| | Tata Indica non-a/c | Tata Indigo non-a/c | Hyundai Accent a/c | Toyota Innova |
|---|---|---|---|---|
| 8 hrs/80 km | Rs 1200 | Rs 1600 | Rs 2200 | Rs 2500 |
| Extra km | Rs 8 | Rs 10 | Rs 15 | Rs 15 |
| Extra hour | Rs 80 | Rs 100 | Rs 200 | Rs 180 |
| **Out of town** | | | | |
| Per km | Rs 8 | Rs 10 | Rs 15 | Rs 15 |
| Night halt | Rs 200 | Rs 200 | Rs 300 | Rs 250 |

**Taxi** Taxi travel in India is a great bargain, and in most cities you can take a taxi from the airport to the centre for under US$10. Yellow-top taxis in cities and large towns are metered, although tariffs change frequently. These changes are shown on a fare chart which should be read in conjunction with the meter reading. Increased night-time rates apply in most cities, and there might be a small charge for luggage. Insist on the taxi meter being flagged in your presence. If the driver refuses, the official advice is to contact the police. This may not work, but it is worth trying. When a taxi doesn't have a meter, you will need to fix the fare before starting the journey. Ask at your hotel desk for a guide price.

At stations and airports it is often possible to share taxis to a central point. It is worth looking for fellow passengers who may be travelling in your direction and get a pre-paid taxi. At night, always have a clear idea of where you want to go and insist on being taken there. Taxi drivers may try to convince you that the hotel you have chosen 'closed three years ago' or is 'completely full'. Say that you have a reservation.

**Rickshaw** Auto-rickshaws (autos) are almost universally available in towns across North India and are the cheapest and most convenient way of getting about. It is best to walk a short distance away from a hotel gate before picking up an auto to avoid paying an inflated rate. In addition to using them for short journeys it is often possible to hire them by the hour, or for a half or full day's sightseeing. In some areas younger drivers who speak some English and know their local area well may want to show you around. However, rickshaw drivers are often paid a commission by hotels, restaurants and gift shops so advice is not always impartial. Drivers generally refuse to use a meter, often quote a ridiculous price or may sometimes stop short of your destination. If you have real problems it can help to note down the vehicle licence number and threaten to go to the police. Beware of some rickshaw drivers who show the fare chart for taxis.

Cycle-rickshaws are in most towns and cities (unless they are hilly) and are a common means of covering short distances (less than 4 km). Agree a price before setting off, or ask a local what the fare should be and hand over the money when you climb down. Less than 1 km should cost Rs 10.

## Where to stay in Delhi and Northwest India

India has an enormous range of accommodation. You can stay safely and very cheaply by Western standards. In the cities there are also high-quality hotels, offering a full range of facilities; in small centres hotels are much more variable. A lifeline for budget travellers are backpacker hotels, found in all major cities and traveller destinations, and nearly always located within walking distance to train and bus stations. Facilities can be sparse – a bed, a few hooks to hang clothes, and a shared bathroom – but they are great places to meet other travellers, and standards are quite good if there's competition in the area. Try to insist on clean sheets (ask for a 'top sheet', as often only a pillow case and one sheet are provided). Another mainstay for economy travellers is the ubiquitous Indian 'business hotel': anonymous but generally decent value, with en suite rooms of variable cleanliness and a TV showing 110 channels of cricket and Bollywood MTV. At the top end, alongside international chains, India boasts several home-grown hotel chains, best of which are the exceptional heritage and palace hotels operated by the **Taj** group. In the peak season (October to April) bookings can be extremely heavy in popular destinations. It is possible to book in advance by phone or email, but double check your reservation, and always try to arrive as early as possible in the day.

### Hotels
**Price categories** The category codes used in this book are based on prices of double rooms excluding taxes. They are **not** star ratings and individual facilities vary considerably. The most expensive hotels charge in US dollars only. Expect to pay more in Delhi for all categories. Prices away from large cities tend to be lower for comparable hotels.

Large discounts are often made by hotels in all categories out of season. Always ask if any is available. You may also request the 10-15% agent's commission to be deducted from your bill if you book direct. Clarify whether the agreed figure includes all taxes.

**Taxes** In general most hotel rooms rated at Rs 3000 or above are subject to a tax of 10%. Many states levy an additional luxury tax of 10-25%, and some hotels add a service charge of 10% on top of this. Taxes are not necessarily payable on meals, so it is worth settling your meals bill separately. Most hotels in the **$$** category and above accept payment by credit card. Check your final bill carefully the evening before departure, and keep all receipts.

**Hotel facilities** You have to be prepared for difficulties which are uncommon in the West. It is best to inspect the room and check that all equipment (air conditioning, TV, water heater, flush) works before checking in at a modest hotel. Don't expect any but the most expensive or tourist-savvy hotels to fit a top sheet to the bed.

In some states **power cuts** are common, or hot water may be restricted to certain times of day. The largest hotels have their own generators but it is best to carry a good torch.

In some regions **water supply** is rationed periodically. Keep a bucket filled to use for flushing the toilet during water cuts. Occasionally, tap water may be discoloured due to rusty tanks. During the cold weather and in hill stations, hot water will be available at certain times of the day, sometimes in buckets, but is usually very restricted in quantity.

Hotels close to temples can be very **noisy**, especially during festivals. Music blares from loudspeakers late at night and from very early in the morning, often making sleep impossible. Mosques call the faithful to prayers at dawn. Some find ear plugs helpful.

## Price codes

**Where to stay**

$$$$ over US$150    $$$ US$66-150
$$ US$30-65    $ under US$30
For a double room in high season, excluding taxes.

**Restaurants**

$$$ over US$12    $$ US$6-12    $ under US$6
For a two-course meal for one person, excluding drinks and service charge.

Modest hotels may not have their own restaurant but will often offer 'room service', bringing in food from outside. In temple towns, restaurants may only serve vegetarian food.

Some hotels offer 24-hour checkout, meaning you can keep the room a full 24 hours from the time you arrive – a great option if you arrive in the afternoon and want to spend the morning sightseeing.

**Homestays**

At the upmarket end, increasing numbers of travellers are keen to stay in private homes and guesthouses, opting not to book large hotel chains that keep you at arm's length from a culture. Instead, travellers get home-cooked meals in heritage houses and learn about a country through conversation with often fascinating hosts. Delhi has many new and smart family-run B&Bs springing up. Tourist offices have lists of families with more modest homestays.

## Food and drink in Delhi and Northwest India

**Food**

You find just as much variety in dishes crossing India as you would on an equivalent journey across Europe. Combinations of spices give each region its distinctive flavour.

The larger hotels, open to non-residents, often offer **buffet** lunches with Indian, Western and sometimes Chinese dishes. These can be good value (Rs 400-500; but Rs 850 in the top grades) and can provide a welcome, comfortable break in the cool. There can, however, be considerable health risks if food is kept warm for long periods, especially if turnover at the buffet is slow.

It is essential to be very careful since food hygiene may be poor, flies abound and refrigeration in the hot weather may be inadequate and intermittent because of power cuts. It is best to eat only freshly prepared food by ordering from the menu (especially meat and fish dishes). Avoid salads and cut fruit, unless the menu advertises that they have been washed in mineral water.

If you are unused to spicy food, go slow. Food is often spicier when you eat with families or at local places. Popular local restaurants are obvious from the number of people eating in them. Try a traditional *thali*, which is a complete meal served on a large stainless steel plate. Several preparations, placed in small bowls, surround the central serving of wholewheat chapati and rice. A vegetarian *thali* would include *dhal* (lentils), two or three curries (which can be quite hot) and crisp poppadums. A variety of pickles are offered –

mango and lime are two of the most popular. These can be exceptionally hot, and are designed to be taken in minute quantities alongside the main dishes. Plain *dahi* (yoghurt), or *raita*, usually acts as a bland 'cooler'. Simple *dhabas* (rustic roadside eateries) are an alternative experience for sampling authentic local dishes.

Many city restaurants and backpacker eateries offer a choice of so-called **European options** such as toasted sandwiches, stuffed pancakes, apple pies, fruit crumbles and cheesecakes. Italian favourites (pizzas, pastas) can be very different from what you are used to, although **ice creams** can be exceptionally good; there are excellent Indian ones as well as some international brands.

India has many delicious tropical **fruits**. Some are seasonal (eg mangoes, pineapples and lychees), while others (eg bananas, grapes and oranges) are available throughout the year. It is safe to eat the ones you can wash and peel.

In cities and larger towns, you will see all types of regional Indian food on the menus, with some restaurants specializing in South Indian food such as *dosas*, *uttapams* and *idlis*. North Indian kebabs and the richer flavoursome cuisine of Lucknow are also worth seeking out. The local Himachali food uses yoghurt to temper the spices – delicious – while in the Punjab you will find lots of ghee and butter in the cooking. Some people believe that the Punjabi flag should have a tandoori chicken on it!

### Drink

**Drinking water** used to be regarded as one of India's biggest hazards. It is still true that water from the tap or a well should never be considered safe to drink since public water supplies are often polluted. Bottled water is now widely available although not all bottled water is mineral water; most are simply purified water from an urban supply. Buy from a shop or stall, check the seal carefully and avoid street hawkers.

There is growing concern over the mountains of plastic bottles that are collecting so travellers are being encouraged to carry their own bottles and take a portable water filter. It is important to use pure water for cleaning teeth.

**Tea** and **coffee** are safe and widely available. Both are normally served sweet, and with milk. If you wish, say 'no sugar' (*chini nahin*), 'no milk' (*dudh nahin*) when ordering. Alternatively, ask for a pot of tea and milk and sugar to be brought separately. Freshly brewed coffee is a common drink in South India, but in the North, ordinary city restaurants will usually serve the instant variety.

Bottled **soft drinks** such as Coke, Pepsi, Teem, Limca and Thums Up are universally available; always check the seal when you buy from a street stall. There are also several brands of fruit juice sold in cartons, including mango, pineapple and apple – Indian brands are very sweet. Don't add ice cubes as the water source may be contaminated.

Indians rarely drink **alcohol** with a meal. In the past wines and spirits were generally either imported and extremely expensive, or local and of poor quality. Now, the best Indian whisky, rum and brandy (IMFL or 'Indian Made Foreign Liquor') are widely accepted, as are good Champagnoise and other wines from Maharashtra. If you hanker after a bottle of imported wine, you will only find it in the top restaurants or specialist liquor stores for at least Rs 1000. For the urban elite, refreshing Indian beers are popular when eating out and so are widely available. 'Pubs' have sprung up in the major cities.

Most states have alcohol-free days or enforce degrees of Prohibition. Some upmarket restaurants may serve beer even if it's not listed, so it's worth asking. In some states there are government-approved wine shops where you buy your alcohol through a metal grille.

## Festivals in Delhi and Northwest India

India has a wealth of festivals with many celebrated nationwide, while others are specific to a particular state or community or even a particular temple. Many fall on different dates each year depending on the Hindu lunar calendar so check with the tourist office, or see the thorough calendar of upcoming major and minor festivals at www.drikpanchang.com.

### The Hindu calendar

Hindus follow two distinct eras: The *Vikrama Samvat* which began in 57 BC and the *Salivahan Saka* which dates from AD 78 and has been the official Indian calendar since 1957. The *Saka* new year starts on 22 March and has the same length as the Gregorian calendar. The 29½-day lunar month with its 'dark' and 'bright' halves based on the new and full moons, are named after 12 constellations, and total a 354-day year. The calendar cleverly has an extra month (*adhik maas*) every 2½ to three years, to bring it in line with the solar year of 365 days coinciding with the Gregorian calendar of the West.

Some major national and regional festivals are listed below. A few count as national holidays: **26 January**: Republic Day; **15 August**: Independence Day; **2 October**: Mahatma Gandhi's Birthday; **25 December**: Christmas Day.

### Major festivals and fairs

**Jan** New Year's Day (1 Jan) is accepted officially when following the Gregorian calendar but there are regional variations which fall on different dates, often coinciding with spring/harvest time in Mar and Apr.

**14 Jan** Makar Sankranti marks the end of winter and is celebrated with kite flying.

**Feb** Vasant Panchami, the spring festival when people wear bright yellow clothes to mark the advent of the season with singing, dancing and feasting.

**Feb-Mar** Maha Sivaratri marks the night when Siva danced his celestial dance of destruction (*Tandava*), which is celebrated with feasting and fairs at Siva temples, but preceded by a night of devotional readings and hymn singing.

**Mar** Holi, the festival of colours, marks the climax of spring. The previous night bonfires are lit symbolizing the end of winter (and conquering of evil). People have fun throwing coloured powder and water at each other and in the evening some gamble with friends. If you don't mind getting covered in colours, you can risk going out but celebrations can sometimes get very rowdy (and unpleasant). Some worship Krishna who defeated the demon Putana.

**Apr/May** Buddha Jayanti, the 1st full moon night in Apr/May marks the birth of the Buddha.

**Jul/Aug** Raksha (or Rakhi) Bandhan symbolizes the bond between brother and sister, celebrated at full moon. A sister says special prayers for her brother and ties coloured threads around his wrist to remind him of the special bond. He in turn gives a gift and promises to protect and care for her. Sometimes *rakshas* are exchanged as a mark of friendship. **15 Aug** is **Independence Day**, a national secular holiday is marked by special events. **Ganesh Chaturthi** was established just over 100 years ago by the Indian nationalist leader Tilak. The elephant-headed God of good omen is shown special reverence. On the last of the 5-day festival after harvest, clay images of Ganesh are taken in procession with dancers and musicians, and are immersed in the sea, river or pond.

**Aug/Sep** Janmashtami, the birth of Krishna is celebrated at midnight at Krishna temples.

**Sep/Oct** Dasara has many local variations. Celebrations for the 9 nights (*navaratri*) are marked with **Ramlila**, various episodes of the Ramayana story are enacted with particular reference to the battle between the forces of good and evil. In some parts of India it celebrates *Rama*'s victory over the Demon king *Ravana* of Lanka with the help of loyal *Hanuman* (Monkey). Huge effigies of *Ravana* made of bamboo and paper are burnt on the 10th day (*Vijaya dasami*) of **Dasara** in public open spaces.

**Oct/Nov** Gandhi Jayanti (2 Oct), Mahatma Gandhi's birthday, is remembered with prayer meetings and devotional singing.

Diwali/Deepavali (*Sanskrit ideepa* lamp), the festival of lights. Some Hindus celebrate Krishna's victory over the demon *Narakasura*, some Rama's return after his 14 years' exile in the forest when citizens lit his way with oil lamps. The festival falls on the dark *chaturdasi* (14th) night (the one preceding the new moon), when rows of lamps or candles are lit in remembrance, and *rangolis* are painted on the floor as a sign of welcome. Fireworks have become an integral part of the celebration which

are often set off days before Diwali. Equally, Lakshmi, the Goddess of Wealth (as well as Ganesh) is worshipped by merchants and the business community who open the new financial year's account on the day. Most people wear new clothes; some play games of chance.

**Guru Nanak Jayanti** commemorates the birth of Guru Nanak. **Akhand Path** (unbroken reading of the holy book) takes place and the book itself (*Guru Granth Sahib*) is taken out in procession.

**Dec** Christmas Day (25 Dec) sees Indian Christians celebrate the birth of Christ in much the same way as in the West; many churches hold services/mass at midnight. There is an air of festivity in city markets which are specially decorated and illuminated. Over **New Year's Eve** (31 Dec) hotel prices peak and large supplements are added for meals and entertainment in the upper category hotels. Some churches mark the night with a Midnight Mass.

## Muslim holy days

These are fixed according to the lunar calendar. According to the Gregorian calendar, they tend to fall 11 days earlier each year, dependent on the sighting of the new moon.

**Ramadan**, known in India as 'Ramzan', is the start of the month of fasting when all Muslims (except young children, the very elderly, the sick, pregnant women and travellers) must abstain from food and drink, from sunrise to sunset.

**Id ul Fitr** is the 3-day festival that marks the end of Ramzan.

**Id-ul-Zuha/Bakr-Id** is when Muslims commemorate Ibrahim's sacrifice of his son according to God's commandment;

the main time of pilgrimage to Mecca (the Hajj). It is marked by the sacrifice of a goat, feasting and alms giving. **Muharram** is when the killing of the Prophet's grandson, Hussain, is commemorated by Shi'a Muslims. Decorated *tazias* (replicas of the martyr's tomb) are carried in procession by devout wailing followers who beat their chests to express their grief. Shi'as fast for the 10 days.

# Essentials A-Z

## Accident and emergency

Contact the relevant emergency service (police T100, fire T101, ambulance T102) and your embassy. Make sure you obtain police/medical reports required for insurance claims.

## Customs and duty free
### Duty free

Tourists are allowed to bring in all personal effects 'which may reasonably be required', without charge. The official customs allowance includes 200 cigarettes or 50 cigars, 0.95 litres of alcohol, a camera and a pair of binoculars. Valuable personal effects and professional equipment including jewellery, special camera equipment and lenses, laptop computers and sound and video recorders must in theory be declared on a Tourist Baggage Re-Export Form (TBRE) in order for them to be taken out of the country (though in practice it's unlikely that your bags will be inspected beyond a cursory x-ray). It is essential to keep these forms for showing to the customs when leaving India, otherwise considerable delays are very likely at the time of departure.

### Prohibited items

The import of live plants, gold coins, gold and silver bullion and silver coins not in current use are either banned or subject to strict regulation. Enquire at consular offices abroad for details.

## Drugs

Be aware that the government takes the misuse of drugs very seriously. Anyone charged with the illegal possession of drugs risks facing a fine of Rs 100,000 and a minimum 10 years' imprisonment. Several foreigners have been imprisoned for drugs-related offences in the last decade.

## Electricity

India's supply is 220-240 volts AC. Some top hotels have transformers. There may be pronounced variations in the voltage, and power cuts are common. Power back-up by generator or inverter is becoming more widespread, even in humble hotels, though it may not cover a/c. Socket sizes vary so take a universal adaptor; low-quality versions are available locally. Many hotels, even in the higher categories, don't have electric razor sockets. Invest in a stabilizer for a laptop.

## Embassies and consulates

For information on visas and immigration, see page 22. For details of Indian embassies and consulates around the world, go to embassy.goabroad.com.

## Health

Obviously 5-star travel is going to carry less risk than backpacking on a budget. Health care in India is varied. There are many excellent private and government clinics/hospitals. Your embassy or consulate will be able to tell you where the recommended clinics are. You can also ask about locally recommended medical dos and don'ts. If you do get ill, and you have the opportunity, you should also ask your medical insurer whether they are satisfied that the medical centre/hospital you have been referred to is of a suitable standard.

### Before you go

Ideally, you should see your GP or travel clinic at least 6 weeks before your departure for general advice on travel risks, malaria and vaccinations. Make sure you have travel insurance, get a dental check (especially if you are going to be away for more than a month), know your own blood group and if you suffer a long-term condition such as diabetes or epilepsy make sure someone knows or that you have a Medic Alert bracelet/necklace with this information on it. Remember that it is risky to buy medicinal tablets abroad because the doses may differ and India has a huge trade in counterfeit drugs.

## Vaccinations

If you need vaccinations, see your doctor well in advance of your travel. The following vaccinations are recommended: typhoid, polio, tetanus, infectious hepatitis and diptheria. For details of malaria prevention, contact your GP or local travel clinic.

The following vaccinations may also be considered: rabies, possibly BCG (since TB is still common in the region) and in some cases meningitis and diphtheria (if you're staying in the country for a long time). Yellow fever is not required in India but you may be asked to show a certificate if you have travelled from Africa or South America. Japanese encephalitis may be required for rural travel at certain times of the year (mainly rainy seasons). An effective oral cholera vaccine (Dukoral) is now available as 2 doses providing 3 months' protection.

## Websites

**British Travel Health Association (UK), www.btha.org** This is the official website of an organization of travel health professionals. **Fit for Travel, www.fitfortravel.scot. nhs.uk** This site from Scotland provides a quick A-Z of vaccine and travel health advice requirements for each country. **Foreign and Commonwealth Office (FCO) (UK), www.fco.gov.uk** This is a key travel advice site, with useful information on the country, people, climate and lists the UK embassies/consulates. **The Health Protection Agency, www.hpa. org.uk** Up-to-date malaria advice guidelines for travel around the world. It gives specific advice about the right drugs for each location. It also has useful information for those who are pregnant, suffering from epilepsy or planning to travel with children.

**Medic Alert (UK), www.medicalalert.com** This is the website of the foundation that produces bracelets and necklaces for those with existing medical problems. **Travel Screening Services (UK), www. travelscreening.co.uk** A private clinic dedicated to integrated travel health. **World Health Organisation, www.who. int** The WHO site has links to the *WHO Blue Book* on travel advice. This lists the diseases in different regions of the world and describes vaccination schedules.

## Language

Hindi, spoken as a mother tongue by over 400 million people, is India's official language. The use of English is also enshrined in the Constitution for a wide range of official purposes, notably communication between Hindi and non-Hindi speaking states. The most widely spoken Indo-Aryan languages are: Bengali (8.3%), Marathi (8%), Urdu (5.7%), Gujarati (5.4%), Oriya (3.7%) and Punjabi (3.2%).

English now plays an important role across India. It is widely spoken in towns and cities and even in quite remote villages it is usually not difficult to find someone who speaks at least a little English. Outside of major tourist sites, other European languages are almost completely unknown.

## Money

Indian currency is the Indian Rupee (Re/Rs). It is **not** possible to purchase these before you arrive. If you want cash on arrival it is best to get it at the airport bank, although see if an ATM is available as airport rates are not very generous. Rupee notes are printed in denominations of Rs 1000, 500, 100, 50, 20, 10. The rupee is divided into 100 paise. Coins are minted in denominations of Rs 10, 5, Rs 2, Rs 1 and (the increasingly uncommon) 50 paise. **Note** Carry cash, rupees or foreign currency in a money belt worn under clothing. Have a small amount in an easily accessible place.

**Exchange rates** ➜ *UK £1 = Rs 101,*
*€1 = Rs 83, US$1 = Rs 61 (Jan 2014).*

## ATMs

By far the most convenient method of
accessing money, ATMs are all over India,
usually attended by security guards, with
most banks offering some services to holders
of overseas cards. Banks whose ATMs will
issue cash against **Cirrus** and **Maestro** cards,
as well as Visa and MasterCard, include **Bank
of Baroda**, **Citibank**, **HDFC**, **HSBC**, **ICICI**,
**IDBI**, **Punjab National Bank**, **State Bank of
India** (SBI), **Standard Chartered** and **UTI**.
A withdrawal fee is usually charged by
the issuing bank on top of the conversion
charges applied by your own bank. Fraud
prevention measures quite often result
in travellers having their cards blocked
by the bank when unexpected overseas
transactions occur; advise your bank of
your travel plans before leaving.

## Credit cards

Major credit cards are increasingly
acceptable in the main centres, though in
smaller cities and towns it is still rare to be
able to pay by credit card. Payment by credit
card can sometimes be more expensive
than payment by cash, whilst some credit
card companies charge a premium on cash
withdrawals. **Visa** and **MasterCard** have an
ever-growing number of ATMs in major
cities and several banks offer withdrawal
facilities for Cirrus and Maestro cardholders.
It is however easy to obtain a cash advance
against a credit card. Railway reservation
centres in major cities take payment for train
tickets by Visa card which can be very quick
as the queue is short, although they cannot
be used for Tourist Quota tickets.

## Currency cards

If you don't want to carry lots of cash,
prepaid currency cards allow you to
preload money from your bank account,
fixed at the day's exchange rate. They look
like a credit or debit card and are issued

by specialist money changing companies,
such as **Travelex** and **Caxton FX**. You can
top up and check your balance by phone,
online and sometimes by text.

## Changing money

The **State Bank of India** and several others
in major towns are authorized to deal in
foreign exchange. Some give cash against
Visa/MasterCard (eg **ANZ**). American Express
cardholders can use their cards to get cash
in Delhi. The larger cities have licensed
money changers with offices usually in
the commercial sector. Changing money
through unauthorized dealers is illegal.
Large hotels change money 24 hrs a day for
guests, but banks often give a substantially
better rate of exchange. Many international
flights arrive during the night and it is
generally far easier and less time consuming
to change money at the airport than in the
city. You should be given a foreign currency
encashment certificate when you change
money through a bank or authorized dealer;
ask for one if it is not automatically given.
It allows you to change Indian rupees back
to your own currency on departure. It also
enables you to use rupees to pay hotel
bills or buy air tickets for which payment
in foreign exchange may be required. The
certificates are only valid for 3 months.

## Cost of travelling

Most food, accommodation and public
transport, especially rail and bus, is
exceptionally cheap, although the price
of basic food items such as rice, lentils,
tomatoes and onions has skyrocketed.
There is a widening range of moderately
priced but clean hotels and restaurants
outside the big cities, making it possible
to get a great deal for your money. Budget
travellers sharing a room, taking public
transport, avoiding souvenir stalls, and
eating nothing but rice and *dhal* can get
away with a budget of Rs 400-600 a day.
This sum leaps up if you drink alcohol, smoke
foreign-brand cigarettes or want to have

your own wheels. Those planning to stay in fairly comfortable hotels and use taxis sightseeing should budget at US$50-80 a day. Then again you could always check into Imperial Hotel for Christmas and notch up an impressive US$600 bill on your B&B alone. India can be a great place to pick and choose, save a little on basic accommodation and then treat yourself to the type of meal you could only dream of affording back home. Also, be prepared to spend a fair amount more in Delhi, where not only is the cost of living significantly higher but where it's worth coughing up extra for a half-decent room. A newspaper costs Rs 5 and breakfast for 2 with coffee can come to as little as Rs 100 in a basic 'hotel', but if you intend to eat banana pancakes or pasta in a backpacker restaurant, you can expect to pay more like Rs 100-150 a plate.

## Opening hours

**Banks** are open Mon-Fri 1030-1430, Sat 1030-1230. Top hotels sometimes have a 24-hr money-changing service. **Post offices** open Mon-Fri 1000-1700, often shutting for lunch, and Sat mornings. **Government offices** Mon-Fri 0930-1700, Sat 0930-1300 (some open on alternate Sat only). **Shops** open Mon-Sat 0930-1800. Bazars keep longer hours.

## Safety
### Personal security

In general the threats to personal security for travellers in India are remarkably small. However, incidents of petty theft and violence directed specifically at tourists have been on the increase so care is necessary in some places, and basic common sense needs to be used with respect to looking after valuables. Follow the same precautions you would when at home. There have been much-reported incidents of severe sexual assault in Delhi and some more rural areas in 2013. Avoid wandering alone outdoors late at night in these places. During daylight hours be careful in remote places, especially

when alone. If you are under threat, scream loudly. Be cautious before accepting food or drink from casual acquaintances, as it may be drugged – though note that Indians on a long train journey will invariably try to share their snacks with you, and balance caution with the opportunity to interact.

As a general rule, travellers are advised to be vigilant in the lead up to and on days of national significance, such as Republic Day (26 Jan) and Independence Day (15 Aug) as militants have in the past used such occasions to mount attacks.

### Travel advice

It is better to seek advice from your consulate than from travel agencies. Before you travel you can contact: British Foreign & Commonwealth Office Travel Advice Unit, T0845-850 2829 (Pakistan desk T020-7270 2385), www.fco.gov.uk. US State Department's Bureau of Consular Affairs, Overseas Citizens Services, Room 4800, Department of State, Washington, DC 20520-4818, USA, T202-647 1488, http://travel.state.gov. Australian Department of Foreign Affairs Canberra, Australia, T02-6261 3305, www.smartraveller.gov.au. Canadian official advice is on www.voyage.gc.ca.

### Theft

Theft is not uncommon. It is best to keep passports and valuables with you at all times. Don't regard hotel rooms as being automatically safe; even hotel safes don't guarantee secure storage. Avoid leaving valuables near open windows even when you are in the room. Use your own padlock in a budget hotel when you go out. Pickpockets and other thieves operate in the big cities. Crowded areas are particularly high risk. Take special care of your belongings when getting on or off public transport.

If you have items stolen, they should be reported to the police as soon as possible. Keep a separate record of vital documents, including passport details and numbers of TCs. Larger hotels will be able to assist in contacting and dealing with the police. Dealings with the police can be very difficult. The paperwork involved in reporting losses can be time consuming and irritating and your own documentation (eg passport and visas) may be demanded.

In some states the police occasionally demand bribes, though you should not assume that if procedures move slowly you are automatically being expected to offer a bribe. Traffic police have the right to make on-the-spot fines for speeding and illegal parking. If you face a fine, insist on a receipt. If you have to go to a police station, try to take someone with you.

Confidence tricksters are particularly common where people are on the move, notably around railway stations or places where budget tourists gather.

## Telephone

The international code for India is +91. International Direct Dialling is available in privately run call booths, usually labelled on yellow boards with the letters 'PCO-STD-ISD'. You dial the call yourself, and the time and cost are displayed on a computer screen. Telephone calls from hotels are usually more expensive (check price before calling), though some will allow local calls free of charge. Internet phone booths, usually associated with cybercafés, are the cheapest way of calling overseas.

**Directory enquiries**, T197, can be helpful but works only for the local area code.

**Mobile phones** are for sale everywhere, as are local SIM cards that allow you to make calls within India and overseas at much lower rates than using a 'roaming' service from your normal provider at home – sometimes for as little as Rs 0.5 per min. **Univercell**, www.univercell.in, and **The Mobile Store**, www.themobilestore.in, are 2 widespread and efficient chains selling phones and SIM cards.

India is divided into a number of 'calling circles' or regions, and if you travel outside the region where your connection is based, eg from Delhi into, you will pay higher 'roaming' charges for making and receiving calls. In Jammu and Kashmir, sim cards will only work within the state itself, for security reasons, and are more difficult to obtain.

## Time

India doesn't change its clocks, so from the last Sun in Oct to the last Sun in Mar the time is GMT +5½ hrs, and the rest of the year it's +4½ hrs (USA, EST +10½ and +9½ hrs; Australia, EST -5½ and -4½ hrs).

## Tipping

A tip of Rs 10 to a bellboy carrying luggage in a modest hotel (Rs 20 in a higher category) would be appropriate. In upmarket restaurants, a 10% tip is acceptable when service is not already included, while in places serving very cheap meals, round off the bill with small change. Indians don't normally tip taxi drivers but a small extra is welcomed. Porters at airports and railway stations often have a fixed rate displayed but will usually press for more. Ask fellow passengers what a fair rate is.

## Tourist information

There are **Government of India** tourist offices in the state capitals, as well as state tourist offices (sometimes **Tourism Development Corporations**) in the Delhi and some towns and places of tourist interest. They produce their own tourist literature, either free or sold at a nominal price, and some also have lists of city hotels and paying guest options. The quality of material is improving though maps are often poor. Many offer tours of the city, neighbouring sights and overnight and regional packages. Some run modest hotels and midway motels with restaurants and may also arrange car hire and guides. The staff in the regional and local offices are usually helpful.

## Visas and immigration

For embassies and consulates, see page 17. Virtually all foreign nationals, including children, require a visa to enter India. The rules regarding visas change frequently and arrangements for application and collection also vary from town to town so it is essential to check details and costs with the relevant embassy or consulate. These remain closed on Indian national holidays. Many consulates and embassies are currently outsourcing the visa process; it's best to find out in advance how long it will take. Note that visas are valid from the date granted, not from the date of entry.

Recently the Indian government has decided to issue 'visas on arrival' for some 40 countries (including the UK, the USA, France and Germany), as well as for citizens of all countries who are over the age of 60. The exact time frame for the change is not yet clear, so check the latest situation online before travelling.

No foreigner needs to register within the 180-day period of their tourist visa. All foreign visitors who stay in India for more than 180 days need to get an income tax clearance exemption certificate from the Foreign Section of the Income Tax Department in Delhi.

Applications for visa extensions should be made to the Foreigners' Regional Registration Offices at New Delhi, or an office of the Superintendent of Police in the District Headquarters. After 6 months, you must leave India and apply for a new visa.

## Weights and measures

Metric is in universal use in the cities. In remote areas local measures are sometimes used. One lakh is 100,000 and 1 crore is 10 million.

## Contents

24    Arriving in Delhi
25    Background

**27    Places in Delhi**
27    Old Delhi
33    New Delhi
39    South Delhi
45    East of the Yamuna
46    Listings

Delhi

## Arriving in Delhi

### Getting there

Delhi is served by **Indira Gandhi International (IGI) Airport**, which handles both international and domestic traffic. The new T3 (International Terminal) has one of the longest runways in Asia and is connected to the city centre by Metro. It is about 23 km from the centre. During the day, it can take 30-45 minutes from the Domestic Terminal and 45 minutes to an hour from the International Terminal to get to the centre. With the Metro, it should take 20 minutes. A free shuttle runs between the terminals. To get to town take a pre-paid taxi (see Transport, page 55) or an airport coach, or ask your hotel to collect you.

The **Inter State Bus Terminus (ISBT)** is at Kashmere Gate, near the Red Fort, about 30 minutes by bus from Connaught Place. Local buses connect it to the other ISBTs.

There are three main railway stations. The busy **New Delhi Station**, a 10-minute walk north of Connaught Place, can be maddeningly chaotic; you need to have all your wits about you. The quieter **Hazrat Nizamuddin** (which has some south-bound trains) is 5 km southeast of Connaught Place. The overpoweringly crowded **Old Delhi Station** (2 km north of Connaught Place) has a few important train connections. ▸▸ *See Transport, page 55.*

### Getting around

The Metro makes the sprawling city very navigable: it's possible to get from Connaught Place to Old Delhi in a cool five minutes; while Connaught Place to Qutb Minar is about 30 minutes, and all the way down to the final stop in Gurgaon is about one hour. It is a strange experience to go from air-conditioned high tech to the bustling streets of Chandi Chowk. There is a women-only carriage at the front of each train, clearly marked inside and on the platform – this prevents women from having to succumb to the crush of the other carriages. There is a fine for men ignoring all the signs in pink and, in early 2011, a posse of women made men do sit-ups on the train for trespassing into the pink zone! Like any city Metro service, try and avoid rush hour if you can. At each Metro station you have to go through airport-like security and have your bag x-rayed, etc.

Auto-rickshaws and taxis are widely available, and new rate cards mean that drivers will now use their meters, even with foreigners. It's best to use pre-paid stands at stations, airport terminals and at the junction of Radial Road 1 and Connaught Place if possible. The same applies to cycle rickshaws, which ply the streets of Old Delhi. City buses are usually packed. Be on your guard from thieves around New Delhi Station. State Entry Road runs from the southern end of Platform 1 to Connaught Place. This is a hassle-free alternative to the main Chelmsford Road during the day (gate closed at night). Also watch your change or cash interactions even at the pre-paid booths – sometimes they do a switch of a Rs 100 note for a Rs 10 for example. Fleets of Radio Taxis are the newest additions to the city's transport options. These include: **Delhi Cab** ① *T011-4433 3222*; **Easy Cab** ① *T011-4343 4343*; **Mega Cabs** ① *T011-4141 4141*; and **Quick Cab** ① *T011-4533 3333*. ▸▸ *See Transport, page 55.*

### Orientation

The **Red Fort** and **Jama Masjid** are the focal point of Old Delhi, 2 km northeast of Connaught Place. Chandni Chowk, the main commercial area, heads west from the fort. Around this area are narrow lanes packed to the rafters with all different types of wares for sale. To the southeast are **New Delhi Railway Station** and the main backpackers' area, **Paharganj**, with **Connaught Place**, the notional 'centre' of New Delhi, about 1 km south.

Running due south of Connaught Place is **Janpath** with small shops selling craft products, and hotels such as the **Imperial**. Janpath is intersected by **Rajpath** with all the major state buildings at its western end. Immediately south is the diplomatic enclave, **Chanakyapuri**. Most of the upmarket hotels are scattered across the wide area between Connaught Place and the airport to the southwest. As Delhi's centre of gravity has shifted southwards, a series of new markets has grown up to serve extensive housing colonies such as **South Extension**, **Greater Kailash** and **Safdarjang Enclave**. This development has brought one of the major historic sites, the **Qutb Minar**, within the limits of the city, about half an hour by Metro south of Connaught Place. **Gurgaon**, which is strictly not in Delhi but in Haryana, is the new business hub with many shopping malls to boot.

## Tourist information

Most tourist offices are open Monday-Friday 1000-1800, www.delhitourism.com. **The Government of India Tourist Office** ① *88 Janpath, T011-332 0005, Mon-Sat 0900-1800; also at the international airport*, is helpful and issues permits for visits to Rashtrapati Bhavan and gardens. There are several branches of **Delhi Tourism** ① *N-36 Connaught Pl, T011-2331 5322 (touts pester you to use one of many imposters; the correct office is directly opposite 'Competent House')*; the branch at **Coffee Home Annexe** ① *Baba Kharak Singh Marg, T011-336 5358*, offers hotel, transport and tour bookings (T011-2462 3782, 0700-2100). There are also branches at the airport terminals, the Inter-State Bus Terminal; **New Delhi Railway Station** ① *T011-2373 2374*; and **Nizamuddin Railway Station** ① *T011-2251 1083*. Also contact the **India Tourism Development Corporation (ITDC)** ① *L-1 Connaught Circus, T011-2332 0331*.

## Best time to visit

October to March are the best months to visit, but December and January can get quite cold and foggy at night. Pollution can affect asthma sufferers – in fact a lot of people develop respiratory problems and sore throats if they spend more than a few days in Delhi; echinacea can help. Monsoon lasts from the end of June to mid-September. May and June are very hot and dry and, with the whole city switching on its air-condioning units, power cuts are suffered more frequently at this time. Even the malls in Saket were having to keep their air conditioning on low during the summer of 2012.

# Background

In the modern period, Delhi has only been India's capital since 1911. It is a city of yo yo-ing fortunes and has been repeatedly reduced to rubble. There have been at least eight cities founded on the site of modern Delhi.

According to Hindu mythology, Delhi's first avatar was as the site of a dazzlingly wealthy city, Indraprastha, mentioned in the Mahabharata and founded around 2500 BC. The next five cities were to the south of today's Delhi. First was Lalkot, which, from 1206, became the capital of the Delhi Sultanate under the Slave Dynasty. The story of the first Sultan of Delhi, Qutb-ud-din Aybak, is a classic rags-to-riches story. A former slave, he rose through the ranks to become a general, a governor and then Sultan of Delhi. He is responsible for building Qutb Minar, but died before its completion.

The 1300s were a tumultuous time for Delhi, with five cities built during the century. Siri, the first of these, has gruesome roots. Legend has it that the city's founder, Ala-ud-din, buried the heads of infidels in the foundation of the fort. Siri derives its name from the

Hindi word for 'head'. After Siri came Tughlaqabad, whose existence came to a sudden end when the Sultan of Delhi, Muhammad Tughlaq, got so angry about a perceived insult from residents, he destroyed the city. The cities of Jahanpanah and Ferozebad followed in quick succession. Delhi's centre of gravity began to move northwards. In the 1500s Dinpanah was constructed by Humayun, whose wonderful tomb (1564-1573) graces Hazrat Nizamuddin. Shahjahanabad, known today as Old Delhi, followed, becoming one of the richest and most populous cities in the world. The Persian emperor Nadir Shah invaded, killing as many as 120,000 residents in a single bloody night and stealing the Kohinoor Diamond (now part of the British royal family's crown jewels).

The next destroyers of Delhi were the British, who ransacked the city in the wake of the Great Uprising/Mutiny of 1857. The resulting bloodbath left bodies piled so high that the victors' horses had to tread on them. For the next 50 years, while the port cities of Calcutta and Bombay thrived under the British, Delhi languished. Then, in 1911, King George, on a visit to India, announced that a new city should be built next to what remained of Delhi, and that this would be the new capital of India. The British architect Edwin Lutyens was brought in to design the city. You could argue that the building hasn't stopped since ...

The central part of New Delhi is an example of Britain's imperial pretensions. The government may have been rather more reticent about moving India's capital, if it had known that in less than 36 years time, the British would no longer be ruling India. Delhi's population swelled after the violence of partition, with refugees flooding to the city. In 10 years the population of Delhi doubled, and many well-known housing colonies were built during this period.

The economic boom that began in the 1990s has lead to an explosion of construction and soaring real estate prices. Delhi is voraciously eating into the surrounding countryside. It is a city changing at such breakneck speed that shops, homes and even airports seem to appear and disappear almost overnight.

# Places in Delhi

The sites of interest are grouped in three main areas. In the centre is the British-built capital of **New Delhi**, with its government buildings and wide avenues. The heart of **Shahjahanabad** (Old Delhi) is about 2 km north of Connaught Circus. Some 10 km to the south is the **Qutb Minar** complex, with the old fortress city of **Tughluqabad**, 8 km to its east. Across the Yamuna River is the remarkable new Akshardham Temple. You can visit each separately, or link routes together into a day-tour to include the most interesting sites.

## Old Delhi → *For listings, see pages 46-58.*

Shah Jahan (ruled 1628-1658) decided to move back from Agra to Delhi in 1638. Within 10 years the huge city of **Shahjahanabad**, now known as Old Delhi, was built. The plan of Shah Jahan's new city symbolized the link between religious authority enshrined in the Jama Masjid to the west, and political authority represented by the Diwan-i-Am in the Fort, joined by Chandni Chowk, the route used by the emperor. The city was protected by rubble-walls, some of which still survive. These walls were pierced by 14 main gates. The **Ajmeri Gate**, **Turkman Gate** (often referred to by auto-rickshaw wallahs as 'Truckman Gate'), **Kashmere Gate** and **Delhi Gate** still survive.

### Chandni Chowk

Shahjahanabad was laid out in blocks with wide roads, residential quarters, bazars and mosques. Its principal street, Chandni Chowk, had a tree-lined canal flowing down its centre which became renowned throughout Asia. The canal is long gone, but the jumble of shops, alleys crammed with craftsmen's workshops, food stalls, mosques and temples, cause it to retain some of its magic. A cycle rickshaw ride gives you a good feel of the place. Make sure you visit **Naughara Street**, just off Kinari Bazar; it's one of the most atmospheric streets in Delhi, full of brightly painted and slowly crumbling *havelis*.

   The impressive red sandstone façade of the **Digambar Jain Mandir** (temple) standing at the eastern end of Chandni Chowk, faces the Red Fort. Built in 1656, it contains an image of Adinath. The charity bird hospital (www.charitybirdshospital.org) within this compound releases the birds on recovery instead of returning them to their owners; many remain within the temple precincts. Beyond Shahjahanabad to the north lies Kashmiri Gate, Civil lines and the Northern Ridge. The siting of the railway line which effectively cut Delhi into two unequal parts was done deliberately. The line brought prosperity, yet it destroyed the unity of the walled city forever. The Northern Ridge was the British cantonment and Civil Lines housed the civilians. In this area the temporary capital of the British existed from 1911-1931 until New Delhi came. The Northern Ridge is a paradise for birds and trees. Follow the **Mutiny Trail** by visiting Flagstaff Tower, Pir Ghaib, Chauburj, Mutiny Memorial. Around Kashmire Gate and Civil Lines, you can discover the Old Residency, St James Church, Nicholson's Cemetery and Qudsia Bagh.

### Red Fort (Lal Qila)

ⓘ *Tue-Sun sunrise to sunset, Rs 250 foreigners, Rs 10 Indians, allow 1 hr. The entrance is through the Lahore Gate (nearest the car park) with the admission kiosk opposite; keep your ticket as you will need to show it at the Drum House. There are new toilets inside, best to avoid*

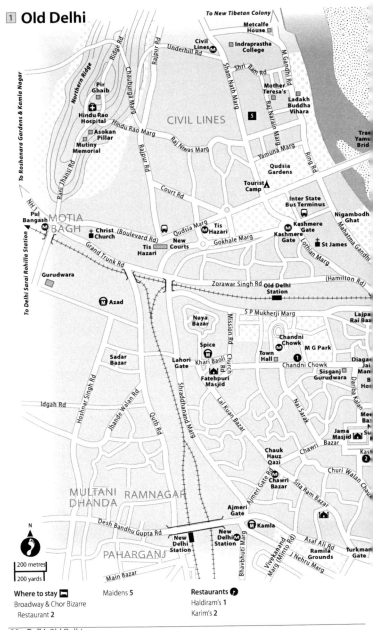

# 1 Old Delhi

**Where to stay** 🏠
Broadway & Chor Bizarre
Restaurant **2**

Maidens **5**

**Restaurants** 🍴
Haldiram's **1**
Karim's **2**

➡ **Delhi maps**
1 Old Delhi, page 28
2 New Delhi, page 34
3 Connaught Place, page 38

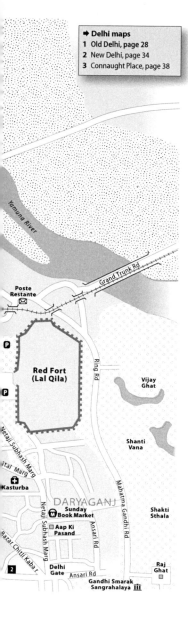

the ones in Chatta Chowk. You must remove shoes and cover all exposed flesh from your shoulders to your legs.

Between the new city and the River Yamuna, Shah Jahan built a fort. Most of it was built out of red *lal* (sandstone), hence the name **Lal Qila** (Red Fort), the same as that at Agra on which the Delhi Fort is modelled. Begun in 1639 and completed in 1648, it is said to have cost Rs 10 million, much of which was spent on the opulent marble palaces within. In recent years much effort has been put into improving the fort and gardens, but visitors may be saddened by the neglected state of some of the buildings, and the gun-wielding soldiers lolling around do nothing to improve the ambience. However, despite the modern development of roads and shops and the never-ending traffic, it's an impressive site.

**The approach** The entrance is by the Lahore Gate. The defensive barbican that juts out in front of it was built by Aurangzeb. A common story suggests that Aurangzeb built the curtain wall to save his nobles and visiting dignitaries from having to walk – and bow – the whole length of Chandni Chowk, for no one was allowed to ride in the presence of the emperor. When the emperor sat in the Diwan-i-Am he could see all the way down the chowk, so the addition must have been greatly welcomed by his courtiers. The new entrance arrangement also made an attacking army more vulnerable to the defenders on the walls.

**Chatta Chowk and the Naubat Khana** Inside is the **Covered Bazar**, which was quite exceptional in the 17th century. In Shah Jahan's time there were shops on both upper and lower levels. Originally they catered for the Imperial household and carried stocks of silks, brocades, velvets, gold and silverware, jewellery and gems. There were coffee shops too for nobles and courtiers.

The **Naqqar Khana** or **Naubat Khana** (Drum House or music gallery) marked the entrance to the inner apartments of the fort. Here everyone except the princes of the royal family had to dismount and leave their horses or *hathi* (elephants), hence its other name of **Hathi Pol** (Elephant Gate). Five times a day ceremonial music was played on the kettle drum, *shahnais* (a kind of oboe) and cymbals, glorifying the emperor. In 1754 Emperor Ahmad Shah was murdered here. The gateway with four floors is decorated with floral designs. You can still see traces of the original panels painted in gold or other colours on the interior of the gateway.

**Diwan-i-Am** Between the first inner court and the royal palaces at the heart of the fort, stood the **Diwan-i-Am** (Hall of Public Audience), the furthest point a normal visitor would reach. It has seen many dramatic events, including the destructive whirlwind of the Persian Nadir Shah in 1739 and of Ahmad Shah the Afghan in 1756, and the trial of the last 'King of Delhi', **Bahadur Shah II** in 1858.

The well-proportioned hall was both a functional building and a showpiece intended to hint at the opulence of the palace itself. In Shah Jahan's time the sandstone was hidden behind a very thin layer of white polished plaster, *chunam*. This was decorated with floral motifs in many colours, especially gilt. Silk carpets and heavy curtains hung from the canopy rings outside the building; such interiors were reminders of the Mughals' nomadic origins in Central Asia, where royal durbars were held in tents.

At the back of the hall is a platform for the emperor's throne. Around this was a gold railing, within which stood the princes and great nobles separated from the lesser nobles inside the hall. Behind the throne canopy are 12 marble panels inlaid with motifs of fruiting trees, parrots and cuckoos. Figurative workmanship is very unusual in Islamic buildings, and these panels are the only example in the Red Fort.

As well as matters of official administration, Shah Jahan would listen to accounts of illness, dream interpretations and anecdotes from his ministers and nobles. Wednesday was the day of judgement. Sentences were often swift and brutal and sometimes the punishment of dismemberment, beating or death was carried out on the spot. The executioners were close at hand with axes and whips. On Friday, the Muslim holy day, there would be no business.

**Inner palace buildings** Behind the Diwan-i-Am is the private enclosure of the fort. Along the east wall, overlooking the River Yamuna, Shah Jahan set six small palaces (five survive). Also within this compound are the Harem, the Life-Bestowing Garden and the Nahr-i-Bihisht (Stream of Paradise).

**Life-Bestowing Gardens (Hayat Baksh Bagh)** The original gardens were landscaped according to the Islamic principles of the Persian *char bagh*, with pavilions, fountains and water courses dividing the garden into various but regular beds. The two pavilions **Sawan** and **Bhadon**, named after the first two months of the rainy season (July-August), reveal something of the character of the garden. The garden used to create the effect of the monsoon and contemporary accounts tell us that in the pavilions – some of which were especially erected for the **Teej** festival, which marks the arrival of the monsoon – the royal ladies would sit in silver swings and watch the rains. Water flowed from the back wall of the pavilion through a slit above the marble shelf and over the niches in the wall. Gold and silver pots of flowers were placed in these alcoves during the day whilst at night candles were lit to create a glistening and colourful effect.

**Shahi Burj** From the pavilion next to the Shahi Burj (**Royal Tower**) the canal known as the **Nahr-i-Bihisht** (Stream of Paradise) began its journey along the Royal Terrace. The three-storey octagonal tower was seriously damaged in 1857 and is still unsafe. In Shah Jahan's time the Yamuna lapped the walls. Shah Jahan used the tower as his most private office and only his sons and a few senior ministers were allowed with him.

**Moti Masjid** To the right are the three marble domes of Aurangzeb's 'Pearl Mosque' (shoes must be removed). Bar the cupolas, it is completely hidden behind a wall of red sandstone, now painted white. Built in 1662 of polished white marble, it has some exquisite decoration. All the surfaces are highly decorated in a fashion similar to rococo, which developed at the same time as in Europe. Unusually the prayer hall is on a raised platform with inlaid outlines of individual *musallas* ('prayer mats') in black marble. While the outer walls were aligned to the cardinal points like all the other fort buildings, the inner walls were positioned so that the mosque would correctly face Mecca.

**Hammam** The **Royal Baths** have three apartments separated by corridors with canals to carry water to each room. The two flanking the entrance, for the royal children, had hot and cold baths. The room furthest away from the door has three basins for rose water fountains.

**Diwan-i-Khas** Beyond is the single-storeyed **Hall of Private Audience**, topped by four Hindu-style *chhattris* and built completely of white marble. The *dado* (lower part of the wall) on the interior was richly decorated with inlaid precious and semi-precious stones. The ceiling was silver but was removed by the Marathas in 1760. Outside, the hall used to have a marble pavement and an arcaded court. Both have gone.

This was the Mughal office of state. Shah Jahan spent two hours here before retiring for a meal, siesta and prayers. In the evening he would return to the hall for more work before going to the harem. The hall's splendour moved the 14th-century poet Amir Khusrau to write the lines inscribed above the corner arches of the north and south walls: "*Agar Firdaus bar rue Zamin-ast/Hamin ast o Hamin ast o Hamin ast*" (If there is a paradise on earth, it is here, it is here, it is here).

**Royal palaces** Next to the Diwan-i-Khas is the three-roomed **Khas Mahal** (Private Palace). Nearest the Diwan-i-Khas is the **Tasbih Khana** (Chamber for the Telling of Rosaries) where the emperor would worship privately with his rosary of 99 beads, one for each of the mystical names of Allah. In the centre is the **Khwabgah** (Palace of Dreams) which gives on to the octagonal **Mussaman Burj** tower. Here Shah Jahan would be seen each morning. A balcony was added to the tower in 1809 and here George V and Queen Mary appeared in their Coronation Durbar of 1911. The **Tosh Khana** (Robe Room), to the south, has a beautiful marble screen at its north end, carved with the scales of justice above the filigree grille. If you are standing with your back to the Diwan-i-Khas you will see a host of circulating suns (a symbol of royalty), but if your back is to the next building (the Rang Mahal), you will see moons surrounding the scales. All these rooms were sumptuously decorated with fine silk carpets, rich silk brocade curtains and lavishly decorated walls. After 1857 the British used the Khas Mahal as an officer's mess and sadly it was defaced.

The **Rang Mahal** (Palace of Colours), the residence of the chief *sultana*, was also the place where the emperor ate most of his meals. It was divided into six apartments. Privacy and coolness were ensured by the use of marble *jali* screens. Like the other palaces it was beautifully decorated with a silver ceiling ornamented with golden flowers to reflect the water in the channel running through the building. The north and south apartments were both known as **Sheesh Mahal** (Palace of Mirrors) since into the ceiling were set hundreds of small mirrors. In the evening when candles were lit a starlight effect would be produced.

Through the palace ran the **Life-bestowing Stream** and at its centre is a lotus-shaped marble basin which had an ivory fountain. As might be expected in such a cloistered and cosseted environment, the ladies sometimes got bored. In the 18th century the **Empress of Jahandar Shah** sat gazing out at the river and remarked that she had never seen a boat sink. Shortly afterwards a boat was deliberately capsized so that she could be entertained by the sight of people bobbing up and down in the water crying for help.

The southernmost of the palaces, the **Mumtaz Mahal** (Palace of Jewels) ① *Tue-Sun 1000-1700*, was also used by the harem. The lower half of its walls are of marble and it contains six apartments. After the Mutiny of 1857 it was used as a guardroom and since 1912 it has been a museum with exhibits of textiles, weapons, carpets, jade and metalwork as well as works depicting life in the court. It should not be missed.

### Spice market
Outside the Red Fort, cycle rickshaws offer a trip to the spice market, Jama Masjid and back through the bazar. You travel slowly westwards down Chandni Chowk passing the town hall. Dismount at Church Road and follow your guide into the heart of the market on Khari Baoli where wholesalers sell every conceivable spice. Ask to go to the roof for an excellent view over the market and back towards the Red Fort. The ride back through the bazar is equally fascinating – look up at the amazing electricity system. The final excitement is getting back across Netaji Subhash Marg. Panic not, the rickshaw wallahs know what they are doing. Negotiate for one hour and expect to pay about Rs 100. The spice laden air may irritate your throat. Also ask a cycle rickshaw to take you to Naughara Street, just off Kinari Bazar, a very pretty street amidst the chaos of Old Delhi.

### Jama Masjid (Friday Mosque)
① *Visitors welcome from 30 mins after sunrise until 1215; and from 1345 until 30 mins before sunset, free, still or video cameras Rs 150, tower entry Rs 20.*
The magnificent Jama Masjid is the largest mosque in India and the last great architectural work of Shah Jahan, intended to dwarf all mosques that had gone before it. With the fort, it dominates Old Delhi. The mosque is much simpler in its ornamentation than Shah Jahan's secular buildings – a judicious blend of red sandstone and white marble, which are interspersed in the domes, minarets and cusped arches.

**The gateways** Symbolizing the separation of the sacred and the secular, the threshold is a place of great importance where the worshipper steps to a higher plane. There are three huge gateways, the largest being to the east. This was reserved for the royal family who gathered in a private gallery in its upper storey. Today, the faithful enter through the east gate on Fridays and for **Id-ul-Fitr** and **Id-ul-Adha**. The latter commemorates Abraham's (Ibrahim's) sacrificial offering of his son Ishmael (Ismail). Islam (unlike the Jewish and Christian tradition) believes that Abraham offered to sacrifice Ishmael, Isaac's brother.

**The courtyard** The façade has the main *iwan* (arch), five smaller arches on each side with two flanking minarets and three bulbous domes behind, all perfectly proportioned. The *iwan* draws the worshippers' attention into the building. The minarets have great views from the top; well worth the climb for Rs 10 (women may not be allowed to climb alone).

The **hauz**, in the centre of the courtyard, is an ablution tank placed as usual between the inner and outer parts of the building to remind the worshipper that it is through the ritual of baptism that one first enters the community of believers. The **Dikka**, in front of the ablution tank, is a raised platform. Muslim communities grew so rapidly that by the eighth century it sometimes became necessary to introduce a second *muballigh* (prayer leader) who stood on this platform and copied the postures and chants of the *imam* inside to relay them to a much larger congregation. With the introduction of the loudspeaker and amplification, the *dikka* and the *muballigh* became redundant. In the northwest corner of the mosque there is a small shed. For a small fee, the faithful are shown a hair from the beard of the prophet, as well as his sandal and his footprint in rock.

---

## New Delhi → *For listings, see pages 46-58.*

Delhi's present position as capital was only confirmed on 12 December 1911, when George V announced at the Delhi Durbar that the capital of India was to move from Calcutta to Delhi. The new city, New Delhi, planned under the leadership of British architect Edwin Lutyens with the assistance of his friend Herbert Baker, was inaugurated on 9 February 1931.

The city was to accommodate 70,000 people and have boundless possibilities for future expansion.

### India Gate and around
A tour of New Delhi will usually start with a visit to India Gate. This war memorial is situated at the eastern end of **Rajpath**. Designed by Lutyens, it commemorates more than 70,000 Indian soldiers who died in the First World War. Some 13,516 names of British and Indian soldiers killed on the Northwest Frontier and in the Afghan War of 1919 are engraved on the arch and foundations. Under the arch is the Amar Jawan Jyoti, commemorating Indian armed forces' losses in the Indo-Pakistan War of 1971. The arch (43 m high) stands on a base of Bharatpur stone and rises in stages. Similar to the Hindu *chhattri* signifying regality, it is decorated with nautilus shells symbolizing British maritime power. Come at dusk to join the picnicking crowds enjoying the evening.

### National Gallery of Modern Art
ⓘ *Jaipur House, near India Gate, T011-2338 4640, www.ngmaindia.gov.in, Tue-Sun 1000-1700, Rs 150 foreigners, Rs 10 Indians.*
There is now a new air-conditioned wing of this excellent gallery and select exhibits in the old building housed in a former residence of the Maharaja of Jaipur. The *'In the Seeds of Time...'* exhibition traces the trajectory of modern Indian art. Artists include: Amrita Shergil, with over 100 exhibits, synthesizing the flat treatment of Indian painting with a realistic tone; Rabindranath Tagore (ground floor) has examples from a brief but intense spell in the 1930s; The Bombay School or Company School (first floor) includes Western painters who documented their visits to India. Realism is reflected in Indian painting of the early 19th century represented by the schools of Avadh, Patna, Sikkim and Thanjavur; The Bengal School (the late 19th-century Revivalist Movement) showcases artists such as Abanindranath Tagore and Nandalal Bose have their works exhibited here. Western influence was discarded in response to the nationalist movement. Inspiration derived from Indian folk art is evident in the works of Jamini Roy and YD Shukla. Prints from the gallery shop are incredibly good value – up to Rs 80 for poster-size prints of famous works.

**➡ Delhi maps**
1 Old Delhi, page 28
2 New Delhi, page 34
3 Connaught Place, page 38

N

700 metres
700 yards

**Where to stay** 🛏
Amarya Haveli **24** *F2*
Claridges **5** *C3*
Jyoti Mahal **1** *A3*
K One One **28** *D4*
Life Tree **12** *E4*
Lutyens Bungalow **10** *D3*
Manor **13** *E5*
Master **14** *B2*
Oberoi **15** *C4*
Prince Polonia **3** *A3*
Rak Internacional **4** *A3*
Taj Mahal **19** *C3*
Tree of Life **16** *F3*
Vivanta by Taj **2** *C4*
Youth Hostel **22** *C2*

**Restaurants** 🍴
Baci **21** *C4*
Bukhara **1** *C1*
Café Sim Tok **2** *A3*
Dum Pukht **1** *C1*
Grey Garden **3** *F2*
Indian Accent **13** *D5*
Kainoosh **34** *E1*
Khan Cha Cha **33** *C4*
Latitude **27** *C3*
Lodi **10** *D3*

Magique **35** *F2*
Naivedyam & Elma's **4** *F2*
Nathu's & Bengali Sweet
  House **18** *B4*
Olive at the Qutb **12** *F2*
Park Baluchi **6** *E2*
Sagar Ratna **8** *E4*
Tadka **14** *A3*
Triveni Tea Terrace **5** *B4*

**Bars & clubs** 🍸
Blue Frog **36** *F2*
Café Morrisons **38** *E3*
Living Room **7** *F2*
Shalom **44** *F4*
Stone **45** *D4*
Urban Pind **47** *E4*
Zoo **48** *F2*

Metro Stops (Yellow Line) Ⓜ
Metro Stops (Videt Line) Ⓜ

## National Museum

ⓘ *Janpath, T011-2301 9272, www.nationalmuseumindia.gov.in, daily 1000-1700, foreigners Rs 300 (including audio tour), Indians Rs 10, camera Rs 300; free guided tours 1030, 1130, 1200, 1400, films are screened every day (1430), marble squat toilets, but dirty.*

The collection was formed from the nucleus of the Exhibition of Indian Art, London (1947). Now merged with the Asian Antiquities Museum it displays a rich collection of the artistic treasure of Central Asia and India including ethnological objects from prehistoric archaeological finds to the late Medieval period. Replicas of exhibits and books on Indian culture and art are on sale. There is also a research library.

**Ground floor  Prehistoric**: seals, figurines, toy animals and jewellery from the Harappan civilization (2400-1500 BC). **Maurya Period**: terracottas and stone heads from around the third century BC include the *chaturmukha* (four-faced) *lingam*. **Gandhara School**: stucco heads showing the Graeco Roman influence. **Gupta terracottas** (circa AD 400): including two life-size images of the river goddesses Ganga and Yamuna and the four-armed bust of Vishnu from a temple near Lal Kot. **South Indian sculpture**: from Pallava and early Chola temples and relief panels from Mysore. Bronzes from the Buddhist monastery at Nalanda. Some of Buddha's relics were placed in the Thai pavilion in 1997.

**First floor  Illustrated manuscripts**: include the *Babur-i-nama* in the emperor's own handwriting and an autographed copy of Jahangir's memoirs. **Miniature paintings**: include the 16th-century Jain School, the 18th-century Rajasthani School and the Pahari schools of Garhwal, Basoli and Kangra. **Aurel Stein Collection** consists of antiquities recovered by him during his explorations of Central Asia and the western borders of China at the turn of the 20th century.

**Second floor  Pre-Columbian and Mayan artefacts**: anthropological section devoted to tribal artefacts and folk arts. **Sharad Rani Bakkiwal Gallery of Musical Instruments**: displays over 300 instruments collected by the famous *sarod* player.

## Rashtrapati Bhavan and Nehru Memorial Museum

Once the Viceroy's House, Rashtrapati Bhavan is the official residence of the President of India. The Viceroy's House, New Delhi's centrepiece of imperial proportions, was 1 km around the foundations, bigger than Louis XIV's palace at Versailles. It had a colossal dome surmounting a long colonnade and 340 rooms in all. It took nearly 20 years to complete, similar to the time it took to build the Taj Mahal. In the busiest year, 29,000 people were working on the site and buildings began to take shape. The project was surrounded by controversy from beginning to end. Opting for a fundamentally classical structure, both Baker and Lutyens sought to incorporate Indian motifs, many entirely superficial. While some claim that Lutyens achieved a unique synthesis of the two traditions, Tillotson asks whether "the sprinkling of a few simplified and classicized Indian details (especially *chhattris*) over a classical palace" could be called a synthesis. The Durbar Hall, 23 m in diameter, has coloured marble from all parts of India.

To the south is **Flagstaff House**, formerly the residence of the commander-in-chief. Renamed Teen Murti Bhawan it now houses the **Nehru Memorial Museum** ⓘ *T011-2301 4504, Tue-Sun 1000-1500, planetarium Mon-Sat 1130-1500, library Mon-Sat 0900-1900, free.* Designed by Robert Tor Russell, in 1948 it became the official residence of India's first prime minister, Jawaharlal Nehru. Converted after his death (1964) into a national memorial, the reception, study and bedroom are intact. A *Jyoti Jawahar* (torch) symbolizes the eternal values he inspired and a granite rock is carved with extracts from his historic speech at midnight on 14 August 1947; an informative and vivid history of the Independence Movement.

The **Martyr's Memorial**, at the junction of Sardar Patel Marg and Willingdon Crescent, is a magnificent 26-m-long, 3-m-high bronze sculpture by DP Roy Chowdhury. The 11 statues of national heroes are headed by Mahatma Gandhi.

## Eternal Gandhi Multimedia Museum

ⓘ *Birla House, 5 Tees Jan Marg (near Claridges Hotel), T011-3095 7269, www.eternal gandhi.org, closed Mon and 2nd Sat, 1000-1700, free, film at 1500.*

Gandhi's last place of residence and the site of his assassination, Birla House has been converted into a whizz-bang display of 'interactive' modern technology. Over-attended by young guides eager to demonstrate the next gadget, the museum seems aimed mainly at those with a critically short attention span, and is too rushed to properly convey the story of Gandhi's life. However, a monument in the garden marking where he fell is definitely worth a visit.

Other museums in the city related to Gandhi include: **National Gandhi Museum** ⓘ *opposite Raj Ghat, T011-2331 1793, www.gandhimuseum.org, Tue-Sat 0930-1730*, with five pavilions – sculpture, photographs and paintings of Gandhi and the history of the *Satyagraha* movement (the philosophy of non-violence); **Gandhi Smarak Sangrahalaya** ⓘ *Raj Ghat, T011-2301 1480, Fri-Wed 0930-1730*, displays some of Gandhi's personal belongings and a small library includes recordings of speeches; and the **Indira Gandhi Museum** ⓘ *1 Safdarjang Rd, T011-2301 0094, Tue-Sun 0930-1700, free*, charting the phases of her life from childhood to the moment of her death. Exhibits are fascinating, if rather gory – you can see the blood-stained, bullet-ridden sari she was wearing when assassinated.

## Parliament House and around

Northeast of the Viceroy's House is the **Council House**, now **Sansad Bhavan**. Baker designed this based on Lutyens' suggestion that it be circular (173 m diameter). Inside are the library and chambers for the Council of State, Chamber of Princes and Legislative Assembly – the **Lok Sabha**. Just opposite the Council House is the **Rakabganj Gurudwara** in Pandit Pant Marg. This 20th-century white marble shrine, which integrates the late Mughal and Rajasthani styles, marks the spot where the headless body of Guru Tegh Bahadur, the ninth Sikh Guru, was cremated in 1657. West of the Council House is the **Cathedral Church of the Redemption** (1927-1935) and to its north the Italianate Roman Catholic **Church of the Sacred Heart** (1930-1934), both conceived by Henry Medd.

## Connaught Place and Connaught Circus

Connaught Place and its outer ring, Connaught Circus (now officially named **Rajiv Chowk** and **Indira Chowk**, but still commonly referred to by their old names), comprise two-storey arcaded buildings, arranged radially around a circular garden that was completed after the Metro line was installed. Designed by Robert Tor Russell, they have become the main commercial and tourist centre of New Delhi. Sadly, the area also attracts bands of insistent touts.

## Lakshmi Narayan Mandir

To the west of Connaught Circus is the Lakshmi Narayan **Birla Temple** in Mandir Marg. Financed by the prominent industrialist Raja Baldeo Birla in 1938, this is one of the most popular Hindu shrines in the city and one of Delhi's few striking examples of Hindu architecture. Dedicated to

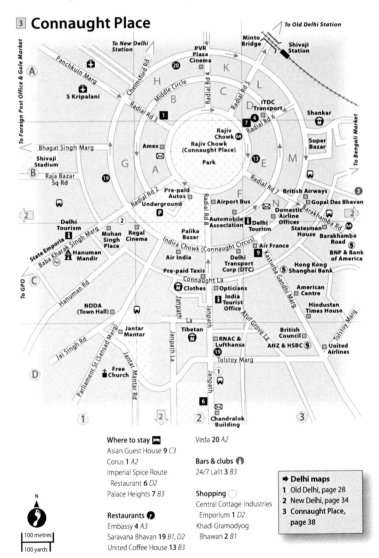

**③ Connaught Place**

**Where to stay** 🛏
Asian Guest House **9** C3
Corus **1** A2
Imperial Spice Route
  Restaurant **6** D2
Palace Heights **7** B3

**Restaurants** 🍴
Embassy **4** A3
Saravana Bhavan **19** B1, D2
United Coffee House **13** B3

Veda **20** A2

**Bars & clubs** 🍸
24/7 Lalit **3** B3

**Shopping** 🛍
Central Cottage Industries
  Emporium **1** D2
Khadi Gramodyog
  Bhawan **2** B1

**➜ Delhi maps**
1  Old Delhi, page 28
2  New Delhi, page 34
3  Connaught Place,
   page 38

N

100 metres
100 yards

Lakshmi, the goddess of well-being, it is commonly referred to as **Birla Mandir**. The design is in the Orissan style with tall curved *sikharas* (towers) capped by large *amalakas*. The exterior is faced with red and ochre stone and white marble. Built around a central courtyard, the main shrine has images of Narayan and his consort Lakshmi while two separate cells have icons of Siva (the Destroyer) and Durga (the 10-armed destroyer of demons). The temple is flanked by a *dharamshala* (rest house) and a Buddhist *vihara* (monastery).

## Gurudwara Bangla Sahib
① *Baba Kharak Singh Rd, free.*
This is a fine example of Sikh temple architecture, featuring a large pool reminiscent of Amritsar's Golden Temple. The 24-hour reciting of the faith's holy book adds to the atmosphere, and there's free food on offer, although don't be surprised if you're asked to help out with the washing up! You must remove your shoes and cover your head to enter – suitable scarves are provided if you arrive without.

Further northeast on Baba Kharak Singh Marg is **Hanuman Mandir**. This small temple was built by Maharaja Jai Singh II of Jaipur. **Mangal haat** (Tuesday Fair) is a popular market.

## Jantar Mantar
Just to the east of the Hanuman Mandir in Sansad Marg (Parliament Street) is Jai Singh's **observatory** (Jantar Mantar) ① *sunrise to sunset, Rs 100 foreigners, Rs 5 Indians.* The Mughal Emperor Mohammad Shah (ruled 1719-1748) entrusted the renowned astronomer Maharaja Jai Singh II with the task of revising the calendar and correcting the astronomical tables used by contemporary priests. Daily astral observations were made for years before construction began and plastered brick structures were favoured for the site instead of brass instruments. Built in 1725 it is slightly smaller than the later observatory at Jaipur.

## Memorial Ghats
Beyond Delhi Gate lies the **Yamuna River**, marked by a series of memorials to India's leaders. The river itself, a kilometre away, is invisible from the road, protected by a low rise and banks of trees. The most prominent memorial, immediately opposite the end of Jawaharlal Nehru Road, is that of Mahatma Gandhi at **Raj Ghat**. To its north is **Shanti Vana** (Forest of Peace), landscaped gardens where Prime Minister Jawaharlal Nehru was cremated in 1964, as were his grandson Sanjay Gandhi in 1980, daughter Indira Gandhi in 1984 and elder grandson, Rajiv, in 1991. To the north again is **Vijay Ghat** (Victory Bank) where Prime Minister Lal Bahadur Shastri was cremated.

---

## South Delhi → *For listings, see pages 46-58.*

South Delhi is often overlooked by travellers. This is a real pity as it houses some of the city's most stunning sites, best accommodation, bars, clubs and restaurants, as well as some of its most tranquil parks.

## Lodi Gardens
These beautiful gardens, with mellow stone tombs of the 15th- and 16th-century Lodi rulers, are popular for gentle strolls and jogging. In the middle of the garden facing the east entrance from Max Mueller Road is **Bara Gumbad** (Big Dome), a mosque built in 1494. The raised courtyard is provided with an imposing gateway and *mehman khana* (guest rooms). The platform in the centre appears to have had a tank for ritual ablutions.

The **Sheesh Bumbad** (Glass Dome, late 15th century) is built on a raised incline north of the Bara Gumbad and was once decorated with glazed blue tiles, painted floral designs and Koranic inscriptions. The façade gives the impression of a two-storeyed building, typical of Lodi architecture. **Mohammad Shah's Tomb** (1450) is that of the third Sayyid ruler. It has sloping buttresses, an octagonal plan, projecting eaves and lotus patterns on the ceiling. **Sikander Lodi's Tomb**, built by his son in 1517, is also an octagonal structure decorated with Hindu motifs. A structural innovation is the double dome which was later refined under the Mughals. The 16th-century **Athpula** (Bridge of Eight Piers), near the northeastern entrance, is attributed to Nawab Bahadur, a nobleman at Akbar's court.

## Safdarjang's Tomb
ⓘ *Sunrise to sunset, Rs 100 foreigners, Rs 5 Indians.*
Safdarjang's Tomb, seldom visited, was built by Nawab Shuja-ud-Daulah for his father Mirza Mukhim Abdul Khan, entitled Safdarjang, who was Governor of Oudh (1719-1748), and Wazir of his successor (1748-1754). Safdarjang died in 1754. With its high enclosure walls, *char bagh* layout of gardens, fountain and central domed mausoleum, it follows the tradition of Humayun's tomb. Typically, the real tomb is just below ground level. Flanking the mausoleum are pavilions used by Shuja-ud-Daulah as his family residence. Immediately to its south is the battlefield where Timur and his Mongol horde crushed Mahmud Shah Tughluq on 12 December 1398.

## Nizamuddin's Tomb
ⓘ *Dress ultra-modestly if you don't want to feel uncomfortable or cause offence.*
At the east end of the Lodi Road, Hazrat Nizamuddin Dargah (Nizamuddin 'village's' Tomb) now tucked away behind the residential suburb of Nizamuddin West, off Mathura Road, grew up around the shrine of Sheikh Nizamuddin Aulia (1236-1325), a Chishti saint. This is a wonderfully atmospheric place. *Qawwalis* are sung at sunset after *namaaz* (prayers), and are particularly impressive on Thursdays – be prepared for crowds. Highly recommended.

West of the central shrine is the **Jama-at-khana Mosque** (1325). Its decorated arches are typical of the Khalji design also seen at the Ala'i Darwaza at the Qutb Minar. South of the main tomb and behind finely crafted screens is the grave of princess Jahanara, Shah Jahan's eldest and favourite daughter. She shared the emperor's last years when he was imprisoned at Agra Fort. The grave, open to the sky, is in accordance with the epitaph written by her: "Let naught cover my grave save the green grass, for grass suffices as the covering of the lowly". Pilgrims congregate at the shrine twice a year for the **Urs** (fair) held to mark the anniversaries of Hazrat Nizamuddin Aulia and his disciple Amir Khusrau, whose tomb is nearby.

## Humayun's Tomb
ⓘ *Sunrise to sunset, Rs 250 foreigners, Rs 10 Indians, video cameras Rs 25, located in Nizamuddin, 15-20 mins by taxi from Connaught Circus, allow 45 mins.*
Eclipsed later by the Taj Mahal and the Jama Masjid, this tomb is the best example in Delhi of the early Mughal style of tomb. Superbly maintained, it is well worth a visit, preferably before visiting the Taj Mahal. Humayun, the second Mughal emperor, was forced into exile in Persia after being heavily defeated by the Afghan Sher Shah in 1540. He returned to India in 1545, finally recapturing Delhi in 1555. The tomb was designed and built by his senior widow and mother of his son Akbar, Hamida Begum. A Persian from Khurasan, after her pilgrimage to Mecca she was known as Haji Begum. She supervised the entire construction of the tomb (1564-1573), camping on the site.

**The approach** The tomb enclosure has two high double-storeyed gateways: the entrance to the west and the other to the south. A *baradari* occupies the centre of the east wall, and a bath chamber that of the north wall. Several Moghul princes, princesses and Haji Begum herself lie buried here. During the 1857 Mutiny Bahadur Shah II, the last Moghul emperor of Delhi, took shelter here with his three sons. Over 80, he was seen as a figurehead by Muslims opposing the British. When captured he was transported to Yangon (Rangoon) for the remaining four years of his life. The tomb to the right of the approach is that of Isa Khan, Humayun's barber.

**The dome** Some 38 m high, the dome does not have the swell of the Taj Mahal and the decoration of the whole edifice is much simpler. It is of red sandstone with some white marble to highlight the lines of the building. There is some attractive inlay work, and some *jalis* in the balcony fence and on some of the recessed keel arch windows. The interior is austere and consists of three storeys of arches rising up to the dome. The emperor's tomb is of white marble and quite plain without any inscription. The overall impression is that of a much bulkier, more squat building than the Taj Mahal. The cavernous space under the main tombs is home to great colonies of bats.

### Hauz Khas

ⓘ *1-hr cultural show, 1845, Rs 100 (check with Delhi Tourism, see page 25).*
South of Safdarjang's Tomb, and entered off either Aurobindo Marg on the east side or Africa Avenue on the west side, is Hauz Khas. Ala-ud-din Khalji (ruled 1296-1313) created a large tank here for the use of the inhabitants of Siri, the second capital city of Delhi founded by him. Fifty years later Firoz Shah Tughluq cleaned up the silted tank and raised several buildings on its east and south banks which are known as Hauz Khas or Royal Tank.

Firoz Shah's austere tomb is found here. The multi-storeyed wings, on the north and west of the tomb, were built by him in 1354 as a *madrasa* (college). The octagonal and square *chhattris* were built as tombs, possibly to the teachers at the college. Hauz Khas is now widely used as a park for early-morning recreation – walking, running and yoga *asanas*. Classical music concerts, dance performances and a *son et lumière* show are held in the evenings when monuments are illuminated by thousands of earthen lamps and torches. Wandering the streets of Haus Khaz village, you can almost forget that you are in India. Labyrinthine alleys lead to numerous galleries, boutiques and restaurants, and there are a lot of little design studios.

### Qutb Minar Complex

ⓘ *Sunrise to sunset, Rs 250 foreigners, Rs 10 Indians. The Metro goes to Qutb Minar. Bus 505 from New Delhi Railway Station (Ajmeri Gate), Super Bazar (east of Connaught Circus) and Cottage Industries Emporium, Janpath. Auto Rs 110, though drivers may be reluctant to take you. This area is also opening up as a hub for new chic restaurants and bars.*
Muhammad Ghuri conquered northwest India at the very end of the 12th century. The conquest of the Gangetic plain down to Benares (Varanasi) was undertaken by Muhammad's Turkish slave and chief general, Qutb-ud-din-Aibak, whilst another general took Bihar and Bengal. In the process, temples were reduced to rubble, the remaining Buddhist centres were dealt their death blow and their monks slaughtered. When Muhammad was assassinated in 1206, his gains passed to the loyal Qutb-ud-din-Aibak. Thus the first sultans or Muslim kings of Delhi became known as the **Slave Dynasty**

(1026-1290). For the next three centuries the Slave Dynasty and the succeeding Khalji (1290-1320), Tughluq (1320-1414), Sayyid (1414-1445) and Lodi (1451-1526) dynasties provided Delhi with fluctuating authority. The legacy of their ambitions survives in the tombs, forts and palaces that litter Delhi Ridge and the surrounding plain. Qutb-ud-din-Aibak died after only four years in power, but he left his mark with the **Qutb Minar** and his **citadel**. Qutb Minar, built to proclaim the victory of Islam over the infidel, dominates the countryside for miles around. Visit the *minar* first.

**Qutb Minar** In 1199 work began on what was intended to be the most glorious tower of victory in the world and was to be the prototype of all *minars* (towers) in India. Qutb-ud-din-Aibak had probably seen and been influenced by the brick victory pillars in Ghazni in Afghanistan, but this one was also intended to serve as the minaret attached to the Might of Islam Mosque. From here the muezzin could call the faithful to prayer. Later every mosque would incorporate its minaret.

As a mighty reminder of the importance of the ruler as Allah's representative on earth, the Qutb Minar (literally 'axis minaret') stood at the centre of the community. A pivot of Faith, Justice and Righteousness, its name also carried the message of Qutb-ud-din's (Axis of the Faith) own achievements. The inscriptions carved in Kufi script tell that "the tower was erected to cast the shadow of God over both east and west". For Qutb-ud-din-Aibak it marked the eastern limit of the empire of the One God. Its western counterpart is the Giralda Tower built by Yusuf in Seville.

The Qutb Minar is 73 m high and consists of five storeys. The diameter of the base is 14.4 m and 2.7 m at the top. Qutb-ud-din built the first three and his son-in-law Iltutmish embellished these and added a fourth. This is indicated in some of the Persian and Nagari (North Indian) inscriptions which also record that it was twice damaged by lightning in 1326 and 1368. While repairing the damage caused by the second, Firoz Shah Tughluq added a fifth storey and used marble to face the red and buff sandstone. This was the first time contrasting colours were used decoratively, later to become such a feature of Mughal buildings. Firoz's fifth storey was topped by a graceful cupola but this fell down during an earthquake in 1803. A new one was added by a Major Robert Smith in 1829 but was so out of keeping that it was removed in 1848 and now stands in the gardens.

The original storeys are heavily indented with different styles of fluting, alternately round and angular on the bottom, round on the second and angular on the third. The beautifully carved honeycomb detail beneath the balconies is reminiscent of the Alhambra Palace in Spain. The calligraphy bands are verses from the Koran and praises to its patron builder.

**Quwwat-ul-Islam Mosque** The Quwwat-ul-Islam Mosque (The Might of Islam Mosque), the earliest surviving mosque in India, is to the northwest of the Qutb Minar. It was begun in 1192, immediately after Qutb-ud-din's conquest of Delhi and completed in 1198, using the remains of no fewer than 27 local Hindu and Jain temples.

The architectural style contained elements that Muslims brought from Arabia, including buildings made of mud and brick and decorated with glazed tiles, *squinches* (arches set diagonally across the corners of a square chamber to facilitate the raising of a dome and to effect a transition from a square to a round structure), the pointed arch and the true dome. Finally, Muslim buildings came alive through ornamental calligraphy and geometric patterning. This was in marked contrast to indigenous Indian styles of architecture. Hindu, Buddhist and Jain buildings relied on the post-and-beam system in which spaces were traversed by corbelling, ie shaping flat-laid stones to create an arch. The arched screen that runs along the western end of the courtyard beautifully illustrates the fact that it was Hindu methods that still prevailed at this stage, for the 16-m-high arch uses Indian corbelling, the corners being smoothed off to form the curved line.

**Screens** Qutb-ud-din's screen formed the façade of the mosque and, facing in the direction of Mecca, became the focal point. The sandstone screen is carved in the Indo-Islamic style, lotuses mingling with Koranic calligraphy. The later screenwork and other extensions (1230) are fundamentally Islamic in style, the flowers and leaves having been replaced by more arabesque patterns. Indian builders mainly used stone, which from the fourth century AD had been intricately carved with representations of the gods. In their first buildings in India the Muslim architects designed the buildings and local Indian craftsmen built them and decorated them with typical motifs such as the vase and foliage, tasselled ropes, bells and cows.

**Iltutmish's extension** The mosque was enlarged twice. In 1230 Qutb-ud-din's son-in-law and successor, Shamsuddin Iltutmish, doubled its size by extending the colonnades and prayer hall – 'Iltutmish's extension'. This accommodated a larger congregation, and in the more stable conditions of Iltutmish's reign, Islam was obviously gaining ground. The arches of the extension are nearer to the true arch and are similar to the Gothic arch that appeared in Europe at this time. The decoration is Islamic. Almost 100 years after Iltutmish's death, the mosque was enlarged again, by Ala-ud-din Khalji. The conductor of tireless and bloody military campaigns, Ala-ud-din proclaimed himself 'God's representative on earth'. His architectural ambitions, however, were not fully realized, because on his death in 1316 only part of the north and east extensions were completed.

**Ala'i Minar and the Ala'i Darwaza** To the north of the Qutb complex is the 26-m **Ala'i Minar**, intended to surpass the tower of the Qutb, but not completed beyond the first storey. Ala-ud-din did complete the south gateway to the building, the **Ala'i Darwaza**; inscriptions testify that it was built in 1311 (Muslim 710 AH). He benefited from events in Central Asia: since the early 13th century, Mongol hordes from Central Asia fanned out east and west, destroying the civilization of the Seljuk Turks in West Asia, and refugee artists, architects, craftsmen and poets fled east. They brought to India features and techniques that had developed in Byzantine Turkey, some of which can be seen in the Ala'i Darwaza.

**Iltutmish's Tomb** Built in 1235, Iltutmish's Tomb lies in the northwest of the compound, midway along the west wall of the mosque. It is the first surviving tomb of a Muslim ruler in India. Two other tombs also stand within the extended Might of Islam Mosque. The idea of a tomb was quite alien to Hindus, who had been practising cremation since around 400 BC. Blending Hindu and Muslim styles, the outside is relatively plain with three arched and decorated doorways. The interior carries reminders of the nomadic origins of the first Muslim rulers. Like a Central Asian *yurt* (tent) in its decoration, it combines the familiar Indian motifs of the wheel, bell, chain and lotus with the equally familiar geometric arabesque patterning. The west wall is inset with three *mihrabs* that indicate the direction of Mecca.

## Tughluqabad
ⓘ *Sunrise to sunset, foreigners Rs100, Indians Rs 5, video camera Rs 25, allow 1 hr for return rickshaws, turn right at entrance and walk 200 m. The site is often deserted so don't go alone. Take plenty of water.*

Tughluqabad's ruins, 7.5 km east from Qutb Minar, still convey a sense of the power and energy of the newly arrived Muslims in India. From the walls you get a magnificent impression of the strategic advantages of the site. **Ghiyas'ud-Din Tughluq** (ruled 1321-1325), after ascending the throne of Delhi, selected this site for his capital. He built a massive fort around his capital city which stands high on a rocky outcrop of the Delhi Ridge. The fort is roughly octagonal in plan with a circumference of 6.5 km. The vast size, strength and obvious solidity of the whole give it an air of massive grandeur. It was not until Babur (ruled 1526-1530) that dynamite was used in warfare, so this is a very defensible site.

East of the main entrance is the rectangular **citadel**. A wider area immediately to the west and bounded by walls contained the **palaces**. Beyond this to the north lay the **city**. Now marked by the ruins of houses, the streets were laid out in a grid fashion. Inside the citadel enclosure is the **Vijay Mandal tower** and the remains of several halls including a long underground passage. The fort also contained seven tanks.

A causeway connects the fort with the tomb of Ghiyas'ud-Din Tughluq, while a wide embankment near its southeast corner gave access to the fortresses of **Adilabad** about 1 km away, built a little later by Ghiyas'ud-Din's son Muhammad. The tomb is very well preserved and has red sandstone walls with a pronounced slope (the first Muslim building in India to have sloping walls), crowned with a white marble dome. This dome, like that of the Ala'i Darwaza at the Qutb, is crowned by an *amalaka*, a feature of Hindu architecture. Also Hindu is the trabeate arch at the tomb's fortress wall entrance. Inside are three cenotaphs belonging to Ghiyas'ud-Din, his wife and son Muhammad.

Ghiyas'ud-Din Tughluq quickly found that military victories were no guarantee of lengthy rule. When he returned home after a victorious campaign the welcoming pavilion erected by his son and successor, Muhammad-bin Tughluq, was deliberately collapsed over him. Tughluqabad was abandoned shortly afterwards and was thus only inhabited for five years. The Tughluq dynasty continued to hold Delhi until Timur sacked it and slaughtered its inhabitants. For a brief period Tughluq power shifted to Jaunpur near Varanasi, where the Tughluq architectural traditions were carried forward in some superb mosques.

### Baha'i Temple (Lotus Temple)

ⓘ *1 Apr-30 Sep 0900-1900, 1 Oct-31 Mar Tue-Sun 0930-1730, free entry and parking, visitors welcome to attend services, at other times the temple is open for silent meditation and prayer. Audio-visual presentations in English are at 1100, 1200, 1400 and 1530, remove shoes before entering.*

Architecturally the Baha'i Temple is a remarkably striking building. Constructed in 1980-1981, it is built out of white marble and in the characteristic Baha'i temple shape of a lotus flower – 45 lotus petals form the walls – which internally creates a feeling of light and space (34 m high, 70 m in diameter). It is a simple design, brilliantly executed and very elegant in form. All Baha'i temples are nine-sided, symbolizing 'comprehensiveness, oneness and unity'. The Delhi Temple, which seats 1300, is surrounded by nine pools, an attractive feature also helping to keep the building cool. It is particularly attractive when flood-lit. Baha'i temples are "dedicated to the worship of God, for peoples of all races, religions or castes. Only the Holy Scriptures of the Baha'i Faith and earlier revelations are read or recited".

Designated as the site of the athletes' village for the 2010 Commonwealth Games, East Delhi has just one attraction to draw visitors across the Yamuna.

## Swaminarayan Akshardham

ⓘ *www.akshardham.com, Apr-Sep Tue-Sun 1000-1900, Oct-Mar Tue-Sun 0900-1800, temple free, Rs 170 for 'attractions', musical fountain Rs 20, no backpacks, cameras or other electronic items (bag and body searches at entry gate). Packed on Sun; visit early to avoid crowds.*

Opened in November 2005 on the east bank of the Yamuna, the gleaming Akshardham complex represents perhaps the most ambitious construction project in India since the foundation of New Delhi itself. At the centre of a surreal 40-ha 'cultural complex' complete with landscaped gardens, cafés and theme park rides, the temple-monument is dedicated to the 18th-century saint Bhagwan Swaminarayan, who abandoned his home at the age of 11 to embark on a lifelong quest for the spiritual and cultural uplift of Western India. It took 11,000 craftsmen, all volunteers, no less than 300 million hours to complete the temple using traditional building and carving techniques.

If this is the first religious site you visit in India, the security guards and swarms of mooching Indian tourists will hardly prepare you for the typical temple experience. Yet despite this, and the boat rides and animatronic shows which have prompted inevitable comparisons to a 'spiritual Disneyland', most visitors find the Akshardham an inspiring, indeed uplifting, experience, if for no other reason than that the will and ability to build something of its scale and complexity still exist.

**The temple** You enter the temple complex through a series of intricately carved gates. The Bhakti Dwar (Gate of Devotion), adorned with 208 pairs of gods and their consorts, leads into a hall introducing the life of Swaminarayan and the activities of BAPS (Bochasanwasi Shri Akshar Purushottam Swaminarayan Sanstha), the global Hindu sect-cum-charity which runs Akshardham. The main courtyard is reached through the Mayur Dwar (Peacock Gate), a conglomeration of 869 carved peacocks echoed by an equally florid replica directly facing it.

From here you get your first look at the central monument. Perfectly symmetrical in pink sandstone and white marble, it rests on a plinth encircled by 148 elephants, each sculpted from a 20-tonne stone block, in situations ranging from the literal to the mythological: mortal versions grapple with lions or lug tree trunks, while Airavatha, the eight-trunked mount of Lord Indra, surfs majestically to shore after the churning of the oceans at the dawn of Hindu creation. Above them, carvings of deities, saints and *sadhus* cover every inch of the walls and columns framing the inner sanctum, where a gold-plated *murti* (idol) of Bhagwan Swaminarayan sits attended by avatars of his spiritual successors, beneath a staggeringly intricate marble dome. Around the main dome are eight smaller domes, each carved in hypnotic fractal patterns, while paintings depicting Swaminarayan's life of austerity and service line the walls (explanations in English and Hindi).

Surrounding the temple is a moat of holy water supposedly taken from 151 sacred lakes and rivers visited by Swaminarayan on his seven-year barefoot pilgrimage. Some 108 bronze *gaumukhs* (cow heads) representing the 108 names of God spout water into the tank, which is itself hemmed in by a 1-km-long *parikrama* (colonnade) of red Rajasthani sandstone.

## Delhi listings

*For hotel and restaurant price codes and other relevant information, see pages 12-14.*

### ⊜ Where to stay

Avoid hotel touts. Airport taxis may pretend not to know the location of your chosen hotel so give full details and insist on being taken there. It really saves a lot of hassle if you make reservations. Even if you change hotel the next day, it is good to arrive with somewhere booked especially if you are flying in late at night. **$** accommodation is concentrated around **Paharganj** (New Delhi), and **Chandni Chowk** (Old Delhi).

**Old Delhi and beyond** *p27, map p28*
**$$$$ Maidens**, 7 Sham Nath Marg,
T011-2397 5464, www.maidenshotel.com.
54 large well-appointed rooms, restaurant (slow), barbecue nights are excellent, old-style bar, attractive colonial style in quiet area, spacious gardens with excellent pool, friendly welcome. One of Delhi's oldest hotels.
**$$$ Broadway**, 4/15A Asaf Ali Rd, T011-4366 3600, www.hotelbroadwaydelhi.com. 36 rooms, some wonderfully quirky. Interior designer Catherine Levy has designed some of the rooms in a quirky kitsch style, brightly coloured with psychedelic bathroom tiles. The other rooms are classic design. **Chor Bizarre** restaurant and bar is highly regarded, as is the 'Thugs' pub. Walking tours of Old Delhi. Easily one of the best options.

**New Delhi** *p33, maps p34 and p38*
**Connaught Place**
**$$$$ Imperial**, Janpath, T011-2334 1234, www.theimperialindia.com. Quintessential Delhi. 230 rooms and beautiful 'deco suites' in supremely elegant Lutyens-designed 1933 hotel. Unparalleled location, great bar, antiques and art everywhere, beautiful gardens with spa and secluded pool. Highly recommended.

**$$$ Hotel Corus**, B-49 Connaught Pl, T011-4365 2222, www.hotelcorus.com. Comfortable hotel right at the heart of things. Good value rooms. You get 15% discount in their onsite **Life Caffe.**
**$$$ Palace Heights**, D26-28 Connaught Pl, T011-4358 2610, www.hotelpalace heights.com. Recently given a complete facelift, the bright, modern rooms with good attention to detail, represent the best choice in Connaught Pl in this price bracket. There's also an attractive glass-walled restaurant overlooking the street.
**$ Asian Guest House**, 14 Scindia House, off Kasturba Gandhi Marg, the sign is hidden behind petrol pump, T011-2331 0229, www.asianguesthouse.com. Friendly faces greet you here, although it's a bit tricky to find – call ahead for directions. Great central location. Clean basic rooms, some with a/c, some with TV.

**Paharganj**
Parharganj is where backpackers congregate. Sandwiched between the main sights and near the main railway station
**$$$$-$$$ Jyoti Mahal**, 2488 Nalwa St, behind Imperial Cinema, T011-2358 0524, www.jyotimahal.net. An oasis in Paharganj with large and atmospheric rooms in a beautiful converted *haveli* and new deluxe rooms in stylish new wing. Top-notch rooftop restaurant serving continental and Indian dishes.
**$$ Prince Polonia**, 2325-26 Tilak Gali (behind Imperial Cinema), T011-4762 6600, www.hotelprincepolonia.com. Very unusual for Paharganj in that it has a rooftop pool. Safe, clean. Recently refurbished.
**$ Rak International**, 820 Main Bazar, Chowk Bowli, T011-2358 6508, www.hotelrak international.com. 27 basic but clean rooms. Professionally run. Quiet, friendly hotel with a rooftop restaurant and water feature.

## Rajendra Nagar

**$$$-$$ Master Guest House**, R-500 New Rajendra Nagar (Shankar Rd and GR Hospital Rd crossing), T011-2874 1089, www.master bedandbreakfast.com. 3 beautiful rooms, a/c, Wi-Fi, rooftop for breakfast, *thalis*, warm welcome, personal attention, secure, recommended. Each room has the theme of a different god, complete with appropriate colour schemes. Very knowledgeable, caring owners run excellent tours of 'hidden Delhi'. They make Delhi feel like home. Recommended.

## South Delhi *p39*

Most of the city's smartest hotels are located south of Rajpath, in a broad rectangle between Chanakyapuri and Humayun's Tomb.

**$$$$ Claridges**, 12 Aurangzeb Rd, T011-3955 5000, www.claridges.com. 138 refurbished, classy rooms, art deco-style interiors, colonial atmosphere, attractive restaurants (**Jade Garden** is good), slick **Aura** bar, impeccable service, more atmosphere than most. Recommended.

**$$$$ Manor**, 77 Friends Colony, T011-2692 5151, www.themanordelhi.com. Contemporary boutique hotel with 10 stylish rooms, heavenly beds, polished stone surfaces and chrome, relaxing garden, a haven. Beautiful artwork and relaxed vibe. Acclaimed restaurant **Indian Accent**. Charming service.

**$$$$ Oberoi**, Dr Zakir Hussain Marg, T011-2436 3030, www.oberoihotels.com. 300 rooms and extremely luxurious suites overlooking golf club, immaculate, quietly efficient, beautiful touches, carved Tree of Life in lobby, all 5-star facilities including 2 pools and spa, superb business centre, good restaurants – **360°** gets rave reviews.

**$$$$ Taj Mahal**, 1 Mansingh Rd, T011-2302 6162, www.tajhotels.com. 1 of 3 Taj hotels in Delhi. 300 attractive rooms, comfortable, new club levels outstanding, excellent restaurants and service, lavishly finished with 'lived-in' feel, friendly 1920s-style bar. There is also a **Vivanta by Taj** hotel close to Khan Market with a more business mood.

**$$$$-$$$ Amarya Haveli**, P5 Hauz Khas Enclave, T011-4175 9268, www.amarya group.com. Luxury, boutique, hip guesthouse, run by 2 Frenchmen. Unique, bright, en suite rooms, with TV, Wi-Fi. Fantastic roof garden. Book ahead. They have a sister property **Amarya Villa** in Safdarjung Enclave – the decor there is inspired by *Navratna* (nine gems) – both properties are effortlessly chic. Highly recommended.

**$$$ K One One**, K11, Jangpura Extn, 2nd floor, T011-4359 2583, www.pari gold.com. Run by wonderful ex-TV chef, who also gives cooking lessons. All rooms en suite with a/c, minibar, Wi-Fi, some with balconies. Wonderful roof terrace with views of Humayan's Tomb. Rooftop room is lovely. Book ahead.

**$$$ Lutyens Bungalow**, 39 Prithviraj Rd, T011-2469 4523, www.lutyensbungalow. co.in. Private guesthouse in a bungalow that has been running for over 35 years. Eccentric, rambling property with 15 a/c rooms, a wonderful pool and beautiful gardens. Free airport pickup/drop off, full services, used for long-stays by NGOs and foreign consultants.

**$$$-$$ Tree of Life B&B**, D-193, Saket, T(0)9810-277699, www.tree-of-life.in. Stylish B&B with beautifully decorated rooms, simple but chic. Kitchen access, excellent on-site reflexology and yoga – really good atmosphere. The owner also runs **Metropole Tourist Service** (page 55). Close to Saket Metro station and to PVR cinema and malls.

**$$ Life Tree**, G 14 Lajpat Nagar Part II, T(0)9910-460898, lifetreebnb@gmail.com. A more simple but charming B&B from the Tree of Life family – well located for Khan Market and centre.

**$ Youth Hostel**, 5 Naya Marg, Chanakyapuri, T011-2611 6285, www.yhaindia.org. Wide range of room from a/c doubles to a basic dorm (a/c dorms much better). Soulless but clean and comfortable. Great location. You need YHA membership to stay (Rs 250 foreigners, Rs 100 Indians).

### Airport
Unless you can afford a 5-star, hotels around the airport are overpriced and best avoided. **$$$-$$ Sam's Snooze at My Space** T3 IGI Airport, opposite Gate 17, T(0)8800-230013, www.newdelhiairport.in. You can book a snooze pod for US$9 per hr – only if you are flying out of T3. There's Wi-Fi, TV and DVD, work stations.

### 🍴 Restaurants

The larger hotel restaurants are often the best for cuisine, decor and ambience. Buffets (lunch or dinner) cost Rs 700 or more. Sun buffets are becoming quite the thing in the top-notch hotels. Others may only open around 1930 for dinner; some close on Sun.

The old-fashioned 'tea on the lawn' is still served at the Imperial and in Claridges (see Where to stay, pages 46 and 47). **Aapki Pasand**, at 15 Netaji Subhash Marg, offers unusual tea-tasting in classy and extremely professional surroundings; it's quite an experience.

### Old Delhi *p27, map p28*
In **Paranthewali Gali**, a side street off Chandni Chowk, stalls sell a variety of *paranthas* including *kaju badam* (stuffed with dry fruits and nuts). For sweets you have to seek out **Old Famous Jalebi Wala**, 1797 Dariba Corner, Chandni Chowk – as they are old and famous!

**$$$-$$ Chor Bizarre**, Broadway Hotel (see Where to stay, page 46), T011- 4366 3600. Tandoori and Kashmiri cuisine (Wazwan, Rs 500). Fantastic food, quirky decor, including salad bar that was a vintage car. Well worth a visit.

**$ Haldiram's**, 1454/2 Chandni Chowk. Stand-up counter for excellent snacks and sweets on the run (try *dokhla* with coriander chutney from seller just outside), and more elaborate sit-down restaurant upstairs.

**$ Karim's**, Gali Kababiyan (south of Jama Masjid), Mughlai. Authentic, busy, plenty of local colour. The experience, as much as the food, makes this a must. Not a lot to tempt vegetarians though.

### New Delhi *p33, maps p34 and p38*
### Connaught Place and around
**$$$ Sevilla**, Claridges Hotel (see Where to stay, page 47). Beautiful restaurant with lots of outdoor seating serving up specialities such as tapas and paella as well as wood fired pizza and the dangerous house special sangria.

**$$$ Spice Route**, Imperial Hotel (see Where to stay, page 46). Award-winning restaurant charting the journey of spices around the world. Extraordinary temple-like surroundings (took 7 years to build), Kerala, Thai, Vietnamese cuisines.

**$$$ Veda**, 27-H, T011-4151 3535, www.
vedarestaurants.com. Owned by fashion
designer Rohit Bal with appropriately
beautiful bordello-style decor, done out like
a Rajasthani palace with high-backed leather
chairs and candles reflecting from mirror
work on ceilings. Food is contemporary
Indian. Great atmosphere at night. There
is another branch at DLF Vasant Kunj.

**$$ Embassy**, D-11, T011-2341 6434.
International food. Popular with artistic-
intellectual-political crowd, good food,
long-standing local favourite.

**$$ United Coffee House**, E-15 Connaught
Pl, T011-2341 1697. Recommended more
for the colonial-era cake-icing decor than
for the fairly average food. Often someone
waxing lyrical over a Casio keyboard. Always
attracts a mixed crowd, well worth a visit.

**$ Nathu's**, and **Bengali Sweet House**, both
in Bengali Market (east of Connaught Pl).
Sweet shops also serving vegetarian food.
Good dosa, *iddli, utthapam* and North Indian
*chana bathura, thalis*, clean, functional.
Try *kulfi* (hard blocks of ice cream) with
*falooda* (sweet vermicelli noodles).

**$ Saravana Bhavan**, P-15/90, near
McDonalds, T011-2334 7755; also at
46 Janpath. Chennai-based chain, light
and wonderful South Indian, superb
chutneys, unmissable *kaju anjeer* ice
cream with figs and nuts. Can take
hours to get a table at night or at weekends.
Highly recommended.

**$ Triveni Tea Terrace**, Triveni Kala Sangam,
205 Tansen Marg, near Mandi House
Metro station (not Sun). Art galleries,
an amphitheatre and this little café in
quite an unusual building close to CP –
the tea terrace is a bit of an institution.

## Paharganj
**$$-$ Café Sim Tok**, Tooti Chowk, above
Hotel Navrang, near **Hotel Rak**, T(0)9810-
386717. Tucked away little gem of a Korean
restaurant. No signage, ask for **Hotel
Navrang** and keep going up stairs to find
delicious *kimbab* (Korean sushi) and *kimchi*.

**$ Tadka**, off Main Bazar. Great range of all
the usual Indian favourites, with nice decor,
friendly staff and good hygiene levels.

## South Delhi *p39*
**$$$ Baci**, 23 Sunder Nagar Market, near
HDFC Bank, T011-4150 7445. Classy, top-
quality Italian food, run by gregarious Italian-
Indian owners. There are also branches of
their cheaper café **Amici** springing up in
Khan Market and Hauz Khas.

**$$$ Bukhara**, ITC Maurya Sheraton,
Sardar Patel Marg, T011-2611 2233. Stylish
Northwest Frontier cuisine amidst rugged
walls draped with rich rugs. Outstanding
meat dishes and vegetarians will miss out
on the best food.

**$$$ Dum Pukht**, ITC Maurya Sheraton,
Sardar Patel Marg, T011-2611 2233,
www.itcwelcomgroup.com. Open evenings;
lunch only on Sun. Voted one of the best
restaurants in the world, it marries exquisite
tastes and opulent surroundings.

**$$$ Grey Garden**, 13a Hauz Khaz Village,
near the lake, T011-2651 6450. New kid on the
block in the lovely Hauz Khaz village, this boho
chic little number serves up a small menu
but with great attention to detail. Delicious
banana-wrapped fish or thin-crust pizzas, lotus
stem chips and other assorted goodies. Book
ahead at weekends. Highly recommended.

**$$$ Indian Accent**, at The Manor, 77
Friends Colony West, T011-4323 5151.
With a menu designed by Manish Mehotra,
who runs restaurants in Delhi and London,
this acclaimed restaurant offers up Indian
food with a modern twist. Your *dosas* will
reveal masala morel mushrooms, rather
than the traditional Goan prawns *balchao*
here you will find it with roasted scallops.
The menu reflects the changing of the
seasons and there is live fusion music on Sat.
Highly recommended.

**$$$ Kainoosh**, 122-124 DLF Promenade
Mall, Vasant Kunj, T(0)9560-715544. Under
the watchful eye of celebrity chef Marut
Sikka, delicious *thalis* marry the traditional
and modern faces of Indian food. These are

bespoke *thalis* with sea bass mousse and chicken cooked in orange juice and saffron.

**$$$ Latitude**, 9 Khan Market, above Good Earth, T011-2462 1013. Like sitting in someone's very posh, very chic living room and getting served delicious Italian numbers like bruschetta, yummy salads and pastas. Topped off with top-notch coffees.

**$$$ Lodi**, Lodi Gardens, T011-2465 5054. Continental lunch, Indian dinner menu in pleasant, Mediterranean-style surroundings, nice terrace and garden. Come more for the setting than the food which can be mediocre.

**$$$ Magique**, Gate No 3, Garden of 5 Senses, Mehrauli Badarpur Rd, T97175-35533. High-class quality food, in a magical setting. Sit outside among the candles and fairy lights. One of Delhi's most romantic restaurants.

**$$$ Olive at the Qutb**, T011-2957 4444, www.olivebarandkitchen.com. Branch of the ever popular Mumbai restaurant and some people say the Delhi version wins hands down. Serving up delicious platters of Mediterranean food and good strong cocktails. Or head to their sister restaurant in the **Diplomat Hotel – Olive Beach** especially for their legendary blow-out Sun brunches: for Rs 2195 you get open access to a mind-boggling buffet and as many martinis as you can drink.

**$$$ Park Baluchi**, inside Deer Park, Hauz Khas Village, T011-2685 9369. Atmospheric dining in Hauz Khas Deer Park. The lamb wrapped in chicken served on a flaming sword comes highly recommended. Can get crowded, book ahead.

**$$ Elma's**, 24/1 Hauz Khas Village, T011-2652 1020. Lovely little café serving up all manner of tea and cakes and more hearty options like shepherds pie! Mismatched china and funky furniture make this a great little hang-out.

**$$ Naivedyam**, Hauz Khas Village, T011-2696 0426. Very good South Indian, great service and very good value in a very beautiful restaurant. Highly recommended.

**$ Khan Cha Cha**, Khan Market, 75 Middle Lane. This no-frills joint serves some of the best kebabs in the city from a window in the middle lane of Khan Market. Fantastic value. You can recognize the place from the crowd clamouring at the counter.

**$ Sagar Ratna**, 18 Defence Colony Market, T011-2433 3110. Other branches in Vasant Kunj, Malviya Nagar and NOIDA. Excellent South Indian. Cheap and "amazing" *thalis* and coffee, very hectic (frequent queues). One of the best breakfasts in Delhi.

## 🌙 Bars and clubs

Many national holidays are 'dry' days. Delhi's bar/club scene has exploded over the last few years. Expect to pay a lot for your drinks and, when in doubt, dress up. Delhi's 'in' crowd is notoriously fickle; city magazines (*Time Out, First City*) will point you towards the flavour of the month.

### South Delhi *p39*

**24/7**, Lalit Hotel, Barakhamba Av, Connaught Pl. Boasting molecular mixology with their cocktails and regular turns by prominent DJs and more alternative acts, 24/7 is putting itself in the scene.

**Blue Frog**, near Qutb Minar, www.blue frog.co.in. For years, **Blue Frog** has been the best venue in Mumbai with supreme live acts and star DJs doing a turn and now it's coming to Delhi.

**Café Morrisons**, Shop E-12, South Extension Part II, T011-2625 5652. Very popular rock bar. Come for live bands or to mosh to the DJ.

**The Living Room**, 31 Haus Khaz, T011-4608 0533, www.tlrcafe.com. Recently done-up, this place has a funky laid-back atmosphere day and night over 3 floors. By day there's cosy armchairs and sofas. By night, things kick up a gear with live music, open mics and DJs spinning electronica and dubstep, and all manner of themed nights. Recommended.

**Rick's**, Taj Mahal Hotel, 1 Mansingh Rd, T011-2302 6162, www.tajhotels.com.

Suave Casablanca-themed bar with long martini list, a long-time fixture on Delhi's social scene.

**Shalom**, 'N' Block Market, Greater Kailash 1, T011-4163 2280. Comfortable, stylish lounge bar serving Lebanese cuisine; the resident DJ plays ambient music.

**Urban Pind**, N4, N-block market, GK1, T011-3951 5656. Multi-level bar, with large roof terrace, popular.

**Zoo**, at **Magique** (see Restaurants, page 50), one of the latest and most popular places on the scene serving up big portions of beats in a beautiful location.

## ⊙ Entertainment

**Delhi** *p27, maps p28, p34 and p38*
For advance notice of upcoming events see www.delhievents.com. Current listings and reviews can be found in *First City* (monthly, Rs 50) and *Time Out* (fortnightly, Rs 50). Cinema listings in the daily *Delhi Times*. Also check out www.bringhomestories.com for inspiration on what to do in Delhi.

### Music, dance and culture
**Goethe Institute**, 3 Kasturba Gandhi Marg, T011-2332 9506. Recommended for arts, film festivals, open-air cinema, plays and events.
**India Habitat Centre**, Lodi Rd, T011-2468 2222. Good programme of lectures, films, exhibitions, concerts, excellent restaurant.
**Indian International Centre**, 40 Lodhi Estate, Max Mueller Marg, T011-2461 9431, www.iicdelhi.nic.in. Some fantastic debates and performances, well worth checking the 'forthcoming programmes' section of their website.
**Kingdom of Dreams**, Great Indian Nautanki Company Ltd. Auditorium Complex, Sector 29, Gurgaon, Metro IFFCO, T0124-452 8000, www.kingdomofdreams.in. Ticket prices Rs 750-3000 depending on where you sit and more pricey at the weekend. The highlight is a much acclaimed all-singing, all-dancing Bollywood style performance. A little like an Indian Disneyland showcasing

Indian tastes, foods, culture, dress and dance all in one a/c capsule, but done impeccably.
**Triveni Kala Sangam**, 205 Tansen Marg (near Mandi House Metro station), T011-2371 8833. Strong programme of photography and art exhibitions, plus an excellent North Indian café.

### Son et lumière
**Red Fort** (see page 27), Apr-Nov 1800-1900 (Hindi), 1930-2030 (English). Entry Rs 50. Tickets available after 1700. Take mosquito cream.

## ⊙ Festivals

**Delhi** *p27, maps p28, p34 and p38*
For exact dates consult the weekly *Delhi Diary* available at hotels and many shops and offices around town.
  Muslim festivals of **Ramadan**, **Id-ul-Fitr**, **Id-ul-Zuha** and **Muharram** are celebrated according to the lunar calendar.

### January
**26 Jan** Republic Day Parade, Rajpath. A spectacular fly-past and military march-past, with colourful pageants and tableaux from every state, dances and music. Tickets through travel agents and most hotels, Rs 100. You can see the full dress preview free, usually 2 days before; week-long celebrations during which government buildings are illuminated.
**29 Jan** Beating the Retreat, Vijay Chowk, a stirring display by the armed forces' bands marks the end of the Republic Day celebrations.
**30 Jan** Martyr's Day, marks the anniversary of Mahatma Gandhi's death; devotional *bhajans* and Guard of Honour at Raj Ghat.
**Kite Flying Festival**, Makar Sankranti above Palika Bazar, Connaught Pl.

### February
**2 Feb** Vasant Panchami, celebrates the 1st day of spring. The Mughal Gardens are opened to the public for a month.

Thyagaraja Festival, South Indian music and dance, Vaikunthnath Temple.

## April
Amir Khusrau's Birth Anniversary, a fair in Nizamuddin celebrates this with prayers and qawwali singing.

## August
Janmashtami, celebrates the birth of the Hindu god Krishna. Special puja, Lakshmi Narayan Mandir.

**15 Aug** Independence Day, Impressive flag-hoisting ceremony and prime ministerial address at the Red Fort.

## October-November
**2 Oct** Gandhi Jayanti, Mahatma Gandhi's birthday; devotional singing at Raj Ghat.
Dasara, with over 200 Ramlila performances all over the city recounting the Ramayana story.
Ramlila Ballet, the ballet, which takes place at Delhi Gate (south of Red Fort) and Ramlila Ground, is performed for a month and is most spectacular. Huge effigies of Ravana are burnt on the 9th night; noisy and flamboyant.
Diwali, the festival of lights; lighting of earthen lamps, candles and firework displays.
National Drama Festival, Rabindra Bhavan.
**Oct/Nov** Dastkar Nature Bazaar, working with over 25,000 crafts people from across India, Dastkar's main objective is to empower rural artisans and keep alive the traditional crafts of India. They hold many events each year, but this is the pinnacle. Knowing that shopping here will bring a difference to the lives of rural people.

## December
**25 Dec** Christmas, Special Christmas Eve entertainments at major hotels and restaurants; midnight mass and services at all churches.

## ⊙ Shopping

**Delhi** p27, maps p28, p34 and p38
There are several state emporia around Delhi including the **Cottage Industries Emporium** (CIE), a huge department store of Indian handicrafts, and those along Baba Kharak Singh Marg (representing crafts from most states of India). Shops generally open 1000-1930 (winter 1000-1900). Food stores and chemists stay open later. Most shopping areas are closed on Sun.

### Art galleries
Galleries exhibiting contemporary art are listed in First City.
**Delhi Art Gallery**, Hauz Khas Village. A newly expanded gallery with a good range of moderately priced contemporary art.
**Nature Morte**, A-1 Neethi Bagh, near Kamla Nehru College, www.naturemorte. com. With a twin gallery in Berlin, you can expect the most profound and inspiring of contemporary art here.
**Photo Ink**, Hyundai MGF building, 1 Jhandewalan Faiz Rd, www.photoink.net. Close to Paharganj, this gallery offers up top notch contemporary photography.

### Books and music
Serious bibliophiles should head to the Sun book market in Daryaganj, Old Delhi, when 2 km of pavement are piled high with books – some fantastic bargains to be had.
**Central News Agency**, P 23/90, Connaught Pl. Carries national and foreign newspapers and journals.
**Full Circle**, 5 B, Khan Market, T011-2465 5641. Helpful knowledgeable staff. Sweet café upstairs for a quick drink – food is hit and miss though.
**Kabaadi Bazaar**, Netaji Subhash Marg, Old Delhi. Sun market with thousands of very cheap used books, great for browsing.
**Manohar**, 4753/23 Ansar Rd, Daryaganj, Old Delhi. A real treasure trove for books on South Asia and India especially, most helpful, knowledgeable staff. Highly recommended.

**Munshiram Manoharlal**, Nai Sarak, Chandni Chowk. Books on Indology.

**Rikhi Ram**, G Block Connaught Circus, T011-2332 7685. This is the place to come if you've wondered about how easy it is to learn to play and travel with a sitar. Has a range of guitars and other stringed instruments too.

## Carpets

Carpets can be found in shops in most top hotels and a number round Connaught Pl, not necessarily fixed price. If you are visiting Agra, check out the prices here first.

## Clothing

For designer wear, try **Ogaan** and for more contemporary, less budget blowing try **Grey Garden** both in Hauz Khas Village, **Sunder Nagar Market** near the Oberoi hotel, or the Crescent arcade near the Qutab Minar.

For inexpensive (Western and Indian) clothes, try shops along Janpath and between Sansad Marg and Janpath; you can bargain down 50%.

The **Khadi shop** (see Emporia, below) has Indian-style clothing.

**Fab India**, 14N-Gt Kailash I (also in B-Block Connaught Pl, Khan Market and Vasant Kunj). Excellent shirts, Nehru jackets, *salwar kameez*, linen, furnishing fabrics and furniture. The most comprehensive collection is in N block.

## Earthenware

Unglazed earthenware *khumba matkas* (water pots) are sold round New Delhi Railway Station (workshops behind main road).

## Emporia

Most open 1000-1800 (close 1330-1400). **Central Cottage Industries Emporium**, corner of Janpath and Tolstoy Marg. Offers hassle-free shopping, gift wrapping, will pack and post overseas; best if you are short of time.

**Dilli Haat**, opposite INA Market. Rs 15, open 1100-2200. Well-designed open-air complex with rows of brick alcoves for craft stalls from different states; local craftsmen's outlets (bargaining obligatory), occasional fairs (tribal art, textiles, etc). Also good regional food – hygienic, safe, weighted towards non-vegetarian. Pleasant, quiet, clean (no smoking) and uncrowded.

**Khadi Gramodyog Bhawan**, near the Regal building, Baba Kharak Singh Marg. For inexpensive homespun cotton *kurta pajama* (loose shirt and trousers), cotton/silk waistcoats, fabrics and Jaipuri paintings.

## Jewellery

Traditional silver and goldsmiths in Dariba Kalan, off Chandni Chowk (north of Jama Masjid). Cheap bangles and along Janpath; also at Hanuman Mandir, Gt Kailash I, N-Block. Also Sunder Nagar market. Bank St in Karol Bagh is recommended for gold.

**Amrapali**, Khan Market has an exceptional collection from affordable to mind-blowing.

**Ashish Nahar**, 1999 Naughara St, Kinari Bazaar, Chandni Chowk, T011-2327 2801. On quite possibly the prettiest street in Delhi, full of brightly painted and slowly crumbling *havelis*, you will find a little gem of a jewellery shop.

## Markets and malls

Beware of pickpockets in markets and malls. **Hauz Khas village**, South Delhi. Authentic, old village houses converted into designer shops selling handicrafts, ceramics, antiques and furniture in addition to luxury wear. Many are expensive, but some are good value. A good place to pick up old Hindi film posters with many art galleries and restaurants.

**Khan Market**, South Delhi. Great bookshops, cafés, restaurants and boutiques. Full of expats so expect expat prices.

**Sarojini Nagar**, South Delhi. Daily necessities as well as cheap fabric and clothing. Come for incredible bargains. This is where a lot of the Western brands dump their export surplus or end-of-line clothes. Haggle hard.

**Select City Walk**, Saket. An enormous, glitzy mall for the ultimate in upmarket shopping. Lots of chains, cinemas, etc.

**Shahpur Jat**, is a new up and coming shopping area, south of **South Extension**. **Tibetan Market**, North Delhi. Stalls along Janpath have plenty of curios – most are new but rapidly aged to look authentic.

### Souvenirs
**Aap ki Pasand**, opposite Golcha cinema, Netaji Subhash Marg, Old Delhi. Excellent place to taste and buy Indian teas.
**Dastkari Haat**, 39 Khan Market, www.indian craftsjourney.in. Charming selection of conscious crafts from around India working with rural artisans and women's collectives.
**Gulabsingh Johrimal Perfumers**, 467 Chandni Chowk, T011-2326 3743. Authentic *attars* (sandalwood based perfumes), perfumes and incense. High-quality oils are used.
**Haldiram's**, Chandni Chowk near Metro. Wide selection of sweet and salty snack foods.
**Khazana India**, 50A Hauz Khaz Village. Little treasure trove of Bollywood posters, old photographs and all sorts of interesting bric-a-brac.
**People Tree**, 8 Regal Building, Connaught Pl. Handmade clothing, mostly T-shirts with arty and people conscious slogans. Great posters made up of all those weird signs that you see around India and wide-range of ecological books. A real find.
**Playclan**, F51 Select Citywalk, Saket, www. the playclan.com. Fantastic shop selling all manner of clothes, notebooks, lighters and pictures with great colourful cartoon designs created by a collective of animators and designers – giving a more animated view of India's gods, goddesses, gurus, Kathakali dancers and the faces of India.
**Purple Jungle**, 16 Hauz Khaz Village, T(0)9650-973039, www.purple-jungle.com. Offering up kitsch India with bollywood pictures and curious road signs refashioned onto bags, clothes, cushions, etc.

### ⚙ What to do

### Body and soul
**Integral Yoga**, Sri Aurobindo Ashram, Aurobindo Marg, T011-2656 7863. Regular yoga classes (Tue-Thu and Sat 0645-0745 and 1700-1800) in *asana* (postures), *pranayama* (breathing techniques) and relaxation.
**Laughter Club of Delhi**, various locations, T011-2721 7164. Simple yogic breathing techniques combined with uproarious laughter. Clubs meet early morning in parks throughout the city.
**Sari School**, Jangpura Extension, near Lajpat Nagar, T011-4182 3297. Author of *Saris in India* Rta Christi Kapur holds classes every Sat in different styles of sporting a sari.
**Tree of Life Reflexology**, T(0)9810-356677. Reflexology with acclaimed teacher Suruchi. She also does private and group yoga classes on the roof and in the park.
**The Yoga Studio**, Hauz Khaz, www.the yogastudio.info. Regular yoga classes with Seema Sondhi, author of several yoga books, and her team.
**Yogalife**, Shapur Jat main market, T(0)9811-863332, www.yogalife.org. Closed Mon. Bright, friendly centre.

### Tours and tour operators
### Delhi Tourism tours
Departs from **Delhi Tourism**, Baba Kharak Singh Mg near State Govt Emporia, T011-2336 3607, www.delhitourism.nic.in. Book a day in advance. Check time.
**Evening Tour** (Tue-Sun 1830-2200): Rajpath, India Gate, Kotla Firoz Shah, Purana Qila, *son et lumière* (Red Fort). Rs 150.
**New Delhi Tour** (0900-1400): Jantar Mantar, Qutb Minar, Lakshmi Narayan Temple, Baha'i Temple (Safdarjang's Tomb on Mon only).
**Old Delhi Tour** (1415-1715): Jama Masjid, Red Fort, Raj Ghat, Humayun's Tomb. Both Rs 100 plus entry fees.

## ITDC Tours

Guides are generally good but tours are rushed, T011-2332 0331. Tickets booked from **Hotel Indraprastha**, T011-2334 4511. **New Delhi Tour**: departs from L-1 Connaught Circus and **Hotel Indraprastha** (0800-1330), Rs 125 (a/c coach): Jantar Mantar, Lakshmi Narayan Temple, India Gate, Nehru Pavilion, Pragati Maidan (closed Mon), Humayun's Tomb, Qutb Minar. **Old Delhi Tour**: departs Hotel Indraprastha. (1400-1700), Rs 100: Kotla Firoz Shah, Raj Ghat, Shantivana, Jama Masjid and Red Fort.

## Taj Mahal tours

Many companies offer coach tours to Agra (eg **ITDC**, from L1 Connaught Circus, Sat-Thu 0630-2200, Rs 600, a/c coach). However, travelling by road is slow and uncomfortable; by car, allow at least 4 hrs each way. Train is a better option: either *Shatabdi* or *Taj Express*, but book early.

## Walking tours

**Chor Bizarre**, Hotel Broadway, T011-2327 3821. Special walking tours of Old Delhi, with good lunch, 0930-1330, 1300-1630, Rs 350 each, Rs 400 for both.
**Delhi Metro Walks**, T(0)9811-330098, www.delhimetrowalks.com. With the charismatic Surekha Narain guiding your every step, informative **Heritage Walks** around Delhi. The walking tours around Old Delhi, Qutb Minar and the shrines of Mehrauli are fantastic.
**Master Guest House** (see Where to stay, page 47). Highly recommended walking tours for a more intimate experience.
**Salaam Baalak Trust**, T(0)9873-130383, www.salaambaalaktrust.com. NGO-run tours of New Delhi station and the streets around it, guided by Javed, himself a former street child. Your Rs 200 goes to support the charity's work with street children.

## Tour operators

**Ibex Expeditions**, 30 Community Centre East of Kailash, New Delhi, T011-2646 0244, www.ibexexpeditions.com. Offers a wide range of tours and ticketing, all with an eco pledge. Recommended.
**Kunzum Travel Café**, T-49 Hauz Khaz Village, T011-2651 3949. Unusual travel centre and meeting place for travellers. Free Wi-Fi, walls lined with photos, magazines, and buzzing with people. Also hosts photography workshops and travel writing courses.
**Metropole Tourist Service**, 224 Defence Colony Flyover Market (Jangpura Side), New Delhi, T011-2431 2212, T(0)9810-277699, www.metrovista. co.in. Car/jeep (US$45-70 per day), safe, reliable and recommended, also hotel bookings and can help arrange homestays around Delhi. Highly recommended.
**Namaste Voyages**, I-Block 28G/F South City, 2 Gurgaon, 122001, T0124-221 9330, www. namastevoyages.com. Specializes in tailor-made tours, tribal, treks, theme voyages.
**Shanti Travel**, F-189/1A Main Rd Savitri Nagar, T011-4607 7800, www.shantitravel. com. Tailor-made tours throughout India.

## ⊖ Transport

### Air

All international flights arrive at the shiny new terminal of **Indira Gandhi International Airport**, 20 km south of Connaught Pl. Terminal 1 (Domestic) enquiries T011-2567 5126, www.newdelhiairport.in; Terminal 3 (International) T0124-377 6000. At check-in, be sure to tag your hand luggage, and make sure it is stamped after security check, otherwise you will be sent back at the gate to get it stamped.

The most extensive networks are with **Air India**, T140/T011-2562 2220, www.airindia.com; and **Jet Airways**, T011-3989 3333, airport T011-2567 5404, www.jetairways.com. **Indigo**, T(0)9910-383838, www.goindigo.in, has the best record for being on time etc, and **Spicejet**, T(0)9871-803333, www.spicejet.com.

### Transport to and from the airport

It is now possible to travel by Metro from New Delhi train station to the airport in

20 mins. There is a booth just outside 'Arrivals' at the International and Domestic terminals for the **bus** services. It is a safe, economical option. A free **shuttle** runs between the 2 terminals every 30 mins during the day. Some hotel buses leave from the Domestic terminal. Bus 780 runs between the **airport** and **New Delhi Railway Station**.

The International and Domestic terminals have **pre-paid taxi** counters outside the baggage hall (3 price categories) which ensure that you pay the right amount (give your name, exact destination and number of items of luggage). Most expensive are white 'DLZ' **limousines** and then white 'DLY' **luxury taxis**. Cheapest are 'DLT' **ordinary Delhi taxis** (black with yellow top Ambassador/Fiat cars and vans, often very old). 'DLY' taxis charge 3 times the DLT price. A 'Welcome' desk by the baggage reclamation offers expensive taxis only. Take your receipt to the ticket counter outside to find your taxi and give it to the driver when you reach the destination; you don't need to tip, although they will ask. From the International terminal DLT taxis charge about Rs 240 for the town centre (Connaught Pl area); night charges double 2300-0500.

## Bus
### Local
The city bus service run by the **Delhi Transport Corporation** (DTC) connects all important points in the city and has more than 300 routes. Information is available at www.dtc.nic.in, at DTC assistance booths and at all major bus stops. Don't be afraid to ask conductors or fellow passengers. Buses are often hopelessly overcrowded so only use off-peak.

### Long distance
Delhi is linked to most major centres in North India. Services are provided by **Delhi Transport Corporation** (DTC) and State Roadways of neighbouring states from various **Inter-State Bus Termini** (ISBT).

Allow at least 30 mins for buying a ticket and finding the right bus. If any of the numbers below have changed since writing check www.delhitourism.gov.in.

**Kashmere Gate**, north of Old Delhi, T011-2296 0290 (general enquiries), is the main terminus, with a restaurant, left luggage, bank (Mon-Fri 1000-1400; Sat 1000-1200), post office (Mon-Sat 0800-1700) and telephones (includes international calls). The following operators run services to neighbouring states from here: **Delhi Transport Corp**, T011-2386 5181. **Haryana Roadways**, T011-2296 1262; daily to **Agra** (5-6 hrs, quicker by rail), **Varanasi** and many others.

**Sarai Kale Khan Ring Rd**, smaller terminal near Nizamuddin Railway Station, T011-2469 8343 (general enquiries), for buses to Haryana, Rajasthan and UP: **Haryana Roadways**, T011-2296 1262. **Rajasthan Roadways**, T011-2291 9537. For **Agra**, **Gwalior**, etc.

**Anand Vihar**, east side of Yamuna River, T011-2215 2431, for buses to Uttar Pradesh, Uttarakhand and Himachal Pradesh.

### Car hire
The main roads out of Delhi are very heavily congested; the best time to leave is in the very early morning.

Hiring a car is an excellent way of getting about town either for sightseeing or if you have several journeys to make.

Full day local use with driver (non a/c) Rs 900 and for (a/c) is about Rs 13-1600, 80 km/8 hrs, driver overnight *bata* Rs 150 per day; to Jaipur, about Rs 6 to 8000 depending on size of car We highly recommend **Metropole** see below. **Cozy Travels**, N1 BMC House, Middle Circle, Connaught Pl, T011-4359 4359, cozytravels@vsnl.net.com.

### Metro
The sparkling new Metro system (T011-2436 5202, www.delhimetrorail.com) is set to revolutionize transport within Delhi. For travellers, the yellow line is the main aorta

and useful as it stops Chandni Chowk, Connaught Pl and Qutb Minar. The blue line connects to Paharganj. The violet line for Khan Market. And the Orange Line linking airport to New Delhi train station.

**Line 1 (Red)** Running northwest to east, of limited use to visitors; from Rithala to Dilshad Garden.

**Line 2 (Yellow)** Running north–south through the centre from Jahangipuri to Huda City via Kashmere Gate, Chandni Chowk, New Delhi Station, Connaught Pl (Rajiv Chowk), Hauz Khaz, Qutb Minar and Saket – probably the most useful line for visitors.

**Line 3 (Blue)** From Dwarka 21 to Valshall or City Centre (splits after Yamuna Bank) Intersecting with Line 2 at Rajiv Chowk and running west through Paharganj (RK Ashram station) and Karol Bagh.

**Line 4 (Orange)** Just 4 stations for now including I.G.I Airport to New Delhi Train Station.

**Line 5 (Green)** From Mundka to Inderlok.

**Line 6 (Violet)** From Central Secretariat to Badarpur, including Khan Market and Lajpat Nagar. Useful.

Trains run 0600-2200. Fares are charged by distance: tokens for individual journeys cost Rs 6-19. **Smart Cards**, Rs 100, Rs 200 and Rs 500, save queuing and money. **Tourist Cards** valid for 1 or 3 days (Rs 70/200) are useful if you plan to make many journeys. Luggage is limited to 15 kg; guards may not allow big backpacks on board. Look out for the women-only carriages at the front of each train, clearly marked in pink.

## Motorcycle hire
**Chawla Motorcycles**, 1770, Shri Kissan Dass Marg, Naiwali Gali, T(0)9811-888918. Very reliable, trustworthy, highly recommended for restoring classic bikes.
**Ess Aar Motors**, Jhandewalan Extn, west of Paharganj, T011-2367 8836, www.essaarmotors.com. Recommended for buying Enfields, very helpful.

Also for scooter rentals **U Ride**, T(0)9711-701932, find them on facebook.

## Rickshaw
**Auto-rickshaws** Widely available at about half the cost of taxis. Normal capacity for foreigners is 2 people (3rd person extra); the new fare system is encouraging rickshaw wallahs to use the meter. Expect to pay Rs 30 for the shortest journeys. Allow Rs 150 for 2 hrs' sightseeing/shopping. It is best to walk away from hotels and tourist centres to look for an auto.

**Cycle-rickshaws** Available in the Old City. Be prepared to bargain: Chandni Chowk Metro to Red Fort. They are not allowed into Connaught Pl.

## Taxi
Yellow-top taxis, which run on compressed natural gas, are readily available at taxi stands or you can hail one on the road. Meters should start at Rs 13; ask for the conversion card. Add 25% at night (2300-0500) plus Rs 5 for each piece of luggage over 20 kg.

**Easy Cabs**, T011-4343 4343. Runs clean a/c cars and claim to pick up anywhere within 15 mins; Rs 20 per km (night Rs 25 per km). Waiting charges Rs50/30 mins.

## Train
Delhi stations from which trains originate have codes: **OD** – Old Delhi, **ND** – New Delhi, **HN** – Hazrat Nizamuddin, **DSR** – Delhi Sarai Rohilla. The publication *Trains at a Glance'* (Rs 30) lists important trains across India, available at some stations, book shops and newsagents,

New Delhi Railway Station and Hazrat Nizamuddin Station (500 m north and 5 km southeast of Connaught Pl respectively) connect Delhi with most major destinations. The latter has many important southbound trains. **Old Delhi Station**, 6 km north of the centre, has broad and metre-gauge trains. **Delhi Sarai Rohilla**, northeast of CP, serves Rajasthan.

Train enquiries T131. Reservations T1330. Each station has a computerized reservation counter where you can book any Mail or Express train in India.

**International Tourist Bureau (ITB)**, 1st floor, Main Building, New Delhi Station, T011-2340 5156, Mon-Fri 0930-1630, Sat 0930-1430, provides assistance with planning and booking journeys, for foreigners only; efficient and helpful if slow. You need your passport; pay in US\$, or rupees (with an encashment certificate/ ATM receipt). Those with **Indrail** passes should confirm bookings here. At the time of writing the station was under renovation, so the layout may change, but be wary of rickshaw drivers/ travel agents who tell you the ITB has closed or moved elsewhere. (There are also counters for foreigners and NRIs at **Delhi Tourism**, N-36 Connaught Pl, 1000-1700, Mon-Sat, and at the airport; quick and efficient.)

New Delhi and Hazrat Nizamuddin stations have pre-paid taxi and rickshaw counters with official rates per km posted: expect to pay around Rs 25 for 1st km, Rs 8 each km after. Authorized *coolies* (porters), wear red shirts and white *dhotis;* agree the charge, there is an official rate, before engaging one. For left luggage, you need a secure lock and chain.

Some useful services are: **Agra:** *Shatabdi Exp 12002*, ND, 0600, 2 hrs; *Taj Exp 12280*, HN, 0710, 2¾ hrs. **Amritsar:** *Swarna Shatabdi 12029*, 0720, 6½ hrs (NDLS); **Amritsar:** *Shatabdi 12013*, 1630, 6 hrs (NDLS); **Chandigarh:** *Kalka Shatabdi 12011*, 0740, 3½ hrs, (NDLS) goes onto Kalka for Shimla 4 hrs. **Pathankot** (for Dharamsala) *Jammu Mail 14033*, 2010, 10 hrs (goes onto Jammu, 15 hrs).

## 🛈 Directory

**Delhi** *p27, maps p28, p34 and p38*
**Embassies and consulates** Most are in the diplomatic enclave/Chanakyapuri. For details, go to embassy.goabroad.com.
**Medical services** Ambulance (24 hrs): T102. Hospitals: Embassies and high commissions have lists of recommended doctors and dentists. Doctors approved by IAMAT (International Association for Medical Assistance to Travellers) are listed in a directory. Casualty and emergency wards in both private and government hospitals are open 24 hrs. **Ram Manohar Lohia**, Willingdon Crescent, T011-2336 5525, 24-hr A&E. **Bara Hindu Rao**, Sabzi Mandi, T011-2391 9476. **JP Narayan**, J Nehru Marg, Delhi Gate, T011-2323 2400. **Safdarjang General**, Sri Aurobindo Marg, T011-2616 5060. **S Kripalani**, Panchkuin Rd, T011-2336 3728. **Chemists:** Many hospitals have 24-hr services: **Hindu Rao Hospital**, Sabzi Mandi; **Ram Manohar Lohia Hospital**, Willingdon Crescent; **S Kripalani Hospital**, Panchkuin Rd. In Connaught Pl: **Nath Brothers**, G-2, off Marina Arcade; **Chemico**, H-45. **Useful contacts** Fire: T101. Foreigners' Registration Office: East Block-VIII, Level 2, Sector 1, RK Puram, T011-2671 1443. Police: T100.

# Contents

**60 Chandigarh and around**
- 60 Chandigarh
- 62 Chandigarh to Himachal Pradesh
- 63 Chandigarh to Delhi
- 64 Listings

**67 Amritsar and around**
- 67 Arriving in Amritsar
- 67 Background
- 69 Golden Temple
- 73 Around Amritsar
- 73 Listings

**76 Southern Himachal**
- 76 Shimla
- 79 Around Shimla
- 80 Old Hindustan Tibet Road
- 81 Sarahan
- 82 Listings

**87 Kinnaur and Spiti**
- 87 Kinnaur and around
- 90 Spiti
- 93 Shimla to the Kullu Valley
- 96 Listings

**100 Kullu Valley**
- 100 Kullu
- 101 Parvati Valley
- 103 Kullu to Manali
- 104 Manali and around
- 108 Listings

**116 Lahaul and the Manali–Leh road**
- 116 Arriving at Lahaul and the Manali–Leh road
- 116 Background
- 116 Manali to Leh
- 118 Pattan Valley
- 119 Keylong
- 120 Keylong to Leh
- 121 Listings

**122 Northern Himachal**
- 122 Dharamshala
- 126 Kangra Valley
- 129 Chamba Valley
- 132 Listings

**143 Trekking in Himachal**
- 143 Trekking from Shimla
- 143 Trekking in Lahaul, Kinnaur and Spiti
- 146 Trekking in the Kullu and Parvati valleys
- 147 Trekking in Kangra
- 148 Trekking from Chamba

## Footprint features

- 72 Jallianwala Bagh Massacre
- 101 Dasara in Kullu
- 118 Motorcycling from Manali to Leh
- 124 Open your heart volunteering in Mcleodganj
- 147 The Valley of the Gods

North from Delhi

# Chandigarh and around

In 1947 when Lahore, Punjab's former capital, was allocated to Pakistan, the Indian government decided to build a new capital for the Indian state of the Punjab. The result is Chandigarh, a planned city in the post-war modernist style, acting as the dual capital of Punjab and Haryana states. Some critics describe Chandigarh as soulless; anyone familiar with England may find themselves reminded of Milton Keynes. Not quite the garden city it was dreamt to be, it is nevertheless a convenient stop en route to Himachal Pradesh, or before flying to Leh.

## Chandigarh → *For listings, see pages 64-66.*

Chandigarh's major centres are: the Capitol Complex consisting of the Secretariat, Legislative Assembly and High Court in the northeast with the Shiwalik Hills as a backdrop; Sector 17, the central business district with administrative and state government offices, shopping areas and banks; a Cultural Zone in Sector 14, for education which includes a museum and a campus university with institutions for engineering, architecture, Asian studies and medicine. A vast colonnaded Shopping Mall has opened in Sector 35, with hotels, restaurants, banks, a well-stocked supermarket and internet/international phones. Sector 7 also has a high density of shops.

### Arriving in Chandigarh
**Getting there** The airport and railway stations are some distance from the centre with pre-paid auto rickshaws to town. From the large Inter-State Bus Terminus (ISBT) in the busy Sector 17, you can walk to several budget hotels and restaurants. ▸▸ *See Transport, page 65.*

**Getting around** Buses serve the different sectors but if you are only here for a few hours, it is best to hire transport as there are long distances to cover in this widely spread out city and it is not always easy to find a taxi or auto-rickshaw for single journeys. Half-day tours 'Fun on Wheels' offer a hop-on hop-off service around the attractions; contact CITCO (below) for information.

**Tourist information** Chandigarh Tourism ① *ISBT, Sector 17, T0172-270 3839, www.chandigarhtourism.gov.in.* **Himachal Tourism** ① *1st floor, ISBT, T0172-270 8569.* **Uttarakhand and Uttar Pradesh Tourism** ① *ISBT, T0172-271 3988.*

**Climate** Temperatures in summer reach a maximum 39°C/minimum 25°C; in winter, maximum 20°C/minimum 7°C. Over 250 mm of rain falls from June to August. The best time to visit is November to March.

## Background

The initial plans for the creation of the city were drawn in New York by Mayer and Novicki. When the latter died in 1950 the work was entrusted to the internationally renowned architect **Le Corbusier** who supervised the layout and was responsible for the grand buildings. Fry and Drew designed the residential and commercial areas.

Jawaharlal Nehru said of Chandigarh "Let this be a new town symbolic of the freedom of India, unfettered by the traditions of the past, an expression of the nation's faith in the future". Its detractors describe it as a concrete prairie, the product of "the ivory tower school of architecture" and, despite its planning, many regard Chandigarh as a characterless failure. Today there is a growing scarcity of land, despite the complete ban on industrial activity. However, the ban has had the advantage of greatly limiting air pollution.

## Places in Chandigarh

The multi-pillared **High Court** stands nearby with a reflective pool in front. Primary colour panels break up the vast expanses of grey concrete but this classic work of modernist architecture looks stark and bleak. The **Legislative Assembly** has a removable dome and a mural by Le Corbusier that symbolizes evolution. In the same sector is the **Open Hand Monument**. The insignia of the Chandigarh Administration, it symbolizes "the hand to

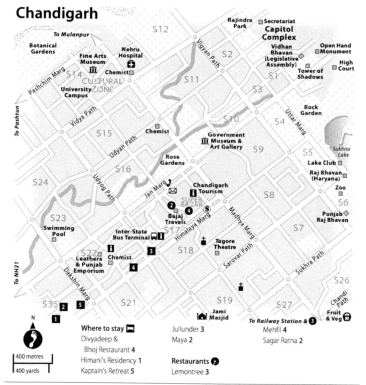

# Chandigarh

**Where to stay**
Divyadeep &
  Bhoj Restaurant 4
Himani's Residency 1
Kaptain's Retreat 5

Jullunder 3
Maya 2

**Restaurants**
Lemontree 3

Mehfil 4
Sagar Ratna 2

give and the hand to take; peace and prosperity, and the unity of humankind". The metal monument, 14 m high and weighing 50 tonnes, rotates in the wind and sometimes resembles a bird in flight. The geometrical hill nearby, known as the **Tower of Shadows** ① *tours 1030-1230 and 1420-1630, ask at Secretariat reception desk (you may need special permission to enter)*, was designed to beautify the complex, breaking its symmetrical lines.

The **Government Museum and Art Gallery** ① *Sector 10, Tue-Sun 1000-1630*, has a collection of stone sculptures dating back to the Gandhara period, as well as miniature paintings, modern art, prehistoric fossils and artefacts. The **Museum of Evolution of Life** ① *Sector 10, Tue-Sun 1000-1630*, has exhibits covering 5000 years from the Indus Valley Civilization to the present day. The **Fine Arts Museum** ① *Punjab University, Sector 14 (all the faculties of the university are in Gandhi Bhavan, Sector 14), Mon-Fri 1000-1700 (closed between 1300-1400)*, specializes in Gandhi studies. The **Chandigarh Architecture Museum** ① *Sector 10-C, Tue-Sun 1000-1645* charts the planning and creation of Chandigarh.

The **Rock Garden** or **Garden of Nek Chand** ① *Apr-Sep 0900-1900, Oct-Mar closes 1800, Rs 15, allow 3 hrs*, an unusual place, is the creation of Nek Chand, a road inspector in the Capitol City project. The 'garden' comprises an extraordinary collection of stones from the nearby Shiwaliks (carried on his bike) and domestic rubbish transformed into sculptures. Nek Chand dreamed of "creating a temple to Gods and Goddesses" out of discarded items of everyday use, for example bottle tops, fluorescent lights, mud guards, tin cans, and by highly imaginative re-assembling made models of people and animals. These have been set out along a maze of paths, creating an amusing and enjoyable park. First opened in 1976 the park is still being extended. The low archways make visitors bow to the gods who have blessed the park. Definitely challenges the uniformity of the rest of Chandigarh.

Just below the rock garden is the man-made **Sukhna Lake**, the venue of the Asian rowing championships which is circled by a walk. It gets crowded on holidays and Sunday. There are cafés, boating and fishing (permits needed).

The **Rose Gardens** ① *Sector 16, until sunset*, are one of the largest in Asia (25 ha), contains over 1500 varieties of rose; well worth visiting in spring. There's a rose show in early March.

The **Zoological Park** ① *Chaat Bir, a few kilometres out of the city centre, Rs 30 per person*, has a lion and deer safari park.

## Chandigarh to Himachal Pradesh → *For listings, see pages 64-66.*

### Pinjore (Pinjaur)

The **Yadavindra Gardens**, at Pinjore, 20 km on the Kalka road, were laid out by Aurangzeb's foster brother Fidai Khan, who also designed the Badshahi Mosque in Lahore. Within the Mughal *char bagh* gardens are a number of palaces in a Mughal-Rajasthani style: **Shish Mahal**, which has mirror-encased ceiling and is cooled by water flowing underneath (remove a slab to see!); **Rang Mahal**, a highly decorated pavilion; and **Jal Mahal**, set among fountains, cool and delightful. There are also camel rides and fairground attractions to tempt city dwellers. Keep a close eye on your belongings at all times; thefts have been reported.

### Anandpur Sahib

Anandpur Sahib (City of Divine Bliss), in a picturesque setting at the foot of the Shiwaliks by the River Sutlej, was established by the ninth guru, Tegh Bahadur, in 1664, when the Sikhs had been forced into the foothills of the Himalaya by increasing Mughal opposition.

Guru Tegh Bahadur himself was executed in Chandni Chowk, Delhi, and his severed head was brought to Anandpur Sahib to be cremated. The event added to the determination of his son, Guru Gobind Singh, to forge a new body to protect the Sikh community. The Khalsa Panth was thus created on Baisakhi Day in 1699. Anandpur Sahib became both a fortress and a centre of Sikh learning. **Hola Mohalla** is celebrated the day after **Holi** when battles are re-enacted by *nihangs* (Guru Gobind Singh's army) on horseback, dressed in blue and huge turbans, carrying old weapons. The stunning blossom of **The Khalsa Heritage Complex** is a dramatic addition to the architecture of Anandpur Sahib – it will house galleries, a state of the art museum, a research library, 400-seat auditorium, water gardens and restaurant. www.khalsaheritagecomplex.org. Anandpur Sahib is also the home of **Dashmesh Sadan**– former residence of Yogi Bhajan and now popular with students of Kundalini Yoga as a retreat and training space, www.dashmeshsadan.org.

## Chandigarh to Delhi → *For listings, see pages 64-66.*

### Kurukshetra

The battlefield where Arjuna learned the meaning of *dharma* has left no trace. The plain around Kurukshetra is described in Sanskrit literature as "Brahmavarta" (Land of Brahma). Like many other sacred sites it becomes the special focus of pilgrimage at the time of exceptional astronomical events. In Kurukshetra, eclipses of the sun are marked by special pilgrimages, when over one million people come to the tank. It is believed that the waters of all India's sacred tanks meet together at the moment of eclipse, giving extra merit to anyone who can bathe in it at that moment.

### Panipat

Panipat is the site of three great battles which mark the rise and fall of the Mughal Empire. It stands on the higher ground made up of the debris of earlier settlements near the old bank of the River Yamuna. Today it is an important textile town with over 30,000 looms. A high proportion of the products, carpets, curtains and tablewear, is exported.

In the first battle of Panipat on 21 April 1526 Babur, the first Mughal emperor, fought Ibrahim Lodi, the Sultan of Delhi, reputedly resulting in the death of 20,000 of the sultan's army, including Ibrahim Lodi. The second battle, on 5 November 1556, changed the course of India's history, as it secured Mughal power. Akbar, who had just succeeded his father Humayun and his general, defeated Hemu, the nephew of the Afghan Sher Shah. There was a mass slaughter of the captives, and in the gruesome tradition of Genghis Khan, a victory pillar was built with their heads plastered in. The third battle took place on 13 January 1761. The once great Mughal Empire was threatened from the west by the resurgent Rajputs and from the northwest by the Afghans. The distracted Mughal minister called in the Marathas. Despite their numbers, the Marathas lost and their soldiers fled. However, the Afghan leader Ahmad Shah Durrani was unable to take advantage of his victory as his followers mutinied for the two years' arrears of pay he owed them. North India was thus left in a political vacuum which adventurers tried to fill during the next 40 years. The main old building in Panipat is a **shrine** to the Muslim saint Abu Ali Kalandar.

## Chandigarh and around listings

*For hotel and restaurant price codes and other relevant information, see pages 12-14.*

### 😑 Where to stay

**Chandigarh** *p60, map p61*
**$$$$ Lemontree**, Chandigarh Industrial and Business Park Phase-I, T0172-442 3232, www.lemontreehotels.com. Lemontree offers citrus smelling rooms with all the mod cons. Extensive buffet breakfasts on offer as well as multi-cuisine restaurant for the rest of the day.
**$$$$-$$$ Maya**, SCO 325-28, S35-B, T0172-260 0547. After quite the nip and tuck, Maya is a stylish, boutique hotel with comfortable rooms and chicrestaurant. Definitely worth checking out.
**$$$ Deep Roots Retreat**, Village Ranjitpur, 25 km from Chandigarh, T(0)98784 30085, www.deeprootsretreat.com. Out in the countryside beyond Chandigarh, you get insight into the life of a Punjabi farm. Stylish rooms, great homecooked food and good for dipping into Chandigarh for sightseeing. Picnics, tractor rides and bonfires can all be arranged. They have another fort property close to Anandapur Sahib.
**$$$ Kaptain's Retreat**, 303 S35-B, T0172-500 5599, kaptainsretreat@hotmail.com. Owned by the legendary cricketer, Kapil Dev, this is Chandigarh's first boutique hotel. Each room is named after one of the great man's achievements, eg 'nine wickets', although the interiors are more than cricket chic with nice decor and excellent attention to detail. There's also an attractive bar and restaurant. Good value. Recommended.
**$$$-$$ Classic**, S35-C, T0172-260 6092, www.hotelclassicchandigarh.com. Comfortable modern hotel (buffet breakfast included), bar, reasonable value, lively bar and disco.
**$$$-$$ Himani's Residency**, 469-70, S35-C, T0172-266 1070, www.himanihotels.com.

17 adequate rooms in a good location close to bars and restaurants, friendly, good value.
**$$$-$$ Jullunder**, S22, opposite ISBT, T0172-270 6777, www.jullunderhotel.com. 17 average a/c rooms with restaurant on site.
**$$-$ Divyadeep**, S22-B, Himalaya Marg. T0172-270 5191. 15 rooms, some a/c, neat and clean, great value, good Bhoj restaurant. Recommended.

**Anandpur Sahib** *p62*
It is possible to stay in one of the many *gurudwaras* in town. Also at time of writing a 3-star government (PTDC) hotel is under construction, all to help accommodate people visiting the stunning Khalsa Heritage Complex.
**$$$-$$ Dashmesh Sadan**, Bani Village, 4 km from Anandpur Sahib, www.dashmesh sadan.org. For students and teachers of Kundalini Yoga, this is Yogi Bhajan's home and its doors have reopened as an ashram and teaching centre. It's possible to come and stay here independently, but there are also regular retreats, yatras and teacher trainings. You must book in advance. Beautiful gardens and inspiring vibration. Within walking distance of the main *gurudwaras*. "Walk where the gurus walked". Check the website for full programme.
**$$-$ Kissan Haveli**, Dashmesh Academy Rd, T01887-232 650. 10 rooms in this characterful 'heritage-style' property.
**$ Holy City**, Dashmesh Academy Rd, T01887-232 330, www.hotelholycity.com. Clean basic rooms and good value restaurant.

**Kurukshetra** *p63*
**$ Neelkanthi Yatri Niwas**, well sign-posted, T01744-291 1615. Haryana Tourism offers over-priced simple rooms, but there are dorm beds at Rs 300 a pop, restaurant.

## 🍴 Restaurants

**Chandigarh** *p60, map p61*
**$$$ Elevens**, Kaptain's Retreat (see Where to stay). Unusual combination of Pakistani, Indian and Thai cuisines in Mediterranean-style interior. Recommended.
**$$$ Mehfil**, 183, S17-C, T0172-270 4224. International. Upmarket, a/c, comfortable seating, spicy meals.
**$$ Bhoj**, S22-B, Divyadeep (see Where to stay). Indian Vegetarian. Good set *thalis* only, pleasant, clean, busy at lunch, good value.
**$$ Pashtun**, S35-B. Excellent frontier-style cuisine in pleasant ground-floor restaurant plus 'Wild West' bar in basement, complete with cowboy waiters. Formerly called **Khyber**. Recommended.
**$$ Sagar Ratna**, S35-C. High-quality South Indian. Well-presented, nationwide chain, very professional.
**$ Sindhi's Sweets**, Sco-108, Sector-17C. Serving up good snacks, veg food and sweet treats.

## ✴ Festivals

**Chandigarh** *p60, map p61*
**Apr** All the Hindu festivals are celebrated especially Baisakhi, celebrated by both Hindus and Sikhs as **New Year's Day** (13-14 Apr). Bhangra dancers perform.

## ⊙ What to do

**Chandigarh** *p60, map p61*
**Tour operators**
**Chandigarh Tourism**, T0172-505 5462, www.chandigarhtourism.com, or book at ISBT (see page 60). Local tours including good-value open-top bus (Rs 75 all day), and further afield to Pinjore Gardens, Bhakra Dam, Amritsar, Shimla, Kullu and Manali. They do half-day tours of the city in their double decker fun bus.
**Cozy Tours**, SCF I Sector 10, T0172-274 0850.

## ⊖ Transport

**Chandigarh** *p60, map p61*
**Air** Airport, 11 km. Taxis charge Rs 300 to centre. Air India: reservations, S17, T0172-265 4941, airport, T0172-622 6029, 1000-1630. Daily to **Mumbai** and **Delhi**. Jet Airways, 14 S 9D Madhya Marg, T011-3939 3333 (Delhi), airport T0172-507 5675, daily to **Delhi**.
**Bicycle hire** Free to CITCO hotel guests.
**Bus** It is easier to get a seat on the **Shimla** bus from Chandigarh than from Kalka. Many buses daily from ISBT, S17. A 2nd terminal in S43 has some buses to **Himachal Pradesh**, **Jammu** and **Srinagar**; city buses connect the 2. Transport offices: ISBT, S17, 0900-1300, 1400-1600; Chandigarh, T0172-260 6672; Haryana, T0172-260 3443; Himachal, T0172-266 8943; Punjab, T0172-260 6672. Buy bus tickets from the designated booths next to platforms before boarding. Seat numbers (written on the back of tickets) are often assigned. **Shimla** buses (via Kalka) leave from platform 10. To **Amritsar**, 6 hrs (from Aroma Hotel, T0172-270 0045); **Pathankot**, 7 hrs; **Dharamshala**, 10 hrs; **Kalka** (from Platform 10), Rs 11-28. Buses to **Shimla** also stop at **Kalka**; **Kullu** 12 hrs. Also Himachal Tourism coaches during the season, to **Delhi**, 5 hrs; **Manali**, 0800, 10 hrs; **Shimla**, 5 hrs.
**Motorcycle** Sikhs are officially exempt from wearing motorcycle helmets, although strictly speaking the length of cloth used to form the turban should be not less than 5 m as anything less is not deemed to give adequate protection.
**Rickshaw** Auto-rickshaws are metered with a minimum fare, but you can bargain. Stands at bus station, railway station and the Rock Garden. Cycle rickshaws are unmetered.
**Taxi** Private taxi stands in S22, S17, S35. Chandigarh Tourism (CITCO), S17, T0172-270 3839. Mega Cabs, T0172-414 1414. To **Kalka**, up to Rs 400.
**Train** The station (8 km) has a clean waiting room but a poor bus service to the

city. Pre-paid auto-rickshaws, Rs 45 to S22; to bus stand Rs 34; to Kalka (for the brave) Rs 200. Enquiries/reservations, T1333, T0172-264 1651, 1000-1700; City Booking Office, 1st floor, Inter-State Bus Terminal (ISBT), S17, T0172-270 8573, Mon-Sat 0800-1345, 1445-2000, Sun 0800-1400. Tourist office, 0600-2030. **New Delhi**: *Shatabdi Exp 12006*, 0650, 3¾ hrs; *Shatabdi Exp 12012*, 1820, 3½ hrs; **Shimla (via Kalka)**: *Himalayan Queen 14095*, 1028, 1 hr to **Kalka**, then 40 mins' wait for *Himalayan Queen 52455* to **Shimla** (1210, 6 hrs, book ahead).

**Anandpur Sahib** *p62*
**Bus** From **Chandigarh** and **Ropar**.

## Directory

**Chandigarh** *p60, map p61*
**Medical services** Ambulance: T102. 24-hr chemists. General Hospital, S16, T0172-278 0756; PG Institute, S12, T0172-274 7610.

# Amritsar and around

Amritsar ('Pool of the Nectar of Immortality') is named after the sacred pool in the Golden Temple, the holiest of Sikh sites. The temple itself, the city's singular attraction, is a haven of peace amidst an essentially congested city. The atmosphere is particularly powerful during *amritvela* (dawn to early light), when the surrounding glistening white-marble pavement is still cold under foot and the gold begins to shimmer on the lightening water. Sunset and evening prayers are also a special time to visit. You cannot help but be touched by the sanctity and radiance of the place, the friendly welcome of the people and the community spirit. Music constantly plays from within the inner sanctum of the Hari Mandir.

## Arriving in Amritsar

### Getting there

Sri Guru Ram Das Jee International Airport is 11 km away with taxi or auto-rickshaw transfers. The railway is central, the bus station 2 km east; both are a 15-minute auto-rickshaw ride from the Golden Temple to the south. If you have a couple of hours to spare between connections, you can fit in a visit. ▶▶ *See Transport, page 74.*

### Getting around

The city is quite spread out. Cycle-rickshaws squeeze through the crowded lanes. Auto-rickshaws are handy for longer journeys unless you get a bike.

### Tourist information

**Tourist office** ① *opposite the railway station, T0183-240 2452.* There is another branch outside the Golden Temple ① *T07837-613200.*

## Background

The original site for the city was granted by the Mughal Emperor Akbar (ruled 1556-1605) who visited the temple, and it has been sacred to the Sikhs since the time of the fourth guru, Guru Ram Das (1574-1581). He insisted on paying its value to the local Jats who owned it, thereby eliminating the possibility of future disputes on ownership. Guru Ram Das then invited local merchants to live and trade in the immediate vicinity. In 1577 he heard that a cripple had been miraculously cured while bathing in the pool here. The pool was enlarged and named Amrit Sarovar (Immortality). Guru Arjan Dev (1581-1601), Guru Ram Das' son and successor, enlarged the tank further and built the original temple at its centre from 1589-1601. The Afghan Ahmad Shah Durrani, desecrated the Golden Temple in

1757. The Sikhs united and drove him out, but four years later he defeated the Sikh armies, sacking the town and blowing up the temple. Later, the Sikhs re-conquered the Punjab and restored the temple and tank. Under their greatest secular leader, Maharaja Ranjit Singh, the temple was rebuilt in 1764. In 1830 he donated 100 kg (220 lbs) of gold which was applied to the copper sheets on the roof and much of the exterior of the building, giving rise to the name the 'Golden Temple'. Now Punjab's second largest town, Amritsar was a traditional junction of trade routes. The different peoples, Yarkandis, Turkomans, Kashmiris, Tibetans and Iranians indicate its connections with the Old Silk Road.

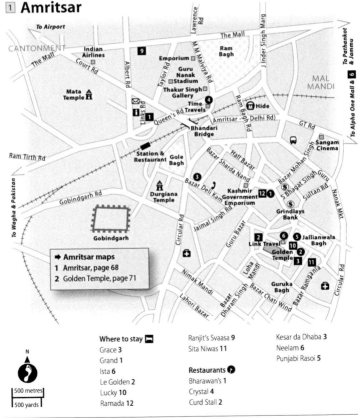

**1 Amritsar**

| Where to stay 🛏 | Ranjit's Svaasa **9** | Kesar da Dhaba **3** |
| Grace **3** | Sita Niwas **11** | Neelam **6** |
| Grand **1** | | Punjabi Rasoi **5** |
| Ista **6** | **Restaurants** 🍴 | |
| Le Golden **2** | Bharawan's **1** | |
| Lucky **10** | Crystal **4** | |
| Ramada **12** | Curd Stall **2** | |

500 metres
500 yards

## Golden Temple → *For listings, see pages 73-75.*

The spiritual nerve centre of the Sikh faith, every Sikh tries to make a visit and bathe in the holy water. It is immensely powerful, spiritual and welcoming to all, with an all-pervasive air of strength and self-sufficiency.

### Visiting the temple
Shoes, socks, sticks and umbrellas can be left outside the cloakroom free of charge. Visitors should wash their feet outside the entrance. It is best to go early as for much of the year the marble gets too hot by noon. Dress appropriately and cover your head in the temple precincts. Head scarves are available during the day but not at night; a handkerchief suffices. Avoid sitting with your back towards the temple or with your legs stretched out. Tobacco, narcotics and intoxicants are not permitted. The community kitchen provides food all day, for a donation. The **information office** ① *near the main entrance, T0183-255 3954*, is very helpful.

### Worship
Singing is central to Sikh worship, and the 24-hour chanting at the Golden Temple adds greatly to the reverential atmosphere. After building the temple, Guru Arjan Dev compiled a collection of hymns of the great medieval saints and this became the *Adi Granth* (Original Holy book). It was installed in the temple as the focus of devotion and teaching. Guru Gobind Singh, the 10th and last Guru (1675-1708) revised the book and also refused to name a successor saying that the book itself would be the Sikh Guru. It thus became known as the *Guru Granth Sahib* (The Holy Book as Guru).

### The temple compound
Entering the temple compound through the main entrance or clock tower you see the **Harmandir** (the Golden Temple itself, also spelt Harimandir, and known by Hindus as the Durbar Sahib) beautifully reflected in the stunning expanse of water that surrounds it. Each morning (0400 summer, 0500 winter) the *Guru Granth Sahib* is brought in a vivid procession from the **Akal Takht** at the west end to the Harmandir, to be returned at night (2200 summer, 2100 winter). The former represents temporal power, the latter spiritual – and so they do not quite face each other. Some like to attend **Palki Sahib** (night ceremony).

 All pilgrims walk clockwise round the tank, stopping at shrines and bathing in the tank on the way round to the Harmandir itself. The tank is surrounded by an 8-m-wide white marble pavement, banded with black and brown Jaipur marble.

### East End
To the left of the entrance steps are the bathing ghats and an area screened off from public view for women to dip. Also on this side are the **68 Holy Places** representing 68 Hindu pilgrimage sites as referenced in Guru Nanak's Japji Sahib. When the tank was built, Guru Arjan Dev told his followers that rather than visit all the orthodox Hindu places of pilgrimage, they should just bathe here, thus acquiring equivalent merit.

 A shrine contains a copy of the **Guru Granth Sahib**. Here and at other booths round the tank the Holy Book is read for devotees. Sikhs can arrange with the temple authorities to have the book read in their name in exchange for a donation. The *granthi* (reader) is a temple employee and a standard reading lasts for three hours, while a complete reading takes 48 hours. The tree in the centre at the east end of the tank is popularly associated with a healing miracle.

### Dining Hall, Kitchen, Assembly Hall and Guesthouses

The surrounding *bunghas* (white arcade of buildings), are hostels for visitors. Through the archway a path leads to the **Guru Ram Das Langar** (kitchen and dining hall) immediately on the left, while two tall octagonal minarets, the 18th-century **Ramgarhia Minars**, provide a vantage point over the temple and inner city. At the far end of the path are a series of guesthouses including **Guru Ram Das Sarai**, where pilgrims can stay free for up to three nights. Sikhs have a community kitchen where all temple visitors, regardless of their religious belief, can eat together. The third Guru, Guru Amar Das (1552-1574), abolished the custom of eating only with others of the same caste. He even refused to bless the Mughal Emperor Akbar unless he was prepared to eat with everyone else who was present. *Seva* (voluntary service), which continues to be a feature of modern Sikhism, extends to the kitchen staff and workers; visitors are also welcome to lend a hand. The Amritsar kitchen may feed up to 10,000 people a day, with 3000 at a sitting and up to 1 Lakh (100,000) visitors at the weekends. It is free of charge and vegetarian, though Sikhs are not banned from eating meat. Lunch is 1100-1500 and dinner 1900 onwards. Next to the Guru Amar Das Langar is the **residence of Baba Kharak Singh** who is hailed by Sikhs as a saint. His followers are distinguished by their orange turbans while temple employees and members of the militant Akali sect wear blue or black turbans.

Returning to the temple tank, the **shrine** on the south side is to Baba Deep Singh. When Ahmad Shah Durrani attacked Amritsar in 1758, Baba Deep Singh was copying out the *Guru Granth Sahib*. He went out to fight with his followers, vowing to defend the temple with his life. He was mortally wounded, 6 km from town; some say that his head was hacked from his body. Grimly determined and holding his head on with one hand he fought on. On his way back to the temple he died on this spot. The story is recounted in the picture behind glass.

### West end

The complex to the west has the Akal Takht, the flagstaffs, and the Shrine of Guru Gobind Singh. The **flagstaffs** symbolize religion and politics, in the Sikh case intertwined. They are joined in the middle by the emblem of the Sikh nation, the two swords of Hargobind, representing spiritual and temporal authority. The circle is inscribed with the Sikh rallying call *Ek Onkar* (God is One).

Started when Arjan Dev was Guru (1581-1605), and completed by Guru Hargobind in 1609, the **Akal Takht** is the seat of the Sikhs' religious committee. It is largely a mixture of 18th- and early 19th-century building, the upper storeys being the work of Ranjit Singh. It has a first-floor room with a low balcony which houses a gilt-covered ark, central to the initiation of new members of the Khalsa brotherhood.

To the side of the flagstaffs is a **shrine** dedicated to the 10th and last guru, Gobind Singh (Guru 1675-1708). In front of the entrance to the temple causeway is a square, a gathering place for visitors.

Sometimes you may see Nihang (meaning 'crocodile') Sikhs, followers of the militant Guru Gobind Singh, dressed in blue and armed with swords, lances and curved daggers.

At the centre of the tank stands the most holy of all Sikh shrines, the **Harmandir** (The Golden Temple). Worshippers obtain the sweet *prasad* before crossing the causeway to the temple where they make their offering. The 60-m-long bridge, usually crowded with jostling worshippers, is built out of white marble like the lower floor of the temple. The rest of the temple is covered in copper gilt. On the doorways verses from the *Guru Granth Sahib* are inscribed in Gurumukhi script while rich floral paintings decorate the walls and excellent silver work marks the doors. The roof has the modified onion-shaped dome, characteristic of Sikh temples, but in this case it is covered in the gold that Ranjit Singh added for embellishment.

The ground floor of the three-storey temple contains the Holy Book placed on a platform under a jewel-encrusted canopy. *Guru Granth Sahib* contains approximately 3500 hymns. Professional singers and musicians sing verses from the book continuously from 0400-2200 in the summer and 0500-2130 in winter. An excited crowd of worshippers attempts to touch the serpent horn. Each evening the holy book is taken ceremoniously to the Akal Takht and brought back the next morning; visitors are welcome. The palanquin used for this, set with emeralds, rubies and diamonds with silver poles and a golden canopy, can be seen in the treasury on the first floor of the entrance to the temple. Throughout the day, pilgrims place offerings of flowers or money around the book. There is no ritual in the worship or pressure from temple officials to donate money. The marble walls are decorated with mirror-work, gold leaf and designs of birds, animals and flowers in semi-precious stones in the Mughal style.

On the first floor is a balcony on which three respected Sikhs always perform the **Akhand Path** (Unbroken Reading). In order to preserve unity and maintain continuity, there must always be someone practising devotions. The top floor is where the gurus used to sit and here again someone performs the *Akhand Path*; this is the quietest part of the building and affords a good view over the rest of the complex.

On the edge of the tank just west of the entrance is the **Tree Shrine**, a gnarled, 450-year-old *jubi* tree, reputed to have been the favourite resting place of the first chief priest of the temple. Women tie strings to the ingeniously supported branches, hoping to be blessed with a son by the primaeval fertility spirits that choose such places as their home. It is also a favourite spot to arrange and sanctify marriages, despite the protests of the temple authorities. The **Sikh Museum** ① *at the main entrance to the temple (just before steps leading down to the parikrama)*, 0700-1830, free, is somewhat martial, reflecting the struggles against the Mughals, the British and the Indian Army. The **Sikh Library** ① *in the Guru Nanak Building, Mon-Sat 0930-1630*, has a good selection of books in English as well as current national newspapers.

## 2 Golden Temple

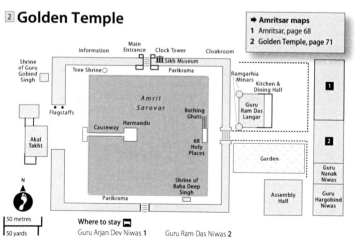

➡ Amritsar maps
1 Amritsar, page 68
2 Golden Temple, page 71

## Jallianwala Bagh Massacre

Relations with the British had soured in 1919. *Hartals* (general strikes) became a common form of demonstration. The Punjab, which had supplied 60% of Indian troops committed to the First World War, was one of the hardest hit economically in 1918 and tension was high. The lieutenant governor of the province decided on a 'fist force' to repulse the essentially non-violent but vigorous demonstrations. Some looting occurred in Amritsar and the British called in reinforcements. These arrived under the command of General Dyer.

Dyer banned all meetings but people were reported to be gathering on Sunday 13 April 1919 as pilgrims poured into Amritsar to celebrate Baisakhi, the Sikh New Year and the anniversary of the founding of the *khalsa* in 1699. That afternoon thousands were crammed into Jallianwala Bagh, a piece of waste ground popular with travellers, surrounded on all sides by high walls with only a narrow alley for access. Dyer personally led some troops to the place, gave the crowd no warning and ordered his men to open fire leaving 379 dead and 1200 wounded. Other brutal acts followed.

The massacre was hushed up and the British government in London was only aware of it six months later at which time the Hunter Committee was set up to investigate the incident. It did not accept Dyer's excuse that he acted as he did in order to prevent another insurrection on the scale of the Mutiny of 1857. He was asked to resign and returned to England where he died in 1927. However, he was not universally condemned. A debate in the House of Lords produced a majority of 126 to 86 in his favour and the *Morning Post* newspaper launched a fund for 'The Man who Saved India'. More than £26,000 was raised to comfort the dying general.

India was outraged by Dyer's massacre. **Gandhi**, who had called the nationwide *hartal* in March, started the Non Co-operation Movement, which was to be a vital feature of the struggle for Independence. This was not the end of the affair. O'Dwyer, the governor of the province, was shot dead at a meeting in Caxton Hall, London, by a survivor of Jallianwala Bagh who was hanged for the offence. For a modern take on the whole story, check out the Bollywood movie *Rang de Basanti*.

### The town

The old city is south of the railway station encircled by a ring road, which traces the line of the city walls built during the reign of Ranjit Singh.

**Jallianwala Bagh**, noted for the most notorious massacre under British rule (see below), is 400 m north of the Golden Temple. Today the gardens are a pleasant enclosed park. They are entered by a narrow path between the houses, opening out over lawns. A **memorial plaque** recounts the history at the entrance, and a large memorial dominates the east end of the garden. There is an interesting museum. On the north side is a well in which many who tried to escape the bullets were drowned, and remnants of walls have been preserved to show the bullet holes.

The old town has a number of mosques and Hindu temples – the **Durgiana Temple** (16th century), and the new **Mata Lal Devi Temple**, which imitates the difficult access to the famous Himalayan Mata Vaishno Devi Cave Temple of Katra by requiring the worshipper to wade awkwardly through water and crawl through womb-like tunnels is well worth a visit. The whole temple area is Disneyesque with plastic grottoes and statues. Women who wish to have children come here to pray, there is community food and a charity hospital run from the temple's trust. It's a very popular and lively temple, definitely worth a visit. Northeast of the railway station are the **Ram Bagh gardens**, the Mall and Lawrence Road shopping areas.

## Around Amritsar → *For listings, see pages 73-75.*

### Wagah
The changing of the guards and the ceremonial lowering of the flags ceremony at sundown, carried out with great pomp and rivalry, are quite a spectacle. There is much synchronized foot stamping, gate slamming and displays of scorn by colourful soldiers! It is the ministry of funny walks. New viewing galleries have been built but crowds still clamour to get the best view. Women are allowed to get to the front, and there is a VIP section (open to foreign visitors) next to the gate. It is best to get there near closing time though photography is difficult with the setting sun.

### Goindwal and Tarn Taran
On the way from Amritsar to Jalandar, there are important *gurudwaras* where Sikhs on pilgrimage traditionally stop. There are separate bathing places for men and women at Goindwal, with a small market place outside the temple. The *gurudwara* at Taran Tarn is surrounded by a busy bazar. The *gurudwara* itself is very beautiful, with a very large water tank and cloisters providing welcome shade.

## Amritsar and around listings

*For hotel and restaurant price codes and other relevant information, see pages 12-14.*

### ○ Where to stay

**Amritsar** *p67, map p68*
**$$$$ Hyatt**, next to Alpha One Mall, GT Rd, T0183-287 1234, www.hyatt.com. Formerly Ista hotel, this is a beautiful boutique hotel. There is a stunning spa with all the usual ayurvedic fare, but also rose quartz and amethyst facials. Food-wise, you can choose between the all-day **Collage** with food from around the globe and a *teppenyaki* station or Thai-Chi, evenings only.
**$$$$ Ramada**, near Town Hall, www.ramada.com. More chain hotels are opening up in Amritsar, there is also a **Radisson** near the airport. The **Ramada** has a great location, closer to the centre of town than any other 4star. All the mod cons are here in this attractive hotel.
**$$$$-$$$ Ranjit's Svaasa**, 47-A The Mall Rd, T0183-256 6618, www.welcomheritage

hotels.in. Tastefully restored rooms with huge windows in a 250-year-old red-brick manor surrounded by palms and lawns, elegant service, great food, beautiful Spa Pavilion offering Ayurvedic and international treatments. Recommended.
**$$$-$$ Hotel Le Golden**, clock tower Extension, outside Golden Temple complex, T0183-255 8800, www.hotellegolden.com. Modern rooms close to the temple, with views of Akal Takht, rooftop restaurant **The Glass** has view of Siri Harmandir Sahib.
**$$ Grand**, Queens Rd, opposite train station, T0183-256 2424, www.hotelgrand.in. 32 modern but characterful rooms, some a/c, set around attractive garden, popular restaurant and attractive bar with Kingfisher on draught, good food, very friendly management.
**$ Grace**, 35 Braham Buta Market, close to Golden Temple, T0183-255 9355. Good range of rooms, friendly management.
**$ Lucky**, Mahna Singh Rd, near Golden Temple and Jallianwala Bagh, T0183-254 2175. Basic rooms some with a/c. Good value.

**$ Rest houses**, in/near the Golden Temple, eg **Guru Ram Das Niwas** and for foreigners especially **Guru Gobind Singh Niwas**. Some free (up to 3 nights), very simple food; please leave a donation. Tobacco, alcohol and drugs are prohibited. Can be noisy as sometimes so busy people stay in the courtyard, but an eye-opening experience.

**$ Sita Niwas**, east of Golden Temple, T0183-254 3092, sitaniwas@yahoo.co.in. 100 rooms from very basic to TVs and mod cons, fans or a/c, bit run-down, room service (cheap Indian meals), can be noisy at dawn (pilgrims), very helpful, friendly manager. Recommended.

## 🍴 Restaurants

**Amritsar** *p67, map p68*
Eating with pilgrims in the *langar* (Golden Temple community kitchen) can be a great experience. Remember to hold out both hands (palms upwards) when receiving food. The corner of the Mall and Malaviya Rd comes alive with ice cream and fast-food stalls in the evening. *Dhabas* near the station and temple sell local *daal, saag paneer* and mouthwatering stuffed *parathas*.

**$$$ The Glass**, at Le Golden Hotel close to Golden Temple. Glass rooftop restaurant serves up range of foods and great views of the temple.

**$$ Crystal**, Queens Rd, T0183-222 5555. Good international food, excellent service, pleasant ambience, huge portions. There is **Crystal** on the ground floor proclaiming that there is only one branch. And there is **Crystal** on the 2nd floor proclaiming the same thing – the 2 brothers have fallen out and both refuse to change the name.

**$$ Punjabi Rasoi**, near Jallianwala Bagh. The best option near the Golden Temple. Very good *thalis*, south Indian food and traditional Punjabi fare. Internet café upstairs too. Recommended.

**$ Bharawan's**, near Town Hall. Excellent breakfast and lunch *thalis* and good vegetarian.

**$ Kesar da Dhaba**, Passian Darwaza, near Durgiana Temple. Serves extremely popular sweet *phirni* in small earthenware bowls. Also Punjabi *thalis*.

**$ Neelam**, near Jallianwalla Bagh. Indian, Chinese. Cheap, plentiful and really tasty.

## ✳️ Festivals

**Amritsar** *p67, map p68*
The birth anniversaries of the 10 gurus are observed as holy days and those of Guru Nanak (**Nov**), and Guru Gobind Singh (**Dec/Jan**), are celebrated as festivals with *Akhand Path* and processions.

**Apr** Baisakhi, for Sikhs, the Hindu New Year marks the day in 1699 Guru Gobind Singh organized the Sikhs into the Khalsa, see page 63. The vigorous *bhangra* dance is a common sight in the villages. Falls on 13 or 14 Apr.

**Oct/Nov** Diwali Illumination of the Golden Temple, fireworks.

## 🅞 What to do

**Amritsar** *p67, map p68*
**Time Travels**, 14 Kapoor Plaza, Crystal Sq, T0183-240 0131, www.travelamritsar.com. Organizes homestays, tours to Dharamshala, Manali, Shimla, etc, local villages, as well as to important Gurudwaras in the state. Very efficient, helpful. Recommended.

## ⊖ Transport

**Amritsar** *p67, map p68*
**Air** Rajsansi Airport, T0183-259 2166; taxi (Rs 550) or auto-rickshaw (Rs 200) to town.
**Domestic flights** Daily flights to **New Delhi** with Indian Airlines, 39A Court Rd, T0183-221 3393, Jet Airways T0183-320 9847.
**International flights** Weekly flights to/from **London** and **Birmingham** on Air India, Jet Airways, both via Delhi.
**Bicycle hire** A bicycle is worthwhile here; available for hire from Hide Market.

**Bus** Daily services to **Delhi** (tiring 10 hrs); **Dharamshala** (7 hrs); **Dalhousie** (8 hrs), **Jammu** (5 hrs); **Pathankot** (3 hrs); **Chandigarh** (5 hrs); **Shimla** 0530 and 0730, 10 hrs. **Link Travels** and other private operators leave for Delhi from outside railway station, 2200; for **Jammu** and **Chandigarh** from Hall Gate. Cross-border bus service to **Lahore** (Tue, Wed, Fri and Sat). Contact International Bus Terminal, T0183-258 7070. Advance booking must).

**Rickshaw** Auto-rickshaw/*tonga*: full day, Rs 600, half day Rs 4.

**Taxi** Non-a/c car from **Time Travels** near Crystal restaurant, Queens Rd, T0183-240 0131/4, www.travelamritsar.com, and **Link Travels**, outside Golden Temple Clock Tower Car Park: full day, Rs 1200, half day Rs 800, Wagah Rs 900. To **Delhi** from Rs 7500, **Dharamshala** Rs 32.

**Train** Enquiries T131. There is a free shuttle bus from the station to the Golden Temple. Computerized reservations in the Golden Temple Complex (far right of the office), open until 2000 on weekdays. **New Delhi**: *Amritsar Shatabdi Exp 12014*, 050, 6¼ hrs; *Shan-e-Punjab Exp 12498*, 1510, 8 hrs (HN); *Swarna Shatabdi 1203*, 1655, 6 hrs. **Pathankot (for Kangra and Dharamsala)**: *Jammu Tawi Exp 18101/18601*, 0820, 2¾ hrs, continues to Jammu, 6 hrs. From Pathankot, you can continue onto Kangra for Dharamsala on the spectacular narrow-gauge Kangra Valley Railway, built in 1928, which runs to **Jogindernagar**, 56 km northwest of Mandi in HP or you can get a taxi direct to Dharamsala and Mcleod Ganj.

# Southern Himachal

Southern Himachal offers an intriguing mix of experiences. Shimla's colonial past, with its Little England architecture and anachronistic air, seems to be fighting for survival amidst the modern-day bustle of Himachal's capital city. The area around Shimla offers stunning views of the foothills of the Himalaya and plenty of attractive places to stay nestled amongst the cool pine forests. This area is also the gateway to the altogether more rugged landscapes of Kinnaur, a world far less affected by the advance of time.

## Shimla → *For listings, see pages 82-86.*

Once a charming hill station and the summer capital of the British, an air of decay hangs over many of Shimla's Raj buildings, strung out for 3 km along a ridge. Below them a maze of narrow streets, bazaars and shabby 'local' houses with corrugated-iron roofs cling to the hillside. There are some lovely walks with magnificent pines and cedars giving a beautifully fresh scent to the air.

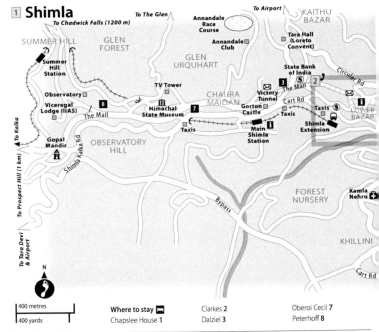

**1 Shimla**

| | Where to stay 🛏 | Clarkes 2 | Oberoi Cecil 7 |
|---|---|---|---|
| 400 metres | Chapslee House 1 | Dalziel 3 | Peterhoff 8 |
| 400 yards | | | |

## Arriving in Shimla

**Getting there** Despite the romance of the narrow-gauge railway from Kalka, see page 79, most arrive in Shimla by bus or taxi as it is so much quicker. The bus stand and the station are on Cart Road, where porters and hotel touts jostle to take your luggage up the steep hill – possibly the best few rupees you will ever spend. If you are staying on the western side of town it is worth getting off the bus at the railway station. Buses from the east, including Rampur and Kinnaur, stop at the Rivoli Bus Stand. Shimla (Jabbarhatti) airport has a coach (Rs 50) in season, and taxis (Rs 400-500) for transfer.

**Getting around** The Mall can only be seen on foot; it takes about half an hour to walk from the Viceroy's Lodge to Christ Church. The main traffic artery is Cart Road, which continues past the station to the main bus stand, taxi rank and the two-stage lift which goes to The Mall above. The Victory Tunnel cuts through from Cart Road to the north side of the hill. ➠ See Transport, page 85.

**Tourist offices** Himachal Pradesh Tourism Development Corportation (HPTDC) ⓘ *The Mall, T0177-265 2561, www.hptdc.nic.in, 0900-1800, in season 0900-1900; also at Cart Rd, near Victory Tunnel, T0177-265 4589, 1000-1700,* is very informative and helpful.

**Climate** October and November are very pleasant, with warm days and cool nights. December-February is cold and there are snowfalls. March and April are changeable; storms are not infrequent and the air can feel very chilly. Avoid May-June, the height of the Indian tourist season prior to the monsoon.

### Places in Shimla

Shimla is strung out on a long crescent-shaped ridge that connects a number of hilltops from which there are good views of the snow-capped peaks to the north: Jakhu (2453 m), Prospect Hill (2176 m), Observatory Hill (2148 m), Elysium Hill (2255 m) and Summer Hill (2103 m). For the British, the only way of beating the hot weather on the plains in May and June was to move to hill stations, which they endowed with mock-Tudor houses, churches, clubs, parks with bandstands of English county towns.

**Christ Church** (1844), on the open area of The Ridge, dominates the eastern end of town. Consecrated in 1857, a clock and porch were added later. The original chancel window, designed by Lockwood Kipling, Rudyard's father, is no longer there. The mock tudor **library** building (circa 1910) is next door. The Mall joins The Ridge at Kipling's **'Scandal Point'**, where today groups gather to exchange gossip.

Originally the name referred to the stir caused by the supposed 'elopement' of a lady from the Viceregal Lodge and a dashing Patiala prince after they arranged a rendezvous here.

The **Gaiety Theatre** (1887) and the **Town Hall** (circa 1910) are reminiscent of the 'arts and crafts' style, as well as the timbered **General Post Office** (1886). Beyond, to the west, is the **Grand Hotel**. Further down you pass the sinister-looking **Gorton Castle**, designed by Sir Samuel Swinton Jacob, which was once the Civil Secretariat. A road to the left leads to the railway station, while one to the right goes to Annandale, the racecourse and cricket ground. The Mall leads to the rebuilt **Cecil Hotel**. On Observatory Hill, the **Viceregal Lodge** (1888) is the most splendid of Shimla's surviving Raj-era buildings, built for Lord Dufferin in the Elizabethan style. Now the **Rashtrapati Niwas** ① *1000-1630, Rs 10 including a brief tour*, it stands in large grounds with good views of the mountains. Reminders of its British origins include a gatehouse, a chapel and the meticulously polished brass fire hydrants imported from Manchester. Inside, you can visit the main reception rooms and the library which are lined from floor to ceiling with impressive teak panelling. It is a long up the hill walk from the gate. It is now the Indian Institute of Advanced Study.

**Himachal State Museum** ① *near Chaura Maidan, Tue-Sun 1000-1330, 1400-1700, free*, is a 30-minute walk west from the GPO along The Mall; then it's a short climb from the Harsha Hotel. Small, with a good sculpture collection and miniatures from the Kangra School, it also houses contemporary art including work by Nicholas Roerich, costumes, jewellery, bronzes and textiles (everything is well labelled).

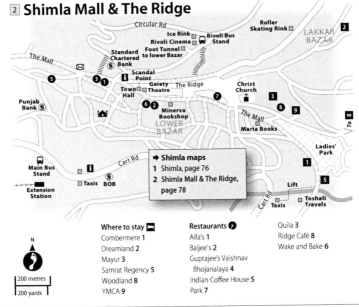

## 2 Shimla Mall & The Ridge

| Where to stay ▭ | Restaurants ● | Quila 3 |
| --- | --- | --- |
| Combermere 1 | Alfa's 1 | Ridge Café 8 |
| Dreamland 2 | Baljee's 2 | Wake and Bake 6 |
| Mayur 3 | Guptajee's Vaishnav | |
| Samrat Regency 5 | Bhojanalaya 4 | |
| Woodland 8 | Indian Coffee House 5 | |
| YMCA 9 | Park 7 | |

➡ Shimla maps
1 Shimla, page 76
2 Shimla Mall & The Ridge, page 78

200 metres
200 yards

## Walks

**Jakhu Temple** on a hill with excellent views (2455 m), dedicated to Hanuman the monkey god, is 2 km from Christ Church. Walking sticks (handy for warding off monkeys, which can be vicious – keep all food out of sight) are available at *chai* shops at the start of the ascent. **The Glen** (1830 m), to the northwest, is a 4-km walk from the centre past the **Cecil Hotel**. **Summer Hill** (1983 m), a pleasant 'suburb' 5 km from town, is a stop on the Shimla-Kalka railway. **Chadwick Falls** (1586 m), 3 km further, drops 67 m during the monsoon season.

**Prospect Hill** (2175 m) is 5 km from The Ridge and a 20-minute walk from Boileauganj to the west. **Tara Devi** (1851 m), with a hilltop temple, 11 km southwest from the railway station, can also be reached by car or train.

## Around Shimla → *For listings, see pages 82-86.*

### Kufri

About 16 km from Shimla, at 2500 m, Kufri hosts a winter sports festival in January which includes the **National Snow Statue Competition**. Don't expect European or American resort standards though. There are some attractions around and about the town. At **Danes Folly** (2550 m), 5 km away, is a government-run orchard. **Mahasu Peak** (bus, Rs 15) 20 minutes from a path behind the Kufri Resort cottages, offers fabulous mountain views on a clear day and there is a small but interesting temple at the start of the walk. The best time to visit is in January and February.

### Chharabra

Chharabra is an enjoyable 3-km forest walk down from Kufri. The Wildflower Hall which once stood here was the residence of **Lord Kitchener**, commander-in-chief of the Indian Army. The original building was replaced; its successor was converted into a hotel which burnt down in 1993. **Oberoi** has opened a new luxury hotel (see Where to stay, page 83).

### Naldera

Off the Hindusthan–Tibet road, 26 km north of Shimla, Naldera has a nine-hole golf course, possibly the oldest in India and one of the highest in the world, and the beautiful Mahung temple. The colourful **Sipi Fair** in June attracts handicraft-sellers from surrounding villages.

### Chail

In a superb forest setting with fine snow views, 45 km southeast of Shimla (2½ hours by bus), off the NH22, Chail was once the Maharaja of Patiala's summer capital. Built across three hills, it claims to have the country's highest cricket ground at 2444 m, a 2-km walk from the bus stand. The old palace on Rajgarh Hill has been converted to a hotel while the old residency, Snow View, and a Sikh temple stand on the other hills. The **Chail Sanctuary**, once a private hunting reserve, is popular with birders and has a Cheer pheasant-breeding programme. It is an idyllic spot until the weekend when day-trippers descend on the tiny resort.

### Kalka

Kalka is the terminus for the narrow-gauge railway from Shimla. The Kalka-Shimla line (0.76 m), completed in 1903, runs 97 km from Kalka in the foothills to Shimla at over 2000 m. The magnificent journey takes just over five hours. The steepest gradient is 1:33; there are 107 tunnels covering 8 km and 969 bridges over 3 km. Take snacks or order a meal in advance at Kalka or Shimla station.

## Nalagarh

The area around Nalagarh was once ruled by the Chandela Rajputs. The fort has wonderful views above an estate of forests and orchards and is built on five levels around manicured grassy courts. Originally built in the 15th century; the **Diwan-i-Khas** (1618) is now the Banquet Hall. The present raja has opened his home to guests. You can request the **Nalagarh Fort** hotel pickup from Ropar (20 km) or Kalka (40 km).

---

## Old Hindustan Tibet Road → *For listings, see pages 82-86.*

The Old Hindustan Tibet road runs east from Shimla to the Tibetan border through a landscape of lush tropical valleys, snow-clad peaks and precipitous gorges. Connecting a string of prosperous-looking farms, villages and towns, it passes through terraced slopes covered with orchards before entering the high-altitude deserts of Spiti. As the narrow road winds even deeper towards the Tibetan border its unprotected sides plunge hundreds of metres to the roaring monsoon-swollen River Sutlej below, grasping at huge boulders brought down by thundering landslides into the gloomy gorges. By bus or jeep, this road is not for the faint-hearted, and it may be severely damaged in the rains.

### Arriving on the Old Hindustan Tibet Road

**Inner Line Permits**, which are needed for travel close to the Tibetan border (essentially the area between Kaza and Jangi), are easy enough to get. Permits are issued free to individuals for seven days from the date of issue (easily renewable for three days at Kaza or Recong Peo). Take your passport, two copies of the details and Indian visa pages, and three passport photos and complete the form from the **Sub-Divisional Magistrate's office (SDM)** in **Shimla** ① *T0177-265 5988*; **Recong Peo** ① *T01786-222452*; or **Kaza** ① *T01906-222212*, where you need the additional 'No Objection' certificate from the chief of police (a mere formality of a stamp and signature). In Recong Peo, the whole process takes about an hour, which may include *chai* or breakfast with the SDM. Permits are also available (in theory) from the **Resident Comissioner of Himachal Pradesh** ① *Himachal Bhavan, 27 Sikandra Rd, New Delhi, T011-2371 6574*, and other magistrates offices. In Shimla, travel agents charge Rs 150. Permits are checked at Jangi if coming from Shimla and at Sumdo coming from Spiti. Carry about 10 photocopies as some checkpoints demand to keep one. Rules regarding overnight stays have been relaxed considerably; it is now possible to sleep in Puh and Nako. Accommodation is limited to simple rest houses, lodges or tents. In some places enterprising local families are opening their modest homes to paying guests. Local village shops often stock canned food and bottled water. It is virtually impossible to get foreign exchange in this area.

### Narkanda

The small market town at 2700 m occupies a superb position. The town offers a base from which to ski but the skiing does not compare with that found in Western resorts. Enquire at the Marketing Office in Shimla for skiing excursions in winter and the seven-day beginners' course.

### Rampur Bushahr

This is one of Himachal's most important market towns. **Padam Palace** (1920s), opposite the bus stand, once the residence of the raja, has interesting carved wooden panels and wall murals, but is difficult to enter. **Sat Narain Temple** in the main bazar (1926) has a beautiful but decaying façade. **Lavi Fair** (November) draws large crowds of colourful hill people who bring their produce – handicrafts, carpets, rugs, fruit and nuts and animals – to the special market. There are sporting competitions in the day, and dancing and making music around bonfires after dark.

## Rampur to Sarahan

From Rampur the highway enters one of the most exciting (and geologically active) stretches of road in the region. During the rains, the Sutlej River is a surging torrent of muddy water, dropping over 450 m in under 30 km and passing through gorges and deeply incised valleys. Although an ancient trade route, the road is comparatively recent and is constantly being upgraded particularly in connection with the Nathpa-Jhakhri HEP scheme, with a 28-km-long tunnel from **Nathpa**, near Wangtu, to **Jhakhri**, about 10 km beyond Rampur. When completed this will be one of the largest Hydel schemes in the world. The blasting both for the shafts and for road widening has further destabilized the already landslide-prone hillsides and during the rains the road may be blocked. Blockages are usually cleared within hours, though travelling times are wholly unpredictable. You also need a strong stomach, both for the main road and for diversions, especially up the Baspa Valley to Sangla. Some 9 km west of Jeori the river passes through a dramatic gorge.

# Sarahan → *For listings, see pages 82-86.*

An important market for traders of neighbouring regions, Sarahan is an attractive town, surrounded by high peaks, with a pheasant-breeding centre nearby (see below). The bazar is interesting: friendly villagers greet travellers, shops sell flowers, bright red and gold scarves and other offerings for worshippers among local produce, fancy goods, clothes and jewellery. It is also a stop on the trekkers' route.

Sarahan was the old capital of the local Rampur Bushahr rulers and has a palace complex containing the strikingly carved wood-bonded **Bhimakali Temple** (rebuilt circa 1927), in a mixture of Hindu and Buddhist styles. The two temples stand on a slope among apple and apricot orchards behind the bazar. The Bhimakali is dedicated to Durga as the destroyer of the *asuras* (demons) and has a Brahmin priest in attendance. Plan for an early-morning visit to the temple to see morning prayers; evening prayers are around 1900. Leave shoes and leather objects with the attendant and wear the saffron cap offered to you before entering. You may only photograph the outside of the temples. It is worth climbing around the back of the complex for a picturesque view.

According to some sources the ancient temple on the right (closed for safety reasons) is many centuries olde. Built in traditional timber-bonded style it has whitewashed dry stone and rubble masonry alternating with horizontal deodar or spruce beams to withstand earthquakes. The upper floors have balconies and windows with superb ornamental woodcarving; the silver repoussée-work doors are also impressive. The first floor has a 200-year-old gold image of goddess Bhimkali which is actively worshipped only during the **Dasara festival** when animals and birds are sacrificed in the courtyard, while on the second floor daily early-morning *puja* is carried out to a second image. The sacrificial altar and the old well are in the courtyard with three other shrines. The palace of the Rampur rajas behind the temple has a drawing room with ornate furniture and a painted ceiling; the caretaker may let you in.

**Pheasant Breeding Centre** ① *summer 0830-1830, winter 0930-1630, free*, on a hill, a 1-km strenuous walk from the main road, on a wooded trail, has Monal, Khalij, Western Tragopan and other varieties in cages.

A pilgrimage route encircles **Shrikhand Mahadev peak** (5227 m), which takes pilgrims seven days to go round. On a clear day you get fantastic panoramic views of the snow-covered peaks.

## Southern Himachal listings

*For hotel and restaurant price codes and other relevant information, see pages 12-14.*

### 🛌 Where to stay

**Shimla** *p76, map p76*

Prices soar May-Jun when modest rooms can be difficult to find especially after midday, so book ahead. Some places close off-season; those that remain open may offer discounts of 30-50%. From the railway or bus station it is a stiff climb up to hotels on or near the Ridge. Porters are available (Rs 20 per heavy bag).

**\$\$\$\$ Clarkes**, The Mall, near Lift, T0177-265 1010, www.clarkesshimla.com. 39 large, comfortable rooms, those with mountain views at rear may suffer from traffic noise at night, front rooms with town views quieter, impressive dining room (good buffets), pleasant bar, has character, well run but lacks some facilities (eg no pool).

**\$\$\$\$ Oberoi Cecil**, Chaura Maidan (quiet end of The Mall), T0177-280 4848, www.oberoihotels.com. 79 sumptuous rooms, colonial grandeur on the edge of town, with superb views, beautifully renovated, stylishly furnished, good restaurant, special ultra-modern pool, full-board. Recommended.

**\$\$\$\$-\$\$\$ Woodville Palace** (Heritage), Raj Bhavan Rd, The Mall, T0177-262 4038, www.woodvillepalacehotel.com. 30 rooms (variable), some good suites with period furniture (freezing in winter), dining hall worth visiting for eclectic mixture of portraits, weapons and hunting trophies (non-residents on advance notice), owned by the Raja of Jubbal's family and featured in *Jewel in the Crown*.

**\$\$\$ Combermere**, 2 entrances, next to the lift at top and bottom, T0177-265 1246, www.hotelcombermere.com. Good central location, 40 decent rooms (including penthouses) on 6 levels (partly served by lift), well located, friendly, efficient, very helpful, pleasant terrace café and bar, games room, central heating/a/c, super deluxe rooms worth spending little extra on.

**\$\$\$-\$\$ Peterhoff** (HPTDC), Chaura Maidan, near All India Radio, T0177-265 2538, www.hptdc. nic.in. 35 sombre but spacious rooms in very quiet location with beautiful lawn terrace and friendly, helpful staff.

**\$\$ Aapo Aap Homestay**, Panthaghati Bazar, Sargheen Chowk, 10 km outside Shimla, T(0)8091-208353, www.aapoaapshimla.com. In a beautiful location outside of Shimla with stunning views, this homestay has 3 lovely guest rooms. There is also Wi-Fi and a meditation room.

**\$\$ Dalziel**, The Mall, above station, T0177-645 1306, www.dalzielhotel.com. 30 clean enough, comfy, creaky valley-facing rooms with bath (hot water) in heritage building, Indian meals, prices depend on size of TV.

**\$\$ Samrat Regency**, near upper lift station on The Mall, T0177-265 8272, www.hotelsamratshimla.com. 20 rooms, restaurant, helpful.

**\$\$-\$ Mayur**, above Christ Church, T0177-265 2393, www.hotelmayur.com. 30 rooms in 1970s style, some with mountain views, some with tub, good restaurant but check bill, modern and clean, great central location.

**\$\$-\$ Dreamland**, The Ridge, T0177-280 6897, www.hoteldreamlandshimla.com. 31 clean rooms that vary in size and quality of bathroom, check first, plus good views.

**\$\$-\$ Woodland**, Daisy Bank, The Ridge, T0177-281 1002, www.hotelwoodland shimla.com. 21 rooms, some wood-panelled, some with great views, all with bath, cleanliness varies, avoid noisy downstairs rooms near reception, friendly, room service, safe luggage storage, off-season bargain.

**\$\$-\$ YMCA**, The Ridge, above Christ Church, T0177-265 2375. 40 rooms in annexe (best with bath), hot water in mornings, clean bathrooms on 2nd floor, avoid west side near noisy cinema, popular but very efficient/institutionalized, gym and billiards.

### Kufri p79
**$$$$ Kufri Holiday Resort**, T0177-264 8341, www.kufriholidayresort.com. 30 rooms and 8 modern cottages (2-3 bedrooms), limited hot water, cold in winter, but attractive design and setting with flower-filled gardens, outstanding views from cottages above and good walks.

### Chharabra p79
**$$$$ Wildflower Hall**, T0177-264 8585, www.oberoihotels.com. Standing on the grounds of the former residence of Lord Kitchener, retains period exterior but has been completely refurbished inside. 87 sumptuous rooms, beautifully decorated, mountain views, good restaurants and lovely gardens surrounded by deodar forest with beautifully peaceful walks, plus extensive spa, yoga classes under pine trees.

### Naldera p79
**$$$$ The Chalets Naldehra**, Durgapur Village, T0177-274 7715, www.chalets naldehra.com. 14 alpine-style pine chalets plus restaurant and a wide range of outdoor activities including world's highest golf course.
**$$$ Koti Resort**, T0177-274 0177, www.kotiresort. net. 40 modern, if slightly spartan rooms in beautifully located hotel surrounded by deodar forest, friendly manager, very relaxing.
**$$ Golf Glade** (HPTDC), T0177-274 7739, www.hptdc.nic.in. 5 simple rooms, plus 7 log huts (2 bedrooms), restaurant, bar, golfing requirements including clubs and instructors.
**$$-$ Mitwa Cottage**, near Koti Resort, T0177-201 2279. Sweet little homestay with kitchens and balconies. Lovely food as well and plenty of nature walks around. Recommended.

### Chail p79
**$$$$-$$$ Tarika's Jungle Retreat**, Chail, T01792-248684, www.tarikasjungleretreat. com. 35 well-appointed 'suite' cottages with lots of wood panelling. Geodesic glass reception. Popular family resort.
**$$$-$$ Chail Palace**, T01792-248141, www.hptdc. nic.in. 19 rooms and 3 suites in old stone-built mansion; avoid basement rooms 21, 22, 23, dark, dingy wooden chalets but others OK, billiards, tennis, orchards, well-maintained lawns and gardens, slightly institutional feel, interesting museum.
**$ Himneel**, T01792-248141, www.hptdc. nic.in. 16 rooms, modest but full of character. Kailash restaurant serves good-value breakfasts and lunches.

### Kalka p79
If using your own transport, there are many hotels, guesthouses and *dhabas* along the Kalka–Shimla road. Kasauli is an attractive hill resort with a distinctly English feel, 16 km off the main road with a few hotels, notably:
**$$$$ Baikunth**, Village Chabbal, near Kasauli, T(0)9857-166230, www.baikunth.com. Red brick building in the hills. Lovely airy, sunny rooms with all mod cons. Recommended for its spa.
**$$$ Alasia**, T01792-272008. 13 rooms in hugely atmospheric Raj-era hotel, remarkably authentic English cuisine, impeccable staff.
**$ Railway Retiring Rooms**. Good for early-morning departures. Reserve ahead at Kalka or Shimla.

### Nalagarh p80
**$$$ Nalagarh Fort**, T01795-223179, www. nalagarh.com. 15 comfortable rooms (some suites), with modern baths, traditional furniture, good food (buffets only), small pool, tennis, rural surroundings, plenty of atmosphere. Recommended. Book ahead.

### Narkanda *p80*

**$$$$ Banjara Orchard Retreat**, Thanedar Village, 15 km from Narkanda (80 km from Shimla), T(0)9418-077180, www.banjara camps.com. 6 double rooms, 2 suites and 2 lovely log cabins, set in apple orchards with stunning views down the Sutlej Valley. Evenings round the fire under the stars, trekking and excellent food. Recommended.
**$$$$ Tethy's Narkanda Resort**, T01782-242641. Comfortable rooms and some swiss cottage tents with stunning views. They organize snow skiing, hiking, mountain biking, river rafting, horse riding. Meals are included.
**$$$-$$ The Hatu**, (HPTDC), T01782-242430. Typical government fare, but with great views.

### Rampur Bushahr *p80*

**$$ Bushehar Regency**, 2 km short of Rampur on NH22, T01782-234103. 20 rooms, some a/c, well positioned. Restaurant, huge lawn, bar nearby.
**$ Bhagwati**, below bus stand near river, T01782-233117, www.hotelbhagwati ramputbsr.com. Friendly hotel, 24 clean rooms with bath (hot water), TV, restaurant.

### Sarahan *p81*

**$$-$ Srikhand** (HPTDC), T01782-274234, www.hptdc.nic.in. Superb hilltop site, overlooking the Sutlej Valley, Srikhand peak and beyond. 19 rooms with bath and hot water (3 large with balcony, 8 smaller with views, 4 in annexe cheaper), dorm (Rs 75), 2-bedroom royal cottage, restaurant but limited menu. Very close to stunning temple.
**$ Sagarika**, near Police Assistance, T01782-274491. 6 rooms with Western toilets on 1st floor, 8 others with Indian toilets, family-run, home-cooked meals.
**$ Bhimakali Temple**. You cn stay in the temple itself – very basic rooms with clean bathrooms and shared balconies, highly atmospheric.

## ❷ Restaurants

### Shimla *p76, map p76*

Below The Mall, towards Lower Bazar, good cheap *dhabas* sell snacks (eg *tikki channa*).
**$$$ Cecil**, Oberoi Cecil (see Where to stay, page 82). Atmospheric, plush, modernized.
**$$$ Woodville Palace** (see Where to stay, page 82). Attractive dining room full of antiquities, good buffet.
**$$ Alfa's**, The Mall. Modern interior, range of continental dishes in addition to good *thalis*, courteous service.
**$$ Baljees**, 26 The Mall, opposite Town Hall. Good snacks, justifiably packed, cakes and sweets available from takeaway counter.
**$$ Cafe Sol** (Hotel Combermere). Airy glass building with decent Western and Indian foods.
**$$ Qilaa**, The Mall, below Syndicate Bank. Serving up Indian, Chinese and Lebanese food, Qilaa is a relaxed affair with low seating and billowing fabrics.
**$$ Wake & Bake**, The Mall. Up some crickety stairs, you will find good coffee, baked goods and international food – cute place. There is internet café below.
**$ Guptajee's Vaishnav Bhojanalaya**, 62 Middle Bazar. 1st-class Indian vegetarian fare including tasty stuffed tomatoes, great *thali*. Recommended.
**$ Indian Coffee House**, The Mall. International. South Indian snacks, excellent coffee, some Western dishes, old-world feel, uniformed waiters, spartan and dim. Recommended.
**$ Park Café**, in hidden park below Christ Church. Indian. Continental menu. Student and traveller hangout, great pizzas, excellent espresso coffee.
**$ Sagar Ratna**, 6/1 The Mall, upstairs, T0177-280 0526. Good vegetarian South Indian food, *dosas*, *idlis*, good value.

## ✹ Festivals

**Shimla** *p76, map p76*
**May-Jun** Summer Festival includes cultural programmes from Himachal and neighbouring states, and art and handicrafts exhibitions.
**25 Dec** An ice skating carnival is held on Christmas Day.

## ✪ What to do

**Shimla and around** *p76, map p76*
**Golf**
There is a 9-hole course in Naldera. Casual members: green fee and equipment, about Rs 100, see page 79.

**Ice skating**
Skating rink: below Rivoli, winter only, Rs 50 to skate all day to loud Indian film hits.

**Skiing**
Early Jan to mid-Mar. Ski courses at Narkanda (64 km) organized by **HPTDC**, 7- and 15-day courses, Jan-Mar, Rs 1700-3000; see page 80.

**Tour operators**
**Band Box**, 9 The Mall, T0177-265 8157, bboxhv@satyam.net.in. Jeep safaris round Kinnaur and Spiti (around Rs 2500 per day), helpful advice, safe drivers and guides who clearly love the mountains. Recommended.
**Hi-Lander**, 62 The Mall, T(0)9816-007799, www.hilandertravels.com. Adventure tours and treks, hotel and transport bookings.
**HPTDC**'s various tours during the season are well run, usually 1000-1700. All start from Rivoli, enquire when booking for other pickup points. Return drop at Lift or Victory Tunnel. 2 tours visit Kufri, Chini Bungalow and Nature Park; 1 returns to Shimla via Fagu, Naldehra and Mashobra, the other by Chail and Kairighat. A further tour visits Fagu, Theog, Matiana and Narkanda. Book in advance at HPTDC office on The Mall.

## ✆ Transport

**Shimla** *p76, map p76*
**Air** Shimla (Jabbarhatti) airport (23 km from town) had flights with Kingfisher until their demise, at the time of writing no other airline was operating flights.
**Local bus** From Cart Rd. Lift: 2-stage lift from the Taxi Stand on Cart Rd and near **Hotel Samrat** on The Mall, takes passengers to and from The Mall, 0800-2200. Porters at bus stand and upper lift station will ask anything from Rs 10 to Rs 50 per bag; lower prices mean hotel commission.
**Long-distance bus** From main bus stand, Cart Rd, T0177-280 6587. Buy tickets from counter before boarding bus (signs in Hindi so ask for help) some long-distance buses can be reserved in advance: HPTDC coaches during the season are good value and reliable. **Kalka**, 3 hrs quicker than train but requires strong stomach; **Chandigarh**, 4 hrs **Dehra Dun**, 9 hrs; **Delhi**, 10-12 hrs; overnight to **Dharamshala**, 10 hrs. **Manali**, departs outside the 'Tunnel', 8-10 hrs, tickets from main bus stand. HPTDC deluxe buses between Shimla and **Delhi** in the summer, 9 hrs.
From **Rivoli Bus Stand** (Lakkar Bazar) T0177-281 1259: frequent buses to **Kufri**, **Rampur**, hourly from 0530, 8 hrs, and **Chitkul**, 2 daily; **Jeori** for **Sarahan** (8 hrs).
**Car hire** HPTDC (see page 77), has a/c cars. **Shimla Taxis** T(0)94180-82385, www.shimlataxis.in – have a wide range of cars.
**Taxi** Local taxis have fixed fares and run from near the lift on Cart Rd, T0177-265 7645. Long-distance taxis run from Union Stands near the lift, T0177-280 5164, and by the main bus stand on Cart Rd. **Chandigarh**, Rs 2500; **Kalka** (90 km), Rs 1600; **Mussoorie**, Rs 5500, 8 hrs, including stops; **Rekong-Peo**, around Rs 7000 (11 hrs).
**Train** Enquiry T131. Computerized reservations at main station (T0177-265 2915), 1000-1330, 1400-1700, Sun 1000-1400, and by tourist office on The Mall. The

newer extension station, where some trains start and terminate, is just below the main bus stand. Travel to/from Shimla involves a change of gauge to the slow and cramped but extremely picturesque 'toy train' at Kalka. To reach Shimla from **Delhi** in a day by train, catch the *Himalayan Queen* or *Shatabdi Exp 12011* leaving New Delhi station at 0740 to arrive in Kalka by 1200 (see Kalka, below). In the reverse direction, the 1030 train from Shimla has you in Kalka at 1600 in time to board the Delhi-bound *Himalayan Queen 14096*. Book tickets for the toy train in advance; the 'Ticket Extension Booth' on Kalka station sells out by 1200 when the *Shatabdi* arrives, and the train often arrives on the Kalka platform already full of locals who board it while it waits in the siding. Worth paying Rs 150-170 plus reservation fee of Rs 20 to guarantee a seat on 1st class.

**Kalka to Shimla**: *Kalka Shimla Passenger 52457*, 0400, 5½ hrs; *Shivalik Exp Deluxe 52451*, 0530, 4¾ hrs (has bigger windows and comfy seats); *Kalka Shimla Express 52453*, 0600, 5 hrs; *Himalayan Queen 52455*, 1210, 5 hrs. Extra trains in season (1 May-15 Jul; 15 Sep-30 Oct; 15 Dec-1 Jan): You can book a special train carriage which can be attached to regular trains with elegant furnishings and big windows which accommodates 8 people through IRCTC Chandigarh. **Shimla to Kalka**: *Himalayan Queen*, 1030, 5½ hrs; *Shivalik Exp Deluxe 52452*, 1740, 4¾ hrs.

## Kalka *p79*

**Bus or taxi** Easily reached from **Shimla**, by bus or taxi (Rs 1600), and from **Chandigarh** by taxi (Rs 500).

**Train  Kalka to Delhi**: *Shatabdi Exp 12006*, 0615, 4 hrs; *Shatabdi Exp 12012*, 1745, 4 hrs; *Himalayan Queen 14096*, ND, 1650, 5½ hrs; *Kalka Mail 12312*, OD, 2345, 6¾ hrs; day trains are better). All via Chandigarh, 45 mins. **Delhi to Kalka**: *Himalayan Queen 14095*, DSR, 0600, 5¼ hrs; *Shatabdi Exp 12011*, ND, 0740 (4 hrs); *Howrah Kalka Mail 12311*, OD, 2215 (7½ hrs).

## Rampur Bushahr *p80*

**Bus** Buses are often late and overcrowded. To **Chandigarh**, **Delhi**; **Mandi** (9 hrs); **Recong Peo** (5 hrs) and **Puh**; **Sarahan** (2-3 hrs), better to change at Jeori; **Shimla**, several (5-6 hrs); **Tapri** (and Kalpa) 0545 (3¼ hrs), change at Karchham for Sangla and Chitkul.

## Sarahan *p81*

**Bus** Daily buses between **Shimla** (Rivoli Bus Stand) and **Jeori** on the Highway (6 hrs), quicker by car. Local buses between Jeori and the army cantonment below Sarahan.

## ⓘ Directory

**Shimla** *p76, map p76*
**Medical services** Tara Hospital, The Ridge, T0177-280 3785: Dr Puri, Mehghana Complex, The Mall, T0177-281 1936, speaks fluent English, is efficient, and very reasonable. **Post** GPO, The Mall, T0177-265 2518. Open Sun 1000-1600. **Poste Restante**: Counter 10 (separate entrance), chaotic, 0800-1700, Sun 1000-1600. **CTO** nearby.
**Useful contacts** Police: T0177-265 2860.

# Kinnaur and Spiti

The regions of Kinnaur and Spiti lie in the rainshadow of the outer Himalayan ranges. The climate in Spiti is much drier than in the Kullu Valley and is similar to that of Ladakh. The temperatures are more extreme both in summer and winter and most of the landscape is barren and bleak. The wind can be bitingly cold even when the sun is hot. The annual rainfall is very low so cultivation is restricted to the ribbons of land that fringe rivers with irrigation potential. The crops include potatoes, wheat, barley and millet. The people are of Mongol origin and almost everyone follows a Tibetan form of Buddhism.

Kinnaur and Spiti can only be seen by following a circular route, first along the Old Hindustan Tibet Road by the Sutlej River, then crossing into the wild Spiti Valley, which has the evocative Tibetan Buddhist sites of Tabo and Kaza set against the backdrop of a rugged mountain landscape. The road continues round to the Rohtang Pass and Manali, or on up to Ladakh. It's also worth making a side trip up the Baspa Valley via Sangla to Chitkul for its views and landscapes, villages, pagodas and culture.

---

### Kinnaur and around → For listings, see pages 96-99.

Most Kinnauri Buddhist temples only accept visitors at around 0700 and 1900. You must wear a hat and a special belt available locally. ▶▶ For trekking, see page 143.

### Along the Sutlej

An exciting mountain road runs through cliffside cuttings along the left bank of the Sutlej – frequently blocked by rockfalls and landslides during the monsoons. At **Choling** the Sutlej roars through a narrow gorge, and at **Wangtu** the road re-crosses the river where vehicle details are checked. Immediately after crossing the Wangtu bridge a narrow side road goes to **Kafnoo village** (2427 m), in the Bhabha Valley (a camping site and the start for an attractive 10-day trek to the Pin Valley). From Wangtu the road route runs to **Tapri** (1870 m) and **Karchham** (1899 m) both of which have hot springs. Here the Baspa River joins the Sutlej from the south. A hair-raising excursion by a precipitous winding rough road leads 16 km up the Baspa Valley to Sangla; buses take approximately 1½ hours.

### Baspa Valley

The valley carries the marks of a succession of glacial events which have shaped it, although the glaciers which formed the valley have now retreated to the high slopes above Chitkul at over 4500 m. Recently the valley has been terribly scarred by the Baspa Hydroelectric

Project, with blasting, dust and truck logjams commonplace, but persevere and carry on up the valley and the rewards are worth it. All villages in Baspa are characterized by exaggerated steeply sloping slate roofs, rich wood carving and elaborate pagoda temples. Although Kinner Kailash (sacred to Hindus and Buddhists) is not visible from here, the valley is on the circumambulating **Parikrama/Kora** route which encircles the massif. Fields of the pink coloured *ogla*, a small flower seed grown specifically in the Baspa Valley for grinding into grain, add a beautiful colouring in the season.

**Sangla**, at 2680 m, is built on the massive buttress of a terminal moraine which marks a major glacial advance of about 50,000 years ago. The Baspa River has cut a deep trench on its south flank. Immediately above is the flat valley floor, formed on the dry bed of a lake which was once dammed behind the moraine. The village has excellent carving and is full of character. No foreign exchange is available but there are telephone facilities. Sangla is

# Kinnaur & Spiti

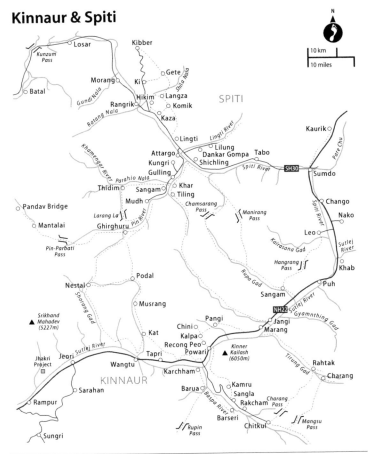

famous for its apples, while a **saffron farm** just north of the village is claimed to be better than that at Pampore in Kashmir.

The old seven-storey **Killa** (Fort) ⓘ *0800-0900, 1800-1900*, where the Kinnaur rajas were once crowned, is 1 km north of new Sangla just before the road enters the village. It was occupied by the local rulers for centuries. It now has a temple to Kamakshi where the idol is from Guwahati, Assam.

**Barseri**, 8 km from Sangla, is situated on an outwash cone which has engulfed part of the Baspa's valley floor. This well-kept 'green village' has solar heaters, *chakkis* (water mills) and water-driven prayer wheels. The **Buddha Mandir**, with *Shakyamuni* and other images and a large prayer wheel, is beautiful inside. Villagers weave shawls and do woodcarving. The beautifully carved pagoda-style **Rakcham temple** is dedicated to Shamshir Debta, Devi and Naga, combining Buddhist and Hindu deities. The ibex horns on the roof are ancient male fertility symbols. There is also a pre-Buddhist, animist **Bon cho shrine** and a Siva temple.

**Chitkul**, some 18 km from Barseri, at an altitude of 3450 m, is the furthest point foreigners can travel without special permits. With its typical houses, Buddhist temple and a small tower, it is worth the trip. The Kagyupa (Oral Transmission School) has a highly valued, old image of the Shakyamuni Buddha. There are four directional kings on either side of the door as well as a Wheel of Life. You can walk along the Baspa River which has paths on both sides. The rough path along the tributary starting at the bridge across the river, below the bus stand, is very steep in places with loose stones. Do not attempt alone.

## Recong Peo to the Spiti River

**Recong Peo**, also called 'Peo', at 2290 m, is the District HQ and a busy little market town. The Sub-Divisional Magistrate's office in a three-storey building below the bus stand deals with Inner Line Permits (see page 80). A short walk above the town takes you to the Kalachakra Temple with a large Buddha statue outside and good views of Kinner Kailash. A shop here sells provisions, medicines and has a telephone, but there's nowhere to change money.

**Kothi village**, reached by a path from the Kalachakra Temple, has ancient Hindu temples associated with the Pandavas. One has a tank of sacred fish, 30 minutes' walk from the bazar.

**Kalpa** (Chini), 12 km from Recong Peo at 2960 m, is reached after a stiff climb. It has an interesting temple complex and Budh mandir and is surrounded by apple, *bemi* (wild apricot) and plum orchards and chilgoza pine forests, with striking views across to Kinner Kailash (6050 m).

A high road from Kalpa/Recong Peo with little traffic passes through Chilgoza pine forests, north to the hamlet of **Pangi**, 10 km away. Pangi is surrounded by apple orchards. The colourful Sheshri Nag temple at the top of the village has an inscription in a strange script above the entrance and standing stones in the courtyard. Apart from two Buddhist temples, the carved pagoda temple to Sheshri's mother encloses a huge boulder representing the Devi. The road then goes over bare and rugged hills beyond to **Morang**, which has impressive monasteries with wood carvings and sculptures.

Inner Line Permits are checked at **Jangi**. From here the road goes to Puh, a steep climb with hairpin bends.

## Into the Spiti Valley

The bridge at **Khab**, 11 km beyond Puh, marks the confluence of the Sutlej and Spiti rivers. The entry into the Spiti Valley at Khab is a rare example of crossing from the Himalaya to the Trans-Himalaya without going over a major pass. The Sutlej now disappears east towards the Tibet border, while the road follows the Spiti. Major deforestation of the mountain slopes has resulted in sections of the road being washed away. The new road, a remarkable feat of engineering, hairpins up to the village of **Nako**, with some basic guesthouses, and rejoins the river at Chango.

**Sumdo**, the last village of Kinnaur, has a border police checkpost and a tea shop, and is the starting point of State Highway 30, which passes through an arid valley with small patches of cultivation of peas and barley near the snow melt streams. It is 31 km from Sumdo to Tabo.

## Tabo

At the crossroads of two ancient trade routes, Tabo was one of the great centres of Buddhist learning and culture. Founded in 996, the **Chos Khor Gompa** (see below) is the oldest living Buddhist establishment in this part of the world. Today, the small town is rapidly being modernized with paved streets and electric lights. Government offices have appeared alongside traditional mud homes and the local shops stock basic provisions for trekkers. There is a post office.

**Chos Khor Gompa** Founded in AD 996 as a scholastic institution, the monastery's original layout was planned as a *mandala* centred around a **Du khang** (Assembly Hall). The deodar wood used was imported from Kullu, Kinnaur, Chamba and Kashmir while the lack of quality structural stone resulted in the extensive use of earth, strengthened with gypsum for the high walls. Today the *gompa* houses 60 *lamas* and has a good collection of scriptures, *thangkas* and art pieces. It is most important and has an immense sense of the spiritual. Carry a torch. No photography allowed.

Many of the **colourful murals** come close to the pure Indian style identified with Ajanta. The technique required the surface to be coated with several thin layers of lime and yak-skin glue and burnished vigorously to provide the 'ground' which was then smoothed and freshened with animal fat and butter. Natural vegetable dyes and powdered stone colours were mixed with *dzo* milk and yak urine for painting. The early Indian style murals used a profusion of reds and yellows with little stress on landscaping, the area around the principal figures being filled with small divinities. These images wear seraphic smiles and have half-shut dreamy eyes denoting introspective meditation. The later 17th-century paintings illustrate the Central Tibetan/Chinese art form where ultramarine takes over from the earlier dominance of reds and yellows, and landscapes become lively and vivid with the appearance of cliffs, swirling clouds, stylized flames, flora and fauna. Here the twists and turns of the limbs and the flowing elaborate drapery show great fluency. This is one of the few *gompas* in the Tibetan Buddhist-influenced areas of Ladakh, Lahaul and Spiti where the highly structured art of painting the complex Tibetan religious iconography is taught. What appears outwardly as a free art form is taught on lined paper where each shape and form is closely measured.

**Nine Temples** **Tsuglhakhang** (academy) The 'resplendent' central *Mahavairochana* – a composite of four figures, each facing a cardinal direction, represents the unity of all

Buddhas. On the walls inside are stucco figures of different Buddhas and Bodhisattvas. The floral ceiling decorations are in the Ajanta style.

**Dri Tsang khang** (Inner Sanctum) and **Kora** (Circumambulatory Path) At the centre of the 'mandala', the five *Dhyani* Buddhas escorted here by four Bodhisattvas, emerge from the darkness lit by a shaft of sunlight.

Masks, weapons and ritual costumes are stored in the **Gon Khang** which is closed to visitors. **Zhalma** (Picture Hall) has a 17th-century entrance temple where the murals are recent and in pure Tibetan style.

**Dromton Lhakhang Chenpo** (17th century) Dominated by Medicine Buddhas. The ceiling, in high Tibetan style, is exceptional, depicting *nagas*, titans, peacocks and parrots amongst rainbows.

**Ser Khang** (Golden Temple) The walls were believed to have been coated with a layer of gold dust as thick as a yak's skin for painting the numerous larger-than-life figures. They were renewed in the 16th and 17th centuries.

**Chamba Chenpo La Khang** Dedicated to the Maitreya (Future) Buddha, this temple has a 6-m-high seated statue. The murals of the eight Buddhas may be some of the earliest in Tabo.

**Buddhist caves** To the north, the small natural caves above the road were an integral part of the monastic complex. **Pho Gompa**, the only surviving, with early murals showing pure Indian influence, has been restored. These post-Ajantan paintings, however, are already fading. On open ground to the east, on both sides of a dyke, there are pre-Buddhist rock carvings on metamorphosed igneous rocks showing ibex, swastikas, *yonis*, horses, panthers and human figures.

### Dankar

Once the capital of Spiti, Dankar is a tiny village. The early 16th-century fort/monastery **Dankar Gompa** (3890 m), which once served as a jail, stands on an impressive overhang, perched on crumbling towers. Today it has more than 160 *lamas* in residence. The 'highest temple' has a collection of Bhotia Buddhist scriptures, a four-in-one *Dhyani Buddha* and interesting murals of Medicine Buddhas and protector deities. The *gompa* is a very steep two-hour climb from a point 2 km away, beyond Shichling on the main road. The 4WD road from the SH30, about 1 km west of Shichling, winds up 8 km to Dankar (a two-hour walk) and is easier. A beautiful large pond at just under 4100 m is reached by a 2.5-km track.

### Lalung Gompa

Lalung Gompa, known for its carved wood panelling, is off the SH30, 22 km from Kaza, reached by 8-km narrow, drivable track. From Dankar Gompa this is a two-hour trek. Carry plenty of water as there are no streams and it can get very hot.

### Pin Valley

About 5 km from Dankar is a sign for the Pin Valley National Park which is on the other side of the river. The Pin River joins the Spiti at Attargo. Above Attargo, 10 km along the Pin Valley, is the **Kungri Gompa** (circa 1330), which though not old is in an established monastic site with old carved wooden sculptures and is commonly understood to be a Bon monastery still practising elements of the pre-Buddhist Bon religion. The trek from the Bhabha Valley ends at the road head at Kungri. One bus a day departs from Kaza at 1200, goes along the Pin Valley as far as Mikkim and turns straight back at 1400, not allowing enough time to visit the *gompa*. You therefore face a long walk unless you can hitch a lift on a passing tractor, truck or yak.

At the confluence of the Pin River and one of its tributaries, 1 km from Mikkim, **Sangam** can be reached by car over a new iron bridge, or more adventurously by a pulley system with a person-sized bucket, 750 m west of the bus stop along the river. It requires a reasonable degree of fitness to negotiate, especially if crossing alone. The local greeting is *joolay, joolay*!

**Pin Valley National Park** is described as the "land of ibex and snow leopard" and was created to conserve the flora and fauna of the cold desert. It adjoins the Great Himalayan National Park (southwest), and Rupi Bhabha Sanctuary (south) with the Bara Shigri Glacier forming its north boundary. The park covers 675 sq km with a buffer zone of 1150 sq km mainly to its east where there are villages, and varies in altitude from 3600 m to 6630 m. The wildlife includes Siberian ibex, snow leopard, red fox, pika, weasels, lammergeier, Himalayan griffon, golden eagle, Chakor partridge, Himalayan snow cock and a variety of rose finches. The Siberian ibex can be sighted at high altitudes, beyond Hikim and Thango village. From July to September the young ibex kids need protection and so the females move up to the higher pastures near cliffs while the adult males concentrate on feeding lower down. The 60-km-long Lingti Valley is famous for its fossils.

## Kaza

Kaza, at 3600 m, is 13 km from Lingti village. Old Kaza has village homes while New Kaza sports government offices. It is a busy bus terminus with a small market, a basic health centre and jeeps for hire. Inner Line Permits are issued by the **SDM's office** ① *T01906-222202, 1030-1700, closed 2nd Sat of each month.* Tourist facilities are open May to October. No foreign exchange is available. If you are in need of supplies, **Kibber**, 19 km away, has post, a bank and several provisions stores for trekkers. For an exceptional insight into the area, check out www.spitiecosphere.com with a focus on conservation.

There is an attractive one-day circular trek from here to **Hikim** and **Komik** villages visiting the monastery midway. **Hikim Gompa** (early 14th century), modelled on a Chinese castle, was built under Mongol patronage. ►► *For trekking in Himachal, see page 143.*

## Kibber-Gete Wildlife Sanctuary

One of the world's highest wildlife sanctuaries, covering an area of 98 sq km, Kibber-Gete has **Mount Gya** (6754 m) to the north and **Kamelong** (5867 m) to the south. On the drive from Kibber to Tashigang, you may spot musk deer and bharal sheep but to see larger mammals (bear, wolf and the rare snow leopard) you would need to trek. Also to be seen are Himalayan birds of prey as well as snowcock and other high-altitude birds. Buses from Kaza take about an hour.

## Tashigang

Tashigang, 18 km away, is one of the highest villages in the world connected by road. **Ki Monastery** on the way is the largest in Spiti and houses 300 *lamas*. Although it has suffered from wars, fires and earthquakes it still has a good collection of *thangkas* and *kangyurs* (scriptures). Although no permit is needed, the monks have instituted their private 'entrance fee' system which, by all accounts, appears quite flexible and linked to the visitor's perceived ability to pay. There are a few cheap guesthouses and camping is possible. If you cannot stay take a bus up and walk down via the Ki Monastery, 11 km from Kaza.

**To Lahaul**
**Losar**, at 4079 m, is the last village in Spiti, reached after driving through fields growing peas and cabbage among poplars, willows and apple orchards. There is a rest house and guesthouse and a couple of cafés serving Tibetan/Spitian food.

The road continues up for 18 km to the **Kunzum La** (Pass) at 4551 m. It means 'meeting place for ibex' and gives access to Lahaul and good views of some of the highest peaks of the Chandrabhaga group that lies immediately opposite the Kunzum La to the west. To the southeast is the Karcha Peak (6271 m). The pass has an ancient *chorten* marker. The temple to **Gyephang**, the presiding deity, is circumambulated by those crossing the pass; the giver of any offering in cash which sticks to the stone image receives special blessing.

The road descends through 19 hairpin curves to reach the rock strewn valley of the River Chandra at **Batal**, where a tea shop serves noodles and sells biscuits and bottled water. It continues to **Chhota Dhara** and **Chhatru**, with rest houses and eateries, and then **Gramphoo** joining the Manali-Keylong-Leh highway around three hours after leaving the pass. From Gramphoo to Manali is 62 km.

---

## Shimla to the Kullu Valley → *For listings, see pages 96-99.*

### Bilaspur and Bhakra-Nangal Dam
**Bilaspur** used to be the centre of a district in which the tribal Daora peoples panned in the silts of the Beas and Sutlej for gold. Their main source, the Seer Khud, has now been flooded by the Bhakra Nangal Lake and they have shifted their area of search upstream. For a bite to eat visit the **Lake View Café**.

The dam on the River Sutlej is one of the highest dams in the world at 225 m and was built as part of the Indus Waters Treaty between India and Pakistan (1960). The Treaty allocated the water of the rivers Sutlej, Beas and Ravi to India. The dam provides electricity for Punjab, Haryana and Delhi. It is also the source for the Rajasthan Canal project, which takes water over 1500 km south to the Thar Desert. There is accommodation should you wish to stay.

### Una to Mandi
Having passed through Una, along the main bus route, **Ghanahatti**, 18 km further on, has the adequate **Monal Restaurant**. There are some magnificent views, sometimes across intensively cultivated land, sometimes through plantations of chilgoza, khir and other species. In **Shalaghat**, further on, accommodation is available. The road descends into a deep valley before climbing again to the small market town of **Bhararighat**. A jeep can take over two hours for this part of the journey. In **Brahmpukar** the road to Beri and Mandi is a very attractive country lane. The more heavily used though still quiet road to the main Bilaspur-Manali road joins it at **Ghaghas**. During the monsoons landslides on the NH21 may cause long delays. Carry plenty of water and some food. The tree-lined and attractive approach to **Sundernagar** from the south gives some indication of the town's rapid growth and prosperity.

### Mandi (Sahor)
Founded by a Rajput prince in circa 1520, Mandi is held sacred by both Hindus and Buddhists. The old town with the main (Indira) bazar is huddled on the left bank of the Beas at the southern end of the Kullu Valley, just below its junction with the River Uhl. The Beas bridge – claimed to be the world's longest non-pillar bridge – is across Sukheti Khad

at the east end of town. The main bus station is across the river, just above the open sports ground. It is worth stopping a night in this quaint town with 81 temples, a 17th-century palace and a colourful bazar. **Tourist information** ① *T01905-225036.*

**Triloknath Temple** (1520), on the riverbank, built in the Nagari style with a tiled roof, has a life-size three-faced Siva image (Lord of Three Worlds), riding a bull with Parvati on his lap. It is at the centre of a group of 13th- to 16th-century sculpted stone shrines. The Kali Devi statue which emphasizes the natural shape of the stone, illustrates the ancient Himalayan practice of stone worship.

**Panchavaktra Temple**, at the confluence of the Beas and a tributary with views of the Trilokinath, has a five-faced image (*Panchanana*) of Siva. The image is unusually conceived like a temple *shikhara* on an altar plinth. Note the interesting frieze of yogis on a small temple alongside.

**Bhutnath Temple** (circa 1520) by the river in the town centre is the focus at **Sivaratri Fair** (see page 98). The modern shrines nearby are brightly painted.

In lower Sumkhetar, west of the main bazar, is the 16th-century **Ardhanarishvara Temple** where the Siva image is a composite male/female form combining the passive Siva (right) and the activating energy of Parvati (left). Although the *mandapa* is ruined, the carvings on the *shikhara* tower and above the inner sanctum door are particularly fine.

From the old suspension bridge on the Dharamshala road, if you follow a narrow lane up into the main market you will see the slate roof over a deep spring which is the **Mata Kuan Rani Temple**, dedicated to the 'Princess of the Well'. The story of this Princess of Sahor (Mandi) and her consort **Padmasambhava**, who introduced Mahayana Buddhism in Tibet, describes how the angry king condemned the two to die in a fire which raged for seven days and when the smoke cleared a lake appeared with a lotus – Rewalsar or *Tso Pema* (Tibetan 'Lotus Lake').

### Around Mandi

The small dark **Rewalsar Lake**, 24 km southeast, with its floating reed islands, is a popular pilgrimage centre. The colourful Tibetan Buddhist monastery was founded in the 14th century, though the pagoda-like structure is late 19th century. The Gurudwara commemorates Guru Gobind Singh's stay here. Start early for the hilltop temples by the transmission tower as it is a steep and hot climb. The **Sisu fair** is held in February/March. There are many buses to the lake from Mandi Bus Stand, one hour; you can also board them below the palace in Indira Bazar.

At **Prashar**, a three-tiered pagoda Rishi temple sits beside a sacred lake in a basin surrounded by high mountains with fantastic views of the Pir Panjal range. The rich woodcarvings here suggest a date earlier than the Manali Dhungri Temple (1553), which is not as fine. No smoking, alcohol or leather items are allowed near the temple or lake. There are basic pilgrim rest houses. A forest rest house is 1 km west of temple. To reach the temple, follow a steep trail from Kandi, 10 km north of Mandi, through the forest of rhododendron, oak, deodar and kail (three hours). After arriving at a group of large shepherd huts the trail to the left goes to the temple, the right to the forest rest house.

You can walk to **Aut**, see below, from Prashar in six to seven hours. A level trail east crosses a col in under a kilometre. Take the good path down to the right side of the *nullah* (valley) and cross the stream on a clear path. Climb a little and then follow a broad path on the left bank to the road. Turn right and down to **Peon village** in the *Chir nullah* and continue to Aut.

## Tirthan Valley and Jalori Pass

From Mandi the NH21 runs east then south along the left bank of the Beas, much diminished in size by the dam at **Pandoh**, 19 km from Mandi, from which water is channelled to the Sutlej. The dam site is on a spectacular meander of the Beas (photography strictly prohibited). The NH21 crosses over the dam to the right bank of the Beas then follows the superb **Larji Gorge**, in which the Beas now forms a lake for a large part of the way upstream to Aut. A large hydroelectric project is being constructed along this stretch. At **Aut** (pronounced 'out') there is trout fishing (season March to October, best in March and April); permits are issued by the Fishery Office in Largi, Rs 100 per day. The main bazar road has a few cheap hotels and eating places. It is also a good place to stop and stock up with trekking supplies such as dried apricots and nuts.

From Aut, a road branches off across the Beas into the **Tirthan Valley** climbing through beautiful wooded scenery up to the Jalori Pass. Allow at least 1½ hours by jeep to **Sojha**, 42 km from Mandi, and another 30 minutes to Jalori. Contact tourist office in Kullu for trekking routes. One suggested trek is Banjar–Laisa–Paldi–Dhaugi/Banogi–Sainj, total 30 km, two days.

**Banjar**, with attractive wood-fronted shops lining the narrow street, has the best examples in the area of timber-bonded Himalayan architecture in the fort-like rectangular temple of **Murlidhar** (Krishna). Halfway to **Chaini**, 3 km away, the large **Shring Rishi Temple** to the deified local sage is very colourful with beautiful wooden balconies and an impressive 45-m-tall tower which was damaged in the last earthquake. The entrance, 7 m above ground, is reached by climbing a notched tree trunk. Such free-standing temple towers found in eastern Tibet were sometimes used for defence and incorporated into Thakur's castles in the western Himalaya. The fortified villages here even have farmhouses like towers.

From Banjar the road climbs increasingly steeply to **Jibhi**, 9 km away, where there are sleeping options and trekking. Some 2 km beyond is **Ghayaghi**, also with accommodation. A few kilometres on is **Sojha**, a Rajput village in the heart of the forest, which offers a base for treks in the Great Himalayan National Park.

Finally you reach the **Jalori Pass** (altitude: 3350 m), open only in good weather from mid-April, which links Inner and Outer Seraj and is 76 km from Kullu. You may wish to take the bus up to the pass and walk down, or even camp a night at the pass. Check road conditions before travelling. A ruined fort, **Raghupur Garh**, sits high to the west of the pass and from the meadows there are fantastic views, especially of the Pir Panjal range. Take the path straight from the first hairpin after the pass and head upwards for 30-40 minutes. The road is suitable for 4WD vehicles. There is a very pleasant, gradual walk, 5 km east, through woodland (one hour), starting at the path to the right of the temple. It is easy to follow. **Sereuil Sar** (Pure Water) is where local women worship Burhi Nagini Devi, the snake goddess, and walk around the lake pouring a line of *ghee*. It is claimed that the lake is kept perpetually clear of leaves by a pair of resident birds. *Dhabas* provide simple refreshments and one has two very basic cheap rooms at the pass.

**Great Himalayan National Park and Tirthan Sanctuary** ⓘ *foreigners Rs 200 per day, Indians Rs 50, students half price, video Rs 300/150,* lies southeast of Kullu town in the Seraj Forest Division, an area bounded by mountain ridges (except to the west) and watered by the upper reaches of the rivers Jiwa, Sainj and Tirthan. The hills are covered in part by dense forest of blue pine, deciduous broadleaved and fir trees and also shrubs and grassland; thickets of bamboo make it impenetrable in places. Attractive species of iris, frittilaria, gagea and primula are found in the high-altitude meadows. Wildlife include the panther, Himalayan black bear, brown bear, tahr, musk deer, red fox, goral and bharal. The rich birdlife includes six species of pheasant. The park is 60,561 ha with an altitude of 1500-5800 m and the sanctuary covers 6825 ha; its headquarters are in Shamshi. Access is easiest from April to June and September to October. Check it out at www. greathimalayannationalpark.com. **Goshiani** is the base for treks into the park. The first 3 km along the river are fairly gentle before the track rises to harder rocky terrain; there are plenty of opportunity to see birds and butterflies. The trout farm here sells fresh fish at Rs 150 per kg. Fishing permits, Rs 100, are obtainable from the Fisheries Department.

## Kinnaur and Spiti listings

*For hotel and restaurant price codes and other relevant information, see pages 12-14.*

### ⊖ Where to stay

**Baspa Valley** *p87*
**$$$$ Banjara Camps**, Barseri, 8 km beyond Sangla, T01786-242536, www.banjara camps.com. Superb riverside site with impressive mountains looming above you. 18 twin-bed rooms and some 4-bed deluxe tents, delicious meals included, hot water bottles in the bed, friendly staff, mountain biking, trekking, Lahaul, Spiti, Ladakh tours. Buses stop 2 km from the site, where road drops down to right, car park at foot of hill is 500-m walk from camp (horn will summon porters). Highly recommended.
**$$ Hotel River Rupin View**, Rakcham Village, 12 km from Sangla, T(0)9999-989548. Pretty little place well off the beaten track, set in garden with basic rooms.
**$$ Kinner Camp**, Barseri, T(0)9769-375993, www.kinnerkamps.com. Small tents with beds/sleeping bags, shared baths, birdwatching, trekking, jeep safaris, meals, cafeteria, superb location.
**$ Amar Guest House**, Chitkul. Clean double rooms (Rs 100), hot water, friendly family atmosphere. Recommended.
**$ Hotel Apple Pie**, Sangla, T07186-226304. Run by a veteran mountaineer.
**$ Mount Kailash**, Sangla, T01786-242527. 8 clean, pleasant rooms (hot shower), 4-bed dorm, too.

**$ Negi Cottage**, Sangla, T(0)94189-04161. 3 rooms with bath, all brightly coloured inside and out so has more character than most.
**$ PWD Rest House**, Chitkul. 4 rooms, lawns, attractive.
**$ Shruti Guest House**, Sanglanear market, www.shrutiguesthouse.com. Comfortable, clean rooms with TV and attached bath. Friendly welcome and good home-cooked food as well as mighty Himalaya views.

**Recong Peo to the Spiti River** *p89*
**$$$-$$ Inner Tukpa** between Kalpa and Recong Peo, T01786-223077, www.inner tukpahotel.com. Nestled in the woods between Kalpa and Recong Peo. There are spacious rooms here and even more spacious views.
**$$ Monk Resort** Roshi Rd, 1.5 km from Kalpa, T(0)9816-737004, www.kinnaurgeo tourism.com. 4 spacious swiss cottage tents, huts and airy rooms available in pretty surroundings. Recommended.
**$$-$ Aucktong Guest House ('Aunties')**, near Circuit House, 1 km north on Pangi road, Kalpa, T01786-226019. Pleasant, 6 clean spacious rooms, large windows, restaurant, very friendly ("arrived for 1 night and stayed a week!").
**$$-$ Kinner Kailash Cottage** (HPTDC), Kalpa, T01786-226159, www.hptdc.nic.in. Open May-Nov. Commanding position, 5 rooms (bathtub Rs 1100), limited menu, camping.
**$$-$ Kinner Villa**, 4 km outside Kalpa, T01786-226006, circuits@vsnl.net.in. 20 rooms with bath, attractively located, seasonal tents and a 6-bed dorm.

**$ Forest Rest House**, Chini, 2 km from Kalpa. Caretaker can prepare meals, modern building, camping overnight (with permission) in school grounds 1600-1000.
**$ Shivling View**, near bus stand, Recong Peo, T01786-222421. Good view of Shivling peak. OK but better to stay up near Kalpa.

## Tabo *p90*

Guesthouses in the village allow camping. There is a good list of homestays throughout Tabo and Spiti on www.spitiecosphere.com and www.himachaltourism.gov.in.
**$$$ Dewachen Retreat**, Tabo T(0)9459-566689, www.dewachenretreats.com. Large comfortable cozy rooms, hot water and great views. They have another property in Rangrik, Kaza.
**$$-$ Millennium Monastery Guest House**, run by monks in monastery complex, 13 colourful rooms, shared dirty toilets, hot water on request, meals.
**$ Tanzin**, near monastery. Tibetan food, friendly, family-run, best in village.

## Dankar *p91*

**$ The *gompa*** has 2 rooms; only 1 has a bed.
**$ Dolma Guest House**. 8 perfectly fine rooms.

## Pin Valley *p91*

**$ Norzang Guest House**. Rooms for Rs 100.
**$ PWD Rest House**.

## Kaza *p92*

Kaza is ideal for camping and there are great opportunities for homestay in this area, see **Spiti Ecospheres** for more information (see What to do, page 98).
**$$$ Kaza Retreat**, T(0)94187-18123, www.banjaracamps.com. 11 clean, modern rooms with attached bathrooms. You can expect high standards here, good food and relaxing atmosphere, with stunning views a bonus. Recommended.
**$$ Monk Resorts**, Shego, 6 km from Kaza, T(0)98167-37004, www.kinaurgeotourism. com. 8 spacious swiss cottage tents in pretty

location surrounded by flowers. They have other camps in Nako and Kalpa.
**$$-$ Sakya's Abode**, T01906-222254. 10 rooms in a fine-looking building with a wide range of rooms and a cheap dorm (Rs 80). It offers a friendly welcome and delicious home-cooked food.
**$$-$ Snow Lion Guest House**, T01906-222525. 8 large, comfortable rooms with great home-cooked food and majestic views.
**$ Kumphen Guest House**. Simple rooms, good service and delicious Tibetan food right inside the Monastery compound.
**$ Mahabuddha Guest House**. Basic but large room, shared bath, very clean, meals.

## Una to Mandi *p93*

**$ Mehman**, Shalaghat. Occupies an extraordinarily bold setting. Restaurant.
**$ Relax Inn**, Sundernagar, on Mandi side of town, T01907-262409. Modern, clean.

## Mandi *p93*

**$$$-$$ Raj Mahal**, lane to right of palace, Indira Bazar, T01905-222401, www.rajmahal palace.com. Former 'palace' has character but in need of attention. 14 rooms, including atmospheric deluxe rooms with bath (sharpened sword in one might be mistaken for a towel rail). Rooms in palace are charismatic, in the other block they are quite dull, but cheap. Restaurant, bar, garden temple. Recommended. Although be persistent – they don't always answer phone.
**$$$-$$ Visco Resorts**, 2 km south of Mandi, T01905-225057, www.viscoresorts.com. 18 large rooms (some for 4) in modern resort, by the river, good cheap vegetarian restaurant, extremely well run.
**$$ Hotel Regent Palms**, near Kargil Park, close to Raj Mahal, T01905-222 777. Bright new hotel with all the mod cons and nice decor.
**$$ Munish Resorts**, on hillside 2 km above New Beas Bridge, T01905-235035, www. munishresorts.com. 15 clean rooms with bath, restaurant, lovely views, colourful garden with tempting fruit, friendly family.

**$ Evening Plaza**, Indira Bazar, T01905-223318. 14 reasonable rooms, some a/c, TV, changes cash and TCs at a good rate.
**$ Hotel Lotus Lake**, Rewalsar, above the lake, T01905 240239. Run by the folks at Ziggar Monastery, this place has had a fresh lick of paint. If going to Rewalsar you can also stay by donation at the Sikh gurudwara (temple).
**$ Rewalsar Inn** (HPTDC), above the lake, T01905-240252, www.hptdc.nic.in. 12 reasonable rooms with bath, some with TV and balcony, dorm (Rs 75), good lake views.

**Tirthan Valley and Jalori Pass** *p95*
**$$$$-$$$ Himalayan Trout House**, below Banjar, T01903-225112, www.mountainhighs.com. All-weather eco-cabins, mud hut suites and stone cottage suites. Stunning location, fine food, great hospitality. Artists studio, gazebo with fire and library. Trekking and fishing. Little shop selling organic wares. Highly recommended.
**$$$ Sojha Retreat**, Sojha, T01903-200070, www.banjaracamps.com. 5 basic double rooms and 4 lovely suites in wooden lodge with fantastic views, good food and trekking information. You can see all the way to the mountains above Manali from here. Stunning.
**$ Dev Ganga**, 9 km from Banjar in Jibhi, T01903-227 005. 8 double rooms, friendly, comfortable, with exceptional views.
**$ Doli Guest house**, Jhibi village, T01903-227 034, www.kshatra.com. Nice little rooms in traditional building. Sweet little café by the river in very pretty little village. Ask about the cottages above the village with sitting rooms and woodburning stove.
**$ Forest Rest House**, near Sojha, spectacular and isolated just below the Jalori Pass.
**$ Fort View Home Stay**, Sojha, just by entrance to Banjara Camp, T(0)9418-626634. Traditional building with 4 rooms inside, shared bathroom. Atmospheric.
**$ Meena**, beyond bus stand, Banjar, T01902-222258. 4 double rooms.

**$ Raju's Place**, Goshaini, is a family-run river-facing guesthouse, 3 rooms with bath. They offer meals – great home-cooked food, treks and safaris. Access by zip wire over the river.
**$ Whispering Woods**, Jibhi village, T(0)9418-776699. Lovely views right by the river, nice little sit-outs. Basic clean rooms.

## ✸ Festivals

**Mandi** *p93*
**Feb/Mar** Sivaratri Fair, a week of dance, music and drama as temple deities from surrounding hills are taken in procession with chariots and palanquins to visit the Madho Rai and Bhutnath temples.

## ⬢ What to do

**Kaza** *p92*
**Tour operators**
**Spiti Ecospheres**, www.spitiecospheres.com. Based in Kaza, this is an exceptional project with a nod towards conservation, environmental and livelihoods; also volunteering projects, unique treks and promoting organic agriculture. They have an interesting range of tours including **Spiritual Sojourns** where you spend time with the *Bhuchens*, a rare sect of Tibetan Buddhist theatrical artists and **Rustic Revelations** and **Spiti Kaleidoscope** where you get real insight into the lives and culture of these Himalayan peoples. There are also several **Carbon Neutral** volunteering projects. Ecosphere also put in 6 Solar installations in 2013 as part of its initiative to provide reliable, green and decentralised energy to the Spiti Valley. Highly recommended.

## ⊖ Transport

**Baspa Valley** *p87*
**Sangla**
**Bus** To **Chitkul** (often 2-3 hrs late); **Shimla** via Tapri (9 hrs); **Recong Peo**, 0630; from

Tapri, 0930. 4WD recommended between Karchham and Chitkul in bad weather.

## Chitkul
**Bus** Twice daily to/from **Karchham** (0930) via **Sangla** (1100) and **Rakcham**; from **Tapri**, 0930; from **Recong Peo** 0600 (prompt).

## Recong Peo to the Spiti River *p89*
## Recong Peo
**Bus** Reserve tickets from booth shortly before departure. Bus to **Chandigarh**; **Delhi** 1030; **Kalpa**, occasional; **Kaza** (9 hrs), gets very crowded so reserve seat before 0700; **Puh**; **Rampur**, frequent (5 hrs); **Sangla/Chitkul** (4 hrs); **Shimla**; **Tabo**, via Kaza (9-10 hrs).

## Kalpa
**Bus** To **Shimla**, 0730; **Chitkul**, 1300. To get to Peo for Kaza bus at 0730, walk down (40 mins) or arrange taxi from Peo. Travellers may not be allowed beyond Jangi without an 'Inner Line' permit. Contact SDM in Recong Peo a day ahead (see page 80).

## Tabo *p90*
**Bus** To **Chandigarh** via Kinnaur, 0900; **Kaza**, 1000.

## Kaza *p92*
**Bus** Reserve a seat at least 1 hr ahead or night before. The road via Kunzum-La and Rohtang Pass can be blocked well into Jul. New bus stand, bottom end of village. In summer: from **Manali** (201 km), 12 hrs via Rohtang Pass and Kunzum La; **Shimla** (412 km) on the route described, 2 days. Approximate times shown: daily to **Chango**, 1400; **Kibber** 0900; **Losar** 0900; **Mikkim** (19 km from Attargo), in the Pin Valley, 1200 (2 hrs); returns 1400. Long-distance buses to **Kullu**, 0400; **Manali** (from Tabo), 0500; **Chandigarh** 0630. The last 3 are heavily used.

## Mandi *p93*
**Bus** Bus information T01905-235538. **Chandigarh** 1100 (203 km, 5 hrs). **Dharamshala** 1215, 6 hrs; **Kullu/ Manali** every 30 mins, 3 hrs (Kullu), 4 hrs (Manali); **Shimla** (5½ hrs, ). Book private buses in town or opposite the bus stand at least 1 day in advance; they do not originate in Mandi. **Dharamshala**, 5 hrs; **Kullu/Manali**, 2 hrs (Kullu), 3½ hrs (Manali).
**Taxi** Rs 1500 to **Kullu**; Rs 2200 to **Manali**; Rs 2000 to **Dharamshala**.
**Train** Jogindernagar (55 km), T01908-222088, is on the narrow gauge from Pathankot.

## Tirthan Valley and Jalori Pass *p95*
**Bus** From **Jibli** the bus to **Jalori** can take 1 hr. Some go via **Ghayaghi** (approximate times): **Kulla–Bagipul**, 0800; **Manali–Rampur**, 1000; **Kullu–Dalash**, 1100; **Manali–Ani**, 1100. If heading for Shimla or Kinnaur, change buses at Sainj on NH22.

Bus from **Ani** and **Khanag** to the south, runs to **Jalori Pass** and back. 4 buses daily traverse the pass in each direction when it is open (8-9 months). Bus to **Sainj**, 3½ hrs, and on to **Shimla**, 5 hrs.
**Taxi** From **Banjar** to Jalori Pass costs Rs 800 (Rs 1200 return), to **Jibhi/Ghayaghi**, Rs 300, to **Kullu**, Rs 600, to **Manali**, Rs 1200, to **Mandi** Rs 700, to **Shimla**, Rs 3000. Buses are rare.

## ❶ Directory

## Mandi *p93*
**Medical services** Hospital, T01905-222102. **Useful contacts** Police: T01905-235536.

# Kullu Valley

The Kullu Valley was the gateway to Lahaul for the Central Asian trade in wool and borax. It is enclosed to the north by the Pir Panjal range, to the west by the Bara Bangahal and to the east by the Parvati range, with the Beas River running through its centre. The approach is through a narrow funnel or gorge but in the upper part it extends outwards. The name Kullu is derived from Kulantapith, 'the end of the habitable world'. It is steeped in Hindu religious tradition; every stream, rock and blade of grass seemingly imbued with some religious significance. Today, the main tourist centre is Manali, a hive of adventurous activity in the summer months, a quiet and peaceful place to relax in the winter snow.

## Kullu → *For listings, see pages 108-115.*

Sprawling along the grassy west bank of the Beas, Kullu, the district headquarters, hosts the dramatically colourful **Dasara festival**. Less commercialized than its neighbour Manali, it is known across India as the home of apple-growing and the locally woven woollen shawls. There is little to occupy you here as a tourist.

### Arriving in Kullu
**Getting there** Kullu-Manali (Bhuntar) airport, 10 km south, has flights from Delhi, Shimla and Ludhiana; transfer by bus or taxi to Manali (Rs 750), Manikaran (Rs 650). If travelling on buses from the south, alight at Dhalpur Bus Stand. ▸▸ *See Transport, page 114.*

**Getting around** The central area, including the main bus stand and Dhalpur (with ample hotels and restaurants) are close enough to cover on foot. Buses and taxis go to nearby sights.

**Tourist information** Himachal Pradesh Tourism Development Corporation (HPTDC) ① *T01902-222349, near Maidan, 1000-1700*, provides maps and advice on trekking.

**Climate** Mid-September to mid-November is the best time to visit. May and June are hot but offer good trekking. March to mid-April can be cold with occasional heavy rain.

### Places in Kullu
Kullu's bulky curvilinear temples seem to have been inspired by the huge boulders that litter the riverbeds and hillsides outside town. A peculiar feature of the Nagari temples is the umbrella-shaped covering made of wood or zinc sheets placed over and around the *amalaka* stone at the top of the spire.

## Dasara in Kullu

The festival of Dasara celebrates Rama's victory over the demon Ravana. From their various high mountain homes about 360 gods come to Kullu, drawn in their raths (chariots) by villagers to pay homage to Raghunathji who is ceremoniously brought from his temple in Kullu.

The goddess Hadimba, patron deity of the Kullu Rajas, has to come before any other lesser deities are allowed near. Her chariot is the fastest and her departure marks the end of the festivities. All converge on the Maidan on the first evening of the festival in a long procession accompanied by shrill trumpeters. Thereafter there are dances, music and a market. During the high point of the fair a buffalo is sacrificed in front of a jostling crowd. Jamlu, the village God of Malana, high up in the hills, follows an old tradition. He watches the festivities from across the river, but refuses to take part. See box, page 147. On the last day Raghunathji's rath is taken to the riverbank where a small bonfire is lit to symbolize the burning of Ravana, before Ragunathji is returned to his temple in a wooden palanquin.

The **Raghunathji Temple** is the temple of the principal god of the **Dasara festival**. The shrine houses an image of Shri Raghunath (brought here from Ayodhya circa 1657) in his chariot. **Bhekhli**, a 3-km climb, has excellent views from the **Jagannathi Temple**. The copper 16th- to 17th-century mask of the Devi inside has local Gaddi tribal features. The wall painting of Durga is in traditional folk style. There are also superb views on the steep but poorly marked climb to the tiny **Vaishno Devi Temple**, 4 km north, on Kullu-Manali road.

### Around Kullu

**Bijli Mahadev**, 11 km from Kullu at 2435 m, is connected by road most of the way with a 2-km walk up steps from the road head. The temple on a steep hill has a 20-m rod on top which is reputedly struck by *bijli* (lightning) regularly, shattering the stone *lingam* inside. The priests put the *lingam* together each time with *ghee* (clarified butter) and a grain mixture until the next strike breaks it apart again. Several buses until late afternoon from Left Bank Bus Stand, the road to Bijli is rough and the buses are in a poor state.

**Bajaura Temple**, on the banks of the Beas River, about 200 m off the NH21 at **Hat** (Hatta), is one of the oldest in the valley. The massive pyramidal structure is magnificently decorated with stone images of Vishnu, Ganesh and Mahishasuramardini (Durga as the Slayer of the Buffalo Demon in the outer shrines. The slender bodies, elongated faces and limbs suggest East Indian Pala influence. Floriated scrollwork decorate the exterior walls.

---

### Parvati Valley → *For listings, see pages 108-115.*

The Parvati (Parbati) Valley runs northeast from Bhuntar. Attractive orchards and the fresh green of terraced rice cultivation line the route. Known for its hot springs at Manikaran, more recently the valley has become infamous for the droves of chillum-smoking Israelis and Europeans who decamp here in the summer months.

Several local buses (and jeep taxis) travel daily to the valley from Kullu via Bhuntar, taking about two hours to Manikaran, which also has buses from Manali. The area is prone to landslides and flash floods – take special care. ➤ *See Transport, page 114. For trekking, see page 113.*

## Kasol

Kasol is the next village en route to Manikaran. The rapidly expanding village has spread on both sides of the road bridge which crosses a tributary that flows into the Parvati, not far from the village itself. Kasol is the main destination for long-stay visitors, many of whom sit in a haze of *charas* smoke by day, repeating the process by night.

**Chhalal** is a 20-minute walk from Kasol. It is a quiet village where families take in guests. A couple of guesthouses have also sprung up here.

## Manikaran

Manikaran, 45 km from Kullu, is at the bottom of a dark gorge with **hot sulphur springs** emerging from the rock-strewn banks of the Parvati. A local legend describes how while Parvati bathed in the river, Naga, the serpent god stole her *manikaran* (earrings). At Siva's

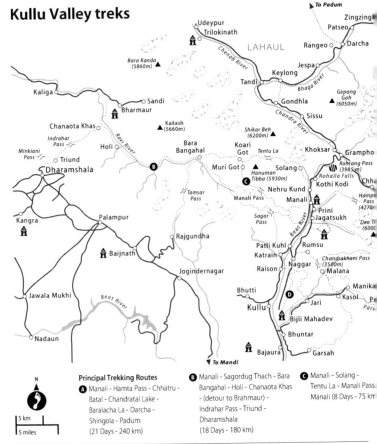

# Kullu Valley treks

**Principal Trekking Routes**

Ⓐ Manali - Hamta Pass - Chhatru - Batal - Chandratal Lake - Baralacha La - Darcha - Shingola - Padum (21 Days - 240 km)

Ⓑ Manali - Sagordug Thach - Bara Bangahal - Holi - Chanaota Khas - (detour to Brahmaur) - Indrahar Pass - Triund - Dharamshala (18 Days - 180 km)

Ⓒ Manali - Solang - Tentu La - Manali Pass - Manali (8 Days - 75 km)

command Naga angrily blew them back from underground causing a spring to flow. Hindu and Sikh pilgrims come to the Rama temple and the *gurdwara* and gather to cook their food by the springs, purportedly the hottest in the world. There are separate baths for men and women. Manikaran, though not attractive in itself, provides a brief halt for trekkers. Short treks go to Pulga and Khirganga beyond while a footpath (affected by landslips in places), leads to the Pin Valley in Spiti. If trekking this route, always go with a registered guide; do not attempt it alone. A road continues for 15 km to **Barseni**, which has become a popular place with long-term travellers.

## Pulga and Khirganga

**Pulga**, a noisy village, is in a beautiful location with some cheap guesthouses. It is a good four-hour walk east of Manikaran. Some long-stay travellers prefer the basic airy guesthouses outside the village which offer meals.

    **Khirganga** is along the trek which winds through the lush Parvati Valley, east of Pulga. It is known for its sacred ancient hot springs marking the place where Siva is thought to have meditated for 2000 years. There is an open bathing pool for men and an enclosed pool for women, next to the humble shrine at the source. A few tents may be hired. *Dhabas* sell vegetarian food. This is the last village in this valley.

## Kullu to Manali → *For listings, see pages 108-115.*

The NH21 continues north along the west side of the Beas. The older road to the east of the river goes through terraced rice fields and endless apple orchards, and is rougher and more circuitous but more interesting. Sections of both roads can be washed away during the monsoon.

### Kullu to Katrain

As you wind out the centre of Kullu along the right bank you'll pass the **Sitaramata Temple** embedded in the conglomerate cliff and **Raison**, a grassy meadow favoured by trekkers. **Katrain**, in the widest part of the Kullu Valley, mid-way between Kullu and Manali, is overlooked by **Baragarh Peak** (3325 m). There are plenty of options for an overnight stay. Across the bridge at **Patli Kuhl**, the road climbs through apple orchards to Naggar.

## Naggar

Naggar's (Nagar) interesting castle sits high above Katrain. Built in the early 16th century, it withstood the earthquake of 1905 and is a fine example of the timber-bonded building of West Himalaya. It was built around a courtyard with verandas, from where there are enchanting views over the valley. With a pleasant, unhurried atmosphere, it is a good place to stop a while. It is also an entry for treks to Malana, see page 146.

The **castle**, probably built by Raja Sidh Singh, was used as a royal residence and state headquarters until the 17th century when the capital was transferred to Sultanpur (see Kullu). It continued as a summer palace until the British arrived in 1846, when it was sold to Major Hay, the first assistant commissioner, who Europeanized part of it, fitting staircases, fireplaces and so on. Extensive renovations have produced fine results, especially in the intricately carved woodwork. In the first courtyard are several black *barselas* (sati stones) with primitive carvings. Beyond the courtyard and overlooking the valley the **Jagti Pat Temple** houses a cracked stone slab measuring 2.5 m by 1.5 m by 2 m believed to be a piece of Deo Tibba, which represents the deity in 'the celestial seat of all the gods'. A priest visits the slab every day.

The small **museum** ⓘ *Rs 10*, has some interesting exhibits, including examples of local *pattu* and *thippu* (women's dress and headdress) and *chola* (folk dance costumes). There are also local implements for butter and tea making, and musical instruments like the *karnal* (broad bell horn) and *singa* (long curled horn).

**Roerich Art Gallery** ⓘ *Tue-Sun 0900-1300 (winter from 1000), 1400-1700, Rs 30*, a 2-km climb from the castle, is Nicholas Roerich's old home in a peaceful garden with excellent views. The small museum downstairs has a collection of photos and his distinctive stylized paintings of the Himalaya using striking colours. It's a beautiful collection from an inspiring family. Nicholas Roerich created the Roerich Pact in the 1930s in order to preserve culture and the arts in the wake of WWI. It was originally signed by 21 countries.

**Uruswati Institute** ⓘ *uphill from the main house, Rs 15*, was set up in 1993. The **Himalayan Folk and Tribal Art Museum** is well presented, with contemporary art upstairs. One room upstairs is devoted to a charming collection of Russian traditional costumes, dolls and musical instruments.

There are a number of **temples** around the castle including the 11th-century Gauri Shankar Siva near the bazar, with some fine stone carving. Facing the castle is the Chaturbhuj to Vishnu. Higher up, the wooden Tripura Sundari with a multi-level pagoda roof in the Himachal style celebrates its fair around mid-May. Above that is the Murlidhar Krishna at Thawa, claimed as the oldest in the area which has a beautifully carved stone base. Damaged in the 1905 earthquake, it is now well restored. There are fine mountain views from here.

---

## Manali and around → For listings, see pages 108-115.

Manali occupies the valley of the Beas, now much depleted by hydroelectric projects, with the once-unspoilt Old Village to the north and Vashisht up on the opposite hillside across the river. Set amidst picturesque apple orchards, Manali is packed with Pahari-speaking Kullus, Lahaulis, Nepali labourers and enterprising Tibetan refugees who have opened guesthouses, restaurants and craft shops. It is a major tourist destination for Indian holidaymakers and honeymooners. In summer months Manali is the start of an exciting two-day road route to Leh.

## Arriving in Manali

**Getting there** Kullu-Manali (Bhuntar) airport is 50 km away with bus and taxi transfers. The bus and taxi stands are right in the centre (though many private buses stop short of

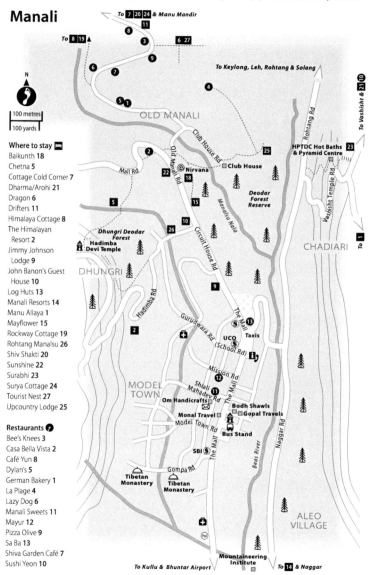

# Manali

To **7** **20** **24** & Manu Mandir

To **8** **19**

To Keylong, Leh, Rohtang & Solang

To Vashisht & **21** **10**

**N**

100 metres
100 yards

OLD MANALI

**Where to stay** 🛏
Baikunth **18**
Chetna **5**
Cottage Cold Corner **7**
Dharma/Arohi **21**
Dragon **6**
Drifters **11**
Himalaya Cottage **8**
The Himalayan
    Resort **2**
Jimmy Johnson
    Lodge **9**
John Banon's Guest
    House **10**
Log Huts **13**
Manali Resorts **14**
Manu Allaya **1**
Mayflower **15**
Rockway Cottage **19**
Rohtang Manalsu **26**
Shiv Shakti **20**
Sunshine **22**
Surabhi **23**
Surya Cottage **24**
Tourist Nest **27**
Upcountry Lodge **25**

**Restaurants** 🍴
Bee's Knees **3**
Casa Bella Vista **2**
Café Yun **8**
Dylan's **5**
German Bakery **1**
La Plage **4**
Lazy Dog **6**
Manali Sweets **11**
Mayur **12**
Pizza Olive **9**
Sa Ba **13**
Shiva Garden Café **7**
Sushi Yeon **10**

Club House Rd

Old Manali Rd

Mall Rd

@ Nirvana

Club House

HPTDC Hot Baths
& Pyramid Centre **23**

Vashisht Temple Rd

Deodar
Forest
Reserve

CHADIARI

To **1**

Manalsu Nala

Dhungri Deodar
Forest
Hadimba
Devi Temple

DHUNGRI

Hadimba Rd

Circuit House Rd

Gurudwara Rd

The Mall

Sa Ba **13**

Taxis

UCO
(School Rd)

Mission Rd

Shlali
Mahadev Rd

The Mall

MODEL
TOWN

Om Handicrafts

Bodh Shawls

Monal Travel

Gopal Travels

Model Town Rd

Bus Stand

SBI

Gompa Rd

Tibetan
Monastery

Tibetan
Monastery

Beas River

Naggar Rd

ALEO
VILLAGE

Pol

Mountaineering
Institute

To Kullu & Bhuntar Airport

To **14** & Naggar

Rohtang Rd

the centre) within easy reach of some budget hotels – the upmarket ones are a taxi ride away. ▶▶ *See Transport, page 114. For trekking in the Himachal, see page 143.*

**Getting around** Manali, though hilly, is ideal for walking. For journeys outside taxi rates are high, so it is worth hiring a motorcycle to explore.

**Tourist information** HPTDC ① *next to Kunzam Hotel, The Mall, T01902-252175,* is helpful.

**Climate** The best season is March-April but there is occasional heavy rain and snow in the villages. May-June and mid-September to mid-November offer better trekking.

### Places in Manali

The **Tibetan Monastery**, built by refugees, is not old but is attractive and is the centre of a small carpet-making industry. Rugs and other handicrafts are for sale. The colourful **bazar** sells Kullu shawls, caps and Tibetan souvenirs.

**Old Manali** is 3 km away, across Manalsu Nala. Once a charming village of attractive old farmsteads with wooden balconies and thick stone-tiled roofs, Old Manali is rapidly acquiring the trappings of a tourist economy: building work continues unchecked in the lower reaches of the village, as ever more guesthouses come up to thwart those seeking an escape from the crowds of modern Manali, while the arrival of the drugs and rave scene in summer extinguishes most of Old Manali's remaining charm. The main road continues through some unspoilt villages to the modern **Manu Mandir**, dedicated to Manu, the Law Giver from whom Manali took its name and who, legend tells, arrived here by boat when fleeing from a great flood centuries ago. Aged rickshaws may not make it up the hill, so visitors might have to get off and walk.

**Vashisht** is a small hillside village that can be reached by road or a footpath, a 30- to 40-minute walk from the tourist office. Note the carvings on the houses of the wealthy farmers. The **Vashisht Temple** dedicated to Lord Rama is very atmospheric. It is built in the local style and has a pretty façade. Inside however you discover separate bathing tanks for men and women with super hot water which many believe has medicinal properties. It's a great way to start the day. **Hot springs** at the top of the hill lead to free communal baths in the village centre. The village, with its messy jumble of old village houses and newer buildings, has cheap places to stay which attract young travellers. A two-hour walk past the village up the hillside leads to a **waterfall**.

**Dhungri Village** is at the top of Hadimba Road. Follow the road uphill, past the gates leading to the temple and take the path 50 m further to arrive at the village centre. The village houses have cedar wood carving and balconies with superb views across the valley. Travellers are welcomed into family homes and traditional village life carries on around the guests, although several new developments, including a fun fair, are starting to change the flavour of the lower half of the village.

**Hadimba Devi Temple**, the Dhungri temple (1553), in a clearing among ancient deodars, is an enjoyable 2-km walk from the tourist office. Built by Maharaja Bahadur Singh, the 27-m-high pagoda temple has a three-tier roof and some fine naturalistic wood carving of animals and plants, especially around the doorway. The structure itself is relatively crude, and the pagoda is far from perfectly perpendicular. Massive deodar planks form the roof but in contrast to the scale of the structure the brass image of the goddess Hadimba inside, is tiny. A legend tells how the God Bhima fell in love with Hadimba, the sister of the demon

Tandi. Bhima killed Tandi in battle and married Hadimba, whose spirituality, coupled with her marriage to a god, led to her being worshipped as a goddess. Today, she is seen as an incarnation of Kali. The small doorway, less than 1 m high, is surrounded by wood-carved panels of animals, mythical beasts, scrolls, a row of foot soldiers and deities, while inside against a natural rock is the small black image of the Devi. To the left is a natural rock shelter where legend has it that Hadimba took refuge and prayed before she was deified. The greatly enlarged footprints imprinted on a black rock are believed to be hers. Hadimba Devi plays a central part in the annual festival in May, at both Kullu and Manali. To prevent the master craftsman producing another temple to equal this elsewhere, the king ordered his right hand to be cut off. The artist is believed to have mastered the technique with his left hand and reproduced a similar work of excellence at Trilokinath (see page 119) in the Pattan Valley. Unfortunately, his new master became equally jealous and had his head cut off. It's a stunning temple, incredibly atmospheric.

A **feast and sacrifice** is held in mid-July when the image from the new temple in Old Manali is carried to the Hadimba Temple where 18 ritual blood sacrifices are performed. Sacrifices include a fish and a vegetable, and culminate with the beheading of an ox in front of a frenzied crowd. This ceremony is not for the faint-hearted. Pickpockets are known to take advantage of awestruck tourists, so take care.

### Walks
Manali is the trail-head for a number of interesting and popular treks (see below). Beyond Old Manali, the **shepherd trail**, which winds its way up and down the hillside, allows you to capture a picture of Himalayan life as well as see some superb birdlife. The path starts at some concrete steps (after The Lazy Dog lounge/bar) on the first hairpin bend along the paved road to Old Manali (or you can pick it up where the road ends and taxis turn around at the top of the hill) and continues along the cemented path, which turns into a dirt trail. Return the same way, four to five hours.

**Walk 1** This walk takes you towards Solang. In Old Manali Village take the right fork and then turn left in front of the new temple. This trail is a classic, following the right bank of the Beas River up towards the Solang Valley passing the villages of **Goshal**, **Shanag**, **Buruwa** to **Solang** (2480 m), a small ski resort with 2.5 km of runs. Solang is 14 km (five hours). You can get tea, biscuits, nuts and plates of steaming spicy noodles along the walk, and there are also places to stay (see Manali, Where to stay, page 109). To return to Manali it is a steady walk down the valley side to the main Rohtang Pass-Manali Highway where you can pick up a bus (Rs 5) or shared jeep (Rs 10).

**Walk 2** Go prepared for cold for this walk as it takes you through woodland shading you from the sun. Keeping the **Hadimba Temple** on your right follow the contour of the hill and bear right to pick up a clear pack-horse trail which heads up the steep valley. This is a steady uphill climb through woodland giving superb views of the river below, abundant Himalayan birdlife and a chance to see all manner of activity in the woods, chopping, cutting and burning. An enjoyable three- to four-hour walk.

**Walk 3** This walk takes you to the village of **Sethan** (12 km). Take a local bus to the Holiday Inn on the Naggar road. With the hotel behind you, cross the road and pass through the orchard and fields which have low mud walls all round which can be walked on. Bear east till you come to a disused track and then bear right and follow it to the once-untouched village of **Prini** which now has several five-star hotels. If you are lucky the *chai* shop will be open. Further east, the trail to Sethan village becomes somewhat indistinct, though local people are at hand to point you in the right direction. It is a superb three-hour hike up a wooded valley to Sethan (3000 m), which is well off the tourist trail.

## Kullu Valley listings

*For hotel and restaurant price codes and other relevant information, see pages 12-14.*

### Where to stay

**Kullu Valley** *p100*
The choice of hotels is widening, some good hotels in all ranges, though very full during Dasara. Large off-season discounts (30-50%).
**$$$$-$$$ Apple Valley Resorts**, Mohal, NH21, on the Beas River, 6 km from airport, T01902-260001, www.applevalleyresorts.co.in. 36 comfortable, very well-designed modern chalets in landscaped grounds, excellent food, friendly reception, rafting nearby.
**$$$-$$ Airport Inn**, next to Bhuntar airport, T01902-268286, airportinncomplex@ gmail.com. A convenient place to stay before taking the 50 km to Manali.
**$$$-$$ Shobla**, Dhalpur, T01902-222800, www.shoblainternational.com. 25 rooms, flashy exterior, central, clean, pleasant atmosphere, airy restaurant, overlooking river.
**$$ Gaur Niwas**, Dhalpur, close to tourist office, T01902-240555. Charming period property with 4 spacious, comfortable rooms, beautiful balconies. Easily the most atmospheric place in town.
**$$-$ Sarwari** (HPTDC), 10-min walk south of Dhalpur Bus Stand, T01902-222471. Peaceful hotel with 16 simple but comfortable rooms (10 in more spacious new wing), 8-bed dorm (Rs 75), good-value restaurant, beer, pleasant gardens, elevated with good views.
**$ Silver Moon** (HPTDC), perched on a hill, 2 km south of centre, T01902-222488, www. hptdc.nic.in. 6 rooms with bath and heaters, each with small sitting room in traditional style, very clean, good food, has character

(enhanced because Mahatma Gandhi stayed here). Taxis Rs 50 from Kullu centre, buses stop at gate if requested – ask for the last barrier south out of Kullu.

**Kasol** *p102*
**$ Alpine**, T01902-273710, www.alpine guesthouse.net. By far the best place in town right next to the river and deservedly popular. Friendly and welcoming with good clean rooms.
**$ Green Valley**, T01902-273869. Friendly place although genuinely surprised if you are not Israeli – clean basic rooms on the way into town.
**$ Panchali Holiday Home**, T01902-273895. Good range of rooms.
**$ Sasi**, new Kasol riverside, T(0)9817-009523. Cheap and cheerful place with basic rooms, often full. Good terrace by the river.

**Manikaran** *p102*
There are a large number of budget guest-houses in the lower part of the village, some with baths fed by the hot springs. However, prices in season rise to unbelievable rates given that most rooms are basic at best.
**$$-$ Country Charm**, main bus stand, T01902-273703. Not really in the country, and not all that charming, but one of the smarter places in town, with 10 brand new rooms, good-value off season.
**$ Padha Family Guest House**, Manikaran bazar, near Gurudwara, T(0)9817-044874. Cheap rooms, super basic but clean with hot shower. Downstairs separate hot bathing room. **Moon Guest House** nearby offers much the same.
**$ Parvati**, near the temple, T01902-273735. 10 simple rooms, sulphur baths, restaurant.

**Katrain and Raison** *p103*
**$$$$ Neeralaya**, Raison, T0 1902-245725,
www.neeralaya.com. Beautiful riverside
cottages and villas made of stone and
wood in the local *kathkuni* style with
private kitchens and large verandas. Great
local food. It's a sedate pace here by the
river with walk through the orchards, trout
fishing possibilities and campfire suppers.
Recommended.
**$$$-$$ Ramgarh Heritage Villa**, near
Raison between Kullu and Manali, T(0)9816-
248514, www.ramgarhheritagevillamanali.
com. A farm since 1928, nicely furnished
rooms with TV and Wi-Fi, but beyond
the front door there are orchards of pear,
pomegranate and walnut trees and great
views of the mountains. You can do trips to
their kiwi plantation and they can organize
paragliding, river rafting, yoga and picnics.
**$ Anglers' Bungalow**, Katrain, T01902-
240136. Superb views from 6 spartan rooms –
although at time of writing, this was no
longer run by HPTDC so details might change.
**$ Orchard Resorts**, Dobhi, 2 km south of
Katrain, T01902-240160. Good off-season
discount. 16 attractive wood-panelled
'cottages', with hot water, TV, heaters.

**Naggar** *p104*
**$$$-$ Castle**, T01902-248316, www.hptdc.
nic.in. Built in 1460, has been a hotel since
1978, 13 rooms, stylish but traditional decor
and furniture, comfortable beds, fireplaces,
modernized baths, best (**$$**) overlook
valley, some share bath, very basic dorm
(Rs 75), restaurant, good service. May-Jun
add Rs 150 for vegetarian meals. Absolutely
beautiful property with amazing temple.
**$ Alliance**, 200 m above castle, T01902-
248263, www.allianceguesthouse.com.
Run by French ex-pat, 6 rooms, hot water,
meals, clean, simple, homely, very good
value. Good for families.
**$ Poonam Mountain Lodge**, close to Castle,
T01902-248248, www.poonam mountain.
in. 6 spotless rooms, hot water, very good

food. Friendly family. They also organize
treks and jeep safaris and have a traditional
cottae to rent.
**$ Ragini**, T01902-248185, raginihotel@
hotmail.com. 16 smart rooms with
modernized baths (hot water), large
windows, good views from rooftop
restaurant, excellent breakfasts, Ayurvedic
massage and yoga, good value, friendly.
**$ Snow View**, down steps past Tripura
Sundari Temple, T(0)9481-388335,
snowviewhomestay@gmail.com. Weaving
co-op outlet, 7 rooms and restaurant.

**Manali and around** *p104, map p105*
Hotels are often full in May and Jun so
better to visit off-season when most offer
discounts. Winter heating is a definite
bonus. There are many cheap hotels on
**School Rd** and in **Model Town** offering
modest rooms often with shared baths
and hot water in buckets.
  In **Old Manali**, generally the further
you walk, the greater the reward. Those
above the Club House are almost out
of Old Manali and are in a great location
overlooking the valley but still close
enough to town.
  **Vashisht** village is another popular choice.
**$$$$ Manu Allaya**, Sunny Side, Chadiari,
overlooking Old Manali, T01902-252235,
www.manuallaya.com. 53 smart,
imaginative rooms, most done in a
contemporary design using wood and
marble, stunning views and good facilities,
a definite cut above the rest, ie an architect
has been involved. Recommended.
**$$$$ The Himalayan**, Hadimba Rd, T01902-
250999, www.thehimalayan.com. One Manali
resident described this place as a bit like
'Hogwarts', it's a new build echoing a Gothic
castle with turrets to boot. You can expect
rooms with 4-posters and fireplaces and there
is a magnificent view from the Crows Nest.
**$$$$-$$$ Banon Resort**, The Mall,
opposite Mayflower, T01902-253026,
www.banonresortsmanali.com.

32 plush rooms, including 12 suites and 6 stylish stone and wooden cottages set in stunning gardens.

**$$$ Baikunth Magnolia**, Circuit House Rd, The Mall, T(0)9816-792888, www.baikunth. com. Definitely the most stylish place to stay in Manali – beautiful decor, heavy wooden doors and floors, chic 4-posters. Come in Apr to catch the magnolia tree in bloom. Great place for a romantic getaway. Highly recommended.

**$$$ Jimmy Johnson Lodge**, The Mall, T01902-253023, www.johnsonhotel.in. 12 very elegant rooms (cottages also available), great bathrooms, pretty gardens, great views, outstanding restaurant (see Restaurants, below). Recommended.

**$$$ Mayflower**, The Mall, opposite Circuit House, T01902-252104, www.mayflower manali.in. 18 rooms, spacious, tastefully decorated wood-panelled suites, TV, good patio restaurant, friendly, well run, but perhaps not the value it once was.

**$$$ Strawberry Garden Cottages**, below Sersai village on the Manali–Nagar road, T(0)9218-924435, www.strawberrygarden manali.com. Stunning location, 4 self-contained, cute, 2-floor cottages in a beautiful garden with great views. Friendly, helpful English owner. Recommended.

**$$ Hymalayan Country House**, near Manu Temple, T01902-252294. 15 smart double rooms, plenty of marble and pine, with great views over Old Manali. Popular, specializes in trekking and motorbike safaris. Getting a bit pricey though.

**$$ Shanti Guest House**, Prini Village, 10 km south of Manali towards Naggar, T(0)9816-929704, www.highmountainstourism.org. In a cluster of little hotels in Prini, near Club Mahindra this is a place to feel at home. Comfy rooms, nice living rooms and open terrace, Spanish and Chilean food.

**$$-$ Rohtang Manalsu** (HPTDC), near Circuit House, The Mall, T01902-252332, www.hptdc.nic.in. 27 large rooms, good restaurant, garden, superb views.

**$$-$ Dharma Guest House**, above Vashisht, T01902-252354, www.hoteldharma manali. com. Perched high on the hill above Vashisht, this place has great views. Rooms are clean and comfortable. Buns of steel guaranteed climbing up there.

**$$-$ Dragon**, Old Manali, T01902-252290, www.dragontreks.com. This hardy perennial of the Old Manali scene has had a chic facelift and offers a smarter alternative in this part of town. Nice decor, lovely outdoor sitting areas, great vibe.

**$$-$ Drifters' Inn**, Old Manali, T(0)98050-33127, www.drifersinn.in. In the heart of Old Manali, comfortable rooms with TV, free Wi-Fi and popular café downstairs.

**$ Arohi**, Vashisht, T01902-254421, www.arohiecoadventures.com. Clean, attractive rooms, big windows facing mountains, owner good for trekking knowledge.

**$ Cottage Cold Corner**, Old Manali, T01902-252312. Strange name and certainly not the vibe, very warm and friendly welcome indeed. Basic rooms, little outdoor seating area.

**$ Didi Guest House**, Vashisht. Through the village and above the school, on the way to waterfall. 10 wood panelled bedrooms. Cheap, chilled and cheerful with yoga and excellent views up and down the valley.

**$ Mango Guest House**, Vashisht. High on the hill above the temple baths. 6 basic bedrooms. Well worth the walk.

**$ Rockway Cottage**, above Old Manali, the last one before the wilderness, a 10-min walk from the road, T01902-254328. Very friendly, 10 well-crafted, but simple rooms, most with woodburners, clean common bath, excellent location. Recommended.

**$ Shiv Shakti**, above Old Manali, beyond Manu Temple, T01902-254170. Fine views across valley and mountains beyond, 4 pleasant rooms and café, attached hot bath, friendly farming family.

**$ Sunshine**, The Mall, next to Leela Huts, T01902-252320. Lots of character, 9 rooms in old traditional house, others in newer cottage, log fires, restaurant, lovely garden, peaceful, family atmosphere, friendly, such good value you might need them to repeat the price! Highly recommended.

**$ Tourist Nest Guest House**, near Dragon, Old Manali, T(09816-266571. Bright clean rooms with balconies – top floors still have views, whereas building in front obscures views from lower floors. There are now family rooms on a new top floor. Recommended.

**$ Upcountry Lodge**, above Club House, Old Manali, T01902-252257. Quiet location in orchards, 9 clean rooms, attached hot bath, pleasant garden.

## 🍴 Restaurants

**Kullu** *p100*

**$$ Ashiyana** in hotel, Sarvari Bazar. Clean, good south Indian.

**$$-$ Planet Food**, next door to Hot Stuff Food Junction. Similar but slightly more upmarket with beer bar as well, good-value *thalis*.

**$ Monal Café**, next to the tourist office. Simple meals.

**Pulga** *p103*

**$ Paradise Restaurant**, in the village. Great vegetarian dishes. Also has information on guides and equipment for treks up the valley and over the Pin-Parvati Pass (5300 m). If you are lucky, you may be able to persuade the watchman of the old **Forest Rest House** to let you in. The 'visitors' registration book' contains entries that date back to the 1930s and include several well-known mountaineers who have passed by.

**Naggar** *p104*

There is also a dhaba up at the Jana waterfall recommended for trying real Himachal food – *dhal* made with sour milk, corn flour *rotis*.

**$$ Nightingale**, 200 m above bus stand. Serves trout and Italian.

**$ German Bakery**, next to Ragini. Sweet little café offering up the usual GB fare, beautiful photography on walls.

**Manali and around** *p104, map p105*

**$$$ Johnson Café**, Circuit House Rd, T01902-253023. Western (varied menu). Elegant restaurant in a large garden, specializes in trout – you can have it oven-baked, curried, masalad or smoked, excellent home-made pasta, good filter coffee, delicious ice creams. Beautiful lighting, quite magical at night. Highly recommended.

**$$$ La Plage**, Old Manali, Sister restaurant of the renowned La Plage from Goa, this is a beautiful restaurant with divine food. You can expect delicious trout cooked with almonds, chicken in soy and sesame with wasabi mash and amazing deserts. It's a stunning location with amazing views, beautiful interiors and garden/terrace dining and great service. Highly recommended.

**$$$ The Lazy Dog**, Old Manali, on left past shops going uphill (before road swings to right). Funky interior design with excellent food, good music, filter coffee, free Wi-Fi and a lovely terrace overlooking the river.

**$$ Adarsh**, The Mall (opposite Kunzam). One of many Punjabi places, but has more style and better menu than others.

**$$ Café Yun**, opposite Drifters Inn, Old Manali. Korean café with lovely vibe serving up trout *sushi* and *sashimi*, as well as other Korean delights and plenty of veggie options. There is an amazing whole-cooked trout on the menu too.

**$$ Chopsticks**, The Mall, opposite bus stand. Tibetan, Chinese, Japanese. Good food, although some say with its growing popularity, its portions have downsized.

**$$ Mayur**, Mission Rd. Vast international menu. Excellent food, smart, efficient service, subdued decor, very pleasant with linen table cloths and candles on tables, Indian classical music, great ambience, cosy with wood-burning stove and generator.

**$$ Peace Café**, behind post office. Good Tibetan, Japanese, some Chinese. Unpretentious, pleasant, warm (wood-burning stove), friendly owner.

**$$ Sa Ba**, Nehru Park. Excellent Indian, snacks, pizzas, cakes, some outdoor seating for people-watching. Recommended.
**$$ Sushi Yoon**, Vashisht. Chic little hole-in-the-wall café with just 12 seats serving up tasty sushi, delicious teas and coffees and the ultimate – green tea ice cream. Highly recommended.
**$$ Vibhuti's**, The Mall, corner of Model Town Rd, up short flight of steps. South Indian vegetarian. Delicious *masala dosas*.
**$ Bee's Knees**, Old Manali. Under the watchful eye of Avi – the man with the greatest smile, you can get big plentiful plates of Mexican food and all the usual Indian fare. Recommended.
**$ Dylan's Toasted and Roasted**, Old Manali, www.dylanscoffee.com. The best coffee this side of Delhi, if not one of the best in India, served up by the affable Raj. The cookies are legendary as is his 'Hello to the Queen' – great atmosphere. Highly recommended.
**$ Green Forest**, Dhungri village, on the forest path, past temple down towards Old Manali, just after leaving the forest. Vegetarian. Excellent breakfasts and meals.
**$ Manali Sweets**, Shiali Mahadev Rd. Excellent Indian sweets (superb *gulab jamuns*), also good *thalis*.
**$ Pizza Olive**, Old Manali. Very tasty wood-oven pizzas, great range of pastas and even tiramisu. Recommended.

## ✹ Festivals

### Kullu *p100*
**End Apr** Colourful 3-day **Cattle Fair** attracts villagers from the surrounding area. Numerous cultural events accompany.
**Oct-Nov** Dasara is sacred to the Goddess Durga which, elsewhere in India, tends to be overshadowed by Diwali which follows a few weeks later. In this part of the Himalaya it is a big social event and a get-together of the gods.

### Manali and around *p104, map p105*
**Mid-Feb** Week-long **Winter Sports Carnival**.
**May** 3-day colourful **Dhungri Forest festival** at Hadimba Devi Temple, celebrated by hill women.

## ○ Shopping

### Kullu *p100*
Best buys are shawls, caps, *gadmas* (blanket). The state weaving cooperative, **Bhutti Weavers Colony**, 6 km south, has retail outlets; **Bhuttico**, 1 store 2 km south of Apple Valley Resorts.
    Akhara Bazar has a **Government Handicrafts Emporium, Himachal Khadi Emporium** and **Khadi Gramudyog. Charm Shilp** is good for sandals.

### Manali and around *p104, map p105*
**Books**
**Bookworm**, NAC Market, behind Bus Station. Huge stock of quality paperbacks, reasonably priced. Highly recommended. New branch near Manali Post, 1000-1800.

### Crafts and local curios
**Bhutico Bodh**, by the Hindu temple in Traders, Gulati Complex. Sikh tailors, quick, good quality, copies and originals (caps to order, ready in hours, Rs 75). There's another branch by the Hindu temple in the bazar, with good range of shawls.
**Charitable Trust Tibetan Handicrafts**, The Mall. Government shop.
**Great Hadimba Weaver's**, near Manu Temple, Old Manali. Excellent value, hand-woven, co-op produced shawls/scarves and there is a little workroom to the side where you can watch them at work. Recommended.
**Manushi**, in the market. Women's co-op producing good quality shawls, hats, socks.
**Om Collection**, The Mall. Good Tibetan T-shirts, dresses, jewellery, jumpers.
**Shree-la Crafts**, near the main taxi stand. Friendly owner, good value silver jewellery. Tibetan Bazar and Tibetan Carpet Centre.

**Hyund Manu Market**. Curios, woollen clothing, arts and crafts.

### Tailors
**Gulati Traders**, Gulati Complex. Sikh tailors, quick, good quality, copies and originals.

### Trekking equipment
**Ram Lal and Sons**, E9 Manu Market, behind bus stand. Good range of well-made products, friendly, highly recommended.

## ⍟ What to do

### Kullu p100
**Look East**, c/o Bajaj Autos, Manikaran Chowk, Shamshi, T01902-065771. Operator recommended for river rafting and bike hire.

### Naggar p104
For trekking to Malana, it is best to employ a local guide. Pawan, from the old *chai* shop in the main village, is recommended.

### Manali and around p104, map p105
### Body and soul
**Spa Magnolia** at Johnson's Lodge Circuit House Road. T(0)9816-100023. Stylish little spa with pricy little treatments – but a bit of a treat. Ayurvedic and Western treatments available.
**Yogena Matha Ashram**, Kanchani Koot, below Vashisht, T(0)9418-240369, www. yogainmanali.com. Swami Yogananda has a great following and offers down-to-earth spirituality with your downward dog. Recommended.

### Skiing and mountaineering
**Mountaineering and Allied Sports Institute**, 1.5 km out of town, T01902-252342. Organizes courses in mountaineering, skiing, watersports, high-altitude trekking and mountain rescue courses; 5- and 7-day ski courses, Jan-Mar. There is a hostel, an exhibition of equipment and an auditorium.

### Tour operators
**Himalayan Adventurers**, opposite tourist office, T01902-252750, www.himalayan adventurers.com. Wide range of itineraries and activities from trekking and motorbiking to ski-touring and bird-watching.
**HPTDC**, T01902-253531/252116. Daily, in season by luxury coach (or car for 5): to Nehru Kund, Rahla Falls, Marhi, Rohtang Pass, 1000-1700, Rs 200 (car Rs 1200); to Solang, Jagatsukh and Naggar; 1000-1600, Rs 190 (car Rs 1200); to Manikaran, 0900-1800, Rs 250 (car Rs 1100).
**Swagatam**, opposite Kunzam, The Mall, T01902-251073. Long-distance buses, trekking, rafting, very efficient.

### Trekking
Clarify details and number of trekkers involved and shop around before making any decisions.
**Above 14000ft**, log huts area, www.above 14000.ft.com, T(0)9816-544803. Expert, environmentally conscious adventure organizers, specializing in treks, mountain biking, climbing expeditions and mountaineering courses throughout the region. Paperless office. Highly recommended.
**Himalayan Journeys**, Park View Building, The Mall, T01902-254397, www.himalayanjourneys india.com. Good range, experienced guides.
**Magic Mountain**, no office as such, but call Raju on T(0)9816-056934, www.magic mountainadventures.com. Manali's most experienced cycling guide, Raju also offers trekking and jeep safaris, and is honest, friendly and reliable. Highly recommended.
**Shangri-la Adventures**, Tibetan Colony, Rohtang Rd, T01902-252734, shang-adv@ hotmail.com. Treks to Zanskar, Ladakh, Spiti, fishing, rafting, experienced Tibetan guides, competitive pricing for small groups, excellent service from Jigme, honest, friendly.

## ⊖ Transport

### Kullu *p100*

**Air** Bhuntar Airport, T01902-265727. Air India, T1-800-180 1407, www.airindia.in.

**Bus** Most buses coming to Kullu continue to Manali. Most long-distance buses use main bus stand, **Sarvari Khad**, with a booking office. For long distance and to **Manali**, left bank bus stand across the bridge: buses for **Naggar** (every 30 mins in summer) and **Bijli Mahadev**, and several to **Manali**; HPTDC deluxe bus to **Chandigarh** (270 km), 0800, 8 hrs; **Delhi**, 512 km, 15 hrs, extra buses during season, often better than private buses, you will pay more for a/c, Volvo service is pricier; **Dharamshala**, 0800-0900, 8 hrs; **Shimla** (235 km), 0900, 8 hrs, Tickets from tourist office.

### Parvati Valley *p101*

**Bus** There are frequent buses from **Bhuntar Bus Stand**, outside the airport, with many connections to/from **Kullu** and **Manali**. To **Manikaran**, 2½ hrs.

### Naggar *p104*

**Bus** The bus stop is in the bazar, below the castle. Several daily between **Kullu** and **Manali** via scenic east bank route (1½ hrs). From Manali, more frequent buses to **Patli Kuhl** (6 km from Naggar, 45 mins), where you can get a local bus (half hourly in summer) or rickshaw.

### Manali and around *p104, map p105*

**Air** Flights connect Bhuntar Airport near Kullu T01902-265037, with **Delhi**. Transport to town: taxi to Manali, Rs 1000 **Himachal Transport** (green) bus, every 15 mins (allow 2½ hrs travel time from Manali).

**Bus** Local bus stand, T01902-252323. Various state RTCs offer direct services to major towns. HRTC Bus Stand, the Mall, T01902-252116, reservations 1000-1200, 1400-1600. HPTDC coaches in season (fewer in winter); deluxe have 2 seats on either side: Harisons and Swagatam (see Tour operators, above), run their own buses. **Chandigarh** 0700, 10 hrs, Rs 415; **Delhi** a/c 1830, 15 hrs, Rs 825; a/c sleeper Rs 1100; non a/c, 1700, Rs 425. **Dharamshala** 0530, 0810, Rs 210, **Keylong** 0600, 6 hrs, Rs 145. **Kullu** via **Naggar**: 2 daily, Rs 30, 1 hr; most Kullu buses go via the national highway and stop at **Patli Kuhl** (see Naggar, above). **Mandi**, Rs 112. **Rohtang Pass** 0900, day trip with photo-stops, striking scenery (take sweater/jacket), 1½ hrs at pass, Rs 120. **Shimla** (280 km), 0830, 1900, 9 hrs, Rs 415.

To **Leh** HPTDC and private coaches run ordinary and luxury buses during the season (mid-Jun to end Sep), but not always daily; usually based on demand. Seats should be reserved ahead. Front seats are best though the cab gets filled by locals wanting a 'lift'. Those joining the bus in Keylong must reserve from Manali to be certain of a seat. Rs 1600 (including tent and meals); usual overnight stop is at Sarchu where other cheaper tents may be available (some choose to sleep on the bus). The 530 km takes about 24-28 hrs on the road, so leave 0600, arrive Leh next afternoon. There are reports of some drivers getting drunk or taking 'medicines' to keep them awake, hence unsafe.

**Motorbike** The uncrowded Kullu–Manali road via Naggar is an ideal place for a test ride.

**Anu Auto Works**, halfway up the hill to Vashisht. Excellent selection; insurance and helmets provided. Mechanical support and bike safaris organized throughout the region.

**Bike Point**, Old Manali. Limited choice of bikes in good condition, mechanical support and competitive rates.

**Enfield Club**, Vashisht Rd, T(0)9418-778899. Enfields and Hondas for hire; reasonable charges, friendly, honest service.

**Local taxi** The local union is very strong, office near tourist office, T01902-254032. Fares tend to be high; from bus stand: Rs 50 for hotels (2-3 km). To Vashisht or top of Old Manali Rd, Rs 90; auto-rickshaws Rs 50.

**Long-distance taxi** Dharamsala,
Rs 3500; **Kaza**, Rs 6000; **Keylong**, Rs 4200;
**Kullu**, Rs 700; **Mandi**, Rs 1500; **Naggar**,
Rs 650; **Rohtang Pass**, Rs 1900.
**Train** Reservations at HPTDC office,
T01902-251925.

**Manali and around** *p104, map p105*
**Medical services** Mission Hospital,
T01902-252379. Men Tsee Khang Hospital,
Gompa Rd, highly recommended for
Tibetan herbal/ mineral treatments.
Chemists: opposite NAC Market. **Post**
GPO, off Model Town Rd, T01902-252324,
Mon-Sat 0900-1700. Very efficient.

# Lahaul and the Manali–Leh road

Lying between the green alpine slopes of the Kullu and Chamba valleys to the south and the dry, arid plateau of Ladakh, the mountainous arid landscapes of Lahaul manage to get enough rain during the monsoon months to allow extensive cultivation, particularly on terraces, of potatoes, green peas and hops (for beer making). Lahaul potatoes are some of the best in the country and are used as seed for propagation. These and rare herbs have brought wealth to the area. Most people follow a curious blend of both Hindu and Buddhist customs though there are a few who belong wholly to one or the other religion.

## Arriving at Lahaul and the Manali–Leh road

The whole region can be approached by road from three directions: Shimla via the Spiti Valley; Manali over the Rohtang Pass (3985 m) into Upper Lahaul; and from Zanskar and Ladakh over the Shingo La and Baralacha La (passes). The Shingo La gives access to Lahaul from Zanskar (see page 143), while the Baralacha La (4880 m) on the Leh–Manali road provides access from Ladakh. There is a trekking route from Manali to Zanskar. Streams cross the road at several places. These may be impassable during heavy rain, and those fed by snow-melt swell significantly during the day as meltwater increases, so travel in the late afternoon can be more difficult than in the early morning when the flow is at its lowest. Rockfalls are also a common hazard. ▸▸ See Transport, page 121.

## Background

Historically there are similarities between this region and Ladakh since in the 10th century Lahaul, Spiti and Zanskar were part of the Ladakh Kingdom. The Hindu rajas in Kullu paid tribute to Ladakh. In the 17th century Ladakh was defeated by a combined Mongol-Tibetan force. Later Lahaul was separated into Upper Lahaul which fell under the control of Kullu, and Lower Lahaul which came under the Chamba rajas. The whole region came under the Sikhs as their empire expanded, whilst under the British Lahaul and Kullu were part of the administrative area centred on Kangra.

## Manali to Leh → For listings, see page 121.

This stunningly beautiful road, one of the highest in the world, is currently the main route for foreigners into the region of Lahaul and on to Leh. The 530-km highway is usually open from July to September, depending on snow fall; most buses stop in mid-September. The first 52 km runs up the Kullu Valley, then climbs through the Rohtang Pass. The pass itself normally opens at the end of May and is the only way into Lahaul, pending the completion of a delayed tunnel, which is currently scheduled to open in 2016. No permits are necessary.

## Leaving Manali

From Manali the NH21 goes through the village of Palchan and then begins a sharp climb to **Kothi**, at 2530 m, set below towering cliffs. Beautiful views of coniferous hillsides and meadows unwind as the road climbs through 2800 m, conifers giving way to poplars and then banks of flowers. The 70-m-high **Rohalla Falls**, 19 km from Manali at an altitude of 3500 m, are a spectacular sight.

The landscape, covered in snow for up to eight months of the year, becomes totally devoid of trees above Marrhi, a seasonal settlement and restaurant stop, as the road climbs through a series of tight hairpins to the Rohtang Pass.

## Rohtang Pass

From the pass you get spectacular views of precipitous cliffs, deep ravines, large glaciers and moraines. Buses stop for photos. From June until mid-October, when **Himachal Tourism** (**HPTDC**) runs a daily bus tour from Manali, the pass becomes the temporary home to a dozen or more noisy roadside 'cafés'.

**Manali to Leh**

The descent to **Gramphoo** (Gramphu), which is no more than a couple of houses at the junction of the road from Tabo and Kaza, offers superb views of the glaciated valley of the Chandra River, source of the Chenab. To the north and east rise the peaks of Lahaul, averaging around 6000 m and with the highest, Mulkila, reaching 6520 m. As the road descends towards Khoksar there is an excellent view of the Lumphu Nala coming down from the Tempo La glacier. An earlier glacial maximum is indicated by the huge terminal moraine visible halfway up the valley.

There is a police check post in **Khoksar**, at 3140 m, where you may be required to show your passport and sign a register. This can take some time if more than one bus arrives at the same time. About 8 km west of Khoksar work is in progress on the Rohtang tunnel, which will link the Solang Valley with the Chandra Valley. If you cross the bridge here you find an attractive waterfall.

### Gondhla to Keylong and the Pattan Valley

It is worth stopping here to see the 'castle' belonging to the local *thakur* (ruler), built around 1700. The seven-storey house with staircases made of wooden logs has a veranda running around the top and numerous apartments on the various floors. The fourth floor was for private prayer,

## Motorcycling from Manali to Leh

Allow four days on the way up, to help acclimatize as the 500 km road will take you from 2000 m to 5420 m and down to 3500 m (Leh). The last petrol station is in Tandi, 7 km before Keylong. A full tank plus five to 10 litres of spare petrol will take you to Leh. Above 3500 m, you should open the air intake on your carb to compensate for the loss of power.

Apart from Keylong, there are no hotels, only a few tented camps, providing basic food and shelter from mid-June to mid-September. Some will be noisy and drafty.

The lack of toilet facilities leads to pollution near the camps (don't forget your lighter for waste paper). A tent and mini-stove plus pot, soups, tea, biscuits, muesli, will add extra comfort, allowing you to camp in the wild expanses of the Moray Plains (4700 m).

Unless you plan to sleep in the camp there, you must reach Pang before 1300 on the way up, 1500 on the way down, as the police will not allow you to proceed beyond the checkpoint after these times. The army camp in Pang has helpful officers and some medical facilities.

while the Thakur held court from the veranda. There is much to see in this neglected, ramshackle house, particularly old weapons, statues, costumes and furniture. The 'sword of wisdom', believed to be a gift from His Holiness the Dalai Lama, is of special interest. On close inspection you will notice thin wires have been hammered together to form the blade, a technique from Toledo, Spain. The huge rock near the Government School, which some claim to be of ancient origin, has larger-than-life figures of *Bodhisattvas* carved on it.

As the road turns north approaching **Tandi**, the Chandra rushes through a gorge, giving a superb view of the massively contorted, folded and faulted rocks of the Himalaya. Tandi itself is at the confluence of the Chandra and Bhaga rivers, forming the Chandrabhaga or Chenab. Keylong is 8 km from here, see page 119. At Tandi you can take a left turn and visit the Pattan Valley before heading to Keylong to continue on the journey.

## Pattan Valley → *For listings, see page 121.*

The Pattan Valley has a highly distinctive agricultural system which despite its isolated situation is closely tied in to the Indian market. Pollarded willows are crowded together all around the villages, offering roofing material for the flat-roofed houses and fodder for the cattle during the six-month winter. Introduced by a British missionary in the 19th century to try and help stabilize the deeply eroded slopes, willows have become a vital part of the valley's village life, with the additional benefit of offering shade from the hot summer sun. Equally important are the three commercial crops which dominate farming: hops, potatoes and peas, all exported, while wheat and barley are the most common subsistence grain crops.

### Tandi to Trilokinath

Just out of **Tandi** after crossing the Bhaga River on the Keylong road, the Udeypur road doubles back along the right bank of the Chenab running close to but high above the river. The road passes through **Ruding**, **Shansha**, 15 km from Tandi, **Jahlma**, 6 km and **Thirot**, another 11 km on (rest house here). A bridge at **Jhooling** crosses the Chenab. Some 6 km further on, the road enters a striking gorge where a bridge crosses the river before taking the road up to **Trilokinath**, 6 km away.

## Trilokinath

Trilokinath, at 2760 m, is approached by a very attractive road which climbs up the left bank of the Chenab. The glitteringly white-painted Trilokinath temple stands at the end of the village street on top of a cliff. The **Siva temple** has been restored by Tibetan Buddhists, whose influence is far stronger than the Hindu. Tibetan prayer-flags decorate the entrance to the temple which is in the ancient wooden-pagoda style. In the courtyard is a tiny stone Nandi and a granite lingam, Saivite symbols which are dwarfed in significance by the Buddhist symbols of the sanctuary, typical prayer-wheels constantly being turned by pilgrims, and a 12th-century six-armed white marble Avalokiteshwara image (Bodhisattva) in the shrine, along with other Buddhist images. The original columns date from Lalitaditya's reign in the eighth century, but there has been considerable modernization as well as restoration, with the installation of bright electric lights including a strikingly garish and flickering *chakra* on the ceiling. Hindus and Buddhists celebrate the three-day **Pauri Festival** in August.

## Udeypur

Some 10 km from the junction with the Trilokinath road is Udeypur (Udaipur). Visited in the summer it is difficult to imagine that the area is completely isolated by sometimes over 2 m of snow during the six winter months. It is supplied by weekly helicopter flights (weather permitting). The helipad is at the entrance to the village. Trekking routes cross the valley here and further west, see page 144.

The unique **Mrikula** (Markula) **Devi temple** (AD 1028-1063) is above the bazar. The temple dedicated to Kali looks wholly unimposing from the outside with a battered-looking wood-tiled 'conical' roof and crude outside walls. However, inside are some beautiful, intricate deodar-wood carvings belonging to two periods. The façade of the shrine, the *mandapa* (hall) ceiling and the pillars supporting it are earlier than those beside the window, the architraves and two western pillars. Scenes from the *Mahabharata* and the *Ramayana* epics decorate the architraves, while the two *dvarapalas* (door guardians), which are relatively crude, are stained with the blood of sacrificed goats and rams. The wood carvings here closely resemble those of the Hadimba Temple at Manali and some believe it was the work of the same 16th-century craftsman (see page 106). The silver image of Kali (*Mahisha-shurmardini*) 1570, inside, is a strange mixture of Rajasthani and Tibetan styles (note the *lama*-like head covering), with an oddly proportioned body.

---

# Keylong → *For listings, see page 121.*

The principal town of the district of Lahaul, Keylong is set amidst fields of barley and buckwheat surrounded by brown hills and snowy peaks and was once the home of Moravian missionaries. Only traders and trekkers can negotiate the pass out of season. Keylong is an increasingly widely used stopping point for people en route to Leh or trekking in the Lahaul/Spiti area. Landslides on the Leh–Manali road can cause quite long delays and the town can be an unintended rest halt for a couple of days. It has little to offer, though the views are very attractive and there are pleasant walks.

There is a pleasant circuit of the town by road which can be done comfortably in under two hours. Tracks run down into the town centre. The **local deity** 'Kelang Wazir' is kept in Shri Nawang Dorje's home which you are welcome to visit. There is a **Tibetan Centre for Performing Arts**. A statue in the centre of Keylong commemorates the Indian nationalist **Rash Behari Bose**, born 15 May 1886 near Kolkata.

**Khardong Monastery**, 3 km away across the Chandra River up a steep tree-shaded path, is the most important in the area. It is believed to have been founded 900 years ago and was renovated in 1912. Nuns and monks enjoy equality; married *lamas* spend the summer months at home cultivating their fields and return to the monastery in winter. The monastery contains a huge barrel drum, a valuable library and collections of *thangkas*, Buddha statues, musical instruments, costumes and ancient weapons.

**Sha-Shur Monastery**, a kilometre away, was in legend reputedly founded as early as AD 17 by a Buddhist missionary from Zanskar, Lama Deva Tyatsho who was sent by the Bhutanese king. It has ancient connections with Bhutan and contains numerous wall paintings and a 4.5-m *thangka*. The annual **festival** is held in June/July.

**Tayul Monastery**, above Satingri village, has a 4-m-high statue of Padma Sambhava, wall paintings and a library containing valuable scriptures and *thangkas*. The *mani* wheel here is supposed to turn on its own marking specially auspicious occasions, the last time having been in 1986.

---

## Keylong to Leh → *For listings, see page 121.*

From Keylong the road passes through very high-altitude desert with extraordinary mountain views. **Jispa**, 21 km on at an altitude of 3200 m, has a hotel, a campsite, a few tea stalls and a mountaineering institute. **Himachal Tourism**'s concrete 'lodge' has three basic rooms with toilets and cheap camping in the yard. About 2 km beyond Jispa is **Teh** which has accommodation. There is a 300-year-old palace, built in the Tibetan style, comprising 108 rooms over four storeys – apparently the largest traditional structure in Lahaul. It is 3.5 km off the main highway (turn off at Ghemur, between Keylong and Jispa) in a village called **Kolong**, and has recently been converted in to a heritage hotel. A museum has also been opened there, with some interesting exhibits depicting the traditional and ceremonial life of the local rulers, who still own the property.

All vehicles must stop for passport checks at **Darcha** checkpost where the Bhaga River is bridged. Tents appear on the grassy riverbank in the summer to provide a halt for trekkers to Zanskar. The road climbs to **Patseo** where you can get a view back of Darcha. A little further is **Zingzingbar**. Icy streams flow across the road while grey and red-brown scree reach down from the bare mountainside to the road edge. The road then goes over the **Baralacha La** (54 km; 4880 m), 107 km from Keylong, at the crossroads of Lahaul, Zanskar, Spiti and Ladakh regions before dropping to **Sarchu** (on the state border). There are a dozen or so tented camps in Sarchu, including on run by **Himachal Tourism** (HPTDC), mostly with two-bed tents (sometimes reported dirty), communal toilet tents, late-night Indian meal and breakfast; private bus passengers without reservations are accommodated whenever possible (Rs 150 per person); open mid-June to mid-September.

The road runs beyond Brandy Nala by the Tsarap River before negotiating 22 spectacular hairpin bends, known as the 'Gata Loops', to climb up to the **Nakli La** (4950 m) and **Lachalung La** (5065 m). It then descends past tall earth and rock pillars to **Pang**, a summer settlement in a narrow valley where you can stop for an expensive 'breakfast' (usually roti, vegetables and omelettes to order). The camp remains open beyond 15 September; an overnight stop is possible in communal tents. The 40-km-wide Moray plains (4400 m) provide a change from the slower mountain road. The road then climbs to **Taglang La** (5370 m), the highest motorable pass along this route and the second highest in the world; the altitude is likely to affect many travellers at this point. You descend slowly towards the Indus valley, passing small villages, before entering a narrow gorge with purple coloured cliffs. The road turns left to continue along the Indus basin passing **Upshi** with a sheep farm and a checkpost, and then **Thikse**, before reaching **Leh**.

# Lahaul and the Manali–Leh road listings

*For hotel and restaurant price codes and other relevant information, see pages 12-14.*

## ⊖ Where to stay

**Udeypur** *p119*
Camping is possible in an attractive site about 4 km beyond the town (permission from Forest Officer) but since there is no water supply, water has to be carried in from a spring about 300 m further up the road. Carry provisions too as there is little in the bazar.
**$ Amandeep Guest House**, T01909-222256. 7 semi deluxe rooms with limited hot water. Good dhaba opposite serves good Indian food.
**$ Forest Rest House**, off the road in a pleasant raised position, T01900-222235. 2 rooms with bath, very basic, bring your own sleeping bag.

**Keylong** *p119*
**$$-$ Chandrabhaga** (HPTDC), T01900-222247. Open mid-Jun to mid-Oct, reserve ahead. 3 rooms with bath, 2-bed tents, dorm (Rs 150), meals to order, solar-heated pool, rates include vegetarian meals.
**$ Dekyid**, below police station, T01900-222217. 3-storey hotel, friendly, helpful reception, decent-sized rooms with bath, quiet, excellent views over fields, good restaurant but service very slow.
**$ Gyespa**, on main road, T01900-222207. 11 basic but adequate rooms plus a good restaurant.

**$ Snowland**, above Circuit House, T01900-222219. Modest but adequate, 15 rooms with bath, friendly reception. Recommended.
**$ Tashi Deleg**, on main road through town, T01900-222450. Does well from being the first place you come to from Tandi, slightly overpriced as a result. Rooms are comfortable though, and the restaurant is one of the best in town. Also has a car park.

**Keylong to Leh** *p120*
**$$ Ibex Hotel**, Jispa, T01900-233204, www.ibexhoteljispa.com. Glass and cement block, 27 comfortable rooms, dorm, impressive location. Reserve ahead.

## ⊖ Transport

**Keylong** *p119*
**Bus** State and private luxury buses are most comfortable but charge more than double the 'B'-class fare. To **Manali** (6-8 hrs); to **Leh** (18 hrs). To board deluxe buses to Leh in Keylong, reserve ahead and pay full fare from Manali (Rs 1300, plus Rs 300 for tent and meals in Sarchu).
**Jeep** To **Manali** by jeep, 4 hrs, weather permitting; **Sarchu** 6 hrs, **Leh** 14 hrs.

## ⊕ Directory

**Keylong** *p119*
**Banks** State Bank of India, but no foreign exchange.

# Northern Himachal

Dominated by Dharamshala, this is a region replete with some of the most breathtaking mountain views imaginable. From Dalhousie eastwards there are tantalizing glimpses of snow-capped peaks, while McLeodganj has been attracting Western travellers for decades, coming in search of peace, tranquillity, the Dalai Lama and sometimes even themselves. The Kangra Valley sees far fewer visitors, but has an unhurried charm all of its own, epitomized by Pragpur, India's first heritage village.

## Dharamshala → For listings, see pages 132-142.

Dharamshala has a spectacular setting along a spur of the Dhauladhar range, varying in height from 1250 m at the 'Lower Town' bazar to 1768 m at McLeodganj. It is this 'Upper' and more attractive part of town that attracts the vast majority of visitors. Although the centre of McLeodganj itself has now become somewhat overdeveloped, it is surrounded by forests, set against a backdrop of high peaks on three sides, with superb views over the Kangra Valley and Shiwaliks, and of the great granite mountains that almost overhang the town.

### Arriving in Dharamshala
**Getting there**  Flights to Gaggal Airport (13 km). Lower Dharamshala is well connected by bus with towns near and far. You can travel from Shimla to the southeast or from Hoshiarpur to the southwest along the fastest route from Delhi. The nearest station on the scenic mountain railway is at Kangra, while Pathankot to the west is on the broad gauge.

**Getting around**  From Dharamshala, it is almost 10 km by the bus route to McLeodganj but a shorter, steeper path (3 km) takes about 45 minutes on foot. Local jeeps use this bumpy, potholed shortcut. Compact McLeodganj itself, and its surroundings, are ideal for walking.

**Tourist information**  HPTDC ⓘ behind post office, McLeodganj, T01892-221205, Mon-Sat 1000-1700, see page 77.

### Background
The hill station was established by the British between 1815 and 1847, but remained a minor town until the **Dalai Lama** settled here after Chinese invasion of Tibet in October 1959. There is an obvious Tibetan influence in McLeodganj. The Tibetan community has tended to take over the hospitality business, sometimes a cause of friction with the local population. Now many Westerners come here because they are particularly interested in Buddhism, meditation or the Tibetan cause. A visitor's attempt to use a few phrases in Tibetan is always warmly responded to: *tashi delek* (hello, good luck), *thukje-chey* (thank you), *thukje-sik* (please), *gong-thag* (sorry), and *shoo-den-jaa-go* (goodbye).

## Places in Dharamshala

**Church of St John-in-the-Wilderness** (1860) ① *open for Sunday morning service*, with attractive stained-glass windows, is a short distance below McLeodganj. Along with other buildings in the area, it was destroyed by the earthquake of 1905 but has been rebuilt. In April 1998 thieves tried to steal the old bell, cast in London, which was installed in 1915, but could only move it 300 m. The eighth Lord Elgin, one of the few viceroys to die in office, is buried here according to his wish as it reminded him of his native Scotland.

The Dalai Lama temple complex, on temple road, is a short walk from Mcleodganj bus station. **Namgyal Monastery** ① *0500-2100*, with the Buddhist School of Dialectics, is mostly attended by small groups of animated 'debating' monks. This Tsuglagkhang (cathedral) opposite the Dalai Lama's residence resembles the centre of the one in Lhasa. It contains large gilded bronzes of the Buddha, Avalokitesvara and Padmasambhava. To the left of the Tsuglagkhang is the **Kalachakra Temple** with very good modern murals of *mandalas*, protectors of the Dharma, and Buddhist masters of different lineages of Tibetan

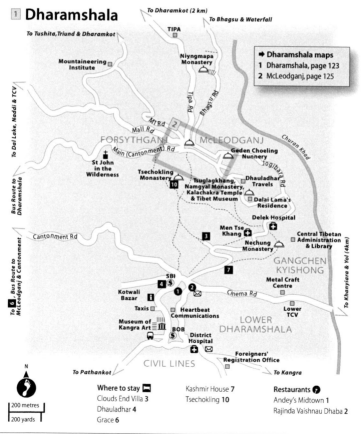

**1 Dharamshala**

➡ **Dharamshala maps**
1 Dharamshala, page 123
2 McLeodganj, page 125

**Where to stay** 🛏
Clouds End Villa **3**
Dhauladhar **4**
Grace **6**

Kashmir House **7**
Tsechokling **10**

**Restaurants** 🍴
Andey's Midtown **1**
Rajinda Vaishnau Dhaba **2**

## Open your heart volunteering in Mcleodganj

There are many opportunities for volunteer work in and around Dharamsala, from conversation to work at the hospital. Many offer a great insight into Tibetan culture and are key in empowering refugees. **Lha Charitable Trust**, Temple Rd, T01892-220992, www.lhasocialwork.org. Office open Mon-Sat 0900-1700, lunch 1200-1300. Volunteers are wanted for language classes, IT and web design, healthcare, fundraising, etc. Short-term or long-term placements are possible, or you can just drop-in. They also offer Tibetan cooking classes, language, meditation, homestay, etc. **Lha** means 'innate goodness'. Also look in at or check the free monthly magazine *Contact*, T(0)98161-55523, www.contactmagazine.net (also a useful resource for restaurant info and goings-on in McLeodganj, Buddhist-related and otherwise). English-language teachers are in high demand to teach newly arrived refugees, for short- or long-term stints. There are a couple of places for teaching and conversation near **Dokebi** restaurant including **Learning and Ideas for Tibet** (www.learningandideasfortibet.org) who have conversation classes, movie parties and talks from ex-political prisoners. You can also volunteer with **Rogpa** (www.tibetrogpa.org ) who provide free childcare for Tibetan people trying to juggle jobs and education – they run a lovely café on the Jogibara road too.

Buddhism, with the central image of Shakyamuni. Sand *mandalas* (which can be viewed on completion) are constructed throughout the year, accompanied by ceremonies. The temple is very important as the practice of Kalachakra Tantra is instrumental in bringing about world peace and harmony. Within the monastery complex is the **Tibetan Museum** ① *Tue-Sun 0900-1700, Rs 5*, with an interesting collection of documents and photographs detailing Tibetan history, the Chinese occupation of Tibet and visions of the future for the country. It is an essential visit for those interested in the Tibetan cause. It is traditional to walk the **Kora** in Mcleodganj, which is a ritual circuit of the Temple complex and the Dalai Lama's residence with stunning views of the mountains and numerous prayer wheels and prayer flags along the way. A very beautiful walk, it is a sacred path which is done clockwise around the complex and finishes by the Namgyal Monastery entrance. The Kora here replicates the ancient Lingkhor path around the Potala Palace in Lhasa.

The **Dalai Lama** ① *www.dalailama.com*, usually leads the prayers on special occasions – 10 days for **Monlam Chenmo** following **Losar**, **Saga Dawa** (May) and his own birthday (6 July). If you wish to have an audience with him, you need to sign up in advance at the Security Office (go upstairs) by **Hotel Tibet**. On the day, arrive early with your passport. Cameras, bags and rucksacks are not permitted. His Holiness is a Head of State and the incarnation of Avalokitesvara, the Bodhisattva of Love and Great Compassion; show respect by dressing appropriately (no shorts, sleeveless tops, dirty or torn clothes); monks may 'monitor' visitors. **Tsechokling Monastery**, in a wooded valley 300 m below McLeodganj (down rather slippery steps), can be seen from above. The little golden-roofed monastery was built between 1984-1986; the monks are known for their skill in crafting *tormas* (butter sculptures) and sand *mandalas*, which decorate the prayer hall (see Where to stay, page 134). Further down the 3-km steep but motorable road to Dharamshala is the Nechung Monastery in **Gangchen Kyishong** with the **Central Tibetan Administration** (CTA), which began work in 1988.

**Norbulingka Institute** ① *T01892-246402, www.norbulingka.org*, is becoming a major centre for Buddhist teaching and practical work. Named after the summer residence of the

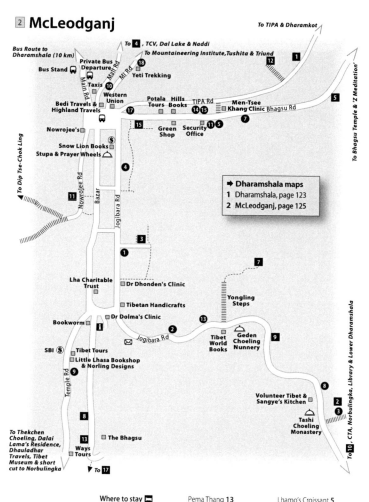

## McLeodganj

50 metres
50 yards

**Where to stay**
Annex 8
Chonor House 17
Drepung Loseling 3
Glenmoor Cottages 4
Green 5
Ladies Venture 9
Mcleod Ganj Homestay 1
Norling Guest House 10
Om & Namgyal Café 11
Paljor Gakyil 12
Pawan House 2

Pema Thang 13
Sidharth House 7
Tibet 15

**Restaurants**
Carpe Diem 2
Common Ground Café 18
Dokebi 3
Gakyi 1
German Bakery 10
Kunga's/Nick's Italian
Kitchen 7

Lhamo's Croissant 5
Lhasa 17
Lung-Ta 8
Moonlight & Sunrise 14
Moonpeak Espresso
 & Thali 9
Rangzen 11
Rogpa Café 13
Snow Lion 4
Tara Café 15

Seventh Dalai Lama built in 1754, it was set up to ensure the survival of Tibetan Buddhism's cultural heritage. Up to 100 students and 300 Tibetan employees are engaged in a variety of crafts in wood, metal, silk and metal, *thangka* painting (some excellent) and Tibetan language. The temple has a 4.5-m-high gilded statue of the Buddha and over 1000 painted images. There is a small **museum** of traditional 'dolls' made by monks and a **Tibetan Library** with a good range of books and magazines. You can attend lectures and classes on Tibetan culture and language and Buddhism or attend two **meditation** classes, free but a donation is appreciated. Those attending regularly pay Rs 100 per meditation session.

**Museum of Kangra Art** ① *Main Rd, Tue-Sun 1000-1330, 1400-1700, free, allow 30 mins*, near the bus stand in Lower Dharamshala, includes regional jewellery, paintings, carvings, a reminder of the rich local heritage contrasted with the celebrated Tibetan presence. Copies of Roerich paintings will be of interest to those not planning to visit Naggar.

Lhamo Tso who runs **Lhamo's Croissant** recommends tuning into the heart of Mcleodganj and the Tibetan people by "walking the Kora (outer-circumnambulation of the temple and palace), and buy the *Essence of the Heart Sutra* at **The Namgyal Bookshop** by the temple. It is a commentary by His Holiness the Dalai Lama on one of the Buddha's main teachings. It is a book that can help and transform your life."

## Around McLeodganj

**Bhagsu**, an easy 2-km stroll east, or Rs 40 auto-rickshaw ride, has a temple to Bhagsunath (Siva). The mountain stream here feeds a small pool for pilgrims, while there is an attractive waterfall 1 km beyond. Unfortunately this has resulted in it becoming very touristy, with increasing building activity and an influx of noisy day-trippers. The hill leading up the valley towards Dharamkot is known as Upper Bhagsu, and is lined with little shops, restaurants and guesthouses. It is a relaxing place with great views, and so attracts many backpackers for long stays here. Outside the rainy season lovely walks are possible.

**Dharamkot**, 3 km away (from McLeodganj by auto Rs 80, or on foot from Bhagsu), has very fine views and you can continue on towards the snowline. Villagers' homes and guesthouses are dotted up the hillside, accessible via pathways, and there is even a Chabbad House for the numerous Israeli tourists. In September, a fair is held at **Dal Lake** (1837 m), 3 km from McLeodganj Bus Stand; it is a pleasant walk but the 'lake', no more than a small pond, is disappointing.

**Naddi Gaon**, 1.5 km further uphill from the bridge by Dal Lake (buses from Dharamshala, 0800-1900), has really superb views of the Dhauladhar Range. **Kareri Lake** is further on. The TCV (Tibetan Childrens' Village) nearby educates and trains children in traditional handicrafts. Big hotels are rapidly appearing next to the traditional Naddi village. Most enjoy excellent views.

It is an 8-km trek to **Triund**, 2827 m, at the foot of the Dhauladhar where there is a **Forest Lodge** on a hill top. Some trekkers pitch tents, whilst others make use of caves or shepherds' huts. Take provisions and warm sleeping gear if planning to stay overnight. It's well worth the effort. A further 5 km, one-hour walk, brings you to **Ilaka**.

---

## Kangra Valley → *For listings, see pages 132-142.*

The Kangra Valley, between the Dhauladhar and the Shiwalik foothills, starts near Mandi and runs northwest to Pathankot. It is named after the town of Kangra but now the largest and main centre is Dharamshala. Chamba State, to its north, occupies part of the Ravi River Valley and some of the Chenab Valley.

## Background

In 1620 Shah Jahan captured Kangra fort for his father Jahangir, and Kangra became a Mughal province. Many of the court artists fled to neighbouring Chamba and Kullu as the Rajas submitted to Mughal rule. When Mughal power weakened, the 16-year-old **Sansar Chand Katoch II** (1775-1823) recaptured the fort and the rajas reasserted their independence. Under his powerful leadership, Kangra sought to extend its boundaries into the Chamba and Kullu Valleys but this was forestalled by the powerful Gurkhas from Nepal. With the rise of the Sikh empire, the valley was occupied until the Treaty of Amritsar. Then under the British, Dharamshala was made the administrative capital of the region which led to the decline of Kangra.

The **Kangra School of Painting** originated by virtue of Raja Goverdhan Singh (1744-1773) of Guler, who gave shelter to many artists who had fled from the Mughals, and during the mid-18th century a new style of miniature painting developed. Based on Mughal miniature style, the subject matter derived from Radha/Krishna legends, the rajas and gods being depicted in a local setting. Under Sansar Chand II the region prospered and the Kangra School flourished. Kangra fort, where he held court for nearly 25 years, was adorned with paintings and attracted art lovers from great distances. The 1905 earthquake damaged many of these buildings though you can still see some miniature wall paintings.

## Kangra

Kangra, 18 km south of Dharamshala, was once the second most important kingdom in the West Himalaya after Kashmir. Kangra town, the capital, was also known as Bhawan or Nagarkot. It overlooks the Banganga River and claims to have existed since the Vedic period with historical reference in Alexander's war records.

**Kangra Fort** ① *foreigners US$2, Indians Rs 5, auto-rickshaw Rs 150 return, taxi Rs 250,* stands on a steep rock dominating the valley. A narrow path leads from the ticket office up steps to the fort, which was once protected by several gates (now reconstructed) and had the palace of the Katoch kings at the top. Just inside the complex is a small museum displaying Hindu and Jain stone statues, while further up the hill is an old Jain temple (still in use) and the ruins of a temple with exquisite carvings on its rear outer wall. At the very top, the remains of Sansar Chand's palace offer commanding views. The fort is worth the effort for these views alone. At its foot is a large modern Jain temple which has pilgrim accommodation (worth considering if you get stuck). There is also an overgrown British cemetery just next to the fort entrance.

**Brajesvari Devi Temple**, in Kangra Town, achieved a reputation for gold, pearls and diamonds and attracted many Muslim invaders from the 11th century, including Mahmud of Ghazni, the Tughlaqs and the Lodis, who periodically plundered its treasures and destroyed the idols. In the intervening years the temple was rebuilt and refurbished several times but in the great earthquake of 1905 both the temple and the fort were badly damaged. The Devi received unusual offerings from devotees. According to Abul Fazal, the pilgrims "cut out their tongues which grew again in the course of two or three days and sometimes in a few hours"! The present temple in which the deity sits under a silver dome with silver *chhatras* (umbrellas) was built in 1920 and stands behind the crowded, colourful bazar. The State Government maintains the temple; the priests are expected to receive gifts in kind only. The area is busy, atmospheric and rather dirty, with mostly pilgrim-oriented stalls. Above these is **St Paul's Church** and a Christian community. Along the river between Old Kangra (where the main road meets the turning to the fort) and Kangra Mandir is a pleasant trail, mostly following long-disused roads past ruined houses and temples which evidence a once sizeable town. Kangra's bus stand is 1.5 km north of the temple.

**Masrur**

A sandstone ridge to the northeast of the village has 15, ninth- to 10th-century *sikhara* temples excavated out of solid rock. They are badly eroded and partly ruined. Even in this state they have been compared with the larger rock-cut temples at Ellora in Maharashtra and at Mamallapuram south of Chennai. Their ridge-top position commands a superb view over the surrounding fertile countryside, but few of the original *shikharas* stand, and some of the most beautifully carved panels are now in the State Museum, Shimla. There are buses from Kangra.

**Jawalamukhi**

This is one of the most popular Hindu pilgrimage sites in Himachal and is recognized as one of 51 *Shakti pitha*. The **Devi temple**, tended by the followers of Gorakhnath, is set against a cliff and from a fissure comes a natural inflammable gas which accounts for the blue 'Eternal Flame'. Natural springs feed the two small pools of water; one appears to boil, the other with the flame flaring above the surface contains surprisingly cold water. Emperor Akbar's gift of gold leaf covers the dome. In March/April there are colourful celebrations during the **Shakti Festival**; another in mid-October. There is accommodation here, and buses to/from Kangra.

**Pragpur**

Pragpur, across the River Beas, 20 km southwest of Jawalamukhi, is a medieval 'heritage village' with cobbled streets and slate-roofed houses. The fine 'Judges Court' (1918) nearby has been carefully restored using traditional techniques. A three- to four-day stay is recommended here and it is advisable to reserve ahead.

**Stops along the Kangra Valley Railway**

**Jogindernagar** is the terminus of the beautiful journey by narrow-gauge rail (enquiries Kangra, T01892-252279) from Pathankot via Kangra. The hydro-power scheme here and at nearby Bassi channels water from the River Uhl. Paragliding and hang-gliding is possible at Billing (33 km), reached via Bir (19 km, see below).

**Baijnath**'s temples are old by hill standards, dating from at least 1204. Note the Lakshmi/Vishnu figure and the graceful balcony window on the north wall. The **Vaidyanatha Temple** (originally circa 800), which contains one of 12 *jyotirlingas*, stands by the roadside on the Mandi-Palampur road, within a vast rectangular enclosure. Originally known as **Kirangama**, its name was changed after the temple was dedicated to **Siva** in his form as the Lord of Physicians. It is a good example of the Nagari style; the walls have the characteristic niches enshrining images of Chamunda, Surya and Karttikeya and the *sikhara* tower is topped with an *amalaka* and pot. A life-size stone Nandi stands at the entrance. There is a bus to and from Mandi taking 3½ hours.

**Palampur**, 16 km from Baijnath, 40 km from Dharamshala (via Yol), is a pleasant little town for walking, with beautiful snow views, surrounded by old British tea plantations, thriving on horticulture. It is a popular stop with trekkers; see page 135. The Neugal Khad, a 300-m-wide chasm through which the Bandla flows is very impressive when the river swells during the monsoons. It holds a record for rainfall in the area.

**Bir**, 30 km east of Palampur, has a fast-growing reputation as one of the best paragliding locations in the world. Bordered by tea gardens and low hills, it also has four Buddhist monasteries worth visiting. Most prominent among these are Choling. You can also pick up fine Tibetan handicrafts from Bir, which has a large Tibetan colony. The village of Billing is 14 km up sharp, hair-raising hairpins and has the hilltop from where paragliders launch. Although unsuitable for beginners, there are courses available for intermediate fliers and a few residential pilots with tandem rigs. One excellent company based in Bir is **Touching Cloud Base**, www.touchingcloudbase.com. They offer great instruction and tandem flights.

**Andretta** is an attractive village 13 km from Palampur. It is associated with **Norah Richards**, a follower of Mahatma Gandhi, who popularized rural theatre, and with the artist **Sardar Sobha Singh** who revived the Kangra School of painting. His paintings are big, brightly coloured, ultra-realistic and often devotional, incorporating Sikh, Christian and Hindu images. There is an art gallery dedicated to his work and memory; prints, books and soft drinks are sold in the shop. The **Andretta Pottery** (signposted from the main road), is charming. It is run by an artist couple (Indian/English), who combine village pottery with 'slipware'. The Sikh partner is the son of Gurcharan Singh (of Delhi Blue Pottery fame) and is furthering the tradition of studio pottery; works are for sale.

---

## Chamba Valley → *For listings, see pages 132-142.*

### Dalhousie

The **Himachal Tourism** ① *near bus stand, T01899-242225, 1000-1700,* is helpful for transport information, but opening hours can be irregular out of season.

Dalhousie, named after the governor-general (1848-1856), was developed on land purchased by the British in 1853 from the Raja of Chamba. It sprawls out over five hills just east of the Ravi River. By 1867 it was a sanatorium and reached its zenith in the 1920s and 1930s as a cheaper alternative to Shimla, and the most convenient hill station for residents of Lahore. Rabindranath Tagore wrote his first poem in Dalhousie as a boy and

## Dalhousie

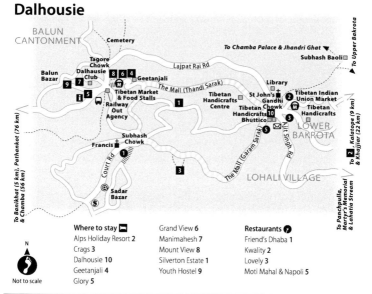

| **Where to stay** 🛏 | Grand View **6** | **Restaurants** 🍴 |
|---|---|---|
| Alps Holiday Resort **2** | Manimahesh **7** | Friend's Dhaba **1** |
| Crags **3** | Mount View **8** | Kwality **2** |
| Dalhousie **10** | Silverton Estate **1** | Lovely **3** |
| Geetanjali **4** | Youth Hostel **9** | Moti Mahal & Napoli **5** |
| Glory **5** | | |

N
Not to scale

Subhash Chandra Bose came secretly to plan his strategies during the Second World War. Its popularity declined after 1947 and it became a quiet hill station with old colonial bungalows, now almost hidden among thick pine forests interspersed with oak, deodar and rhododendron. Its spectacular mountain views mean that it remains a popular bolt hole for tourists from the plains, but its importance today is mainly due to the number of good schools and the presence of the army.

The three Malls laid out for level walks are around Moti Tibba, Potreyn Hill and Upper Bakrota. The last, the finest, is about 330 m above **Gandhi Chowk** around which the town centres. From there two rounds of the Mall lead to Subhash Chowk. The sizeable Tibetan community make and sell handicrafts, woollens, jackets, cardigans and rugs. Their paintings and rock carvings in low relief can be seen along Garam Sarak Mall. Echoes of the colonial past include five functioning churches: diminutive **St John's** (1863) on Gandhi Chowk is open for Sunday service (0930 summer, 1000 winter) and the large Catholic church of St Francis (1894) on Subhash Chowk is often open to visitors. The nostalgic **Dalhousie Club** (1895) displays old Raj-era photos and has preserved the original billiards table. The library contains bizarre English fiction and biographies, but sadly beer is not available in the bar.

Just over 2 km from Gandhi Chowk is the **Martyr's Memorial** at Panchpulla (five bridges), which commemorates Ajit Singh, a supporter of Subhash Bose and the Indian National Army during the Second World War. There are several small waterfalls in the vicinity, and on the way you can see the **Satdhara** (seven springs), said to contain mica and medicinal properties. **Subhash Baoli** (1.5 km from Gandhi Square), is another spring. It is an easy climb and offers good views of the snows. Half a kilometre away **Jhandri Ghat**, the old palace of Chamba rulers, is set among tall pine trees. For a longer walk try the Bakrota Round (5 km), which gives good views of the mountains and takes you through the Tibetan settlement.

## Kalatope and Khajjiar
**Kalatope Wildlife Sanctuary**, 9 km from Dalhousie, with good mountain views, is a level walk through a forest sanctuary with accommodation in a pretty forest resthouse bungalow (permission required from the DFO, Wildlife, Chamba, dfocha-hp@nic.in). There are good walking routes in the area, and wildlife includes black bears, leopards and serows. **Khajjiar**, 22 km further along the motorable road, is a long, wide glade ringed by cedars with a small lake and a floating island. Locals call it 'Mini Switzerland'. You can explore both areas in a pleasant three-day walk, alternatively a 30-km path through dense deodar forest leads from Khajjiar to Chamba. Buses to Khajjiar from Dalhousie take one hour.

## Chamba
Picturesque Chamba is on the south bank of the Iravati (Ravi), its stone houses clinging to the hillside. Some see the medieval town as having an almost Italian feel, surrounded by lush forests and with its Chaugan (or grassy meadow) in the centre. Although that's stretching it a little and recent developments have somewhat diminished its appeal, the warmer climes, unusual temples and mellow ambiance remain most attractive. Most hotels, temples and palaces are within walking distance of the bus stand.

The **Tourist Office** ① *T01899-224002*, Mon-Sat 1000-1630, is in the **Hotel Iravati** complex (see Where to stay, page 136).

Founded in the 10th century, Chamba State was on an important trade route from Lahaul to Kashmir and was known as the 'Middle Kingdom'. Though Mughal suzerainty was accepted by the local rajas, the kingdom remained autonomous but it came under Sikh rule from 1810-1846. Its relative isolation led to the nurturing of the arts – painting, temple sculpture, handicrafts and unique 'rumal'. These pieces of silk/cotton with fine embroidery imitate miniature paintings; the reverse is as good as the front.

The **Chaugan**, once almost 1 km long, is the central hub of the town but sadly, over the last three decades, shops have encroached into the open space. There are several ancient Pahari temples in the town with attractive curvilinear stone towers. Follow the steep and winding road through the market to the **Lakshmi Narayana Temple Complex** (ninth to 11th centuries) containing six *sikhara* temples with deep wooden eaves, several smaller shrines and a tank. Three are dedicated to Vishnu and three to Siva, with some of the brass images inlaid with copper and silver. The **Hari Rai Temple**, next to the Chaugan (14th century), contains a fine 11th-century life-sized bronze Chaturmurti (four-armed Vishnu), rarely visible as it is usually 'dressed'; carved on the outer wall are Tantric couples. Close to the Aroma Hotel is the **Champavati Temple**, with carved wooden pillars, named after the daughter of Raja Sahil Varma who moved the capital here from Bharmour in AD 920 at her request. Others of note in the town centre are the Bansigopal, Sita Ram and Radha Krishna temples.

The 10th-century wooden **Chamunda Devi Temple**, 500 m uphill via steep steps from the bus stand, has some interesting wood carvings on its eaves and a square sanctum decked with bells. A further 500 m along the road to Saho is the elegantly slender **Bajreshwari Temple** with an octagonal roof, adjoined by a small, square unadorned temple.

The eye-catching **Akhand Chandi**, the Chamba Maharajas' palace, beyond the Lakshmi Narayan complex, is now a college. The old **Rang Mahal** (Painted Palace) in the Surara Mohalla was built by Raja Umed Singh in the mid-18th century. A prisoner of the Mughals for 16 years, he was influenced by their architectural style. The wall paintings in one room are splendid. The theme is usually religious, Krishna stories being particularly popular. Some of these were removed, together with carvings and manuscripts, to the Bhuri Singh Museum after a fire. The building now houses a sub-post office and a handicrafts workshop.

**Bhuri Singh Museum** ⓘ *Museum Rd, Mon-Sat 1000-1700, Rs 100*, is a three-storey building (top floor currently closed) housing a heritage collection including some excellent *rumals*, carvings and fine examples of Chamba, Kangra and Basholi schools of miniature paintings. Archaeological finds include the remarkable "fountain slabs" that adorned the spouts of village water sources. Dating from the 10th-18th centuries and hewn from local stone, these were memorials erected to the deceased; they are unique in Indian art. There are also many old photographs showing Chamba in its heyday. Opposite the museum is the finely built **St Andrew's Church**, belonging to the Church of Scotland and completed in 1905.

## Bharmour

Capital of the princely state of Chamba for over 400 years, the tiny town of Bharmour is surrounded by high ranges and is snow-covered for six months of the year. It's 65 km from Chamba along a gruelling but incredibly scenic road, beset by landslides. Bharmour's ancient temples and its proximity to Manimahesh Lake and Manimahesh Kailash peak (5656 m) make it hallowed place, while alpine pastures in the region are home to Gaddi tribespeople (see below). The stone-built villages with slate-roofed houses adjoining Bharmour, and the snowy peaks all round, make it a beautiful spot.

The famous **Chaurasi** temple square has 84 shrines within, of varying architectural styles, built between the 7th-10th centuries. The towering *sikhara* of **Manimahesh (Shiv) Temple** dominates the complex. Giant deodars flank the entrance, which is guarded by a life-size Nandi bull in polished brass; devotees whisper a wish in his ear and crawl under him for good health (a tight squeeze for some). The sanctum of the delicate **Lakshna Devi**

**temple** (circa 700 AD) houses a metre-high idol of the goddess cast in bronze. The wooden exterior, particularly the door jambs, is beautifully carved with romantic couples, flying gandharvas and other unusual figures; a marvellous pair of un-eroded lions flank the door to the inner shrine.

**Manimahesh**, 34 km distant, has a lake in which pilgrims bathe during the Yatra (August-September) and worship at the lakeside temple. Shiva resides on the holy mountain of the same name. Helicopter flights go from the helipad above the Chaurasi complex in Bharmour to Gaurikund during the Yatra, return journey Rs 7000 (www.simmsammairways.com).

Bharmour is the centre of the **Gaddis**, shepherds who move their flocks of sheep and goats, numbering from a couple of hundred to a thousand, from lower pastures at around 1500 m during winter to higher slopes at over 3500 m, after snow-melt. They are usually only found in the Dhauladhar range which separates Kangra from Chamba. Some believe that these herdsmen first arrived in this part of Himachal in the 10th century though some moved from the area around Lahore (Pakistan) in the 18th century, during the Mughal period. Their religious belief combines animism with the worship of Siva; Bharmour's distinctive Manimahesh Temple is their principal centre of worship. In the winter the Gaddis can be seen round Kangra, Mandi and Bilaspur and in the small villages between Baijnath and Palampur. The men traditionally wear a *chola* (a loose white woollen garment), tied at the waist with a black wool rope and a white embroidered cap.

## Northern Himachal listings

*For hotel and restaurant price codes and other relevant information, see pages 12-14.*

### ⊙ Where to stay

**Dharamshala** *p122, maps p123 and p125*
Most visitors stay in McLeodganj (see below). With the new IPL cricket ground in Dharamshala, more 3-star and up hotels are under construction in the area.
**$$$$-$$$ White Haven Tea Estate**, below Dharamshala, T01892-226162, www.hotelwhite haven.in. Charming working colonial tea estate set in 2.8 ha of beautiful gardens. 8 sumptuous rooms with creaking floorboards, log fires, lots of wood panelling and period antiques, exceptional service and tons of history. Recommended.
**$$$ Clouds End Villa**, north of Dharamshala, steep approach off Naoroji Rd, T01892-222109, www.cloudsendvilla.com. 7 rooms and 1 bungalow in Raja of Lambagraon's bungalow (Raj period), not luxurious but very clean, annexe has excellent valley views, authentic local cuisine (everything home-made), tours, peaceful, very friendly, excellent service.
**$$$ Grace Hotel**, 558 Old Chari Rd, Kotwali Bazar, T01892-223265, www.welcom heritagegracehotel.com. 14 comfortable suites in a 200-year-old wooden manor, formerly the residence of India's first Chief Justice. Pleasantly situated slightly out of town, a good place to relax and admire the views. This is a stunning place with beautiful artifacts. There is a meditation room and do try the delicious Himachali food, it's exquisite with subtle spicing and yoghurt.
**$$$-$$ Blossom Village**, Sidhpur, near Dharamshala, T(0)9816-561213, www.blossomsvillage.com. 19 lovely rooms including cottages and suites. Stylishly decorated using local timber and solar energy. New spa in 2013, with treatments and wellbeing therapies. Lovely rooftop bar and restaurant.
**$$ Dhauladhar** (HPTDC), Kotwali Bazar, T01892-224926, www.hptdc.nic.in. Several categories of room, all clean and large, 2 suites (**$$$**), cheaper in

annexe, sombre restaurant, bar, pleasant garden, terrace for meals, friendly staff.

**$$ Kashmir House** (HPTDC), Kotwali Bazar, T01892-222977, www.hptdc.nic.in. 10 large rooms in a period property, hot water, TV, old-fashioned vibes.

## McLeodganj

**$$$ Glenmoor Cottages**, off Mall Rd, T01892-221010, www.glenmoorcottages. com. Very peaceful, 7 large, modern, well-equipped 'cottages' with bedroom, kitchen, veranda, secluded old colonial house surrounded by forest, good valley views, great walks from doorstep.

**$$$-$$ Chonor House**, Thekchen Choeling Rd, T01892-221006, www.norbulingka.org. 11 very comfortable, stylish rooms furnished in Tibetan style (murals of lost monasteries and mythical beasts), good restaurant, clean, well managed, popular with foreign diplomats, beautiful garden, a quiet and lovely place. Book ahead. Accepts credit cards. Highly recommended.

**$$$-$$ Norling Guest House**, Norbulingka Institute, Gangchen Kyishong, T01892-246406, normail@norbulingka.org. Clean, comfortable rooms, in modern facilities in a Tibetan-style house. Café accepts Master/Visa cards. Beautiful setting inside the Norbulingka Institute, so surrounded by art and meditative peace.

**$$ Annex Hotel**, Hotel Surya Rd, T01892-221002, 0941-8020814, www.annexhotel.in. A short walk from the bus stand, all the rooms in this clean hotel have a balcony and are reached by the free Wi-Fi. Lounge and library, plus rooftop restaurant is excellent and has majestic sunset views.

**$$ Pema Thang**, opposite **Hotel Bhagsu**, T01892-221871, www.pemathang.net. 15 rooms with a bit more character than the average, good views from private balconies (better from upper floors), wooden floors, quiet, friendly, hot water and Wi-Fi works in rooms, nice rooftop restaurant.

**$$-$ McLeod Ganj Homestay**, Flourishing Flora, close to TIPA Gate, Dharamkot Rd,

T(0)9736-083878, www.mcleodganj homestay.net. With 3 lovely rooms and 1 hillside hut, this is a short walk towards Dharmkot and has a lovely family vibe. All the rooms have a little touch of Tibet, there's great Indian homecooked food with as much organic as possible and cookery lessons with Nisha. Sometimes there is roast chicken on an open fire. Recommended.

**$$-$ Tibet**, Bhagsu Rd, T01892-221587, hoteltibetdasa@yahoo.com. 20 well-maintained rooms with bath and TV, not much difference between standard and deluxe, those on roadside can be noisy, cosy bar, accepts credit cards.

**$ Drepung Loseling**, Jogibara Rd, T01892-221087. Friendly hotel, 17 clean, well-maintained rooms with bath (some with hot water), dorm (Rs 90), terrace. Profits to Loseling Moanstery in Karnataka.

**$ Green Hotel**, Bhagsu Rd, T01892-221200, www.greenhotel.biz. Popular with backpackers, 30 variable rooms (avoid ground floor ones near the noisy courtyard), restaurant with comfy sofas, good internet.

**$ Ladies Venture**, Jogibara Rd, T01892-221559, www.ipcardesign.com/ ladiesventure. Peaceful hotel with dorm and 13 clean rooms, cheapest with shared bath, standard rooms have bath and TV, while top category are huge with seating areas. Very clean, respectable and popular (in part due to the helpful staff) and a good place to meet people. As they say, it's "just a name" and every body and soul is welcome. Small restaurant (good Chinese and Western food), terrace, often full so book ahead.

**$ Om**, western edge of bazar, T01892-221322, T(0)9857-632037. Friendly hotel with 18 rooms, the en-suite ones are excellent value, while cheap room share baths (but shower is excellent), great views at sunset from patio terrace and rooftop. Free Wi-Fi. The excellent **Namgyal** restaurant which used to be at the Temple has moved here, so expect the best pizza in northern India.

**$ Paljor Gakyil**, TIPA Rd, up steps, T01892-221343. 14 clean rooms with bath (hot shower), dorm (Rs 25), excellent views, charming owners speak French and German, best of nearby bunch.

**$ Pawan House**, next to Dokebi, Jogibara Rd, T01892-220069, www.pawanhouse.com. Good views across the valley. Nice spacious clean rooms – good vibe. Recommended.

**$ Shambhala Guest House**, near prayer wheels, Jogibara Rd. Cosy family run place. Small rooms but nicely decorated, lots of warm blankets, hot shower, TV.

**$ Sidharth House**, bottom of Yongling School Steps off Jogibara Rd, T(0)86795-91907, www.sidharthhouse.in. Great guest house with conscious eco-vibe who established the 'Clean McLeodganj Project' and they have bins for compost as well as encouraging recycling. Much needed. Highly recommended.

**$ Tsechokling Monastery**, Camel Track Rd, 300 m below McLeodganj, down 300 steps, T01892-221726. 20 clean rooms, 3 attached, some singles, hot showers, breakfast and dinner at set times, 'wonderfully peaceful'.

**Around McLeodganj** *p126*
**$$$ Eagles Nest**, Upper Dharamkot, T(0)9218-402822, www.hoteleaglesnest. com. 8 lovely themed rooms and suites in a beautiful old colonial house set in 20 ha of forest. Perched on top of the hill with spectacular views over Kangra and Kullu valleys. All inclusive, with excellent food and plenty of activities. Price includes all meals, horse-riding and guides for trekking. Recommended.

**$$-$ Hotel High Land**, Bhagsu Main Drag, T01892-220501. Big rooms, bit of a view, TV.

**$$-$ Udechee Huts**, Naddi Gaon, T01892-221781, www.udecheehuts.com. Blending in with local style, 10 pleasantly furnished circular huts with bath (hot water), restaurant plus dining terrace, well kept, friendly hosts.

**$ 9 Chimes**, Upper Bhagsu, near Tree House, T(0)9736-130284, www.9chimes.com. 8 spacious rooms with balconies and nice views and one apartment. Recommended.

**$ DK House**, Upper Bhagsu, T01892-220671. 14 comfortable, spacious and clean rooms with big terrace and **Evergreen Restaurant** attached. Friendly family.

**$ Om Tara**, Lower Dharamkot, T(0)981-687949, www.houseomtara.com. Keeping their eye on the environment and with friendly service, this is a popular little guest house among fruit trees. There are big verandas to enjoy the views. Recommended.

**$ Pink House**, between Dharamkot and Bhagsu, T(0)9805-642060. Excellent value place with great views. Really peaceful and run by president of local women's group – she is quite right-on.

**$ Sapna House**, Upper Bhagsu, just above Unity Pizza, T01892-221594. Perennial favourite of the area – friendly family run place with pleasant rooms and garden.

**$ Shiv Shakti Guest House**, off Dharamkot Rd, T(0)9418-247776. Run by friendly father and son, 18 basic rooms with attached bath plus a stand alone, well-equipped cottage available too.

**$ Trimurthi Garden Cafe**, above Unity Pizza, Bhagsu, T(0)9816-869144. Favourite haunt with simple rooms, café and numerous workshops and yoga classes.

**$ ZKL Guesthouse**, above Bhagsu Rd, 500 m before Bhagsu itself, T01892-221581, www.zkl-monastery.com. 12 very basic but clean rooms in this charming monastery, Buddhist teachings and a café in the summer, outstanding value.

**Kangra** *p127*
Most hotels on the busy main road are noisy, even at night.

**$$$$ Raas Kangra**, 20 km from Kangra aiport. Opening Winter 2014 from the team behind the stunning **Raas** in Jodhpur. Boutique hotel with 41 suites all boasting 2 balconies for panoramic views. It will bring innovative design together with natural beauty.

**$ Dilraj Guest House**, near Tehsil Chowk (taxi stand), T01892-265362. Friendly family house with 5 simple rooms, meals available.

**$ Jannat**, Chamunda Rd, T01892-265479. 5 rooms, restaurant, TV, hot water, closest to Kangra Mandir railway station.

## Pragpur *p128*
**$$$ Judge's Court** (Heritage), set in a large orchard, T01970-245035, www.judgescourt. com. Lovely rooms with family hospitality, home-grown vegetables and fruit, fresh river fish, authentic Himachali meals (Rs 350-550), tours of Kangra Fort and other sights included (a ride on a part of the narrow-gauge mountain railway is possible) friendly, efficient management. Pragpur very pretty village with lovely atmosphere. Recommended.

## Stops along the Kangra Valley Railway *p128*
**$$$ Taragarh Palace**, Al-hilal, 11 km southeast of Palampur, T01894-242034, www.taragarh.com. 26 rooms in 1930s summer resort, period furniture and tasteful decor in public spaces, tennis, pool, lovely meandering gardens and mango orchards, luxury Swiss tents in summer. Decent service, but food a bit hit and miss.
**$$ Colonel's Resort**, 1 km out of Bir on the Billing road, T(0)9805-534220, www.colonels resort.com. 10 rooms and 2 cottages, tents in garden (seasonal). Set in pear orchards and working tea plantation, with sublime views down the valley and behind into Dhauladhar mountains. Good food (breakfast and dinner included), warm hospitality, superb value. Popular with paragliders, plus good hiking in the area. 30% discount off-season.
**$$ Darang Tea Estate**, 10 km from Palampur, T(0)9418-012565, www.darang teaestate.com. 2 cottages and 1 room in the main house. Family run homestay in beautiful working tea estate. Exceptional food and warm hospitality. Recommended.
**$$ The Tea-Bud** (HPTDC), 2 km from bus stand, Palampur, T01894-231298, www. hptdc.nic.in. Beautiful setting, 31 rooms, deluxe category are in a newer block, older

rooms are totally acceptable, hot water, restaurant, pleasant lawn, clean and quiet, good service, ayurvedic treatments available.
**$ Standard**, Baijnath, behind bus station, T01894-263714. 5 fairly clean and surprisingly tidy rooms with bath and hot water.
**$ Uhl** (HPTDC), near Power House, on hill outside Jogindernagar, T01908-222002, www.hptdc.nic.in. Unpretentious, clean and peaceful hotel, 16 rooms with bath, best upstairs with balcony, restaurant.

## Dalhousie *p129, map p129*
Some hotels look neglected and run-down, because the cost of maintaining the Raj-built structures is prohibitive. Most have good mountain views and massive discounts out of season.
**$$$ Grand View**, near bus stand, T10899-240760, www.grandviewdalhousie.in. 53 spacious, well-equipped rooms (5 price categories) in the best-preserved of Dalhousie's many Raj-era hotels. The views from the terrace are stunning, while the restaurant and lounge bar (awaiting license at the time of research!) are quintessentially British. Gym and sauna; new Luxury Wing opened 2011, and off-season package deals are worth checking out. Recommended.
**$$$-$$ Silverton Estate Guest House**, near Circuit House, the Mall, T01899-240674, www.heritagehotels.com/silverton. Old colonial building in large grounds, 5 rooms with dressing rooms, TV, closed off season.
**$$ Mount View**, next to bus stand, T01899-242120, www.hotelmountview.com. The elegant, period, oak-panelled reception flatters to deceive; most of the 39 spacious (if unfashionable) rooms are in a modern block to the rear, only the cramped restaurant is in the older building. Kitschy garden has amazing views of the Bathri Valley and Dhauladhar, lots of seating and a pergola. Huge conference hall being constructed at time of research.
**$$ Alps Holiday Resort**, Khajjiar Rd, Bakrota Hills, T01899-240781, www.alpsresort.in.

19 smart rooms in old-fashioned retreat, with lovely large lawns, fine views of the Pir Panjal, 2-km climb.

**$$ Manimahesh** (HPTDC), near bus stand, T01899-242793, www.hptdc.nic.in. The 18 carpeted rooms are rather faded in this typical tourist dept hotel, cheap restaurant, bar with sofas, good mountain views.

**$$-$ Hotel Dalhousie**, Gandhi Square, T(0)981-5550958. Period building with large terrace which lower rooms share, however better quality rooms are on the upper level, all are very spacious. Friendly management, huge discounts off-season.

**$ Crags**, off the Mall, T01899-242124. The 100 steps separating this place from the Mall are the only disadvantage to this excellent budget choice. The rooms are dated but very clean with attached bath (hot water) and a bell to ring for service. Cheap and delicious meals, good views east down the valley from the huge (if not particularly attractive) terrace, very friendly, the elderly owner is pretty stylish and used to catering to foreign travellers. A separate cottage is a more recent addition for a slightly higher price.

**$ Geetanjali** (HPTDC), Thandi Sarak, steep 5-min climb from bus stand, T01899-242155. 10 huge rooms with bath (reliable hot water), towels and clean sheets provided – but expect mildew-scented air as it's a very run-down colonial building.

**$ Glory**, near bus stand, T01899-242533. 4 rooms with bath in this seriously cheap option.

**$ Youth Hostel**, behind Manimahesh, T01899-242189, www.youthhosteldalhousie. org. Well-maintained, modern building with double rooms (Rs 300) and single-sex dorms (Rs 150). Internet, free Wi-Fi and dining hall. Gets busy with groups – book ahead.

### Kalatope and Khajjiar *p130*
**$$$-$$ Mini Swiss**, Khajjiar, T(0)981-0229464, www.miniswiss.in. Comfortable, very clean rooms in a 5-storey building with great views, good restaurant and bar, pool table and ping-pong.

**$$ Devdar** (HPTDC), Khajjiar, T01899-236333, www.hptdc.nic.in. Clean rooms (doubles and suites), dorm (Rs 150) and a nice cottage (Rs 3000), simple restaurant, horse riding, beautiful setting. Free Wi-Fi.

### Chamba *p130*
During Manimahesh Yatra in Sep hotels are often full.

**$$ Hotel City Heart**, Nr Champavati Temple, opposite Chowgan, T01899-222032, www.hotelcityheartchamba.com. Large rather ugly hotel, but modern a/c rooms. Lowest category, are windowless; however, deluxe and super deluxe are spacious with wood floors, big bathrooms and smart furniture. Bar is un-atmospheric, but restaurant is busy and serves good Indian food. Massive discounts off-season

**$$ Iravati** (HPTDC), Court Rd, near bus stand, T01899-222671. Friendly management, 19 variable rooms with bath and hot water. Regular rooms start at Rs 1500, spacious, nicely tiled, clean and overlook the Chaugan. The higher up the building, the better the views and the higher the prices. Decent restaurant.

**$$-$ Aroma Palace**, near Rang Palace, Court Lane, T01899-225577, www.hotel aromapalacechamba.com. Rooms range from economy to sumptuous honeymoon suite, all spotless, plus there's a restaurant and airy terrace. Breakfast included and discounts possible.

**$$-$ Himalayan Orchard Huts**, 10 km out of town, book through **Mani Manesh Travels** next to Lakshmi Narayana Temple, www.himalayanlap.com. Idyllic location (20 mins' walk from nearest road, rooms in guesthouse set in delightful garden with a spring-water pool, beautiful views from large terraces with hammocks, clean shared shower and toilets, or pitch a tent in the garden, superb home cooking (great all-inclusive deal), very friendly family. Recommended. Also own **Ridgemore Cottage**, a trekkers' hut atop a ridge, 4 hrs walk from Orchard Hut.

**$$-$ White House**, near Post Office and Gandhi Gate, Main Bazaar, T01899-224111, rafeevwhitehouse@gmail.com. This red-roofed hotel on the edge of town looks down onto the Ravi River. Many room categories, all clean, bright and modern with pictures on walls, plus the Copper Chimney Restaurant (see Restaurants, page 139) make it a good choice

**$ Akhand Chandi**, College Rd, Dogra Bazar, 1 km from bus stand, T01899-222371. Attractive stone building with 10 rooms, attached bath and TV, restaurant.

**$ Chamba Guesthouse**, Gopal Nivas, near Gandhi Gate, by the Chaugan, T01899-222564, T(0)9805-282372. Simple lodgings with wooden floors and charm, this budget hotel almost hangs over the Ravi River affording amazing views from the balcony. Popular choice, try to book ahead.

### Bharmour *p131*

**$$-$ Chourasi**, Chourasi Rd, T01895-225615. Bright red structure on the road up to the temple. The cheaper basement rooms only have views of rubbish, and the top rooms are a bit overpriced at Rs 2000. Best deal are the Rs 1000 on the mid-levels. The restaurant has good food.

**$ Him Kailash Homestay**, near the bus stop, T01895-225100. Simple, friendly place with clean freshly painted rooms enjoying good valley views. Cheapest rooms (Rs 500) don't have TV or geyser, or indeed curtains; much larger rooms with proper amenities cost Rs1000. Not much English spoken.

## 🍴 Restaurants

**Dharamshala** *p122, maps p123 and p125*
Most memorable food is in McLeodganj.
**$$-$ Andey's Midtown**, Kotwali Bazar. Indian and Chinese, some continental, best in town.

**$ Rajinder Vaishnau Dhaba**, Kotwali Bazar. Very simple sit-down dhaba serving Punjabi basics and thalis, tasty and busy.

### McLeodganj

Try *thukpa* (Tibetan soups), noodle dishes, steamed or fried *momos* and *shabakleb*. Save plastic waste (and money) by refilling your bottles with safe filtered, boiled water at the eco-friendly **Green shop** on Bhagsu Rd, Rs 5 per litre; also recycle used batteries.

**$$ Café Illiterati Books and Coffee**, LHS Jogiwara Rd, near Usho Institute. This trendy mellow café has slate floors and wonderful views, full bookshelves on Buddhism, society or literature and coffee-table tomes, exciting menu (eg. chilli ginger red-bean burger) including good salads.

**$$ Carpe Diem**, past Post Office, Jogibara Rd. Nepali-run joint with excellent Indian, Thai and continental flavours. Good vibe, nice rooftop, beer under the table and open mic nights. Recommended.

**$$ Dokebi Seven Hills**, near Lung Ta, Jogibara Rd. Wonderful cosy restaurant with delicious range of vegetarian food including spicy hotpot style soups, spicy *kkimchi* and *kimbap* (Korean sushi). Upstairs there is lovely airy room with floor seating. Great fresh juices and smoky green tea. Highly recommended.

**$$ Kunga's/Nick's Italian Kitchen**, Bhagsu Rd. Good vegetarian food, Italian including excellent pumpkin ravioli, plus quiches, pies, cakes, etc, but some small portions. With a huge terrace, deservedly popular, recommended.

**$$ Namgyal**, at Om Hotel, western end of bazaar. Open 1000-2200. Cosy and welcoming venue with amazing pizzas such as roquefort and walnut or smoked cheese and spinach – best in the area. Good salads and Tibetan dishes too. Highly recommended.

**$ Common Ground Cafe**, Tushita Rd, above bus stand, behind Asian Plaza, www.commongroundsproject.org. Serving up a Chinese-Tibetan food fusion, their menu underpins their ethos to foster shared understanding and respect between Chinese and Tibetans. It's a lovely place with great teas and deserts too.

**$ Gakyi**, Jogibara Rd. Tibetan. Also excellent porridge, fruit muesli. Lovely lady owner.
**$ Hotel Tibet**, behind old bus stand (see Where to stay, page 133). Good Tibetan/Japanese restaurant and take-out bakery.
**$ Lhamo's Croissant**, Bhagsu Rd. Beautiful café with furniture from **Norbulingka** serving up tip top cappuccino, healthy salads, monumental club sandwiches, home-made soups and outrageously good cakes and tarts all served up by the eponymous Lhamo. They show films about the Tibetan cause every evening. Free Wi-Fi. Highly recommended.
**$ Lhasa**, on 1st floor opposite **Hotel Tibet**. Tucked away, very mellow interior serving good Tibetan dishes, well worth a visit.
**$ Lung-Ta**, Jogibara Rd. Mon-Sat 1200-2030. Classy Japanese vegetarian restaurant, not for profit, daily set menu or à la carte, good breads and cakes, sushi on Tue and Fri. Try the *okononiyak* (Japanese veg omelette). Great value and very popular. Little shop on-site too. Highly recommended.
**$ Pema Thang** (see Where to stay, page 133). Good vegetarian buffet brunch on Sun 1000-1400, plus normal menu featuring great pasta, salads and pizza.
**$ Snow Lion**, near prayer wheels. Offers good Tibetan and Western meals, excellent cakes.

## Cafés and snacks

**German Bakery**, Mirza Ismail Rd, steep road to Dharamkot. Open till 0100. Best bread, brown rice.
**Moonlight** and **Sunrise**, opposite Tibetan Welfare Office, Bhagsu Rd. Small *chai* shops adjacent to each other with basic food. Excellent for meeting other travellers, especially in the evenings when overspill occupies benches opposite.
**Moonpeak**, Temple Rd, www.moonpeak.org. Very atmospheric café where people spill out onto outside tables to enjoy great cappuccinos, sandwiches and fantastic cakes. The first of the many coffee shops.

Often shows photography and art exhibitions. Free Wi-Fi. **Moonpeak Thali** next door has some Himachali dishes.
**Rangzen** (Freedom), Bhagsu Rd. Good health food, cakes.
**Rogpa** Jogibara Rd. Tiny little café serving up lovely cakes and tasty coffee – all for charity. There's a little shop and second-hand stuff too. Recommended.
**Tenyang**, Temple Rd. Delicious coffee and cakes. Recommended.

### Around McLeodganj *p126*
**$$ Unity**, Upper Bhagsu, on path to Dharamkot. English owner creates amazing food, well presented and now a larger restaurant so more opportunity for wood oven pizzas.
**$ Family Pizzeria**, between Upper Bhagsu and Dharamkot. Excellent pizzas, French pastries, quiches and desserts, friendly staff and cider.
**$ Sansu's**, Upper Bhagsu. Renowned for its epic 'fruit-muesli-curd' – the best on the hillside.
**$ Singh Corner**, Bhagsu. Ah Bhagsu cake straight from the fridge – the original and best chocolate, caramel, biscuit combo – beware of imitators!
**$ Wa Blu**, Upper Bhagsu. Climb the steps for tempting Japanese food, miso soups and juices.

### Dalhousie *p129, map p129*
**$$ Kwality**, Gandhi Chowk. Good Indian and Chinese if a bit pricey. Nice place with TV.
**$$ Moti Mahal**, Gandhi Chowk. Good North Indian and tandoor, closed off season.
**$$ Napoli**, near Gandhi Chowk. Similar to Kwality, serving pizza, Indian and Chinese, meat and veg dishes. Very friendly and comfortable. Large portions.
**$ Friend's Dhaba**, Subhash Chowk. Good, unpretentious Punjabi, *paneer burji* to die for.
**$ Lovely**, near Gandhi Chowk. Funky mirrored interiors, tasty North Indian.

**Chamba** *p130*
There are a number of atmospheric little *dhabas* in the alleys through Dogra Market.
**$$-$ Copper Chimney**, 5th floor, White House Hotel (see Where to stay, page 137). Not at all pricey for good tandori, and veg/non-veg Indian and Chinese food. Comfy a/c indoor section or 4 intimate tables on the roof terrace. A long slog up the stairs, however.
**$ Jagaan**, 1st floor, Museum Rd. Reasonable selection, relatively calm, serves *chamba madhra* (Rs 90), a rich stew of kidney beans, ghee and curd that is a local speciality.
**$ Ravi View Café**, next to Chaugan. Reasonable snacks and Indian veg food plus beer (strong, Rs 110), this HPTDC-run circular hut even has outside tables with killer views overlooking the river.

## Entertainment

**Dharamshala** *p122, maps p123 and p125*
See *Contact*, a free, monthly publication. With everyone travelling with laptops now, there is only 1 film-club on the strip now on Jogibara Rd with a programme of Western films at a rather pricey Rs 150. **Lhamos Croissant** shows documentaries on Tibet. There are open mics at **Carpe Diem**. Indian classical music and Tibetan traditional music often at Yongling School. **One Nest**, Lower Dharamkot. Regular live music in the evenings (Indian Classical and Western nomads), contact dance and free dance sessions.
**Tibetan Institute of Performing Arts** (**TIPA**), www.tibetanarts.org, McLeodganj, stages occasional music and dance performances; details at Tourist Office.

## Festivals

**Chamba** *p130*
**Apr** Suhi Mela, lasts 3 days, commemorates a Rani who consented to be buried alive in a dry stream bed in order that it could flow and provide the town with water. Women and children in traditional dress carry images of her to a temple on the hill, accompanied by songs sung in her praise. Men are strictly prohibited from participating.
**Jul-Aug** Gaddis and Gujjars take part in many cultural events to mark the start of harvesting. Minjar is a 7-day harvest festival when people offer thanks to Varuna the rain god. Decorated horses and banners are taken out in procession through the streets to mark its start. Sri Raghuvira is followed by other images of gods in palanquins and the festival ends at the River Irawati where people float *minjars* (tassels of corn and coconut).

## Shopping

**Mcleodganj** *p122, p123 and p125*
**Bookworm**, near Surya Resort, has a good selection of paperbacks, some second-hand. Recommended.
**Dolls 4 Tibet** is an initiative bringing together Tibetan refugees and local Indian women, making beautiful dolls together. 'We see our Doll Makers grow in confidence and their sense of self worth. Their eyes and smiles say it all when a doll they've finished is admired. The skills they learn are empowering, the money they take home spells a new-found independence and their social interactions across our diverse community benefits not only our team but the wider society.' You can buy them at **The Green Shop** and **Common Ground Cafe**.
**Doritsang Tibetan Culture Centre**, Temple Rd, near SBBI. Great range of books, CDs, clothes and Tibetan bits and pieces.
**Jewel of Tibet**, opposite prayer wheels. Best selection of singing bowls, jewellery and Tibetan arts. Maybe not the cheapest, but certainly the best value.
**Green Shop**, Bhagsu Rd. Sells recycled and handmade goods including cards and paper. Also sells filtered drinking water for half the price of bottled water.
**Norbulingka Shop**, Temple Rd, close to Moonpeak. Well-crafted bags, cushion

covers and clothes from **Norbulingka** – preserving Tibetan cultural arts.

**Rogpa**, Jogibara Rd. Charity based shop selling great gifts, notebooks, cards, bags and wallets. And second-hand clothes.

**Tibet Book World**, Jogibara Rd, near Yongling School steps. Best bookshop in town – great range.

**Tibetan Children's Villages (TCVs)**, Main office on Temple Rd and workshops at various locations around town. Fabrics and jewellery at fixed prices.

**Tibetan Handicrafts Centre**, Jogibara Rd, near the tourist office. Ask at the office for permission to watch artisans working on carpets, *thangkas*, etc, reasonable prices.

---

**Dalhousie** *p129*
**Bhuttico**, The Mall (Garam Sarak), www.bhutticoshawls.com. Mon-Sat 0900-1930. Fixed price shop, with branches nationwide, selling top-quality Kullu shawls, socks and *pullas* (slippers with grass soles) that incorporate traditional designs.

---

**Chamba** *p130*
**Handicrafts Centre**, Rang Mahal. Rumal embroidery and leather goods.

### ✪ What to do

**Dharamshala** *p122, maps p123 and p125*
**Body and soul**
See also **Tibetan Library**, page 126.
**Buddha Hall**, Main Rd, Bhagsu, T01892-221749. Yoga, meditation and healing courses.
**Dr Gonpo Kyi Acupuncture**, T(0)9857-119800. Attentive and reliable healer working with acupuncture, massage and Tibetan medicine.
**Himachal Vipassana Centre**, Dhamma Sikhara, next to Tushita, T(0)92184-14051, www.sikhara.dhamma.org. 10-day retreat, meditation in silence, donations only, reserve in advance, information and registration Mon-Sat 1600-1700.
**Himalayan Iyengar Yoga Centre**, Dharamkot, www.hiyogacentre.com.

Offers 5-day course in Hatha yoga, starting every Thu at 0830. Information and registration Mon 1330. Now has retreat centre too.

**Tushita Meditation Centre**, Dharamkot village 2 km north of McLeodganj, T(0)8988-160988, www.tushita.info. Quiet location, offers individual and group meditation; 10-day 'Introduction to Buddhism' including lectures and meditation (residential courses get fully subscribed), enquiries Mon-Sat 0930-1130, 1230-1600, also drop-in guided meditation Mon-Sat 0915-1015 throughout the year, movies relevant to Buddhist interests Mon and Fri 1400, simple accommodation on site.

**"Z Meditation"**, Kandi village, T(0)9418-036956, www.zmeditation.com. Interesting course including yoga and meditation. Retreats offered in silence with separate discussion sessions, 5 days (Mon 1600-Sat 1100), includes a 'humble' breakfast; highly recommended for beginners, run by friendly couple in peaceful location with beautiful views. Tibetan cookery.

**Lhamo's Kitchen** Next to Green Shop, Bhagsu Rd, T(0)9816-468719. Runs 3 courses (soups, bread, *momos*), 1100-1300, 1700-1900, Rs 200 each. Friendly, fun, eat what you cook.

**Tour operators**
**Dhauladhar Travels**, Temple Rd, McLeodganj, T01892-221158, dhauladhar@hotmail.com. Agents for **Indian Airlines**.
**HPTDC** luxury coach in season: Dharamshala to McLeodganj, Kangra Temple and Fort, Jawalamukhi, 1000-1900, Rs 200; Dharamshala to McLeodganj, Bhagsunath, Dal Lake, Talnu, Tapovan, Chamunda, 1000-1700, Rs 200. Tickets from HPTDC Marketing Office, near SBI, Kotwali Bazar in Dharamshala, T01892-0224 928.
**Skyways Travels**, just off main square, Temple Rd, T(0)9857-400001. Reliable travel agent who is a mine of knowledge and even has paypal. Can make travelling in India a whole lot easier. Also for tours to Jammu

and Kashmir, Rajasthan; trekking, camping and paragliding locally.

**Summit Adventures**, main square, Bhagsu Nag, McLeodganj, T01892-221679, www.summit-adventures.net. Specialist in trekking and climbing, also cultural trips and a yoga trekking tour.

**Trans Himalaya**, 6 Skye Cres, Crieff, PH7 3FB, T01764-650604, www.trans-himalaya.com. This UK-based company specializes in touring the Himalayan region. With an indepth knowledge of Buddhist heritage, it offers cultural tours and eco-trekking.

**Ways Tours & Travels**, Temple Rd, T01892-221355, waystour@vsnl.net. Most reliable, Mr Gupta is very experienced, and provides professional service.

### Trekking

Best season Apr-Jun and Sep-Oct. Rates upwards of Rs 1400 per person per day. See Summit Adventures above.

**Highpoint Adventures**, Kareri Lodge, T01892-220931,www.trek.123himachal.com. Organize treks for smaller groups and a range of tours.

**Mountaineering Institute**, Mirza Ismail Rd, T01892-221787. Invaluable advice on routes, equipment, accommodation, campsites, etc. Equipment and porters can be hired for groups of 8 or more, reasonable charges. The deputy director (SR Saini) has described many routes in *Treks and Passes of Dhauladhar and Pir Pinjal* (Rs 150) although the scale of maps can be misleading. Consult the author for detailed guidance. Mon-Sat 1000-1700.

## ⊖ Transport

**Dharamshala** *p122, maps p123 and p125*
It is dangerous to drive at night in the hills. The roads are not lit and the risks of running off the edge are great.
**Air** Nearest airport is at Gaggal, T01892-232374, 13 km (taxi Rs 650). To/from **Delhi** with **Spicejet**, www.spicejet.com. One service each daily.

**Local bus** Buses and share jeeps between Dharamshala and McLeodganj, 10 km, 30 mins, Rs 10/ Rs 25.
**Long-distance bus** Most originate in Dharamshala, T01892-224903, but some super and semi-deluxe buses leave from below the taxi stand in McLeodganj. HRTC enquiries, T01892-221750. HPTDC run luxury coaches in season). **Delhi** (Kashmir Gate, 521 km), semi-deluxe coach departs McLeodganj 1700, 14 hrs; deluxe coach 1830, 1945; super deluxe coach, 1900 (Volvo). Prices vary – deluxe coach is around 880rs and some of the private companies charge 1200. Avoid Bedi Travels with bad suspension. From Delhi at same times. 1930 arrives Lower Dharamshala 1000, recommended for best morning views of the foothills (stops en route). **Dalhousie** and **Chamba**, 0730, 0830, 1730, Rs180, 8 hrs; **Manali**, 1700, Rs 400, 8 hrs; luxury coach 2030, Rs650, **Pathankot**, from Mcleod 1000, 1100, 1320, 1450, 1600, Rs150. HRTC buses to **Baijnath**, 2½ hrs; **Chandigarh** (248 km), 9 hrs, via Una (overnight stop possible); also deluxe buses to **Dehra Dun**, 1420and 2000, Rs 410 and **Shimla**, 6000, 0820 and 2130 (from Dharamshala). **Kangra**, 50 mins, Rs 14; **Kullu** (214 km) 10 hrs; **Manali** (253 km) 11 hrs; best to travel by day (0800), fabulous views but bus gets overcrowded; avoid sitting by door where people start to sit on your lap! Always keep baggage with you; **Pathankot** (90 km), several 1000-1600, 4 hrs, connection for **Amritsar**, 3 hrs; **Shimla** (317 km, via Hamirpur/Bilaspur), 10 hrs.

**Private bus service** **Dalhousie**, 0740, 6 hrs, Rs 250; **Delhi** (Connaught Pl), 1800, 1830, 11 hrs, Rs 600-900. **Dehra Dun**, 1900, 13 hrs, Rs 650; **Kullu** 2100, 8 hrs, Rs 550; **Manali**, 0900, 2030, 9 hrs, Rs 550; **Rishikesh** 1930, 13 hrs. Several private agents, see Sky Travels.
**Local taxi** Shared by 4, pick up shuttle taxi at Kotwali Bazar on its way down before it turns around at the bus stand, as it is usually full when it passes the taxi stand.
**Long-distance taxi** Can be hired from near the bus stands, T01892-221205.

Between Dharamshala and McLeodganj, Rs 150; to Pathankot around Rs 1500-2000 depending on size of vehicle.
**Train** Nearest broad-gauge railhead is at Pathankot. Booking office at bus stand, below tourist office, 1000-1100. For narrow gauge, see below.

___

**Kangra** *p127*
**Air** Gaggal Airport, see Dharamshala, above.
**Bus** To **Dharamshala**, Rs 20, under 1 hr.
**Taxi** A taxi to **Dharamshala** costs Rs 400.
**Train** Narrow-gauge **Kangra Valley Railway**, enquiries T01892-265026. From **Pathankot** to **Jogindernagar** (10 hrs) or **Baijnath**, reaching Kangra after 4½ hrs: 0430, 0710, 0925, 1300, 1640, 1740, 5 hrs (often 1 hr late). **Jogindernagar to Pathankot**: 0720, 1220, reaches Kangra in 5-6 hrs; **Baijnath to Pathankot**: 0420, 0735, 1425, 1800, to Kangra in 3-4 hrs. Kangra station serves Old Kangra with the fort, near the main road, while Kangra Mandir station is near the temple, bazar and most of the hotels. During the day there are regular rickshaw shuttles between Kangra Mandir station and Tehsil Chowk.

___

**Dalhousie** *p129, map p129*
**Air** The nearest airport is at Gaggal, see Dharamshala, above.
**Bus** Dalhousie is on NH1A. **Amritsar**, 0600, 0945, 7 hrs; **Delhi**, 1830, 12 hrs; To **Chamba** 4 buses daily, 2 go via Khajjiar, 2½ hrs; **Dharamshala** 0715, 1115, 1400, 7 hrs; **Jammu**, 1000, 7 hrs; **Pathankot** 1st bus 0530, 1-2 buses per hr until 1630, 3½ hrs (change in Pathankot for frequent services to main towns/cities); **Shimla**,

1245, 14 hrs. Note that Banikhet village, 10 mins down from Dalhousie, has many more bus options.
**Jeep/Taxi** From bus stand up to **Gandhi Chowk**, Rs 100, **Bakrota**, Rs 200.
**Train** Nearest station is at Pathankot, 2 hrs by taxi. There is a helpful Railway Out Agency close to the bus stand.

___

**Chamba** *p130*
**Bus** The hectic bus stand is at the south end of the Chaugan. To **Bharmour** (3 hrs, Rs 70); **Dalhousie** (2½ hrs, Rs 50); and to **Shimla** once per day.
**Jeep** hire is relatively expensive. Special service during **Manimahesh Yatra**.
**Train** Nearest station is at Pathankot, 120 km away.

## ⊙ Directory

**Dharamshala** *p122, maps p123 and p125*
**Medical services** Civil Hospital, T01899-242125. Delek Hospital, T01892-220053/223381, often foreign volunteer doctors, good for dentistry. District Hospital, T01892-222133. Men Tse Khang (Tibetan Medical Institute) T01892-222484, Gangchen Kyishong, for Tibetan herbal medicine. Dr Dolma's and Dr Dhonden's clinics, near McLeodganj Bazar for Tibetan treatment. **Post** GPO, 1 km below tourist office on Main Rd, T01892-222912, Mon-Sat 1000-1630, another in Kotwali Bazar. In McLeodganj, the post office, Jogibara Rd, has poste restante. **Useful contacts** Foreigners' Registration Office: Civil Lines, beyond GPO, near petrol pump. Police: T01892-224893.

# Trekking in Himachal

Himachal has something to offer every type of trekker. From short, leisurely walks through the pine forests that surround Shimla, with ample food and accommodation options meaning that nothing need be carried, to demanding treks over the high passes of Lahaul, Kinnaur and Spiti, the choice is almost as staggering as the views.

## Trekking from Shimla

From Shimla on the Hindustan–Tibet Highway, there are opportunities for short and long treks. These include **Chharabra**, 13 km beyond Shimla at 2593 m, and **Naldera**, 23 km from Shimla, which was Curzon's summer retreat, see page 79.

Still further on at **Narkanda**, 64 km from Shimla, is another trek with very good walks, especially up Hattu Peak. From Narkanda the road runs down to the Sutlej Valley and enters Kinnaur and Spiti. Foreigners are allowed into Spiti if they have a permit.

From just beyond Narkanda you can trek northwest over the **Jalori Pass** (3350 m) in the **Seraj** region. Starting from Ani village reached by bus/jeep from Luhri in the Sutlej Valley below Narkanda, you trek into the lower part of the Kullu Valley, joining the Kullu–Manali road at Aut. There is a road, accessible to jeeps, over much of this route. An alternative is to proceed 65 km from Narkanda to **Rampur** and then trek into the Kullu Valley via the **Bashleo Pass** (3600 m). There are forest rest houses en route so a tent is not essential. The pass is crossed on the third day of this five-day trek. Both treks end at **Banjar** in the Tirthan Valley from where there are buses to Kullu.

## Trekking in Lahaul, Kinnaur and Spiti

The border areas are being opened to trekkers with permits. At the same time the local tribal people are being exposed to outside influences which started with the introduction of television in these valleys. Now enterprising families open their homes to paying guests, youths offer their services as guides and muleteers and shops stock bottled drinks and canned food. However, anyone trekking in this region is advised to carry food, tents and all essentials.

### Lahaul

Lahaul, like Zanskar and Ladakh immediately to the north, is an ideal trekking destination during the monsoon, as it is not nearly as wet as most other regions. The best time to go is from mid-June to mid-October but some passes, eg Shingo-La, Parvati Pass, may remain snow bound until mid-July or even later.

You can take a trek from **Darcha**, see page 120, up the valley over the **Shingo La** and on to **Padum**, the capital of the Zanskar region. Padum is linked with Leh. Shingo-La is over 5000 m so some acclimatization is desirable. The route is well marked.

An alternative route to Zanskar is up the Chandra valley and over **Baralacha La**. From here a trail leads over a high pass Phitsela to Phuktal, where you join the main trail coming from Darcha. Most travellers drive into Darcha; however, a fine trek past the 'Lake of the

Moon' or Chandratal makes a nice and less known addition for those with a little more time. The route taken from **Manali** is over the **Hamta Pass** with good views of Deo Tibba (6001 m), weather permitting, to **Chhatru** village in the Chandra Valley. Here, there is camping in the grounds of a rest house and local families can put up visitors in very basic homes. It is four days' trek from Manali. Two days along the dirt road brings you to **Batal** (to save time you can take the bus from Manali over the Rohtang Pass). The next stage of both variations is to Chandratal.

**Chandratal** (4270 m) is 18 km from Batal. The first section up to Kunzum Pass is on the bus route. The remaining 8.5-km trail is open June-October and brings you to the beautiful clear blue-water lake, about 1 km long and 500 m wide, which lies on a glacial bowl. Carry your own tent and provisions. The lake can also be reached on a lower 14-km trail that directly runs from Batal (no regular buses from Manali). From Chandratal the route crosses several fast flowing streams before reaching the Baralacha La (usually three days). You need to be very careful and take adequate safety precautions while negotiating these stream crossings. It then goes over another pass along the same ridge as the Shingo-La, to join the main Darcha-Padum trail. From here you can continue on to **Padum** or return to Darcha in Lahaul. This second option makes for a very good circular trek.

Another possibility is to trek down the Chenab Valley and either cross the Pir Panjal by one of a number of passes into the Ravi Valley via Bahrmaur, to Chamba or carry on to Kishtwar.

Around lower Lahaul, you can trek from the district town of **Udeypur** at the base of the Miyar Nullah, the upper section of which is glaciated. To the east, high passes give access to the Bhaga valley and to the west to the Saichu Nala (Chenab tributary). The Trilokinath Temple nearby is well worth a visit, see page 119.

Trails run into the Miyar Nullah, renowned for flowers, then over the 5100-m Kang La Pass to Padum. Alternatively, you can follow the Chandrabhaga River to the scarcely visited Pangi valley with its rugged scenery, then over the 4240-m Sach Pass leading to Chamba District.

In the Pangi Valley, the Chandrabhaga flows at over 2400 m after the two rivers meet in this desolate and craggy region. The cheerful and good-looking Pangiwals keep their unique heritage alive through their singing and dancing. The Mindhal temple to Devi is their focus of worship. **Kilar** is the HQ which has a rest house and the Detnag Temple nearby. From Kilar a wide trail follows the steep slopes above the Chandrabhaga (Chenab) River to Dharwas on the Himachal/Kashmir border and then onwards to **Atholi** in the Paddar region of Kishtwar, known for its sapphire mines.

## Kinnaur

Close to the Tibetan border on its east, Kinnaur has the Sutlej flowing through it. Garhwal is to the south, Spiti Valley to the north and Kullu to the west. The rugged mountains and sparse rainfall make Kinnaur resemble Lahaul. The Kinners (Kinnauris) are Hindu but the Tibetan Buddhist influence is evident in the numerous *gompas* that can be seen alongside the temples. The **Phulaich** (Festival of Flowers) takes place in September when some villagers leave for the mountains for two days and nights to collect scented blossoms, then return on the third day to celebrate with singing and dancing. Kinnaur, including the lovely side valleys of **Sangla** and **Bhabha**, is now open and permits are easily available from the District Magistrates in Shimla, Kullu or Keylong. These treks are immensely enjoyable; although there are stone huts and the occasional rest house, always carry a tent in this area.

**Baspa Valley** Starting from **Sangla** (2680 m), you can take a fairly level forest walk up to Batrseri (5 km), then along the road up to Rakcham (8 km; 3130 m) and climb gradually to reach **Chitkul** (18 km; 3450 m), passing through Mastrang. Another option is to start at **Morang**, see page 89, which has a bus from Kalpa. The trail follows the Sutlej River bank for a short distance until the Tirung Gad meets it. Here it turns southeast and after going through a narrow valley reaches **Thangi**, a village connected to Morang by road (4WD only) where mules are available for hire. The track continues along barren hills to Rahtak (camping possible), before rising steeply to Charang Pass (5266 m), then drops down following a mountain stream to Chitkul.

**Bhabha Valley** Starting from **Kafnoo** (2427 m), 22 km from Wangtu, this is another beautiful valley to trek. Permit details have to be entered and stamped at the police post 1 km before Kafnoo reservoir. They are checked at Tabo.

There is level ground at the end of the road by the reservoir suitable for camping, but it can get flooded. Local guides are available. From Kafnoo, the trail follows the right bank of the river for about 1 km before crossing to the left bank over a new bridge. From here, the trail gradually ascends to **Chokhapani**, about a five-hour walk away. The riverside trail is slippery and not recommended. The upper trail climbs past Yangpa II then through fields around Musrang hamlet. There is an adequate campsite at Chokhapani (10 km, 3000 m).

From Chokhapani to **Upper Mulling** (3470 m) is a beautiful 8 km, four hours' walk (including lunch stop), following the left bank of the Bhabha stream. Initially going through forests the track then crosses open meadows. At the far end of the meadows is an ideal camping site by the river. The trail from Mulling enters a forested section leading to a snow bridge across the stream. Cross the stream and follow the steeply rising trail to the **Kara** meadows where the Government Animal Husbandry Department has a merino sheep breeding centre. Ford the Bhabha River with care (either on horseback or by wading across with support from a fixed line), to the campsite at Pasha. This section takes three hours, so you can continue to the **Kara-Taria Pass Base**. The 5-km walk up a steep trail along the right fork of the Bhabha stream takes another four hours. Taria Base Pass (4290 m) camp is below the steep slope leading to the Pass. Camp well away from the slope as it is prone to rock falls.

**Pin Valley** There is a steep descent over scree for the first kilometre from **Taria Pass**, followed by a five-hour 15-km walk along a narrow but clear trail to the first camp in the Pin Valley. None of the apparently promising campsites on the way has a good water source. The **Bara Boulder** site has a stream and good grazing for horses.

The 11-km stretch from Bara Boulder to **Mudh** (3925 m) takes four hours. It is the highest permanently inhabited village in the Pin Valley and is surrounded by summer cultivation. Log bridges cross several streams feeding into the Pin River. There are places to stay and food is available but some villagers charge up to Rs 200-300 for a room. It is possible to camp outside the village. One campsite is on the flat plateau overlooking the river near the summer hut of the lay *lama* (before crossing the narrow foot bridge on the river), another is near the fields immediately below the village where a side stream runs below the old monastery into the Pin. It is worth visiting the old *gompas* in the village. From here you can get a ride back to Kaza.

## Spiti

Spiti is a high-altitude desert, bare, rugged and inhospitable, with the Spiti River running from the slopes of Kunzum La (4551 m) to Sumdo (3230 m). Kunzum La offers seasonal access by road to Kullu from the valley, and it is also directly connected with Shimla via the NH22 and the SH30. Like neighbouring Lahaul, Spiti is famous for its *gompas*. Foreigners are allowed to trek in this region up to Kibber with permits.

At **Tabo**, the Buddhist monastery is one of the region's most famous, see page 90. There is a dispensary and two adequate teashops. Foreigners are now allowed to stay overnight in Tabo. There are other important *gompas* at Dankar, Ki, Kungri and Lalung. Trekkers interested in **fossils** choose a trail starting at **Kaza** and travel to **Langza** (8.5 km), which has a narrow track accessible to 4WD. The trek goes to Hikim, the Tangyut monastery, Komik (8 km) and returns to Kaza (6 km). From Kibber (4205 m) there is a 6-km track through alpine meadows to **Gete** (4520 m) which claims to be one of the highest permanent settlements in the world only reached on foot.

## Trekking in the Kullu and Parvati valleys

Treks here vary in duration and degree of difficulty. There are pleasant walks up the subsidiary valleys from Aut and Katrain with the opportunity to camp in spectacular and high locations without having to spend very long getting there. An option is to take the bus up to the Rohtang Pass, 51 km from Manali, which is spectacular and then walk down. There is a path and it only takes a few hours.

The post-monsoon period (September to mid-November) is the most reliable **season**. Longer treks with crossings of high passes can be undertaken then, before the winter snows arrive. During the monsoon (June to September) it is wet but the rain is not continuous. It may rain all day or for only an hour or two. Visibility is affected and glimpses of mountains through the clouds are more likely than broad clear panoramic views. However, many flowering plants are at their best. There is trekking in the spring, that is April to May, but the weather is more unsettled and the higher passes may still have quite a lot of snow on them. There can be very good spells of fine weather during this period and it can get quite hot in May.

You will need to take your own **equipment** since that hired out by local agencies is often of an inferior quality. Kullu now has pony unions with fixed rates for guides, porters and horses. Ask at the tourist office and the **Mountaineering Institute** for information and assistance.

### Routes
From **Manali** you can go north into **Lahaul** (Map trek **A**) and **Spiti** Valleys by crossing the Rohtang (3985 m) or the Hampta Pass (4270 m). Once over the great divide of the Pir Panjal the treks are briefly described – see Trekking in Lahaul, Kinnaur and Spiti, above. West of Manali there are routes into the **Chamba** and **Kangra** Valleys (Map trek **B**).

The trek to Malana Valley offers an opportunity to see a relatively isolated and comparatively unspoilt hill community. From Manali you go to Naggar (28 km, which can also be reached by bus) and stay at **Rumsu** (2377 m), which is higher. The Chandrakhani Pass (3500 m) takes you into the Malana Valley at the head of which is the glacier. On the third day you can reach **Malana** (2650 m, 20 km from Naggar), which has two guesthouses. In the past you could only enter with permission from the villagers but this is no longer needed. On the fourth day you trek to **Jari** (1500 m) where you can catch a bus to Kullu. The road from Jari to Malana may destroy the distinct character of the community. The whole of the Malana Valley is dominated by **Deo Tibba** peak in the north.

## The Valley of the Gods

No one knows the origin of the village of Malana. People believe that a band of renegade soldiers who deserted Alexander's army in the fourth century BC settled here (some wooden houses have soldiers carved on them); it is more probable that their antecedents were from the Indian plains. Their language, Kanashi, has no script but is linked to Tibetan. The villagers are directly involved in taking decisions on important matters affecting them, thus operating as an ancient democratic 'city state'. Language, customs and religious practices also differ from neighbouring hill tribes, polygamy being permitted.

A charming myth is associated with Jamlu, the principal deity in the valley. Jamlu, possibly of pre-Aryan origin, was carrying a casket containing all the important deities of Hinduism and while crossing the mountains through the Chandrakhani Pass into Kullu, a strong gust of wind blew open the box and spread the deities all over the valley. Since then Malana has been known as 'The Valley of the Gods'.

### Parvati Valley

To extend the trek from Malana it is possible to continue to **Manikaran** and onwards to Pulga and beyond in the scenic Parvati Valley. You can also get to Manikaran by bus from Kullu, see page 114. Up to **Khirganga** the trail is fairly clear but take care since the area is prone to heavy rain and land slips. Beyond Khirganga, the trek follows the valley up-river passing the tree line to Pandav Bridge and eventually arriving at the sacred lake and shrine at **Mantalai**. Here it splits leading up and over the Pin-Parvati Pass, and down into the dry Pin Valley.

Alternatively, you can explore the lower Parvati Valley by walking to **Kasol**, and then to Jari and Naggar via the temple of Bijli Mahadev (Map trek **D**).

### Pin Valley

The difference between the Parvati and the Pin Valley is striking. Immense glaciers and bizarre moonscape rock formations here contrast with the verdant pastures and evergreen forests of the Parvati Valley behind. The trek leads down to the traditional village of **Mudh**, see page 145. The road to Mudh is still incomplete so it takes about five hours to walk to Sangam and Chatral, leading to Kinnaur and Spiti. There are buses from Chatral to Kaza, see page 99. The trek from Manikaran to Kaza with passes over 5300 m, can take 10 to 14 days. Guides and porters are necessary.

## Trekking in Kangra

**Baijnath**, **Palampur** and **Dharamshala** are popular starting points. See pages 128 and 122. From here you go over the **Dhaula Dhar** at passes such as the Indrahar and Minkiani (both from Dharamshala) and the Waru (from Palampur), then enter a feeder of the Upper Ravi Valley.

Midway up the valley, which lies between the Manimahesh Dhar and Dhaula Dhar ranges, is Bara Bangahal. From there you can go downstream to **Chamba** or upstream which offers the choice of at least three passes for crossing into the Kullu Valley. The northernmost of these is the Taintu Pass which passes Beas Kund beneath Hanuman Tibba. In the middle is the Manali Pass whilst the southernmost is Kalihani Pass. A good trip which includes the upper part of this valley is the round trip trek from Manali, see page 104.

## Trekking from Chamba

The Chamba region receives less rain than the Kangra Valley to the south. A trek, particularly over the Pir Panjal into Lahaul is possible during the monsoon months (June to September). The ideal season, though, is just after the monsoon. There are several short and longer treks from Chamba and Bahrmaur in the Upper Ravi Valley.

To the north there are three main passes over the **Pir Panjal** into Lahaul: the Kalicho, Kugti and Chobia passes. At least five days should be allowed for crossing them as their heights are around 5000 m and acclimatization is highly desirable. All the first stages of the walks are along the Budhil River. After the first two days, the services of a guide or porters are recommended for picking the right trail. Views from the passes are very good both of the Himalaya to the north and the Chenab Valley to the south. The descent from the passes is very steep. On reaching the road you can take a bus from **Udeypur** or **Trilokinath** in the Pattan Valley, to the Kullu Valley over Rohtang Pass. Several trails cross the high passes over the Pir Panjal range to give access to the Pattan Valley of Lahaul. The semi-nomadic Gaddi shepherds regularly use these to take their flocks across to the summer grazing grounds located in the high-sided valleys of Lahaul.

**Bahrmaur** (1981 m), also spelt Brahmaur or Bharmaur, is 65 km from Chamba and can be reached by bus. It was the original capital Brahmapura for four centuries and has 8th-10th-century *Pahari* style temples. The best known are the Lakshminarayan group which is the centre of worship for the semi-nomadic Gaddi tribe. From Bahrmaur a three-day trek is possible to **Manimahesh Lake** (3950 m), 34 km, in the Manimahesh Kailash (5575 m), a spur running off the Pir Panjal. The **Manimahesh Yatra** begins in Chamba and ends at the lake, revered by local people as a resting place of Siva. Pilgrims arrive at the Manimahesh temple here and take a holy bath a fortnight after *Janmashtami* (September/October). The temple has a brass *Mahisasuramardini* image. During the *yatra* period buses, minibuses and taxis are laid on from Chamba to Bahrmaur. Many pilgrims trek the next 12 km to Hadsar although jeeps are available. From here it is a two-day climb to the lake with a night halt at Dhanchho. Himachal Tourism tents available at Bahmaur and there is also a rest house, Hadsar, Dhanchho and Manimahesh; contact tourist office, Dalhousie, T01899-242736. Ponies and porters can be hired at each place. The nine-day trek starting from Chamba includes **Rakh** (20 km) on Day 1, **Bahrmaur** on Day 2, a rest stop there, then continuing to **Hadsar** (12 km), **Dhanchho** (7 km) and **Manimahesh** (7.5 km) with a brief halt at **Bhairon Ghati**. The return is by the same route.

## Contents

**150 Kashmir Valley**
- 150 Jammu
- 151 Vaishno Devi
- 152 Srinagar
- 157 Around Srinagar
- 159 Zanskar
- 160 Srinagar to Leh road
- 161 Listings

**171 Ladakh**
- 171 Leh
- 176 Southeast of Leh
- 178 Along the Srinagar road
- 182 Nubra Valley, Nyona and Drokhpa area
- 184 Trekking in Ladakh
- 188 Listings

## Footprint features

- 151 Warning
- 172 Traditional Ladakhi dress
- 175 Prepare for a different lifestyle in Leh
- 185 Who might you meet along the way – birds and wildlife

Jammu & Kashmir

# Kashmir Valley

The beauty of the Vale of Kashmir, with its snow-dusted mountains looming in shades of purple above serene lakes and wildflower meadows, still has the power to reduce grown poets to tears. Nonetheless, the reality of military occupation pervades many aspects of daily life, with army camps, bunkers and checkposts positioned along the highways and throughout the countryside. Travellers not dissuaded by the threat of violence or the official warnings to stay away can expect to encounter extremes of beauty and friendliness, not to mention the warm welcome from Kashmiris – which is unforgettable.

---

## Jammu → *For listings, see pages 161-170.*

Jammu, the second largest city in the state, is the winter capital of government and main entry point for Kashmir by train. While it doesn't possess the charm of Srinagar, it is a pleasant enough city to spend a day in. Built in 1730 by the Dogra rulers as their capital, Jammu marks the transition between the Punjab plains and the Himalaya hills.

### Arriving in Jammu
**Getting there** The airport is within the city; a pre-paid taxi to the centre (Ragunath Bazar) costs around Rs 200. There are daily flights from Delhi and Srinagar, and twice weekly flights to Leh. The railway station is in the New Town, across the Tawi River, a few kilometres from the old hilltop town where most of the budget hotels are located. The general bus stand, where inter-state buses come in, is at the foot of the steps off the Srinagar Road in the Old Town. ▸▸ *See Transport, page 169.*

**Getting around** The frequent, cheap city bus service or an auto-rickshaw comes in handy as the two parts of the town and some sights are far apart.

**Tourist information** Jammu and Kashmir Tourist Reception Centre ① *Vir Marg, T0191-254 8172, www.jktourism.org*, has brochures. **Jammu Tawi** ① *railway station, T0191-247 6078.* JKTDC ① *T0191-257 9554.*

**Climate** Temperatures in summer reach a maximum of 40°C, minimum 28°C. Rainfall in July and August is 310 mm, with other months measuring an average 40 mm. The best time to visit is from November to March.

### Places in Jammu
**Raghunath Temple** ① *0600-2130, inner sanctum closes 1130-1800, museum 0600-1000, cloakroom for bags/cameras* (1857) in the old centre is one of the largest temple complexes in North India. The temple, dedicated to Lord Rama, has a series of glittering gilded spires

and seven shrines. The main shrine's interior is gold-plated, while in surrounding shrines contain literally millions of "saligrams" (mini-lingams fixed onto slabs of stone) most of which are fossils. **Rambiresvar Temple** (1883), centrally located on the Shalimar Road, is dedicated to Siva and named after its founder Maharaja Ranbir Singh. The 75-m orange tower is rather unattractive, but the central 2.3-m sphatik shivling is an extraordinary crystal lingam and this is the largest Siva temple in North India. A fine bronze Nandi bull watches the entrance to the shrine.

About 700 m from the Rambiresvar Temple are the palace buildings of **Mubarak Mandi**. Dating from 1824, it blends Rajasthani, Mughal and baroque architectural elements. Within the dilapidated complex is the **Dogra Art Gallery** ⓘ *Tue-Sun 103-163, foreigners Rs 5* displaying royal memorabilia in the "Pink Hall".

The **Amar Mahal Museum** ⓘ *Apr-Sep 0900-1300, 1400-1800, Oct-Mar 0900-1300, 1400-1700, foreigners Rs100, great views of the river, Rs 150 by auto-rickshaw from the centre of town, or take a minibus*, is superbly sited on the bend of the Tawi, just off Srinagar Road. There is a maharajas portrait gallery and 18th-century Pahari miniature paintings of *Mahabharata* scenes. The early 20th-century palace is a curiosity; its French designer gave it château-like roofs and turrets. Look through a rear window to see Hari Singh's 100 kg golden canopied throne. Other rooms show modern art; admission to the library is only for researchers (fine collection of antique books). The Hari Niwas Hotel is adjacent; the lawns are a nice spot for refreshments when it's not too hot.

Across the Tawi River lies the impressive **Bahu Fort**, thought to have a 3000-year history. The ramparts have been renovated and are now surrounded by a lush terraced garden, the Bagh-e-Bahu.

## Vaishno Devi → For listings, see pages 161-170.

The Vaishno Devi cave, 61 km north of Jammu, is one of the region's most important pilgrimage sites. As the temple draws near you hear cries of 'Jai Matadi' (Victory to the Mother Goddess). Then at the shrine entrance, pilgrims walk in batches through cold ankle-deep water to the low and narrow cave entrance to get a glimpse of the deity. Visitors joining the *yatra* find it a very moving experience.

The main pilgrimage season is March to July. The arduous climb along the 13-km track to the cave temple has been re-laid, widened and tiled, and railings provided. Another road from Lower Sanjichat to the Darbar brings you 2 km closer with 300 m less to climb. Ponies, *dandies* (a kind of local palanquin for carrying tourists) and porters are available from Katra at fixed rates. Auto-rickshaws and taxis can go as far as the Banganga. Yatra slips are issued free of charge by the **Yatra Registration Counter** (**YRC**) in the bus stand in Katra. The slip must be presented at the Banganga checkpoint within six hours (or face disciplinary action if caught). Tea, drinks and snacks are available on the route.

Visitors should leave all leather items in a cloakroom at Vaishno Devi before entering the cave; take bottled water and waterproofs. If you are on your own or in a small group, you can usually avoid having to wait for a group if you present yourself at Gates 1 or 2, and smile.

## Srinagar → *For listings, see pages 161-170.*

Founded by Raja Pravarasen in the sixth century, ringed by mountains and alluringly wrapped around the Dal and Nagin lakes, Srinagar ('beautiful city') is divided in two by the River Jhelum. Once known as the city of seven *kadal*s (bridges), there are now

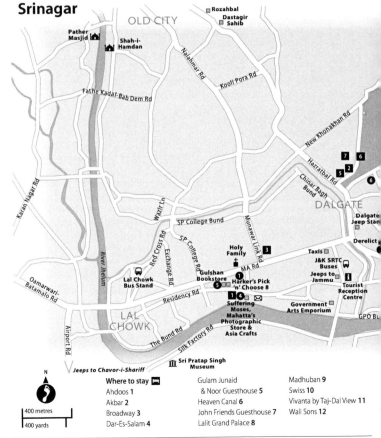

# Srinagar

**Where to stay** 🛏

Ahdoos **1**
Akbar **2**
Broadway **3**
Dar-Es-Salam **4**

Gulam Junaid
  & Noor Guesthouse **5**
Heaven Canal **6**
John Friends Guesthouse **7**
Lalit Grand Palace **8**

Madhuban **9**
Swiss **10**
Vivanta by Taj-Dal View **11**
Wali Sons **12**

12 that connect the two sides, the older ones giving their names to their adjoining neighbourhoods. It is the largest city in the state and the summer seat of government. Sadly the troubles of the past 20 years have scarred the town, leading to the desertion and neglect of many of its fine houses, buildings and Hindu temples. The famous Dal Lake has shrunk to a sixth of its former size and has become badly polluted. Older Srinagaris lament the passing of the formerly spruce city, yet even so, Srinagar is a charming city with a strong character, unique in India for its Central Asian flavour.

## Arriving in Srinagar

**Getting there** The airport is 14 km south of town; a taxi to the main tourist areas takes 30-45 minutes and costs Rs 400. Srinagar has several daily direct flights from Delhi and weekly flights from Leh. Direct buses from New Delhi take 24 hours, but this is an arduous trip. If you want to travel overland, it's more comfortable to take the train as far as Jammu (12 hours), stop for the night and then travel to the valley by jeep or bus the next day (eight to nine hours, including stops for lunch and tea). It's a stunning journey through the mountains to the Jawahar tunnel that burrows through the Pir Panjal, the jade-green Chenab river flowing hundreds of feet below. Emerging from the tunnel on the other side, high in the hills of south Kashmir, travellers are treated to a breathtaking view of the valley spread before out before them.

**Getting around** There are government taxi stands with fixed rates at the Tourist Reception Centre (Residency Road), Dal Gate and Nehru Park, and an abundance of auto-rickshaws. Local buses are cheap, but can be crowded and slow. The days of dusk-to-dawn curfews are over, but even so, the city shuts down relatively early; by 2100 the streets are deserted and it can be tricky to find transport. ▸▸ See Transport, page 169.

**Tourist information** The Tourist Reception Centre ① *Residency Rd, close to the tourist area of Dalgate, T0194-245 2691, www.jktourism.org, open 24/7,* houses the state department of tourism, the **Jammu and Kashmir Tourism Development Corporation** (JKTDC) ① *T0194-2457927, www.jktdc.co.in,* and **Adventure Tourism** for booking accommodation and tours. Also within the complex is the **J&K State Transport Corporation** ① *T0194-245 5107,*

Dal Lake

Floating Post Office & Museum
**9**
Nehru Park
**10**
Checkpoint & entry to Shankaracharya Temple
Boulevard Rd
Old Gagribal Rd
To 11 ❶ ❷ Mughal Garden & Botanical Gardens
eemal Hotel
**3**
**Shankaracharya Reserved Forest** ◆
**Shankaracharya Temple**
To 8
City Forest Hotel
Gupkar Rd
dency Rd
Srinagar-Ladakh Hwy

**Restaurants ❶**
Café Robusta **1**
Krishna Dhaba **2**
Lhasa **3**
Mughal Darbar & Tao Café **4**

Shakti Sweets & Modern Sweets **5**
Shamyana **6**

for bus tickets. You can pick up an excellent map showing both the city and the whole state at the TIC.

**Safety** At time of writing the British **Foreign and Commonwealth Office** ⓘ *www.fco. gov.uk*, advises against all rural travel in Jammu and Kashmir, except in Ladakh, and excepting the cities of Jammu and Srinagar, and along the Jammu-Srinagar highway. For an on-the-ground perspective, check www.greaterkashmir.com, www.kashmirtimes.com and www.freepresskashmir.com. Most travellers report no problems, but it is essential to be careful and keep informed about the situation.

Grenade attacks on army bunkers in the city used to be common, but are currently rare. However, in 2006 six Indian tourists were killed during grenade attacks on two bus loads of tourists from West Bengal. Given the tensions between Kashmir and the Indian government, Indian tourists are more likely to be directly targeted than foreigners.

If you are in town and see the shop shutters coming down before closing time, this is generally a sign that a protest is approaching. Either beat a hasty retreat in an auto-rickshaw, or take shelter in a shop until the demonstrators and police have passed. Always ask how the situation is before heading to the old city ('Downtown') and don't go there on Fridays, when spontaneous demonstrations following afternoon prayers are common.

### Places in Srinagar
The city falls into three parts; the commercial area (**Uptown**), the old city (**Downtown**) and the area around the lakes (**Dalgate**, the **Boulevard, Nehru Park**). Uptown is the place for shopping, particularly Polo View and the Bund, which is a footpath that runs along the Jhelum. Residency Road and Lal Chowk are also in Uptown.

Hotels on the Boulevard are popular – particularly with Indian tourists – but tend to be huge, impersonal and overpriced. The city is famous for its houseboats and staying on one can be a very pleasant experience, but it is necessary to book carefully; if the deal sounds too good to be true, then it probably is and you will end up paying in other ways (ie by being coerced into shopping trips, from which your hosts will take a hefty commission). Don't be bullied into booking a trip by pushy, Kashmiri travel agents in New Delhi – much better try to book through the **Houseboat Owners Association**. Try and find a boat with good references from other travellers, through sites such as www.tripadvisor.com. Also be aware that many boats in the Dal and Nagin lakes can only be accessed by *shikara*. While boat owners will always insist that a *shikara* will always be at your disposal, some tourists have found that this has not been the case and have found themselves marooned on boats with hosts they don't particularly like.

The Uptown area is good to stay in if you are interested in exploring the city and prefer to be away from the tourist rush. There are also some houseboats on the Jhelum River, with walk-on/walk-off access. You can hear the noise of the traffic from these boats, but there are no hawkers in this area.

Hotels around Dalgate tend to offer more budget options and can be very enjoyable. Those actually inside the lake are a good choice (Heaven Canal, Akbar) as the area is interesting with good views, but less hassle than the Boulevard.

**Old City** Srinagar's old city (known locally as 'Downtown') is a fascinating area to wander around with rather a Central Asian feel. Once the manufacturing and trade hub of Kashmir, each *mohalla* (neighbourhood) had its own speciality, such as carpet weaving, goldsmithery and woodcarving. It was said that you could find even the milk of a pigeon in the thriving bazars and its traders grew rich, building themselves impressive brick and wood houses, in a style that is a charming fusion of Mughal and English Tudor.

In the north of the Old City is the distinctive mound of **Hari Parbat Hill**, on which stands a fort built by Shujah Shah Durrani in 1808 (closed to the public). On the southern side of Hari Parbat, the **Makhdoom Sahib shrine** is dedicated to Hazrat Sultan and affords wonderful views of the city. The actual shrine is off-limits to women and non-Muslims, but you can peek through the ornate, carved screen from outside and marvel at the fabulous array of chandeliers. In 2013, a **cable car** ⓘ *tourists Rs 100*, up to the shrine was opened. Alternatively, you can access the steps up the hill from near the Sikh Gurdwara **Chhatti Padshahi**, by the imposing **Kathi Darwaza** (gate) in the Old City walls. This arched gateway (recently restored) was the principle entrance to the fort; a Persian inscription states that it was built by Akbar in 1597-1598. In the city wall on the opposite side of fort is the Sangeen Darwaza, which is more ornate (currently being restored).

From Makhdoom Sahib take an auto-rickshaw (or walk 15 minutes) to the **Jama Masjid** (1674). The mosque is notable for the 370 wooden pillars supporting the roof, each is made from a single *deodar* tree. The building forms a square around an inner courtyard, with a beautiful fountain and pool at its centre. Its four entrance archways are topped by the striking, pagoda-like roofs that are an important architectural characteristic of the valley's mosques and shrines. The mosque was where the sacred hair of the Prophet Mohammed was kept before being moved to the Hazratbal Mosque.

About 10 minutes' walk, to the southeast lies the 17th-century **tomb of Naqash Band Sahib**, a sufi saint. The interior of the shrine is covered with (modern) colourful papier-mâché flower designs; there is a women's section. The ornate mosque adjacent to the shrine is meticulously maintained, and is constructed of brick and wood alternate layers. Next to the shrine lie the graves of the 'martyrs' who died in the 1931 uprising against the Dogras. They are claimed as heroes by both the state government and the separatists – one of the few things both sides agree on.

Continue further in the same direction and you will reach the **Dastagir Sahib shrine**, which houses the tomb of Abdul Qazi Geelani. A fire in June 2012 almost entirely destroyed the main structure, including antique chandeliers, exquisite papier mâché and carved wood decoration. The 300-year-old, giant, handwritten Qu'ran and the holy relic of the saint were saved, as they were in a fireproof vault. The shirine is to be rebuilt according to its original structural character, and many devotees still come to pray here.

A minute's walk away is little **Rozahbal shrine**, which claims to contain the 'tomb of Jesus' (Holger Kersten's *Jesus Lived in India* recounts the legend; also see www.tombofjesus.com). The community here are sensitive about inquiring visitors: do not produce a camera, and don't be surprised if locals warn you away. Head west, towards the river for the beautiful **Shah-i-Hamdan Masjid**, the site of Srinagar's first mosque, built in 1395 by Mir Sayed Ali Hamadni. The original building was destroyed by fire, the current wooden structure dating back to the 1730s. The entrance is worth seeing for its exquisite papier-mâché work and woodcarving, but non-Muslims are not allowed inside the actual shrine. However, there is a women's section at the rear which female non-Muslims can enter and you can linger by the doorway with devotees, peeping inside to see the richly painted walls and chandeliers.

Facing Shah-i-Hamdan, across the river is the limestone **Pathar Masjid** (1623), built for the Empress Nur Jahan and renamed Shahi Mosque. Further up the river, on the same side as Shah-i-Hamdan lies the 15th-century bulbous brick **tomb of Zain-ul-Abidin's mother** ⓘ *daily 0900-1700*, which is embellished with glazed turquoise tiles. The tomb adjoins a graveyard, containing the sultan Zain-ul-Abidin's grave and those of his wives and children, enclosed by an old stone wall that has been reused from an earlier Hindu temple. The area, Zaina Kadal, is interesting to walk around – carved copperwork is still produced here and you can see the craftsmen at work. It's the best place to buy your souvenir samovar.

South of the old city and the river is the remarkable **Sri Pratap Singh Museum** ① *Lal Mandi, Tue-Sun 1030-1630, foreigners Rs 50* (1898). Kashmir's Hindu and Buddhist past literally stares you in the face as 1000-year-old statues of Siva, Vishnu and the Buddha, excavated from all over the valley, casually line the walls. One room houses an eclectic mix of stuffed animals, bottled snakes and birds eggs, topped off by the dissembled skeleton of a woolly mammoth and looked down on by a collection of stags heads, mounted on the papier-mâché walls. There are also miniature paintings, a selection of ancient manuscripts and coins, weapons, musical instruments and an anthropology section. Look out for the extraordinary "Amli" shawl in the textiles room: an embroidered map of Srinagar, showing the Jamia mosque and the Jhelum dotted with houseboats (it took 37 years to complete). The collection will be displayed in full when the museum extends into the larger building being constructed next door.

**Dal Lake and the floating gardens** Of all the city's sights, **Dal Lake** must be its trademark. Over 6.5 km long and 4 km wide, it is divided into three parts by manmade causeways. The small islands are willow covered, while round the lake are groves of *chinar*, poplar and willow. The Mihrbahri people have lived around the lakes for centuries and are market gardeners, tending the floating beds of vegetables and flowers that they have made and cleverly shielded with weeds to make them unobtrusive. Shikaras, the gondola-like pleasure boats that ply the lake, can be hired for trips around the Dal (official rate Rs 300 per hour, but it's possible to bargain for half that). The morning vegetable market is well worth seeing by boat, it starts around 0600 and a one-hour tour is adequate; it is in a Shi'ite area adorned with appropriate flags. If you're curious about the city, take a boat up the Jhelum as far as Shah-i-Hamdan, where you can get out for a walk. If you do this, it's worth taking a guide with you who can speak English.

Set up on a hill, behind the Boulevard (known as Takht-i-Sulaiman or 'Throne of Soloman'), is the **Shankaracharya Temple**, affording great views and a good place to orientate yourself. The temple was constructed during Jahangir's reign but is said to be on the same site as a second-century BC temple built by Asoka's son. The inelegant exterior houses a large lingum, while beneath is a cave where Shankaracharya is said to have performed a puja. The temple is 5.5 km up a steep road from the Boulevard; walking up the road is not permitted, although hitching a ride from the security check at the bottom is possible (open 0900-1700). There is an alternative rough path starting from next to the gate of the City Forest Hotel on Durganag Rd (one hour up, 30 mins down).

Set in front of a triangle of the lake created by intersecting causeways (now demolished) with a slender bridge at the centre lies the famous **Nishat Bagh** (Garden of Gladness) ① *Sat-Thu 0900-sunset, Rs 10*. Sandwiched between the hills and the lake, the steep terraces and central channel with fountains were laid out by Asaf Khan, Nur Jahan's brother, in 1632.

The **Shalimar Bagh** ① *Apr-Oct 0900-sunset, Nov-Mar 1000-sunset, Rs 10*, gardens are about 4 km away and set back from the lake. Built by Jahangir for his wife, Nur Jahan, the gardens are distinguished by a series of terraces linked by a water channel with central pavilions. These are surrounded by decorative pools, which can be crossed by stones. The uppermost pavilion has elegant black marble pillars and niches in the walls for flowers during the day and candles or lamps at night. The chinar (plane trees) have become so huge that some are falling down. **Chashma Shahi** (Royal Spring, 1632) ① *0900-sunset, Rs 10*, is a much smaller garden built around the course of a renowned spring, issuing from a miniature stone dome at the garden's summit. It is attributed to Shah Jahan though it has been altered over the centuries. Nearby are the **Botanical Gardens** (Royal Spring, 1632) ① *Sat-Thu 0800-sunset, Rs 10*. Rather wilder than the other gardens, its tucked-away location makes it a good place for runners to stretch their legs.

West (2.5 km) of Chashmi Shahi, nestling in the hills, is the smallest and sweetest of the Mughal gardens, the charmingly named **Pari Mahal** (Fairy Palace) ① *sunrise-sunset, Rs 10*. Built in the 17th century by the ill-fated prince Dara Shikoh, who was later beheaded by his brother Aurangzeb, the garden has six terraces and the best sunset views of Srinagar. The terraced gardens, backed by arched ruins, are being restored and are illuminated at night.

Close to Nagin Lake, **Hazratbal Mosque** (Majestic Place) is on the western shore of Dal Lake and commands excellent lake views. The modern mosque stands out for its white, marble dome and has a special sanctity as a hair of the prophet Mohammad is preserved here. Just beyond is the **Nazim Bagh** (Garden of the Morning Breeze), one of the earliest Mughal gardens and attributed to Akbar.

At the end of the Boulevard in Nehru Park the tiny **Post Office Museum** ① *daily 1100-2000* is unique in that it floats. You can send your mail from here.

**Dachigam National Park** ① *22 km east, past the Shalimar gardens. Passes available from the Tourist Reception Centre.* This national park is home to the endangered Hangul deer as well as black and brown bears, leopards, musk deer and various migratory birds. Permits and further information about the best time to see the wildlife can be obtained from the Tourist Reception Centre in Srinagar.

---

# Around Srinagar → For listings, see pages 161-170.

## Gulmarg

India's premier winter sports resort, Gulmarg attracts a colourful mix of characters, from the off-piste powder-addict adventurers who stay for months each year to the coach-loads of Indian tourists eager to see snow for the first time. Three times host of the country's annual Winter Games, it is one of the cheapest places in the world to learn to ski, although there are only a few beginners' runs. The resort is served by three ski lifts and boasts the world's second highest **gondola** ① *daily 1000-1800, Rs 800 return*, which stops at the Kangdori mid-station before rising up to Apharwat Top (4000 m), from where you can ski the 5.2 km back to Gulmarg. Or in summertime, take the cable car up and then half-way back, and walk down the remaining distance (take a picnic). Check with **Gulmarg J&K Tourism** ① *T01954-254 439 (or see page 172)*, about opportunities for heli-skiing. The season runs from December to April (best in January to February), and equipment is available for hire for around Rs 400-500 a day. Lift passes cost Rs 700-1250. Outside the winter season, Gulmarg is a popular day trip from Srinagar, with pony rides, walks and the world's highest green golf course being the main attractions.

## Charar-i-Sharief

From Srinagar it's a scenic one-hour drive to Charar-i-Sharief (27 km), the last 10 km of road climbing through orchards and vales of willow. Spread over a series of ridges, the colourful roofs of modern houses denote the fire in 1995, when most of the town was burnt down – including the famed 700-year old wooden **shrine and mosque** – as a result of a battle between militants and Indian troops. The complex is now rebuilt as a grand tiered pagoda with carved walnut-wood screens around the central tombs. Entombed here is Sheikh Noor-u-Din Noorani, one of many names given to the great Sufi poet, seer, philospoher and saint who died in 1438. He preached peace, tolerance and non-violence, and his shrine attracts thousands of visitors both Muslim and Hindu. It's possible to combine a visit to the shrine and a day-trip to Yusmarg (45 minutes away); or there's a nice J&K bungalow on the edge of town, should you get stranded. Shared jeeps to Charar-i-Sharief leave when full from Iqbal Park, in west Srinagar.

## Yusmarg

Yusmarg, a rolling meadowland surrounded by conifer forests and snowy peaks, is an up-and-coming tourist spot for Indian day-trippers. Pony rides are popular, and you will probably be inundated by horsemen on arrival (a board shows official rates). Views over **Nilnag Lake** are a pleasant one-hour walk (or pony ride) through undulating forest. The walk to **Doodh Ganga** river takes 30 minutes through the meadows; you can link Doodh Ganga and Nilnag for a longer day-trek. There's a tourist reception centre and JKTDC have huts and cottages (or locals will offer you cheaper accommodation); there are a couple of very simple eateries near the jeep stop. Jeeps leave Srinagar at 1400 for Yusmarg, and return to Batmulla bus stand at 0800. Or you go via Charar-i-Sharief (last sumo from Yusmarg 1630).

## Pahalgam

Pahalgam ('village of shepherds') sits at an altitude of 2133 m and is the main base for the yearly 'Amarnath Yatra' pilgrimage, which sees thousands of Hindu pilgrims climbing to a cave housing an 'ice lingam'. During the Yatra season, which runs from June to August, it gets very busy. Situated at the convergence of two dramatic river valleys, the town is surrounded by conifer forests and pastures. Central Pahalgam is packed with shawl shops, eateries and hotels; there's a striking mosque and pleasant parks (one of which surrounds the Pahalgam Club). The pointy-roofed Mamleshwar Temple, across Kolahoi stream, is devoted to Shiva, There are many short walks you can take from Pahalgam and it is also a good base for longer treks to the Suru Valley and Kishtwar. A good day walk is the 12 km up the beautiful Lidder Valley to Aru; from there you can continue on to to Lidderwat (22 km) and Kolahoi Glacier (35 km). A wide selection of accommodation caters for all budgets; some of the nicer options are a couple of kilometres up the valley from the town centre.

## Sonamarg

Literally meaning the 'golden valley', Sonamarg gets its name from the yellow crocus blooms that carpet the valley each spring. At an altitude of 2740 m, it's the last major town in Kashmir before the Zoji La Pass – the gateway to Ladakh. Mountains and blankets of pine trees surround the village, and Indian tourists make pony trips to nearby Thajiwas glacier. It's also a start/end point for the Amarnath Yatra (www.amarnathyatra.org). The area is highly regarded for its trekking and fishing; trout were introduced here by the British in the 19th century. Treks to high-altitude Himalayan alpine lakes, including Vishnasar (4084 m), Krishnasar (3810 m), Satsar, Gadsar and Gangabal (3658 m), take 8 days; the trekking season runs from July-October. Accommodation is available through **JKTDC** (see page 150) in the summer months and there are several hotels.

## Kargil

On the bank of the River Suru, Kargil was an important trading post on two routes, from Srinagar to Leh, and to Gilgit and the lower Indus Valley. In 1999 the Pakistan army took control briefly of the heights surrounding the town before being forced to retreat. The town is considered grim by most visitors, however it is the main overnight stop on the Srinagar–Leh highway, and provides road access to the Zanskar Valley. With a largely Shi'ite population, Kargil has a very different vibe to both Srinagar and Leh. Centred around the busy main bazaar are cheap internet cafés (unreliable), ATMs, a tourist office and plenty of hotels. Walking up the valley slope, perpendicular to the main bazaar, takes you past old village houses to finish at Goma Kargil (4 km) for excellent views.

## Suru Valley

The motorable road extends from Kargil south to Padum through the picturesque and relatively green Suru Valley, where willow trees dot a wide valley floor flanked by mountain ridges. The valley's population have been Muslim since the 16th century, but some ancient Buddhist monuments remain. The first (and largest) settlement is **Sankoo**, 42 km from Kargil, which has a 7-m rock-carved relief of the Maitreay Buddha and the ruins of Kartse Khar (fort) 3 km distant. It's also a bus rest-spot and place to pick up last minute supplies. The road continues 15 km to **Purtikchay**, a lonely spot with just a scattering of houses but boasting stunning views down to the **Nun-Kun** peaks. A further 10 km on is **Panikhar**, set in an attractive agricultural bowl of the valley and where a glacier and Nun-Kun frame the horizon. From Panikar you can trek (a hard day) over the Lago La to Parkachik, or take pleasant strolls around the hamlet and the neighbouring village of Te-Suru. It is also possible to cross the mountains to Pahalgam in Kashmir from here, and you should be able to find local guides and ponies to make the one-week trek. The regular bus from Kargil terminates at **Parkachik**, after which is **Rangdum** and the Zanskar Valley. There are J&K Tourist Bungalows at each of the settlements along the Suru Valley (see Where to stay, page 165, for details) and for buses in/out see Transport, page 169.

---

## Zanskar → *For listings, see pages 161-170.*

Zanskar is a remote area of Ladakh contained by the Zanskar range to the north and the Himalaya to the south. It can be cut off by snow for as much as seven months each year when access is solely along the frozen Zanskar River. This isolation has helped Zanskar to preserve its cultural identity, though this is now being steadily eroded; a road is being currently being constructed to link Padum with Nimmu, on the Kargil–Leh highway. Traditional values include a strong belief in Buddhism, frugal use of resources and population control: values which for centuries have enabled Zanskaris to live in harmony with their hostile yet fragile environment. The long Zanskar Valley was 'opened' up for tourism even later than the rest of Ladakh and quickly became popular with trekkers. There is river rafting on the Zanskar River, with excursions as long as 11 days possible.

## Background

Zanskar became an administrative part of Ladakh under Senge Namgyal whose three sons became the rulers of Ladakh, Guge and Zanskar/Spiti. This arrangement collapsed after Ladakh's war with Tibet and the Zanskar royal house divided, one part administering Padum, the other Zangla. Under the Dogras, the rulers were reduced to puppets as the marauding army wreaked havoc on the villages, monasteries and population.

## Rangdum

Making a convenient night's stop between Kargil and the Zanskar Valley (130 km from Kargil, halfway to Padum), Rangum (3657 m) sits on a plateau of wild and incredible beauty. The isolated **Rangdum Monastery** perched on a hillock is particularly striking, and two Buddhist villages surrounded by chortens lie nearby.

## Padum

Padum, the capital, has a population of about 1300 of whom about 40% are Sunni Muslim. The present king of the Zanskar Valley, Punchok Dawa, who lives in his modest home in Padum, is held in high regard. The ruined old town, palace and fort are 700 m from the rather uninspiring new town, where transport, guesthouses and internet are found. Access is by the jeep road over the **Pensi La** (4401 m), generally open from mid-June to mid-October with a twice weekly bus service from Leh via Kargil (highly unreliable and crammed); the alternative method is to trek in. There is accommodation available (see Where to stay, page 166). For information about trekking in the Zanskar Valley, see page 186.

## Srinagar to Leh road

The road to Leh from Srinagar must be one of the most fascinating journeys in the world as it negotiates high passes and fragile mountainsides. There are dramatic scenic and cultural changes as you go from verdant Muslim Kashmir to ascetic Buddhist Ladakh. When there is

# Ladakh & Zanskar

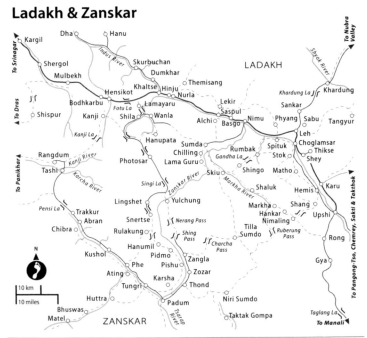

political unrest in Kashmir, the route, which runs very close to the Line of Control, may be closed to travellers. For more details about the monasteries and villages along the way. The alternative route to Leh from Manali is equally fascinating, see page 116.

After passing through **Sonamarg** (see page 158), you reach the pass of **Zoji La** (3528 m). The pass is slippery after rains and usually closed by snow during winter months (November to April). From Zoji La the road descends to **Minamarg meadow** and **Dras** (3230 m). The winter temperatures have been known to go down to -50°C, and heavy snow and strong winds cut off the town. Dras has a spectacular setting and a scruffy centre with restaurants and shops; there's a TIC and decent enough J&K bungalows. The broad Kargil basin and its wide terraces are separated from the Mulbekh Valley by the 12-km-long **Wakha Gorge**.

From Kargil (see page 159) the road continues 30 km to **Shargol** – the cultural boundary between Muslim and Buddhist areas, with a very ambient very tiny monastery located down a side-road – and then after another 10 km reaches **Mulbek**, a pretty village with a large (9 m) ancient Maitreya Buddha relief fronted by a gompa on the roadside. The ruins of Mulbek Khar (fort) sit atop a stalk of cliff next to two small gompas, a steep climb that affords fabulous views (see Where to stay, page 166). Shortly after Mulbek is its larger sister village of Wahka, then the road crosses **Namika La**, at 3720 m (known as the 'Pillar in the Sky'). There is a tourist bungalow in tiny **Haniskut**, set in a pretty river valley marred by roads and pylons, where very ruined fort lies on the northern side of the valley. The road then climbs to **Fotu La** at 4093 m, the highest pass on the route. From here you can catch sight of the monastery at Lamayuru. The road does a series of loops to descend to the ramshackle village of **Khaltse** with a couple of garden-restaurants, shops and lodges, where it meets the milky green Indus River.

**Lamayuru**, 10 km from Khaltse, with a famous monastery and spectacular landscapes, is worth a long lunch break or overnight stop (see page 182). There is a comfortable eco-camp in **Uletokpo**, just by the highway (see Where to stay, page 191). From Uletokpo village a 6-km track leads to dramatic **Rizong**, with a monastery and nunnery, which may accommodate visitors. **Saspol** village marks the wide valley from which you can reach **Alchi** by taking a branch road across the Indus after passing some caves. **Lekir** (see page 180) is off the main road, 8 km after Saspol.

Further along the road you catch sight of the ruins of **Basgo** before it crosses the Chargyal Thang plain with *chortens* and *mani* walls and enters **Nimmu**. The road rejoins the Indus Valley and rises to a bare plateau to give you the first glimpse of Leh, 30 km away. **Phyang** is down a side valley and finally **Spituk** is reached.

## Kashmir Valley listings

*For hotel and restaurant price codes and other relevant information, see pages 12-14.*

### ⬤ Where to stay

**Jammu** *p150*
**$$$$-$$$ Hari Niwas Palace**, Palace Rd, T0191-254 3303, www.hariniwaspalace.com. 40 a/c rooms and suites in a heritage property with elegant bar and classy restaurant. Meals and drinks can be enjoyed on the immaculate lawns, with a sweeping view. The cliff-top location next to Amar Mahal is the chief attraction. Palace Mews rooms (Rs 3600) give you a chance to enjoy the ambiance but are very average, below ground level in side wing. The Royal Deluxe and Semi Suites are the most attractive, huge and with wonderful views from either front or back. Heated pool and health club.
**$$$ Asia Jammu-Tawi**, Nehru Market, north of town, T0191-243 5757, www.asia hotelsjammu.com. The 44 rooms are beginning to show their age a little, but this

Jammu stalwart has an excellent Chinese restaurant, bar and a clean pool. Close to the airport.

**$$$ KC Residency**, Vir Marg, T0191-252 0770, www.kcresidency.com. Rising from the heart of Jammu, the KC tower is a good place to stay if you have a day or so to check out the city. There are 61 good-quality a/c rooms and health club specializing in Ayurvedic massage, all extraordinarily crowned by a superb, multi-cuisine revolving restaurant.

**$$-$ Tourist Reception Centre**, AKA Hotel Jammu Residency, Vir Marg, T0191-257 9554. Set back from the main road, the TRC has 173 rooms with bath ranging in price and quality arranged around well-kept gardens, price is dictated by size and views. The best accommodation is in Blocks NA and A. The restaurant has a very good reputation, in particular for its Kashmiri food, and there's a bar.

**$ Kranti Hotel**, near the railway station, T0191-247 0525. One of the better budget hotels in the railway area with 45 clean rooms with attached bath and a restaurant.

### Vaishno Devi *p151*

**$$$ Asia Vaishnodevi**, Katra, T01991-232061, www.asiavaishnodevi.in. 37 a/c rooms, restaurant, transport to Banganga.

**$ Dormitories**, at the halfway point to Vaishno Devi. Simple rooms provide sheets.

**$ Prem**, Main Bazar, Katra, T01991-232014. Rooms with hot water and a fire, adequate.

**$ Tourist Bungalow**, Katra, T01991-232009. 42 basic but clean rooms.

### Srinagar *p152, map p152*

The room costs quoted reflect peak-season prices (Mar-Aug); if you go in the winter, you can expect to get a hefty discount. Be prepared to haggle.

**$$$$ The Lalit Grand Palace**, Gupkar Rd, a few kilometres outside the city, T0194-250 1001, www.thelalit.com. This former palace was once the residence of Kashmir's last maharajah, Hari Singh. Situated on a hillside overlooking Dal Lake, it has been tastefully kitted out with antiques befitting its history, including India's largest handmade carpet. One wing houses enormous, classically styled suites, while the other has 70 recently refurbished modern rooms. The restaurant, bar and health club are open to non-guests. It's a good place to go on a summer evening for the al fresco buffet.

**$$$$ Vivanta by Taj – Dal View**, Kralsangri Hill, Brein, T0194-246 1111, www.vivantaby taj.com. All-out luxury in this sprawling elegant resort, atop a peak with sublime Dal Lake views. Rooms are chic without being over-the-top, with Kashmiri details and warm colours. 24-hr fitness suite, fantastic restaurants (speciality Sichuan), spa to open soon (check website). Gorgeous place, worth going for a meal if you can't stay here.

**$$$$-$$$ Hotel Broadway**, Maulana Azad Rd, T0194-245 9001, www.hotelbroadway. com. One of Srinagar's oldest and best-known hotels, the **Broadway**'s original 1970s interior has been well maintained. With lots of wood panelling, rooms can be a little dark. The staff are professional and polite, while the comfortable, centrally heated rooms, Wi-Fi service and city location make it popular with business travellers and journalists. It houses one of the city's few drinking spots, has an informal cinema and is attached to the city's 1st coffee shop, **Café Arabica**. Book online for discounts.

**$$$ Dar-Es-Salam**, Nandpora, Rainawari, T0194-242 7803, T(0)9810-899584, www. hoteldaressalam.com. This white Art Deco ex-stately home is the only hotel on Nagin Lake, with an established garden and a sweep of lawn onto the shore overlooking houseboats. Mounted heads over the entrance set the colonial tone, while period furnishings in the 2 lounges include brass antique pots and a Raj-era tiger's head. An enclosed balcony surveys the lake. Modernized rooms (and **$$$$** suites), central heating, white duvets, new floors, meals available in the (formal) dining room.

**$$$-$$ Hotel Akbar**, Dalgate, Gate No 1, T0194-250 0507, www.hotelakbar.com.

Smart, clean hotel with 36 spacious rooms arranged around a pretty lawn with rose arbours. attractive lobby and restaurant, 8 of the rooms have a balcony and it's a great location on the lakeside. Souvenir shop and travel desk.

**$$ Ahdoos**, Residency Rd, T0194-247 2593, www.ahdooshotel.com. A Srinagar institution, **Ahdoos** backs onto the Jhelum river and is well situated for the city's classiest handicraft and shawl shops. The deluxe rooms are huge with new TVs, the standard rooms are not much smaller and all have marble bathtubs. Backside rooms have river views. It's a little old-fashioned, however, and some rooms could do with a revamp. But a good choice for those who want to get a feel of the city. Staff are friendly and the restaurant is renowned among locals for its Kashmiri (Wazwan) food, the chicken patties, and their tea.

**$$ Hotel Madhuban**, Gagribal Rd, T0194-245 3800, www.hotelmadhuban-kashmir.net. The **Madhuban** has bags of character, with a lot of wood going on in its homely rooms. The restaurant has an attractive veranda where guests can sit out in the summer and there is a small, but well-kept garden.

**$$ Hotel Wali Sons**, Boulevard Lane No 1, T0194-250 0345, www.walisonshotel.com. A smart red-brick building, complemented by white window-frames and green roof, containing 17 immaculate spacious rooms. Varying configurations sleep 2-4 persons, white duvets, flatscreen TV, fan, seating, clean carpets and bathrooms with modern fixtures and decor. It's a central location, and a couple of public balconies give views of Shankaracharya Hill. Free use of computer, 24-hr electricity (generator), respectful staff.

**$ Swiss Hotel**, Old Gagribal Rd, T0194-2472766, www.swisshotelkashmir.com. The **Swiss** has 35 clean rooms with attached bath and running hot water (morning and evening) that are given at greatly discounted rates to foreign tourists. The attractive red-painted old house has the best-value budget rooms in town. The new

annex with plate-glass windows has large well-maintained rooms, prices increase as you go up to the 3rd floor. Look at a few rooms, as all washrooms are uniquely decorated, some have wood panelling, others wallpaper, and some are simply enormous. There's a big front garden. One of the few hotels with a stated environmental policy, owner Rouf makes a point of using energy efficient lighting. Recommended.

**$ John Friends Guesthouse**, Pedestrian Mall Rd (opposite Ghat No.1), Dalgate, T0194-245 8342, johna_mondoo@yahoo.com. Set back from Dal Lake, along wooden walkways and gangplanks, is this family guesthouse with 9 rooms across 2 buildings. Charming and quiet flowery garden with seating, surrounded by poplars and willows, with fairy lights at night. Decent budget rooms, some with attached bathroom and TV, shared bathroom very clean, 24-hr hot water, cheap rates. Fascinating snapshot into life on the lake. Free pick-up service.

**$** There's a backpacker-conscious enclave on by the lake at Dalgate, where small and simple guesthouses include **Gulam Junaid** and **Noor Guesthouse**, which has a little garden and internet café at the front, balconies and character. Both cost Rs 250-500.

## Houseboats

Houseboats are peculiar to Srinagar and can be seen moored along the shores of Dal Lake, the quieter and distant Nagin Lake and along the busy Jhelum River. They were originally thought up by the British as a ruse to get around the law that foreigners could not buy land in the state: being in the water, the boats didn't technically count as property.

In the valley's heyday the boats were well kept and delightfully cosy; today some are still lavishly decorated with antiques and traditional Kashmiri handicrafts, but others have become distinctly shabby. Still mostly family-run, they usually include all meals and come in 5 categories: deluxe, A, B, C and D. The tariff for each category is given by the

Houseboat Owners Association, T0194-245 0326, www.houseboatowners.org, through whom you can also make bookings.

Most tourists enjoy their houseboat holidays, however a significant number complain of being ripped off in various ways. It's better to spend extra on a boat with a good reputation than to go for a bargain that is probably too good to be true.

The following all quote **$$$-$$**, but prices are generally negotiable if you go in person. **Athena Houseboats**, opposite Hotel Duke, Dal Lake, T0194-476957. One of the larger houseboat operators with voluminous boats that can comfortably sleep larger groups. Excellent service, with real integrity: discourages hawkers and tries to support only legitimate retail and onward tourism. **Butt's Clermont Houseboats**, west side of Dal Lake, T0194-242 0325, www.butts clermonthouseboat.com. Moored by Naseem Bagh, "Garden of Breezes", shaded by chinar trees by a wall built by Emperor Akbar. Far from the densely packed south side of Dal Lake, four cream painted boats are moored side-on to the shore. Crewelwork on fabrics, carved cedar panels, rosewood tables and a view of Hazratbal mosque. In operation since 1940, they are now on guestbook No.16. Former guests include Lord Mountbatten, George Harrison, PG Wodehouse, Ravi Shankar and Michael Palin. **Gurkha Houseboats**, Nagin Lake, T0194-242 1001, www.nivalink.com/gurkha. The Gurkha group are renowned for their comfortable rooms and stylish boats on peaceful Nagin Lake. Good service and food. **Zaffer Houseboats**, on Nagin Lake, T01954-250 0507, www.zafferhouseboats.com. Deluxe boats with a long history, walnut panelled walls, single-piece walnut tables, old writing desks, backed onto the lake which means front terrace is delightful place to sit. Peaceful and quiet despite the *sikhara* salesmen, excellent food, courteous staff and interesting owners.

## Gulmarg *p157*

As with Srinagar, prices can be negotiated in the winter months, particularly for longer stays.

**$$$$ Khyber Himalayan Resort & Spa**, T01954-254666, www.khyberhotels.com. Absolute luxury in a new resort with an Ayurvedic spa, gym, heated pool, and amazing restaurants. Rooms beautifully furnished with teak floors, silk carpets, walnut carving and rich Kashmiri fabrics. State-of-the-art bathrooms, huge windows make the most of views. Also four cottages, some with own pool.

**$$$ Hotel Highlands Park**, T01954-254430, www.hotelhighlandspark.com. Oozing with old-world charm, rooms and suites are decorated with Kashmiri woodcraft and rugs. Renowned for its atmosphere – the best bar in Gulmarg is here, a large yet cosy lounge, straight out of the 1930s – it's a wonderful place to unwind after a hard day on the slopes. Rooms have *bukharis* (wood stoves) to keep you warm and electric blankets are available on request. Recommended.

**$$$-$$ Nedou's Hotel**, T01954-254428, www.nedoushotel.com. The oldest hotel in Gulmarg, the **Nedous** has the same cosy colonial charm as **Highlands Park**. Its rooms and suites are comfortingly old-fashioned, with spotless bathrooms. The food isn't flash, but it's home-cooked, wholesome and delicious.

**$$ Hotel Yemberzal**, T01954-254523, www.yemberzalhotel.com. Rooms are on the small side, but at least this means they heat up quickly and the bathrooms has 24-hr running hot water. If you ask for the corner room, you can enjoy a panoramic view of the mountains. The restaurant is very good and the management are extremely helpful. It's a 10-min walk to the lifts, but there's a taxi stand next door if you feel lazy. **$$-$ JK Tourism Huts**, T(0)9419-488181. These comfortable huts come with 1-2 bedrooms, a living room and kitchen. Very good value and close to the drag-lift.

**\$\$-\$ Green Heights**, T01954-254404. This wood-built hotel is slightly shabby, but the quirky staff more than compensate, making this a budget choice with character. The decent-sized rooms come with wood stoves and if you ask nicely, you might get a hot-water bottle. Close to the gondola.

## Yusmarg *p158*
**\$ J&KTDC Huts**, T(0)9797-292001, www.jk tourism.org. Dotted around the centre of Yusmarg's meadow, connected by flagged paths, these comfortable huts are well-maintained and fresh, if simple. There are various configurations, some with pine walls, others whitewashed with pretty bedspreads, so check them all out. Basic doubles cost Rs 1000, 30% discount low-season.

## Pahalgam *p158*
**\$\$\$\$ Pahalgam Hotel**, T01936-243252, www.pahalgamhotel.com. Upper-end Raj-era hotel dating back to 1931, 4 buildings, with 36 of 40 rooms enjoying splendid views of forested peaks across the River Lidder. Rooms are tastefully decorated, centrally heated, very spacious, some have been recently renovated but all are pleasing (18 suites). Swimming pool in summer. Prices include all meals. Excellent shop (see Shopping, page 168).
**\$\$-\$ Himalaya House**, 3km from the bus stand, 1km from Laripora village, T(0)9411-9045021, gulzarhakeem@hotmail.com. A cosy hotel on the river with an enchanting island garden and a restaurant of repute. All rooms with attached bath and hot water some with bathtub and balcony, crewelwork curtains and bedspreads. Free Wi-Fi. The hotel is linked to a recommended trekking company, see What to do. Cheaper older rooms in house across laneway all with TV and attached bath.
**\$\$-\$ Brown Palace**, T01936-243255, www.brownpalace.in. Another decent budget option. All rooms have attached bath with hot water, wood panelling abounds, the lounge has bark walls and a fire, 2 newer bungalows at rear.

## Sonmarg *p158*
**\$\$-\$ Snowland**, on the edge of town. This is a good choice, well managed with cottage-style rooms. Those at the back are quieter and have great mountain views; veg restaurant is merely average.

## Kargil *p159*
Hotels are quite expensive, but bargaining is expected and will secure a discount. On Hospital Rd, running uphill off the Main Bazaar, there's a further cluster of budget hotels (not listed here). Restaurants all serve meat; for vegetarian food (hard to find) look for signs advertising Punjabi meals.
**\$\$\$-\$ Green Land**, signed down an alley off Main Bazaar, T01985-232324, www. hotelgreenlandkargil.com. A popular and well-kept place, it's not cheap but prices fairly reflect the standard of the rooms. Old block doubles Rs 1000, new block (much preferable) with a range of rooms including deluxe standard. Open all year round.
**\$\$-\$ PC Palace**, off Main Bazaar, T01985-202189, pcpalace@live.inpcpalace@live.in. Smart white building with well-appointed rooms with flatscreen TV, fawn carpets, blankets and curtains, fancy lights and good bathrooms (Rs 1500). Slightly smaller, darker rooms are at the rear, but they are also cheaper and quieter.
**\$ J&K Tourist Bungalow**, T01985-232266, behind the bus station, it's a bargain at Rs 200 per room, but obviously rather worn and often booked up. The tourist office is adjacent.
**\$ Tourist Marjina**, off Main Bazaar, T09419-831517. An aging pink and blue-painted building that is being encircled by high new hotels, making dark rooms even darker. It's a bearable budget option though, with reliable hot showers, doubles Rs 500-600.

## Suru Valley *p159*
J&K Tourist Bungalows, costing from Rs150-200 per person, are found in villages along the Suru Valley. Sankoo also has plenty of shops and several dhabas, while the Tourist Bungalow in Panikhar enjoys remarkable

views of Nun and Kun, but is isolated – take supplies with you. In Panikhar, the **Dak Bungalow** has 3 basic gloomy rooms and a better choice is **Khayoul Hotel**, T(0)9469-293976, with 2 sunny rooms in a family house, decked with cheerful fabrics and plants, Rs 150 per person, meals Rs 50-70.

### Padum *p160*

Places to stay are limited, but there is a choice of about 4 simple lodges. There is also a **tourist complex** with basic rooms and meals; you can camp there.
**$ Ibex**, has the best rooms in town, a decent restaurant, and a courtyard garden.

### Mulbek *p161*

**$ Karzoo Guesthouse**, T(0)941-9880463. In an impressive old Ladakhi building, with restaurant and camping space, conveniently located for walking to the monastery; all rooms share clean bathrooms, and the family are very hospitable. There are also a couple of other simple guesthouses and a **J&K Tourist Bungalow**. In Wakha, the sister village 3 km on the road towards Leh, there are a few *dhabas* and shops.

## 🍴 Restaurants

### Jammu *p150*

The best eateries tend to be found in the upmarket hotels. However, there are some good snack places dotted around town, which can be fun to check out.
**$$-$ Smokin' Joes Pizza**, Bahu Plaza, near the railway station. Very acceptable veg and non-veg pizza and pasta, but strictly no pork. Take away and home delivery also available.
**$$-$ Sagar Ratna**, Hotel Premier, opposite KC Plaza, Residency Rd. Vegetarian delights, both south and north Indian plus Chinese, at reasonable prices for smart-casual surrounds (a/c), and generous portions. TV blares.
**$ Amritsarian di Hatti**, Raghunath Bazar. Good and popular vegetarian, also sells sweets.

### Vaishno Devi *p151*

Excellent vegetarian food is available – curd and *paneer* (curd cheese) dishes are especially good. For non-*dhaba* food try the 2 vegetarian fast food places on the main street. Both are clean and good. No alcohol.

### Srinagar *p152, map p152*

While Kashmiris generally prefer to eat at home, being a tourist town, Srinagar has its fair share of good restaurants catering for all tastes. For a special treat, do the buffet at the Lalit Grand or a meal at the Taj Vivanta (with killer views).There are 3 wineshops on the left side of the ground floor of the Hotel Heemal building on the Boulevard.

Traditional Kashmiri food is centred around meat, with mutton generally being the favoured flesh. The traditional 36-course banquet served at weddings is known as a *wazwan* and you will find several of its signature dishes on the menu in restaurants. *Yakhnee* is a delicious mutton stew cooked in a spiced curd sauce. *Goshtabas* and *rishtas* are meatballs made from pounded (not ground) meat, which makes a big difference in consistency. *Goshtabas* come in a curd sauce; *rishtas* in red sauce. *Roganjosh* is made with chicken or mutton and is curd based, owing its red colour to red Kashmiri chilies. *Hakh* is the Kashmiri version of spinach and *nadroo* are lotuses, usually served in a *yakhnee* sauce.
**$$ Char Chinar**, Boulevard Rd, near Brein village. You'll need to take a *shikara* to get to this houseboat restaurant, moored on a tiny island in Dal Lake. Named after the 4 giant *chinar* trees that grow there, the food is average, but it's a perfect place to sit in peace with a good book on a sunny day.
**$$ Lhasa**, Boulevard Lane No 2. Daily 1200-2230. Enjoy the lovely back garden with rose bushes and well-spaced tables, each with its own awning. The central fountain is defunct, but old houses surround. The vaguely Tibetan-themed indoor area has fish-tanks and is cosy on a cold night. They serve a varied menu of excellent Chinese, Tibetan, and Indian non-veg and veg food.

**$$ Mughal Darbar**, Residency Rd. Popular with middle-class locals, the cosy Mughal Darbar offers multi-cuisine fare, specializing in Kashmiri *wazwan*. It's located on the 1st floor, up the stairs.

**$$ Shamyana**, Boulevard Rd, www.shamyana.net. Daily 1230-2230. Consistently highly rated by locals and popular with middle-class customers, this restaurant serves high quality Chinese and Indian food (meat and veg, good tikka). The calm front section is separated from a "funkier" back room by wooden lattices.

**$$ Tao Café**, Residency Rd. A popular hangout with local journalists, politicians and artists, the **Tao** serves decent Kashmiri and Chinese food, as well as Tibetan *momos*, fish, and various snacks. Its attractive gardens make it a good summer spot.

**$$-$ Café Robusta**, Maulana Azad Rd, near Polo View. Competes with nearby **Café Arabica** (in the Broadway Hotel) to attract Srinagar's latte lovers. Aside from pizza, kebabs and cake, you can also sample a *shisha* (Middle Eastern water pipe) with a range of flavoured tobaccos on offer. Bring your laptop and make use of the Wi-Fi

**$ Krishna Dhaba**, Durga Nag Rd. Note that the restaurant has a break-time 1600-1900. A haven for vegetarians in a city of meat-eaters, the Krishna's canteen environment gets the thumbs-up from fastidious Indian tourists for its cleanliness and delicious pure veg fare – the best in town.

**$ Shakti Sweets** and **Modern Sweets**, Residency Rd. If you are invited to a Kashmiri home, a box of *burfi* will go down well as a gift. Both serve great snack food at rock-bottom prices, such as *channa bhatura* and *masala dosa*, as well as very popular chowmein.

### Gulmarg *p157*
Most hotels serve their own food but some close their kitchens in low season. In the bazar there is a row of *dhabas* serving a wide variety of Indian vegetarian food including *thalis*, *dosas* and *punjabi*. Outside seating.

**$$ Sahara Hotel**, next to Yemberzal Hotel. Well worth venturing out in the cold for. The owner spent 15 years working as a chef in Saudi Arabia, Japan and China, so has a wide repertoire. If you need a break from Indian food, the continental choice here is good, especially the chicken champion.

**$ Lala's**, close to the JK Tourism Huts (see Where to stay, page 164). Good, honest home-cooked food.

### Pahalgam *p158*
**$$$-$ Trout Beat** restaurant and the welcoming **Café Log Inn**, both at the Pahalgam Hotel, serve the same menu of vegetarian meals and snacks and, of course, fish.

**$ Nathu's Rasoi**. You can't miss this self-service fast-food vegetarian restaurant near the bus stand, which serves excellent North/South Indian and Chinese dishes – but most famed for its South Indian, the best in Kashmir. Open 0800-2230.

## ⊛ Festivals

### Srinagar *p152, map p152*
**Apr Tulip Festival**, Indira Gandhi Memorial Tulip Garden. 1st 2 weeks of Apr, with over 1 million blooms.

## ◉ Shopping

### Jammu *p150*
**J&K Arts Emporium**, next to J&K Tourism, Residency Rd. Mon-Sat 1000-2000. Good selection, cheap.

### Srinagar *p152, map p152*
If you arrived in Srinagar without your thermals or you're craving a bar of chocolate, a bowl of cornflakes, marmite on toast or just about any other Western goods, then look no further than **Harker's Pick 'n' Choose Supermarket** on Residency Rd, for all your expat needs.

**Gulshan Bookstore**, a few mins' walk from Residency Rd, towards Lal Chowk. Here you will find all manner of books about Kashmir, some of them extremely rare. If you are interested in the political situation, it's an excellent place for books on Kashmir's history. **Mahatta's Photographic Store**, next to Suffering Moses. Mon-Sat 1030-1830. Worth stopping by for its old-world charm, its history and above all for the priceless visual memory of old Srinagar it houses. Founded in 1918, this was once the place to have your portrait taken and was patronized by the elite of the day. The walls are lined with large prints of the city, taken up in the 1930s and 1940s. They are not for sale, but they have produced a booklet, 'Srinagar Views 1934-1965' for Rs 300, and sell black and white postcards.

## Handicrafts

There are plenty of handicraft shops, particularly around Dal Lake and Dalgate, but beware of touts who are on commission. Much of what is sold is not even Kashmiri: inferior quality papier mâché products from Bihar and shawls from Amritsar have flooded the market and are bought merrily by tourists who don't know the difference.

For a real understanding of Kashmiri craftwork and to support the local industry, call into any of the quality shops on **Polo View** or the **Bund**. The prices may seem high, but the quality and authenticity are guaranteed and shop-keepers do not usually pay commission.

**Asia Crafts**, next to Suffering Moses (see below). Very fine embroidery and genuine Kashmiri carpets, but much of its stock is now sold in New Delhi.

**Habib Asian Carpets**, Zaldagar Chowk, Downtown, T0194-247 8640. If you are serious about buying a genuine Kashmiri carpet, this is one of the few companies that has its workshop in the city.

**Heritage Woodcrafts**, on the way to Shalimar gardens. It's worth making the trip here for the carved walnut wood. Stuffed with fine pieces including some antiques, the authenticity of the work is guaranteed by the on-site workshop.

**Kashmir Government Arts Emporium**, the Bund. Mon-Sat 1000-1800, closed for noon prayers. Large showroom of fixed-price Kasmiri goods: rugs, papier mâché, crewel-work, furniture and more. In the old British Residency, a beautifully restored building with heritage gardens (and moth-eaten tigers lurking among the wares).

**Sadiq's Handicrafts**, next to Tao Café (see Restaurants, page 167). Owned by the same family as **Suffering Moses** and is almost as much a museum as a shop; many of the antique treasures are not for sale and Mr Sadiq, a man passionate about art, will happily explain their history to you. Prices in both shops are fixed and there is no pressure to buy.

**Suffering Moses**, next to Mughal Darbar restaurant (see Restaurants, page 167). Famous for its exquisite papier mâché goods. The curious name was apparently awarded to the owner's father by the British, who were impressed by the amount of suffering that went into each work. Really beautiful top-quality stock; they can ship overseas.

## Pahalgam p158

**Almirah Books etc**, at Pahalgam Hotel. An OK book selection and some tasteful souvenirs. Also sell "Shepherd's Craft" goods – brightly decorated bags/purses, embellished with the traditional designs of the Bakkarwala nomadic shepherds (who embroider saddlebags and hats with colourful threads).

**Himalayan Products**, T(0)941 9045420, www.himalyancheese.com. Fair-trade cheesemakers, making organic Gouda and local-style Kelari, deep-fried and flavoured with chilli.

## ◑ What to do

## Pahalgam p158

**Himalaya Fun N' Tours**, www.himalaya funandtours.com. Have 25 years trekking experience, 1-10 day circular treks from Pahalgam or even 21-days to Leh via Suru and Zanskar valleys (US$50 per person per day, includes all meals, equipment, ponies, guides) and can also arrange white water rafting along the Lidder River (best May-Jul).

### Zanskar *p159*

Most agents in Leh can arrange trekking expeditions to the Zanskar Valley.
**Aquaterra Adventures**, www.aquaterra.in. Have 12-day rafting trips down the Zanskar River each Aug.
**Ibex Expeditions**, in Delhi organizes trekking and rafting in Zanskar. See page 55.

## ⊖ Transport

### Jammu *p150*

**Air** Rambagh Airport, 6 km. Transport to town: taxis (Rs 200) and auto-rickshaws. Air India, flies to **Delhi** and **Srinagar** daily; **Leh** (Thu, Sat). Jet Konnect, to **Delhi** and **Srinagar** daily. Also **Spicejet**, twice daily flights to Delhi, and GoAir, www.goair.in.
**Bus** J&KSRTC, TRC, Vir Marg, T0191-257 9554 (1000-1700), general bus stand, T0191-257 7475 (0400-2000). To **Amritsar** (6 hrs) at least hourly via **Pathankot** (3 hrs); direct buses to **Srinagar** (9 hrs), **Katra** (for Vaishno Devi), and **Kishtwar**. To **Delhi** (12 hrs), hourly. **Srinagar** buses also leave from the railway station, usually 0600-0700.
**Jeep** Sumos to **Srinagar** leaving early morning (Rs 500, 8-9 hrs), to **Katra** from the station private jeeps cost Rs 900 (Rs 1200 a/c).
**Train** 5 km from centre; allow at least 30 mins by auto. Enquiries T0191-245 3027. Daily to **Delhi** (OD): *Jammu Tawi Mail 14034*, 1615, 14¼ hrs; *Jammu All Exp 12414*, 1815, 10½ hrs*Jat Muri Exp 18110*, 1430, 14 hrs;. **Delhi** (ND): *Jammu Tawi Indore Malwa Exp 12920*, 0900, 10½ hrs; *Duronto Exp 12266*, Mon, Wed, Sat 1920, 9 hrs. **Kolkata** daily: *Sealdah Exp 13152*, 1855, 45 hrs.

### Vaishno Devi *p151*

Buses and taxis leave from the general bus stand, Jammu (or the railway station at peak season) and go to **Katra** (48 km); Rs 30, a/c Rs 60; taxi Rs 500 for 4.

### Srinagar *p152, map p152*

**Air** Srinagar Airport, 14 km south, T0194-230 3000. Taxi to town: Rs 500. Stringent security checks on roads plus 2 hrs' check-in at airport. Tight on hand luggage but you can generally get away with a laptop. Daily flights to **Delhi** and **Mumbai** with: Air India, JetKonnect, Spicejet, GoAir. To **Leh** with Air India and JetKonnect, daily.
**Bus** Srinagar is on NH1A linked to the rest of India by 'all-weather' roads, through superb scenery. To **Jammu** (293 km), by a narrow mountain road, often full of lorries and military convoys, takes 9-10 hrs; few stops for food.
J&KSRTC, TRC, Srinagar, T0194-245 5107. Summer 0600-1800, winter 0700-1700.
Bus to **Kargil** (alternate days in summer), **Leh** (434 km). **Gulmarg**, daily bus at 0800 in ski season from Tourist Reception Centre, returning in the evening. Taxis charge around Rs 2000 for same-day return. Or take J&KSRTC bus to **Tangmarg**, 8 km before Gulmarg and take a *sumo* from there, Rs 20. To **Pahalgam** at 0830 (2-3 hrs).
**Jeep**Jeeps are faster than the bus and leave when full from various locations near Dalgate. To **Jammu**, 8-9 hrs, Rs 500.
**Train** The most nearest railhead is Jammu Tawi with coach (12 hrs) and taxi transfer (8-9 hrs). Govt TRC, 0700-1900. T0191-243 1582 for reservation of 2nd-class sleeper and a/c only. Summer 0830-1900, winter 1000-1800. Connections with several cities including **Guwahati**, **Kolkata**, **Mumbai**, **Chennai** and **Delhi**.

### Kargil *p159*

**Bus** To **Leh** at 0430 (Rs 350, 7 hours); to **Srinagar** at 2230-2300, some are deluxe (Rs 300-400, 9 hrs). Buses to the Suru Valley leave from the crossroads of Main Bazaar and Lal Chowk, to **Panikhar** daily at 0700 (Rs 70, 4 hrs; return bus at 0600, 0800 and 1100.) and to **Parkachik** at 1130 on alternate days (5 hrs, returning at 0700). Bus booking counter T01985-232066.

**Jeep** Shared jeeps to Srinagar leave from taxi stand on Lal Chowk, connected to the bus station by an alleyway, at 0400-0600 and 1300-1500 (Rs 750, 6 hrs). Shared taxi to Leh (Rs 800, 7 hrs).

## ❶ Directory

**Jammu** *p150*
**Banks** State Bank of India, Hari Market, among several. **Medical services** Hospital: T0191-254 7637.

**Srinagar** *p152, map p152*
**Useful contacts** Ambulance: T0194-247 4591. Fire: T0194-247 2222. Police: T100. Foreigners' Registration Office: Supt of Police, Residency Rd. 1000-1600.

# Ladakh

The mountains of Ladakh – literally 'many passes' – may not be as typically spectacular as some parts of the high Himalaya for, as even the valleys are at an altitude of 3500 m, the summits are only 3000 m higher. Because it is desert there is little snow on them and they look like big brown hills, dry and dusty, with clusters of willows and desert roses along the streams. Yet bright blue skies are an almost constant feature, as the monsoon rains do not reach here, and the contrast with the dramatic landscape creates a beautiful and heavenly effect. For thousands of visitors Ladakh is a completely magical place, remote and relatively unspoilt, with delightful, gentle, ungrasping people.

## Arriving in Ladakh

### Getting there and around
**Inner Line Permits** for the Nubra Valley, Dha-Hanu, Tso-moriri and Pangong Tso cost Rs 50 per person per day (for each area; Dha-Hanu is more expensive, at Rs 300 per person for an enrolment fee card, then Rs 70 per person per day) for a maximum of seven days in each place, while trekkers in the Hemis High Altitude Park must pay Rs 25 per day. Permits are available from the District Commissioner's office in Leh (see Directory, page 196), but all trekking/travel agents can arrange them for you – a much easier option. Allow at least half a day for an agent to obtain a permit, given only for groups of two or more. Permits are not extendable, but can be post-dated. Many people opt for permits covering all restricted areas. As a matter of course you should carry your passport with you since Ladakh is a sensitive border region. It's also worth carrying multiple photocopies of your passport and permits, as some checkpoints demand a copy. **Note** Given the darkness of many buildings even at midday it is worth taking a torch wherever you go; a must at night.
▸ *See Transport, page 195.*

### Climate
The temperature can drop to -30°C in Leh and Kargil and -50°C in Dras, remaining sub-zero from December to February. Yet on clear sunny days in the summer, it can be scorching hot and you can easily get sunburnt; take plenty of sun cream. Ladakh lies beyond the monsoon line so rainfall is only 50 mm annually and there are even occasional dust storms.

## Leh → *For listings, see pages 188-196.*

Mysterious dust-covered Leh sits in a fertile side valley of the Indus, about 10 km from the river. Encircled by stark awe-inspiring mountains with the cold desert beyond, it is the nearest experience to Tibet in India. The old Palace sits precariously on the hill to the north and looms over Leh. The wide Main Bazar Street (circa 1840s), which once accommodated caravans, has a colourful vegetable market where unpushy Ladakhi women sell local produce on the street side while they knit or chat. Makeshift craft and jewellery stalls line parts of Fort Road to the east to attract summer visitors along with Kashmiri shopkeepers who have come in search of greener pastures. The Old Town, mainly to the east of the Main Street, with its maze of narrow lanes, sits on the hillside below the palace and is worth exploring.

### Arriving in Leh

**Getting there** For seven to eight months in the year Leh is cut off by snow and the sole link with the outside world is by air. Tickets are in high demand so it is essential to book well ahead (on the internet). From mid-June to the end of September (weather permitting) the Manali-Leh highway opens to traffic, bringing travellers to the New Bus Stand south of town. Taxis wait at both the airport and bus stand to take you to town.

**Getting around** Many hotels are within a few minutes' walk of the Main Bazar Street around which Leh's activities are concentrated. All the places of interest in Leh itself can also be tackled on foot by most visitors though those arriving by air or from Manali are urged to acclimatize for 48 hours before exerting themselves. For visiting monasteries and spots out of town arrange a jeep or taxi, although there are some buses and hitchhiking is possible. ▶ *See Transport, page 195.*

**Tourist information** J&K Tourism ① *2 km south on Airport Rd, T01982-252297, www.jktourism.org; or try the more convenient office on Fort Rd, T01982-253462, 1000-1600.*

### Background

The city developed as a trading post and market, attracting a wide variety of merchants – from Yarkand, Kashgar, Kashmir, Tibet and North India. Tea, salt, household articles, wool and semi-precious stones were all traded in the market. Buddhism travelled along the Silk Road and the Kashmir and Ladakh feeder, which has also seen the passage of soldiers, explorers and pilgrims, forerunners of the tourists who today contribute most to the urban economy.

### Places in Leh

Dun-coloured **Leh Palace** ① *sunrise to sunset, Rs 100,* has been described as a miniature version of Lhasa's Potala Palace. Built in the mid-16th century, the palace was partly in ruins by the 19th century. It has nine storeys, sloping buttresses and projecting wooden

# 1 Leh Orientation

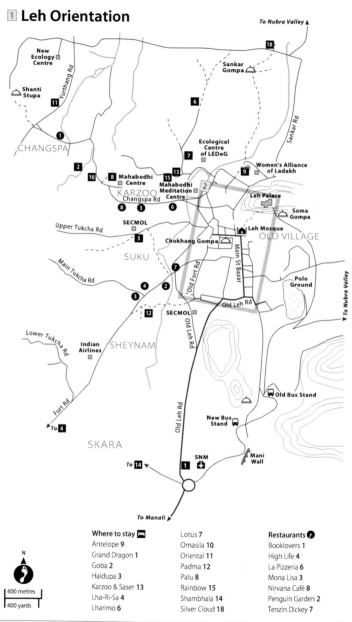

To Nubra Valley

New Ecology Centre

Shanti Stupa

Yurthang Rd

11

1

CHANGSPA

2

10

8  Mahabodhi Centre

Changspa Rd

8  3

Sankar Gompa

6

Ecological Centre of LEDeG

7

13

15  Mahabodhi Meditation Centre

18

Sankar Rd

Women's Alliance of Ladakh

9

2

Leh Palace

Soma Gompa

Upper Tukcha Rd

SECMOL

3

KARZOO

SUKU

Main Tukcha Rd

4  2

3

12  SECMOL

Chokhang Gompa

7

Old Fort Rd

Leh Mosque

Main St Bazar

OLD VILLAGE

Polo Ground

To Nubra Valley

Old Leh Rd

Lower Tukcha Rd

Indian Airlines

SHEYNAM

Old Leh Rd

Old Bus Stand

Fort Rd

To 4

SKARA

Old Leh Rd

To 14

SNM

1

New Bus Stand

Mani Wall

To Manali

N

400 metres
400 yards

**Where to stay** 🛏

Antelope 9
Grand Dragon 1
Goba 2
Haldupa 3
Karzoo & Saser 13
Lha-Ri-Sa 4
Lharimo 6

Lotus 7
Omasila 10
Oriental 11
Padma 12
Palu 8
Rainbow 15
Shambhala 14
Silver Cloud 18

**Restaurants** 🍴

Booklovers 1
High Life 4
La Pizzeria 6
Mona Lisa 3
Nirvana Café 8
Penguin Garden 2
Tenzin Dickey 7

balconies. From the town below it is dazzling in the morning sun and ghostly at night. Built by King Singe Namgyal and still owned by the royal family, it is now unoccupied – they live in the palace at Stok. Visible damage was caused during Zorawar Singh's invasion from Kashmir in the 1830s. The palace is under restoration, with new window and door frames fitted, and structural improvements being made – but still be wary of hazardous holes in the floor. After a steep climb some find the palace disappointing, but the views from the roof are exceptional. Like the Lhasa Potala Palace it has numerous rooms, steps and narrow passages (take a torch). The central prayer room has religious texts lining the walls, and contains dusty deities and time-worn masks. The upper levels have some painted carved wooden lintels and old murals that give a hint of past splendours. The Archaeological Survey of India is responsible for restoration and you will be able to watch work in progress.

South of the palace, the architecturally striking **Leh Mosque** in the main bazar is worth visiting – the inner section is not open to women visitors. The Sunni Muslim mosque is believed to stand on land granted by King Deldan Namgyal in the 1660s; his grandmother was the Muslim Queen of Ladakh.

The new **Central Asian Museum** is housed in a beautifully constructed building in the Tsa Soma gardens, where camel caravans used to camp. The museum explores the history of the caravan trade that for centuries linked Ladakh, until its mid-20th century isolation, with Tibet, Afghanistan, Samarkand, Kashmir and other city states. The museum is shaped like a Ladakhi fortress tower, with four floors inspired by the architecture of Ladakh, Kashmir, Tibet and Baltistan. Exhibits (metalware, coins, masks, etc) reveal the cultural exchange throughout the region; a garden café and museum shop are planned. A walking tour that includes the museum and visits restored buildings of the Old Town leaves from **Lala's Art Café** daily (see Restaurants, page 193), 1000-1300, Rs 300.

The **Chokhang Gompa** (New Monastery, 1957), off Main Bazar, was built to commemorate the 2500th anniversary of the birth of Buddha. The remains of the **Leh Gompa** houses a large golden Buddha.

The 15th-century **Tsemo Gompa** ('Red' Temple) is a strenuous walk north of the city and has a colossal two-storey-high image of Maitreya, flanked by figures of Avalokitesvara (right) and Manjusri (left). It was founded in 1430 by King Graspa Bum-Lde of the Namgyal rulers and a portrait

**2 Leh centre**

Where to stay
Alpine Villa 1
Atisha 7
Indus 2
Kang-lha Chen 3
Malpak 6
Old Ladakh 4
Tsomo-Ri 8
Yak Tail 5

Restaurants
Amdo Food 1
Chansa Traditional
  Ladakhi Kitchen 6
Chopsticks 2
Ibex 3
Il Forno 8
Lala's Art Café 9
Mentokling Apple
  Garden 13
Open Hand Expresso Bar 7
Pumpernickel 10
Shubh Panjabi Dhaba 14
Tibetan Friend's Corner 12

Not to scale

## Prepare for a different lifestyle in Leh

The whitewashed sun-dried brick walls of a typical two-storey, flat-roofed Ladakhi house, often with decorative woodwork around doors and windows and a carefully nurtured garden, look inviting to a traveller after a long hard journey. Many local families have opened up their homes to provide for the increasing demand for accommodation over a very short peak season and new hotels are springing up everywhere. However, prices do not reflect the type of furniture, furnishings and plumbing you might expect elsewhere in India although on the whole the rooms are kept clean. There is usually a space for sitting out – a 'garden' with a tree or two, some flower beds and some grass struggling to establish itself.

Electricity is limited, so expect power cuts, which are random and unpredictable. Some hotels have generators. Those without may run out of tap water but buckets are always at hand. Hot water is a luxury, available only during mornings and evenings. Plumbing allows for flush WCs in most hotels, although compost toilets are the more ecological method.

Guests are encouraged to economize on water and electricity – you will notice the low-power bulbs and scarcity of lights in rooms and public areas, so put away your reading material until sunrise.

of Tashi Namgyal hangs on the left at the entrance. Just bove the gompa is **Tsemo Fort** ① *dawn-dusk, Rs 20*, the classic landmark above Leh which can be seen from miles around.

**Sankar Gompa** (17th-18th centuries) ① *3 km north of the centre, 0700-1000, 1700-1900, prayers at 1830 with chanting, drums and cymbals*, of the Yellow Hat Sect, is one of the few *gompas* built in the valley bottom; it's an enjoyable walk through fields from town. It houses the chief *lama* of Spituk and 20 others. The newer monks' quarters are on three sides of the courtyard with steps leading up to the *dukhang* (Assembly Hall). There are a number of gold statues, numerous wall paintings and sculptures including a large one of the 11-headed, 1000-armed *Avalokitesvara*. It's an atmospheric and beautiful enclave in the increasingly busy valley.

On Changspa Lane, across the stream from Sankar Gompa, you reach the start of the stiff climb up to the white Japanese **Shanti Stupa** (1989). This is one of a series of 'Peace Pagodas' built by the Japanese around the world. There are good views from the top where a café offers a welcome sight after the climb. There is also a road which is accessible by jeep. Below the *stupa*, the **New Ecology Centre**, has displays on 'appropriate technology', as well as a handicrafts centre, a technical workshop and an organic vegetable garden.

The **Ecological Centre of LEDeG** (Ladakh Ecological Development Group) and the **craft shop** ① *T01982-253221, www.ledeg.org, Mon-Fri 1000-1800*, opened in 1984 to spread awareness of Ladakhi environmental issues, encourage self-help and the use of alternative technology. It has a library of books on Ladakhi culture, Buddhism and the environment. Handicrafts are sold, and you can refill water for Rs 10.

The **Women's Alliance of Ladakh (WAL)** ① *Sankar Rd, Chubi, T01982-250293, www.womenallianceladakh.org, video shown Mon-Sat 1500 (minimum 10 people)*, is an alliance of 5000 Ladakhi women, concerned with raising the status of traditional agriculture, preserving the traditionally high status of women which is being eroded in the modern sector, and creating an alternative development model based on self-reliance for Ladakh. The centre has a café selling local and organic foods (see Restaurants, page 193), and a craft shop. They hold festivals, cultural shows, dances, etc which are advertized around Leh; it's mainly aimed at local people, but all visitors are welcome.

The **The Donkey Sanctuary** ① *www.donkeysanctuary.in*, opened in 2008. This charity looks after 40-60 donkeys at any one time – well worth a visit.

From the radio station there are two long *mani* walls. **Rongo Tajng** is in the centre of the open plain and was built as a memorial to Queen Skalzang Dolma by her son Dalden Namgyal. It is about 500 m long and was built in 1635. The stones have been meticulously carved. The other, a 350-m wall down the hill, is believed to have been built by Tsetan Namgyal in 1785 as a memorial to his father the king.

## Southeast of Leh → *For listings, see pages 188-196.*

South and east of Leh is an amazing stretch of road with some fascinating monasteries strung along it. Many of these make good day trips from Leh, and are possible excursions by bus and hitching. If you hire a car or jeep (which is good value when shared by four), you can visit many of the places below in a single day. Camera flash is usually not allowed in monasteries to reduce damage to wall paintings and *thangkas*. Carry a torch.

### Choglamsar

Choglamsar, 7 km south of Leh on the east bank of the Indus, is a green oasis with poplars and willows where there are golf links and a polo ground as well as horticultural nurseries. The road between Leh and Choglamsar is now quite built up and at times clogged with traffic. The Central Institute of Buddhist Studies is here with a specialist library. Past the Tibetan refugee camps, children's village and the arts and crafts centre, the Choglamsar Bridge crosses the Indus. The **Chochot Yugma Imambara**, a few minutes' walk from the bridge, is worth a visit. Buses depart Leh hourly from 0800-1800.

### Stok

Across Choglamsar Bridge, 16 km south of Leh, is the royal palace dating from the 1840s when the King of Ladakh was deposed by the invading Dogra forces. The last king died in 1974 but his widow still lives here. His son continues the royal line and ascended to the throne in July 1993. The palace is a rambling building where only a dozen of the 80 rooms are used. The small **Palace Museum** ① *May-Oct 0900-1300 and 1400-1900, Rs 50*, with three rooms, is a showpiece for the royal *thangkas*, many 400 years old, crown jewels, dresses, coins, *peraks* (headdresses) encrusted with turquoise and lapis lazuli as well as religious objects. There's also a rather lovely café, which beckons with its views.

The **gompa**, a short distance away, has some ritual dance masks. **Tsechu** is in February. A three-hour walk up the valley behind Stok takes you to some extraordinary mountain scenery dominated by the 6121-m-high Stok Kangri.

There is an **archery contest** in July. There are at least three simple guesthouses in town, of which the Yarsta is most comfortable. Buses to Stok leave Leh at 0730 and 1700. Taxis from the Leh central taxi stand are available at fixed rates at any time.

### Shey

① *Palace open all day; try to be there 0700-0900, 1700-1800 when prayers are chanted, Rs 20.* Until the 16th century, Shey was the royal residence, located at an important vantage point in the Indus Valley. Kings of Leh were supposed to be born in the monastery. The royal family moved to Stok in order to escape advancing Dogra forces from Kashmir who came to exploit the trade in pashmina wool. Shey, along with Thikse, is also regarded as an auspicious place for cremation.

Most of the fort walls have fallen into disrepair but the palace and its wall paintings have now been restored. The palace *gompa* with its 17.5-m-high blue-haired Maitreya Buddha, imitating the one at Tsemo Gompa, is attended by Drukpa monks from Hemis. It is made of copper and brass but splendidly gilded and studded with precious gem stones. Paintings in the main shrine have been chemically cleaned by the Archaeological Society of India. The large victory *stupa* is topped with gold. Extensive grounds covering the former lake bed to the east contain a large number of *chortens* in which cremated ashes of important monks, members of the royal family and the devout were buried. A newer temple houses another old giant Buddha statue. There are several rock carvings; particularly noteworthy is that of five *dhyani* Buddhas (circa eighth century) at the bottom of the hill. The small hotel below the *gompa* has spartan but clean rooms. It is 15 km southeast of Leh on the Indus River or can be reached along a stone path from Thikse. Hourly buses depart Leh 0800-1800.

## Thikse

ⓘ *Rs 30, hourly buses from Leh 0800-1800.*

Situated 25 km south of Leh on a crag overlooking the flood plain on the east bank of the Indus, this is one of the most imposing monasteries in Ladakh and was part of the original Gelugpa order in the 15th century. The 12-storey monastery, with typical tapering walls painted deep red, ochre and white, has 10 temples, a nunnery and 80 *lamas* in residence whose houses cling to the hillside below. The complex contains numerous *stupas*, statues, *thangkas*, wall paintings (note the fresco of the 84 Mahasiddhas, high above) swords and a large pillar engraved with the Buddha's teachings.

The new temple interior is dominated by a giant 13-m-high Buddha figure near the entrance. The principal *Dukhang* (assembly hall) at the top of the building has holes in the wall for storing religious texts and contains the guardian deities. At the very top, the Old Library has old wooden bookcases with ancient texts and statues; adjacent is the tiny *Chamsing Lhakhang*. Views from the roof are staggeringly good. The slightly creepy *Gonkhang* has Tibetan-style wall paintings. The **museum** ⓘ *0600-1800, lunch break 1300-1330*, is near the entrance, and also sells souvenirs. There's a restaurant and guestrooms, below the museum. Thikse is a popular place to watch religious ceremonies, usually at 0630 or 1200. An early start by taxi makes even the first possible, or it's possible to stay overnight (see Where to stay, page 190). They are preceded by the playing of large standing drums and long horns similar to *alpenstock*. Masked dances are performed during special festivals.

## Stakna

Across the valley on a hill, Stakna is the earliest Drukpa monastery, built before Hemis though its decorations are not as ancient. It is also called 'Tiger's nose' because of the shape of the hill site. This small but well-kept monastery has a beautiful silver-gilt *chorten* in the assembly hall, installed around 1955, and some interesting paintings in the dark temple at the back. No need for a local guide as the *lamas* are always willing to open the doors. There are excellent views of the Indus Valley and the Zanskar range.

## Hemis

ⓘ *0800-1300, 1400-1800.*

On the west bank of the Indus, 45 km southeast of Leh, the monastery, built on a green hillside surrounded by spectacular mountain scenery, is tucked into a gorge. The

Drukpa monastery was founded by Stagsang Raspa during the reign of Senge Namgyal (circa 1630). It is the biggest (350 lamas) and wealthiest in Ladakh and it's a 'must', thus is busy with tourists. Pass by *chortens* and sections of *mani* walls to enter the complex through the east gate which leads into a large 40 m by 20 m courtyard. Colourful flags flutter in the breeze from posts, and the balconied walls of the buildings have colourfully painted door and window frames. On the north side are two assembly halls approached by steps. The large three-tiered *Dukhang* to the right used for ceremonies is old and atmospheric; the smaller *Tshogskhang* (main temple) contains three silver gilt *chortens* and is covered in murals. The murals in the verandas depict guardian deities, the *kalachakra* (wheel of life) and 'Lords of the four quarters' are well preserved. A staircase alongside the *Tshogskhang* leads to a roof terrace where there are a number of shrines including a bust of the founder. The *Tsom Lakhang* (chapel) has ancient Kashmiri bronzes, a golden Buddha and a silver *chorten*. The largest of the monastery's prized possessions is a heavy silk *thangka*, beautifully embroidered in bright coloured threads and pearls, which is displayed every 12 years (next 2016). The museum contains an important library of Tibetan-style books and an impressive collection of *thangkas*.

Not many people make the walk to the new golden Buddha on a nearby cliff, and there is also a pleasant 3-km walk uphill to another *gompa*. A stay in Hemis overnight enables you to attend early-morning prayers, a moving experience and recommended. Bus services make a day trip possible.

## Chemrey

Picture-perfect Chemrey is a short way off the main road, walkable from where the bus drops passengers. Perched on a little peak above encircling barley fields is **Thekchok Gompa**, home to 70 monks. A road winds to the top, but it's nicer to walk up the steep steps through traditional homesteads. The wonky prayer hall has countless murals of the Buddha, and there are three further *lhakhang* (image halls) to visit; a museum on the roof contains *thangkas* and statues. The beautiful setting and relative lack of visitors makes Chemrey a very worthwhile stop.

## Sakti and Takthok

The road continues through a sloping valley to Takthok, first passing Sakti village with the dramatic ruins of a fortress by the roadside. At ancient **Takthok Gompa** ⓘ *Rs 30*, there is a holy cave-shrines in which the sage Padmasambhava meditated in the 8th century. The walls and ceiling are papered with rupee notes and coins, numerous statues are swathed in prayer scarves, and centuries of butter lamps have left their grime. A highly colourful *dukhang* hall contains three beautiful statues. It is the only monastery in Ladakh belonging to the Nyingma sect of Buddhism; about 60 lamas reside here, and at the new gompa constructed nearby in 1980. It's possible to take a morning bus from Leh to Takthok and walk the 5 km back down the valley to Chemrey. Should you get stranded in Takthok, a **Tourist Bungalow** ⓘ *opposite the Gompa, T(0)9622-959513*, has four jaded but sunny rooms, some with squat toilets.

---

## Along the Srinagar road → *For listings, see pages 188-196.*

The Srinagar road out of Leh passes through a flat dusty basin mostly occupied by army encampments with mile after mile of wire fencing. The scenery is stunning and, as with the Leh-Manali Road, is punctuated with monasteries. A bus leaves Leh each afternoon for Alchi (see below), allowing access to most of the sites described in this section. A few places make for interesting and peaceful overnight stops.

## Spituk

Standing on a conical hill, some 8 km from Leh, Spituk was founded in the 11th century. The buildings themselves, including three chapels, date from the 15th century and are set in a series of tiers with courtyards and steps. The Yellow-Hat Gelugpa monks created the precedent in Ladakh for building on mountain tops rather than valley floors. You can get good views of the countryside around.

The long 16th- to 17th-century dukhang (assembly hall) is the largest building and has two rows of seats along the length of the walls to a throne at the far end. Sculptures and miniature *chortens* are displayed on the altar. Spituk has a collection of ancient Jelbagh masks, icons and arms including some rescued from the Potala Palace in Lhasa.

Also 16th- to 17th-century, the **Mahakal Temple**, higher up the hill, contains a shrine of Vajrabhairava, often mistaken for the Goddess Kali. The terrifying face is only unveiled in January, during the **Gustor festival**. The Srinagar buses can drop you on the highway (four daily, 20 minutes).

## Phyang

**Phyang Gompa**, 16 km from Leh, dominates a beautiful side valley dotted with poplars, homesteads and *chortens* with a village close by. It belongs to the Red-Hat Kagyupa sect, with its 16th-century Gouon monastery built by the founder of the Namgyal Dynasty which is marked by a flagstaff at the entrance. It houses 60 lamas and hundreds of statues including some Kashmiri bronzes (circa 14th century), *thangkas* and manuscript copies of the Kangyur and Tengyur. The temple walls have colourful paintings centring on the eight emblems of happiness. The walls in the main prayer hall are covered with ancient smoke-blackened murals, and a giant rolled-up *thangka* hangs from the ceiling. The faces of the statues in the Protector's Hall have been covered. A grand new wing is being constructed, with rather gawdy paintings by the artists (many of whom come from Bhutan). Morning prayers take place 0600-0730. Phyang is the setting for a spectacular July **Tseruk festival** with masked dancing. There are three buses daily (0900, 1400 and 1630, 45 minutes; return to Leh at 0800, 1000, 1300 from the monastery, 1600 and 1730); the morning bus allows you to explore the valley and walk back to Leh, but the afternoon bus only allows a short visit. However, it is worth overnighting in Phyang as there is a pleasing guesthouse (see Where to stay, page 190), good walks around the traditional village and dramatic valley up to the fort, and stunning views to the pyramid-peak of Stok Kangri.

## Phyang to Nimmu

About 2 km before Nimmu the Indus enters an impressive canyon before the Zanskar joins it; it is a good photo opportunity. As the road bends, a lush green oasis with lines of poplars comes into view. The mud brick houses of Nimmu have grass drying on the flat rooftops to provide fodder for the winter. A dry stone *mani* wall runs along the road; beyond Nimmu the walls become 2 m wide in places with innumerable *chortens* alongside. The rocky outcrops on the hills to the right appear like a natural fortress. Nimmu serves mainly as a bus rest-stop, but there are a couple of small hotels (Nilza Guesthouse is most acceptable) and a collection of *dhabas* and shops.

## Basgo

The road, lined by *mani* walls and *chortens*, passes through Basgo Village with the ruins of a Buddhist citadel impressively sited on a spur overlooking the Indus Valley. It served as a royal residence for several periods between the 15th and 17th centuries. The **fort palace** was once considered almost impregnable having survived a three-year siege by Tibetan and Mongol armies in the 17th century.

Among the ruins two temples have survived. The higher **Maitreya Temple** (mid-16th century) built by Tashi Namgyal's son contains a very fine Maitreya statue at the rear of the hall, flanked by *bodhisattvas*. Some murals from the early period illustrating the Tibetan Buddhist style have also survived on the walls and ceiling; among the Buddhas and *bodhisattvas* filled with details of animals, birds and mermaids, appear images of Hindu divinities. The 17th-century **Serzang Temple** (gold and copper), with a carved doorway, contains another large Maitreya image whose head rises through the ceiling into a windowed box-like structure. The murals look faded and have been damaged by water. The fort is very photogenic, particularly so in the late afternoon light. The Chamba View guesthouse and restaurant is by the road, as you exit the village.

## Lekir (Likir)

Some 5.5 km from Basgo, a road on the right leads up to Lekir Monastery via a scenic route. Lower Lekir, a scattering of houses where most accommodation is found, is about 1 km off NH1 accessed by confusing unpaved tracks. You can walk from Lower Likir up to the monastery, about 5 km on the road, or via short-cuts crossing the river. The picturesque whitewashed monastery buildings rise in different levels on the hillside across the Lekir River. A huge gold-coloured Maitreya Buddha flanks the complex. Lekir was built during the reign of Lachen Gyalpo who installed 600 monks here, headed by Lhawang Chosje (circa 1088). The *gompa* was invested with a collection of fine images, *thangkas* and murals to vie with those at Alchi. The present buildings date mainly from the 18th century since the original were destroyed by fire. A path up leads to the courtyard where a board explains the origin of the name: Klu-Khyil (snake coil) refers to the *nagas* here, reflected in the shape of the hill. Lekir was converted to the Gelugpa sect in the 15th century. The head *lama*, the younger brother of the Dalai Lama, has his apartments here, which were extended in the mid-1990s.

The **dukhang** (assembly hall) contains large clay images of the Buddhas (past, present and future), *thangkas*, and Kangyur and Tengyur manuscripts, the Kangyur having been first compiled in Ladakh during Lachen Gyalpo's reign. The **Nyenes-Khang** contains beautiful murals of the 35 confessional Buddhas and 16 arahats. Wooden steps lead up to the **Gon-Khang** housing a statue of the guardian deity here, as well as *thangkas* and murals. Further steps lead to a small but very interesting **museum** ① *Rs 20, opened on request (climb to a hall above, up steep wooden stairs)*, displays *thangkas*, old religious and domestic implements, costumes, etc, which are labelled in English.

Village craftsmen produce *thangkas*, carved wooden folding seats and clay pottery. If you wish to stay overnight, the monastery has guestrooms which share bathrooms (by donation); for further accommodation options in the villages, see Where to stay, page 191. A bus goes to Leh at 0730 from the monastery.

## Alchi

① *0800-1300, 1400-1800, Rs 50, www.achiassociation.org*

The road enters Saspol, 8 km after the Lekir turn-off. About 2 km beyond the village, a link road with a suspension bridge over the river leads to Alchi, which is hidden from view as you approach. As the road enters the village, impressive old houses in various states of repair can be seen. It's possible to climb up the small rocky peak behind these, to a square white turret with graves around, for good views up the Indus valley and of the village. A patchwork of cultivated fields surrounds the monastery complex.

A narrow path from the car park winds past village houses, donkeys and apricot trees to lead to the **Alchi Monastery**. You will be expected to buy a ticket from one of the three *lamas* on duty. The whole complex, about 100 m long and 60 m wide, is enclosed by a whitewashed mud and straw wall. Alchi's large temple complex is regarded as one of the most important Buddhist centres in Ladakh and a jewel of monastic skill. Founded in the 11th century by Rinchen Zangpo, the 'Great Translator', it was richly decorated by artists from Kashmir and Tibet. Murals of the *mandalas*, which have deep Tantric significance, are particularly fine; some decorations are reminiscent of Byzantine art. The monastery is maintained by monks from Lekir and is no longer a place for active worship. A path on the right past two large prayer wheels and a row of smaller ones leads to the river which attracts deer down to the opposite bank in the evenings. At the rear, small *chortens* with inscribed stones strewn around them, line the wall. It is worth walking around the exterior of the complex, and you'll get a beautiful view of the Indus River with mountains as a backdrop. For accommodation options, see Where to stay, page 191.

**The temple complex** The entrance *chortens* are worth looking into. Each has vividly coloured paintings within, both along the interior walls as well as in the small *chorten*-like openings on the ceilings. The first and largest of these has a portrait of the founder Rinchen Zangpo (closed at the time of research).

The first temple you come to is the **Sum-stek**, the three-tier temple with a carved wooden gallery on the façade, has triple arches. Inside are three giant four-armed, garlanded stucco figures of *Bodhisattvas*: the white *Avalokitesvara* on the left, the principal terracotta-red *Maitreya* in the centre at the back, and the ochre-yellow *Manjusri* on the right; their heads project to the upper storey which is reached by a rustic ladder (inaccessible). The remarkable features here are the brightly painted and gilded decorations on the clothing of the figures which include historical incidents, musicians, palaces and places of pilgrimage. Quite incongruous court scenes and Persian features appear on *Avalokitesvara* while the figures on *Maitreya* have Tantric connotations illustrating the very different styles of ornamentation on the three figures. The walls have numerous *mandalas* and inscriptions, as well as thousands of tiny Buddhas.

The oldest temple is the **dukhang**, which has a covered courtyard (originally open to the sky) with wooden pillars and painted walls; the left wall shows two rowing boats with fluttering flags, a reminder perhaps of the presence in ancient times of lakes in this desert. The brightly painted door to the *dukhang*, about 1.5 m high, and the entrance archway has some fine woodcarving. The subsidiary shrines on either side of the doorway contain *Avalokitesvaras* and *Bodhisattvas* including a giant four-armed Maitreya figure to the extreme right. This main assembly hall, which was the principal place of worship, suffers from having very little light so visitors need a good torch. The 'shrine' holds the principal gilded *Vairocana* (Resplendent) Buddha (traditionally white, accompanied by the lion) with ornate decorations behind, flanked by four important Buddha postures among others. The walls on either side of the main hall are devoted to fine but damaged *Mandala* paintings illustrating the four principal manifestations of the *Sarvavid* (Omniscient) Buddha – *Vairocana*, *Sakyamuni* (the Preacher), *Manjusri* (Lord of Wisdom) and as *Prajna Paramita* (Perfection of Wisdom). There are interesting subsidiary panels, friezes and inscriptions. On exiting, note the terrifying figure of *Mahakala* the guardian deity above the door with miniature panels of royal and military scenes. The one portraying a drinking scene shows the royal pair sanctified with haloes with wine-cups in hand, accompanied by the prince and attendants – the detail of the clothing clearly shows Persian influence.

The **Lotsawa** (Translator's) and **Jampang** (Manjusri) *Lhakhangs* were built later and probably neglected for some time. The former contains a statue of Rinchen Zangpo along with a seated Buddha while the latter has a finely carved doorway and exterior lintels. Ask for the lights to be switched on.

**Lhakhang Soma** (New Temple) is a square hall used as a meditation centre with a *chorten* within; its walls are totally covered with *mandalas* and paintings portraying incidents from the Buddha's life and historic figures; the main figure here is the preaching Buddha. There is an interesting panel of warriors on horseback near the door. Request the temple be opened if it is locked. **Kanjyur Lhakhang** in front of the Lhakhang Soma houses the scriptures.

### Lamayuru

In Lamayuru, 10 km before Khaltse, the famous monastery is perched on a crag overlooking the Indus in a striking lunar landscape between a drained lake and high mountains. Little medieval houses nestle on the steep slope beneath the monastery, and the effect is dramatically photogenic. The monastery complex, which includes a library thought to be the oldest in the region, was founded in the 11th century and belongs to the Tibetan Kagyupa sect. The present monastery dating from the 16th century was partly destroyed in the 19th. You can still see some of the murals, along with the redecorated *dukhang* (assembly hall). A small glass panel in the right hand wall of the *dukhang* protects a tiny holy cave, and there are many beautiful bronzes displayed. In a small temple, below the monastery, is an 11-headed and 1000-armed Avalokiteshvara image; the walls here are coated with murals – you will need to ask someone to get the key. Some of the upper rooms are richly furnished with carpets, Tibetan tables, statues, silver *stupas* and butter lamps. In June/July the monastery holds the famous **Yuru Kabgyat** festival, with colourful masked dancing, special prayers, and burning of sacrificial offerings. There are several guesthouses strung along the road and up the hillside (see Where to stay, page 192); it's also possible to camp near the stream in a willow grove. There are daily buses from Leh at 0800; buses to Leh and Kargil leave Lamayuru at around 0930, and to Chitkan at 1000.

Shortly after Lamayuru, a jeep road leaves the highway heading south down the Yapola Valley to **Wanla** which has a beautiful *gompa*, from the same era as Alchi and decorated by same artists. It has been recently restored, see www.achiassociation.org, and is adjoined on a dramatic ridge by a ruined fort. In Wanla village there are guesthouses. The next village is **Phanjila**, and further along there is a homestay in the delightful village of **Hinju**, from where the track peters out into a fantastic trekking route (see page 186).

---

## Nubra Valley, Nyona and Drokhpa area → *For listings, see pages 188-196.*

These once-restricted areas are now open to visitors with an Inner Line Permit. Permits are issued in Leh to groups of two or more travelling together by jeep, for a maximum of seven days. You can get a joint permit to cover all areas. Allow a day to get a permit, which costs around Rs 250 (more if you include Dha-Hanu). A lot of ground can be covered in the period but it is best to consult a Leh-based trekking and travel agent. Always carry multiple photocopies of your passport and ILP with you, to facilitate the crossing of checkpoints.

## Nubra Valley

For an exhilarating high-altitude experience over possibly the highest motorable pass in the world, travel across the Ladakh range over the 5600-m **Khardung La**. This is along the old Silk Route to the lush green Nubra Valley up to **Panamik**, 140 km north of Leh. Camel caravans once transported Chinese goods along this route for exchanging with Indian produce. The relatively gentle climate here allows crops, fruit and nuts to grow, so some call it 'Ldumra' (orchard). There are guesthouses in villages throughout the valley, and temporary tented camps are occasionally set up by tour companies during the season, but it's still a good idea to take a sleeping bag.

It is possible to visit the Nubra-Shyok valleys over two days, but it's much preferable (and the same cost) to make the journey over three. After crossing the Khardung La, the first village is **Khardung**, 42 km later, boasting a majestic setting. The road continues down the Shyok Valley to **Deskit**, which has an old and a new (less appealing) town centre and several places to stay. On a hill above the old village is a Gelugpa sect **monastery** (the largest in Nubra) built by the Ladakhi king Sohrab Zangpo in the early 1700s. There is large statue of Tsongkhapa, and the Rimpoche of Thikse monastery south of Leh oversees this monastery also. A further 10 km past Diskit is the village of **Hunder**, probably the most popular place to overnight, with several garden-guesthouses to chose from. Highly prized double-humped camels can occasionally be seen on the sand dunes near Hunder, allegedly descendents of the caravan-camels that used to ply the Silk Route, and it is possible to take a 15-30 minute camel ride (on a tame beast). Past Hunder the road continues to **Turtuk**, opened to tourists in 2010. The scenery is impressive and the tiny settlements here are culturally Balti and practise Islam.

The second biggest monastery in Nubra is near **Tiger** village along the road to Panamik in the Nubra Valley. Called the **Samtanling** *gompa*, it was founded in 1842 and belongs to the Gelugpa sect. **Panamik** has several guesthouses and reddish, sulphurous hot springs nearby. The ILP allows travel only up **Ensa Gompa**, included on some itineraries, and approached by foot for the last 30 minutes.

Should you need medical help, there is a health centre at Deskit and a dispensary at Panamik. Traffic into and out of the Nubra Valley is controlled by the army at Pulu. From Leh there are two buses per week from June to September; a few have tried by bike, which can be put on the roof of the bus for the outward journey.

## Pangong-Tso

A popular excursion from Leh (permit required) is to the narrow 130-km-long Pangong-Tso, at 4250 m, the greater part of which lies in Tibet. The road, which is only suitable for 4WD in places, is via **Karu** on the Manali-Leh Highway, where the road east goes through **Zingral** and over the Chang La pass. Beyond are **Durbuk**, a small village with low-roofed houses, and **Tangste**, the 'abode of Chishul warriors' with a Lotswa Temple, which is also an army base with a small bank. The rough jeep track takes you through an impressive rocky gorge which opens out to a valley which has camping by a fresh water stream in the hamlet of **Mugleb** and then on to **Lukung** and finally **Spangmik**, 153 km from Leh. On the way you will be able to see some Himalayan birds including *chikhor* (quail) which may end up in the cooking pot.

An overnight stop on the lake shore allows you to see the blue-green lake in different lights. You can walk between Lukung and Spangmik, 7 km, on the second day, passing small settlements growing barley and peas along the lake shore. You return to Leh on the third day. There are tented camps at Durbuk, Tangtse and Lukung. At Spangmik there is a wider choice of accommodation, in the form of homestays (mats on floor) or in the rather pricey Pangong Tso Resort (rooms have attached bath). Buses go from Leh at 0630 on Saturdays and Sundays, but almost everyone makes the journey by private jeep.

## Tso-Moriri

The Rupshu area, a dry, high-altitude plateau to the east of the Leh-Manali Highway, is where the nomadic Changpas live, in the bleak and windswept Chamathang highlands bordering Tibet. The route to the beautiful Tso-Moriri (*tso* – lake), the only nesting place of the bar-headed geese on the Indus, is open to visitors. It is 220 km from Leh; jeeps make the journey. To the south of the 27-km-long lake is the land of the Tibetan wild ass.

You can travel either via **Chhumathang**, 140 km, visiting the hot spring there or by crossing the high pass at Taglang La, leaving the Manali-Leh Highway at Debring. The route takes you past the **Tsokar** basin, 154 km, where salt cakes the edges. A campsite along the lake with access to fresh water is opposite **Thukje** village which has a *gompa* and a 'wolf-catching trap'. The road then reaches the hot sulphur springs at **Puga** before arriving at the beautiful Tso-Moriri, about four hours' drive from Tsokar. You can follow the lake bank and visit the solitary village of **Karzog**, at 4500 m, north of the lake, which also has a *gompa*. There are some rest houses and guesthouses at Chhumathang and Karzog and camping at Tsokar and Karzog as well as a tent camp at Chhumathang.

## Drokhpa

**Dha** and **Biama** (Bema) are two Drokhpa (aka Brokpa) villages where the so-called pure Aryan tribe speaking a distinct dialect live in a fair degree of isolation; Buddhism here is mixed with animist practices. You may reach these Indus Valley villages from **Khaltse** on the Leh–Srinagar road via the scenic villages of Dumkhar, Tirit, Skurbuchan and Hanu There are homestays and a campsite at Biama, but Dha (3 km further) is the more popular option for overnight stays.

---

# Trekking in Ladakh

Make sure your trekking guide is experienced and competent. A detailed book, although dated, is the Trailblazer guide *Trekking in Ladakh* which can be bought in bookshops in Leh. Some treks, eg Spituk to Hemis and Hemis High Altitude National Park, charge a fee of Rs 25 per person per day or Rs 10 for Indians. For trekking, July and August are pleasant months. Go earlier and you will be trudging through snow much of the time. September and October are also good months, though colder at night.

## Markha Valley Trek, Spituk to Hemis

Both places are in the Indus Valley, just 30 km apart. A very satisfying nine to 10 days can be undertaken by traversing the Stok range to the Markha Valley, walking up the valley and then back over the Zanskar range to Hemis. The daily walking time on this trek is five to six hours so you must be fit. Places to camp are highlighted below, but there are also basic homestays or guesthouses in the villages if you don't want to carry equipment.

There is an interesting monastery at **Spituk**, a short drive from Leh (see page 179). From Spituk proceed southwest of the Indus along a trail passing through barren countryside. After about 7 km you reach the **Zingchen Valley** and in a further five hours, the beautiful village of **Rumbak**. Camp below the settlement. You can also trek here from Stok which takes one-two days and a steep ascent of the **Namlung La** (4570 m).

# Who might you meet along the way – birds and wildlife

The Himalayan range is the longest and the highest mountain range in the world. The sheer diversity of the topography makes it one of the best places to spot some of the rarest wildlife and birds. The forested regions offer a large variety of birds, both resident and migratory. You might see Himalayan griffons, crested serpent eagle, lamagiers, forest owlets, common flameback, golden oriole, scarlet minivets, rose finches, chukors, snow cocks, pigeons, Himalayan blue magpies, monals, khaleej pheasants, the critically endangered western tragopan, or the black-necked cranes around Tso Kar. In fact, the flatlands around Tso Kar in Ladakh is one of my favourite places to see birds. Another great place to venture to in order to see birds and wildlife is the Great Himalayan National park, located in Himachal Pradesh. The park is a habitat to 375 fauna species, which includes 31 mammals, 181 birds, 3 reptiles, 9 amphibians, 11 annelids, 17 mollusks and 127 insects.

In my 16 odd years of trekking and wanderings in the Western Himalayas the sighting that has had me the most excited is seeing a Snow Leopard for the first time in the Rumbak valley of Ladakh in February 1995. Watching a snow leopard right in front of you is not a feeling that is easily explained, it was awe-inspiring. Once I was even offered a chanko cub, which is a Tibetan wolf. I was camped in the village of Rumtse where I met a villager from the Khanag valley who had a two- or three-month-old cub that he had found somewhere on the plateau and was not sure what to do with.

My work as a trekking and climbing guide in the Western Himalayas takes me to some really remote parts and over the years I have seen dramatic changes in not just glaciers receding due to global warming but also extensive deforestation because of so many hydro electric projects in the region. This has affected carnivores like the snow leopard and the chanko due to the loss of prey caused by habitat destruction. A positive development is the increase in nnow leopard tourism in Ladakh which has prompted the locals to stop viewing the big cat as an enemy and has opened doors to alternative income generations in various valleys of Ladakh.

From Rumbak it is a five-hour walk to **Utse** village. The camp is two hours further on at the base of the bleak **Gandha La** (4700 m), open, bare and windswept. To go over the pass takes about three hours, then the same time again to negotiate the wooded ravine to **Skiu**. Here the path meets the Markha Valley. You can make a half-day round trip from Skiu to see the impressive gorges on the Zanskar River. The stage to **Markha**, where there is an impressive fort, is a six-hour walk. The monastery, while not particularly impressive from the outside, has some superb wall paintings and *thangkas*, some dating from the 13th century. You need to take a torch.

The next destination is **Hankar** village, whose ruined fort forms an astonishing extension of the natural rock face, an extremely impressive ruin. From here the path climbs quite steeply to a plateau. There are good views of Nimaling Peak (6000 m) and a number of *mani* walls en route. From **Nimaling** it is a two-hour climb to **Gongmaru La** (5030 m) with views of the Stok range and the Indus Valley. The descent is arduous and involves stream crossings. There is a lovely campsite at **Shogdu** and another at **Sumda** village, 3 km further on. The final stage is down the valley to **Martselang** from where you can walk down 5 km to **Karu** village on the Leh-Manali road or take a 2-km diversion to visit **Hemis** monastery.

## Hemis High Altitude National Park

Set up in 1981, the park adjoining the monastery comprising the catchments of Markha, Rumbak and Sumda *nalas*. The reserve area has been expanded a couple of times, and now covers 4400 sq km making it the largest national park in South Asia. The rugged terrain with valleys often littered with rocks and rimmed by high peaks (some over 6000 m), supports limited alpine vegetation but contains some rare species of flora and fauna, including the ibex, Pallas' cat, *bharal* and *shapu*. It is the habitat of the endangered and elusive snow leopard, now numbering around 200 (mainly in the Rumbak area, best spotted in winter). It is hoped that the activities of local villagers, who graze livestock within the park, can be restricted to a buffer zone so that their animals can be kept safe from attack by wolves and snow leopards. Villages used to trap the leopard, but now they are reimbursed for any livestock lost to snow leopard attacks.

There are camping sites within the park, which can be reserved through the Wildlife Warden in Leh. There are also homestays, see www.himalayan-homestays.com, run in conjunction with the Snow Leopard Conservancy India Trust (SNC-IT), www.snowleopard conservancy.org. SNC-IT also run 10-day winter expeditions, "Quest of the Snow Leopard". Since most of the park lies within 'restricted' areas, you need a special permit for entry, also issued in Leh. Contact a local travel agent for advice.

## Ripchar Valley Trek

This is a shorter trek of four to five days, however, the average daily walking time is seven hours so don't think that the shortness of the trek means less effort. A guide is recommended.

The first stage involves transport from Leh (five to six hours), then an hour's walk to **Hinju** (3750 m); camp or homestay overnight at the village. Stage two continues up through the Ripchar Valley to cross the **Konze La** (4570 m), from where you will see the Zanskar River and gorge and the Stok range. Then descend to **Sumdo Chenmo**, quite a treacherous route as it involves river crossings There is a monastery here with an impressive statue of the Buddha and some attractive wall paintings. A campsite lies just beyond the village. The next day takes you from Sumdo Chenmo to **Lanak** (4000 m), a walk of five to six hours. The final stage, about seven hours, from Lanak to **Chilling** is over the **Dungduchan La** (4700 m) with excellent views. The path continues down the valley following a stream to Chilling. Overnight in Chilling or make the two hours drive back to Leh. Some agents also offer the option of rafting back to Leh from Chilling along the Zanskar River.

## Trekking in Zanskar

Trekking in Zanskar is not easy. The paths are often rough and steep, the passes high and the climate extreme. Provisions, fuel and camping equipment should be bought in advance from Kishtwar, Manali or Leh. You can get necessities such as dried milk, biscuits, noodles and sugar from Padum, though supplies are scare at the beginning of the season. In Padum the Tourism Officer and Government Development Officer will be able to advise and maybe even assist in hiring horses. Porters can be hired at **Sani** village for the traverse of the **Umasi La** into Kishtwar. Horses cannot use this pass. In Padum you may be able to hire porters with whom you can cover rougher terrain. It is best to contact a trekking agent in advance. ▸▸ *See What to do, page 169.*

**Pensi La to Padum** You can trek this three-day route before the road opens (June-October) when it is free of vehicles.

**Karsha to Lamayaru** This is a demanding nine-day trek which includes seven passes, five of which are over 4500 m. The highest is the Singi La (5060 m). It is essential to be very fit before starting the trek. Each day's walking should take under six hours, but with time for rests and lunch this adds up to a full day. An extra day allows for flexibility.

The 16th-century monastery of the Tibetan Gelugpa (Yellow Hat) sect at **Karsha** is the largest and wealthiest in the Zanskar Valley and is occupied by nearly 200 monks. Karsha has an inn with dormitory beds and a vegetarian canteen.

**Padum to Leh** This is another demanding trek which also takes about 10 days. Some are through the spectacular gorges between Markha and Zangla. A local guide is recommended as this is truly a wilderness area. The trek involves walking along stream beds and in July there is still too much snow melt to allow safe crossings. Recommended only for August/September.

It is seven hours' walking from Padum to Zangla and this includes crossing the Zanskar River by a string and twig bridge that spans over 40 m. Ponies are not allowed on it and if it is windy sensible humans don't cross. You can now start your trek at Zangla as there is a motorbike route from Padum to Zangla. At **Zangla** you can see the King's Palace, which has a collection of *thangkas* painted by the king's son (who was once a monk). The third stage takes you over the **Cha Cha La** (5200 m). On the next stage river crossings are again necessary. This is time consuming and if you are travelling in mid-summer, an extra day may be called for.

You then follow the **Khurna River** to a narrow gorge that marks the ancient border between Zanskar and Ladakh, and end up below the **Rubarung La**. When you cross this you get good views of the Stok range. You then descend into the Markha Valley and from here you can reach Leh in six stages by heading west into the heart of the valley and then crossing the Ganda La to Spituk, or in three stages by crossing the Gongmaru La and descending to Martselang and nearby Hemis.

**Padum to Darcha** This is a week-long trek and starts with a walk along the Tsarap Chu to **Bardan**, which has *stupas* and interesting idols, and **Reru**. There is a now a motorable road till Mune from where the trek starts towards Darcha.

After two stages you reach **Purni** (with a couple of shops and a popular campsite), where you can stay two nights and make a side trip to the impressive 11th-century **Phugtal monastery** (a two-hour walk). On a spectacular site, it has been carved out of the mountainside round a limestone cave. Usually there are about 50 monks in attendance. From Purni you continue on to Kargiakh, the last village before the **Shingo La**. It's another day's walk to the camp below this high pass (5200 m).

The mountain scenery is stunning with 6000 m-plus peaks all around. Once over the pass you can stop at **Rumjack** where there is a campsite used by shepherds or you can continue to the confluence of the **Shingo** and the **Barai** rivers where there is now a bridge. From here the trail passes through grazing land and it is about 15 km to **Darcha**, the end of the trek. Keen trekkers can combine this with a trek from Darcha to **Manali**. The average daily walking time of the Padum–Darcha trek is six hours so you have to be very fit. There is now a motorable road from Darcha all the way to Zanskar Sumdo which is after the Shingo La Pass.

### Trekking in the Nubra and Shyok valleys
The easing of controls to visit the Nubra-Shyok valleys has made possible treks that start from points in the Indus Valley not far from Leh, cross the Ladakh Range to enter the Shyok

River valley and then re-cross the Ladakh range further to the west to re-enter the Indus Valley near Phyang monastery. Ask a good local trekking agent for advice on how to get the required 'Restricted Area Permits'.

**Day 1** Drive from Leh south along the Manali road to Karu, near Hemis, where you turn left and drive about 10 km to the roadhead at the village of Sakti, just past **Takthak monastery**. Trek about 90 minutes to **Chumchar** and camp.

**Day 2** Cross the Ladakh range at the **Wari La** (4400 m) and descend to Junlez on the northern flank.

**Day 3** Walk downhill to **Tangyar** (3700 m) with a nice *gompa*.

**Days 4, 5, 6** A level walk along the **Shyok River** valley takes you to **Khalsar** from where you follow the military road west to the confluence of the Shyok and Nubra rivers at **Diskit** (see Nubra Valley, above).

**Days 7, 8, 9** Three days to gradually ascend the northern flanks of the Ladakh Range passing the hamlets of **Hunder**, **Wachan** and **Hunder Dok** to the high pastures of **Thanglasgo** (4700 m).

**Days 10, 11** Trek back over the Ladakh Range via the Lasermo La pass (5150 m) to a campsite on the southern base of the pass.

**Day 12** Camp at Phyang village about 1 km above Phyang monastery before driving back to Leh.

---

## Ladakh listings

*For hotel and restaurant price codes and other relevant information, see pages 12-14.*

### 🛏 Where to stay

**Leh** *p171, maps p173 and p174*
For eco-conscious homestays throughout Ladakh, see www.himalayan-homestays.com. Grand Dragon, Omasila, Oriental remain open throughout the year. There are now scores of guest houses and many traditional Ladakhi homes offer rooms during the summer. Outside the peak period expect discounts (as much as 25-50%). Those in Karzoo and Changspa (some way from the bus stand) are quieter and more rural. There is lots of budget accommodation along Fort Rd and in the Changspa area; some are very basic and you might want to use your own sleeping bag. But generally you will find a clean simple room, without needing to book in advance.

**$$$$-$$$ Grand Dragon**, Old Leh Rd, Sheynam, T01982-257 786, www.thegrand dragonladakh.com. Big hotel with all mod cons, Wi-Fi and great views. Stunning dining room and a nod to eco tourism with double-glazing, under-floor heating and solar panels. Open all year round.

**$$$ Lha-Ri-Sa**, Skara, T01982-252 000, www.ladakh-lharisa.com. With a boutique vibe, they offer stylish rooms and the outside of the building is simply beautiful. In the restaurant they serve up flavours from all over India as well as traditional Ladakhi food. Recommended, although it's on the outskirts of town.

**$$$ Shambhala**, Skara, T01982-251 100, www.hotelshambhala.com. Large airy rooms, excellent restaurant (often caters for German packages), breakfast included, very pleasant staff and lovely owners, peaceful away from crowds, attractive garden with hammocks and fruit trees, free transport to centre.

**$$ Alpine Villa**, Chulung, T01982-252354, www.alpinevilla.co.in. The modern design is rather out of keeping with Leh, but public areas are adorned with Ladakhi furniture, and door jambs and ceilings are painted with traditional motifs. 22 spacious new rooms have bedside lights, flatscreen TV and comfy beds; bathrooms are a cut above the rest, with an attempt at stylish tiling. Large public terraces have mountain views; restaurant, and lawn.

**$$ Antelope**, Chubi Rd, near Women's Alliance, T01982-252086, discoverladakh@yahoo.com. Guesthouse with simple, clean rooms, some wear-and-tear, quiet, small shady garden. Great central location, well-priced, free Wi-Fi, helpful staff.

**$$ Kang-lha Chen**, T01982-252144, www.hotel-klcleh.com. Open May-Oct. 23 simple rooms, with attached bathrooms. Recently renovated with larger dining area, lobby done in traditional style with old family furniture and carpets, restaurant, pleasant shaded inner courtyard garden and lawns with sitting area at hotel entrance, own spring, quiet and peaceful and centrally located, old fashioned but well maintained.

**$$ Lharimo**, Fort Rd, T01982-252101, lharimo@yahoo.com. Attractive central hotel with scarlet window-frames and whitewashed exterior, large comfortable rooms have traditional bamboo ceilings and inoffensive aging wooden furniture, TV, clean tiled bathrooms. The big grassy lawn is perfect for relaxing

**$$ Lotus**, Upper Karzoo, T01982-257265, www.lotushotel.in. 17 high-spec rooms with quality furniture, modern amenities, and a nod to traditional Ladakhi decor. 24-hr hot water, central heating and good multicuisine restaurant. Views from the flowery garden straight onto the palace.

**$$ Omasila**, Changspa, T01982-252119, www.hotelomasila.com. A series of annexes around a pleasant back lawn, plus huge terrace and ornate restaurant (garden vegetables). Rooms have TV, wooden floors, worth paying bit extra for the deluxe rooms with seating areas, all have decent tiled bathrooms. More mature clientele, heating system. Free Wi-Fi. Open throughout the year.

**$$ Tso-Kar**, Fort Rd, T01982-253071, www.lehladakhhotel.com. Very reasonably priced and well-maintained rooms,

bathrooms a little old but clean, TV, and comfortable beds. Astroturf, flowers, and cane chairs and tables in the courtyard.

**$$ Yak-Tail**, Fort Rd, T01982-252118, www.hotelyaktail.com. Open May-Oct. One of Leh's oldest hotels, comfortable and cosy (decent heating), some of the 30 rooms are "houseboat style", others have balconies, some have lots of patterns. Restaurant nicely decorated with murals serves good Indian food, courtyard has been astro-turfed but swinging vines create a pleasing greenhouse effect.

**$$-$ Oriental**, below Shanti Stupa, T01982-253153, www.orientalguesthouse.com. 35 very clean rooms in traditional family home, good home cooking in the dining hall, great views across the valley, friendly, treks and travel arrangements reliable. Open all year. Recommended.

**$$-$ Padma Guesthouse & Hotel**, off Fort Rd down an alley, T01982-252630, T(0)9906-982171, www.padmaladakh.net. Clean, charming rooms with common bath in guesthouse in the old family home, upstairs has mountain views (rooftop restaurant), plus hotel-style rooms in newer block, beautiful and peaceful garden, Buddhist chapel/meditation room, solar panels, good library, but most known for their outstanding hospitality. Highly recommended.

**$ Atisha**, Malpak, off Fort Rd, T(0)9906-992187, atisha_leh@rediffmail.com. Not much to look at on arrival, but simple rooms are spotless with bright paint and shiny tiled bathrooms. Prices increase as you go up from ground to 3rd floor, rooftop terrace is lovely, and although there's not much of an aspect it feels rural and a burbling brook surrounds. Very pleasant low-key family.

**$ Haldupa**, Upper Tukcha Rd, Malpak, T01982-251374. Very budget rooms (Rs 250-300) in the old building share (smelly) bathrooms, hot buckets available, and memorable shrine is in same building. New 2-level wing is swish (Rs 600-1000) and there's a delightful garden with plenty of seating, organic food available.

**$ Indus**, Malpak, off Fort Rd, T01982-252502, masters_ adv@yahoo.co.in. A range of rooms (Rs 500-1000), all large and with clean sheets and attached bath. Basic rooms on the ground floor contain only beds, furniture is added as the price goes up. There's a central sociable yard, and food is available.

**$ Karzoo**, Karzoo Lane, T(0)9906-997015. The usual flowery garden; very cheap rooms with shared bath in an old Ladakhi house and modern clean rooms in the new annex (still waiting for the upper storey to be built), but very relaxed and helpful staff, omelette for breakfast. Recommended.

**$ Malpak**, Upper Tukcha Rd, Malpak, T01982-257380, dollayleh@yahoo.co.in. Quaint 6-room guesthouse in an old building, all rooms with attached bath. Shady outdoor tables next to a luxuriant flower and vegetable garden, and a convenient yet peaceful location. Recommended budget choice.

**$ Old Ladakh**, in the Old Town, T01982-252951. 8 rooms around an inner courtyard (varying in comfort), has bags of character with red lacquered windows and doorframes, the odd cracked window, great views from top floor, pleasant atmosphere (old-school vibes).

**$ Palu Guest House**, Changspa, T(0)9419-218674, gurmatpalu@yahoomail.com. Sweet family home, very spacious rooms have clean sheets, carpets and big windows, some have private bath and TV, others share a bathroom, all have working geysers. Particularly attractive flowery garden and veg patch, with shady seating, secluded and set back from Changspa Rd.

**$ Rainbow**, Karzoo. Big clean rooms, some with wonderful views of mountains and Shanti Stupa, hot water in the morning, great hospitality, and lovely garden with restaurant. Rooms in old house share baths, or new wing has en-suite. Recommended.

**$ Saser**, 500-800, Karzoo Lane, T01982-257162, nam_gyal@rediff.com. A good, clean choice with large freshly painted rooms arranged around a grassy garden.

Pay more for new laminate floors, cheerful bed-covers and better bathrooms. There's a generator and breakfast is available.

**$ Shanti Guest House**, below Shanti Stupa, Changspa, T01982-253084. Guesthouse with well-heated rooms, most with great views, very good food, summer/winter treks arranged with guide, free Wi-Fi, friendly Ladakhi family.

**$ Silver Cloud**, by Sankar Gompa, 15 mins' walk from centre, T01982-253128, T(0)9622-175988, silvercloudpsd@hotmail.com. Ladakhi guesthouse with very clean rooms, friendly helpful family, rural homestay atmosphere, excellent food, large garden, open during the winter months. Recommended.

**$ Tsomo-Ri**, Fort Rd, T01982-2252271, www.ladakhtsomori.com. 15 rooms arranged around a central whitewashed courtyard with trellises of runner beans running up the stairs. Surprisingly quiet, rooms have TV, new carpets, plain wood furniture and clean walls – and plenty of good bedding. Wicker chairs for relaxing in courtyard. Very hospitable manager. Good choice.

---

### Thikse *p177*

**$ Chamba**, T01982-267385, www.thiksey monastery.org. Basic chalet rooms with Indian toilets (Rs 500) lie next to a scruffy yard, or the main building has more comfortable rooms (Rs 1200). The garden restaurant makes for a good lunch-break after exploring the monastery.

---

### Hemis *p177*

Many householders take in guests. Not ideal.
**$ Tourist**, camp or sleep on the floor, own sleeping bag, Rs 100; or in the homestay Rs 150 per person. Basic tented restaurant.

---

### Phyang *p179*

**$ Hidden North Guesthouse**, T01982-226007, T(0)9419218055, www.hidden north.com. This sweet guesthouse, set on a hillside, commands marvellous views. There are 7 unfussy clean rooms, most with views, one with private terrace, some with private bath; run by a nice Ladakhi-German couple. Huge shared terrace and garden. Meals available (Rs 70-150). It's perched at the top end of the village, a 5-min uphill walk from the last bus stop. Treks can also be arranged by their responsible outfit.

## Lekir *p180*

The bus directly to the monastery facilitates staying in 1 of 4 options near the monastery. Or, if you are dropped off on NH1, there are half a dozen choices in Lower Likir, about 1 km on dirt tracks from NH1. Hotels all provide dinner and breakfast. Just below the monastery gate is the **Gonpa Restaurant** (0630-2030) for breakfast and reasonably priced Tibetan and Chinese food.

**$$ Lhukhil**, T01982-253588, www.ladakh packages.com. Grand gateway and luxuriant garden, although outdoor seating is on patchy grass next to scary statues and dragon-wrapped pillars. 24 rooms are well-fitted out and comfortable, with towels, toiletries, and some views. Meals included.

**$ Lotos Guesthouse**, T01982-227171, T(0)9469-297990, opposite Hotel Lhukhil, Lower Likir. 3 clean modern rooms with mats over the floor and plenty of warm bedding, sharing a bathroom, nice front garden and fruit trees, food costs extra. Cheap and cheerful.

**$ Norboo Lagams Chow Guesthouse and Camp**, Lower Likir. A bit of a building site, set at the back of a long scruffy orchard (camping possible) with small un-curtained rooms, 1 with bath (no light or toilet seat), others use traditional Ladakhi toilet in the house behind. It's cheap at Rs 300 per double, Rs 70 for dinner in the traditional kitchen-cum-dining room surrounded by pots of all shapes and sizes.

**$ Norboo Spon Guesthouse and Camping**, Lower Likir. Signed off the road to the monastery, or 300 m walk from Lower Likir on the way to the monastery; worth the slight climb if walking. In a large Ladakhi house, roof decked with prayer flags, bright white paint and red trims, set among trees

in a large garden with plenty of seating. Dining-seating area of little tables, rugs and cushions with the odd decorative mask is cosy and homely; shared balcony. Rooms upstairs have good views, cream carpets, wicker chairs and a very decent shared bathroom. Rs 700 double with breakfast and dinner. Charming and kind family.

**$ Old Likir Guesthouse**. A 10-min walk downhill through the fields from the monastery (signed) has 3 rooms (2 upstairs are best). Very simple, in a farming family's home. Mattresses on floor and little else, but fabulous views either of the valley below or the Buddha's back and the monastery above. Rs 300 per person including breakfast and dinner.

**$** A short walk up from the monastery are **Dolker Tongol** and **Chhuma** guesthouses, both basic but with views.

## Alchi *p180*

Alchi has a several guesthouses, some are not great value, but the ones listed here are well-priced for what they offer. It is a pleasant little village with some shops, dhabas, hotel restaurants, and souvenir stalls, none of which are a long walk from the bus stop or the monastery.

**$$ Alchi Resort**, T(0)9419-218636, www.alchi resort.tripod.com. "The first never before hut type twin roomed resort in Ladakh"! Cross over a little bridge after the unattractive main building (restaurant) to a flowery fruit-filled garden edged by whitewashed cottages in adjoining pairs. Well-appointed motel layout rooms differ slightly in configuration, all have flatscreens, laminate wood floors or carpets, plain tiled bathrooms.

**$$-$ Zimskhang Holiday Home**, on the lane to the monastery, T01982-227086, www.zimskhang.com. Some pricier rooms in a large building that is more attractive outside than in, but with appealing public balcony upstairs, clean spacious rooms with flatscreens, bathrooms with marble basin-tops and floors, but by no means swanky. Cheap clean rooms in an older building share modern bathrooms and are good value, but have the potential downside of overlooking the walled-in open-air restaurant.

**$ Choskor**, 15-min walk back along the road towards Leh, T01982-227084, T(0)9419-826363. Set in a lovely garden this colourful guesthouse has rooms ranging from simple doubles with shared baths, to great-value upstairs rooms with attached bath. A roof terrace has rural views, you can eat outdoors in the garden or inside the restaurant with painted motifs on the wall. Campers can set up their tents for Rs 100. Taxi and laundry services available, and they pride themselves on the cleanliness of their sheets.

**$ Heritage Home**, right next to the monastery entrance. A very pleasant and convenient choice. Rooms are large, carpeted, freshly painted, en-suite (hot water in the evening), soap and clean towel (Rs 500). Upstairs is more expensive (Rs 800), there's a decent restaurant out front with apricot trees above.

### Lamayuru *p182*
Most guesthouses are on NH1 in the lower village, with a couple of homestays on the hill towards the monastery. They all provide food, and little **Zambala Restaurant**, on the highway opposite the Dragon Hotel, does surprisingly good chai and *aloo paratha*.

**$$ Ule Ethnic Resort,** Uletokpo, next to the highway 10 km past Saspol, T01982-253640, www.uleresort.com. 15 cottages and 31 posh canvas tents in a well set up eco-resort. It caters mainly to groups, but is worth considering as an alternative night's stop to Alchi.

**$ Dragon**, Lower Rd, T01982-224501, dragon_skyabu@yahoo.com. A range of spacious carpeted rooms, 4 with en-suite by the garden restaurant, 8 with shared bath in the building to the rear, most are south-facing, and room 10 has attractively painted walls. Clean sheets and very reasonably priced (Rs 300-800). Restaurant serves up excellent Indian meals, and has a diverse menu. Internet available (during the 3 hrs of electricity in the evenings), as is hot water.

**$ Lion's Den**, 300 m from the village centre, T01982-224542, lioondenhouse@gamil.com. Ignore the unfinished-concrete ground floor, as upstairs rooms are given warmth by colourful walls, rugs and bedding (shared bath Rs 500). Good views of the weird rock formations in the valley from the 2 corner rooms with attached bath (Rs 700). Little outdoor restaurant with checked cloths has shade or there's a Ladakhi dining room.

**$ Niranjana Hotel**, T01982-224555. Next to the monastery, this institutional-looking hotel has rooms on 3 levels affording excellent valley views. Rooms are plain but comfortable, they take the time to turn down the sheets. All share communal bathrooms which are modern and clean, hot shower in the evenings, restaurant is good.

**$ Tharpaling**, 100 m past the village centre on main road, T01982-224516. The warm family atmosphere is what appeals most to visitors, who are made wonderfully welcome at this simple guesthouse.

### Nubra Valley *p182*
**$$$ Yarab Tso**, Tiger, T(0)9622-820661, www.hotelyarabtso.com. 13 carpeted rooms with private baths and attractive furnishings; in an idyllic setting with large garden, plus very good food.

**$ Olgok**, Hunder, T01980-221092. Large simple rooms are very clean in this homely guesthouse, where the owners go out of their way to be helpful. Fresh food from the quaint garden. Recommended.

**$ Snow Leopard**, Hunder, T01980-221097. Busy yet cosy place with lovely central garden and fruit trees; choice between older (cheaper) and newer rooms.

## 🍴 Restaurants

### Leh *p171, maps p173 and p174*
**$$ Chopsticks Noodle Bar**, Fort Rd. Great East Asian, Tibetan and regional food in a clean and attractive restaurant. Deservedly popular and worth at least 1 visit when in Leh.

**$$-$ Booklovers' Retreat**, Changspa. Perennial favourite as cosy place for food and hanging out. There's a roof terrace.

**$$-$ Il Forno**, Zangsti Rd. Serves up pretty decent pizzas, pastas and there's beer too.

**$$-$ La Pizzeria**, Changspa Rd, Changspa. Pretty authentic pizza, very pleasant ambiance, some mattress seating, and soft lantern light at night.

**$$-$ Mona Lisa**, Fort Rd. International food covers all bases (pizzas, momos, garlic cheese bread), particularly recommended for tandori selection. Nice atmosphere under lamps on the terrace.

**$$-$ Nirvana Café**. Live music after 2100. Indoor and outdoor seating under lanterns and fairy lights, some Sinai-style slouching areas. Laid-back vibe and varied menu of South Asian, Asian and lots of Italian, prices slightly higher than average. No alcohol.

**$$-$ Open Hand Espresso Bar & Bistro**, off Fort Rd, www.openhand.in. A chic retreat, with loungers and seating on decking by an active vegetable garden, chunky wood furniture inside, great cakes, cappuccinos and home-cooked meals, healthy smoothies and more. Ethical shopping – clothes, silks, cushions, gifts etc – plus wireless connection.

**$ Chansa Traditional Ladakhi Kitchen**, next to Chokhang Vihara, off Main Bazar. A chance to try traditional Ladakhi cuisine (vegetarian); simple indoor seating, or outside under the shade of a parachute. Whiteboard shows the day's dishes, such as *sku* – a delicious chunky wholewheat pasta and veg broth, plus limited offerings of Chinese, Indian (great mushroom masala) and Western food. Cheap and tasty.

**$ High Life Tibetan Restaurant**, Fort Rd. Exceptional range of high quality Tibetan food, plus good salads and Western dishes, inviting indoor seating with gingham table cloths or big outdoor area.

**$ Lala's Art Café**, off Main Bazar, Old Town. Quaint restored Ladakhi house in the Old Town with a roof terrace, and shrine on the ground floor. Coffee and cakes are the order of the day.

**$ Local Food Café**, see page 175. Mon-Sat 1100-1630. Serves good Ladakhi snacks, while promoting traditional farming methods threatened by the modern cash economy, run by the Women's Alliance.

**$ Mentokling Apple Garden**, Changspa Road, Zangsti. Great paratha breakfasts, good menu generally, with Indian and Thai dishes, lovely garden. Free Wi-Fi with orders over Rs100.

**$ Shubh Panjabi Dhaba**, Main Bazar. Typical Sikh-style *thalis* and cheap dishes in a basic restaurant; half-plates available, great lassis and good paratha breakfasts.

**$ Tenzin Dickey**, Fort Rd. Delicious *kothay* (fried *momos*), soups, and other Tibetan/Chinese dishes, some Western food, all veg, and the Tibetan herbal tea is pretty good. Simple and neat little place with checked table cloths.

**$ Tibetan Friend's Corner**, Main St, Bazar. Clean and cheerful, *kothay* and wide menu of Tibetan/Chinese veg and non-veg, thick pancakes and great hot drinks, locally popular.

**$** Also recommended are the kebab stalls near the mosque.

### Bakeries

Four German bakeries sell good bread (trekking bread keeps for a week) and excellent cakes and muesli. There are also traditional ovens turning out delicious local bread in the laneway next to the Museum, behind the mosque.

**Pumpernickel**, Zangsti Rd. The original German bakery is the best and friendliest, indoor/outdoor seating, excellent apricot and apple crumble/pie, message board for trekkers.

### Alchi *p180*

**$$-$ Zimskhang** and **Heritage** both have good drop-in restaurants, other hotels provide meals when there are guests.

**$ Golden Oriole German Bakery**, has good cake selection but doesn't always have bread; serves Chinese and Indian dishes, pizza, good place for breakfast, same menu as Zimskhang but at lower prices; terrace is a nice place to sit and watch folks pass on their way to the monastery.

There are a couple of *dhabas* near the bus stop, although the **Tibetan** has bad chowmein. **Dil Dil Restaurant**, opposite the Tibetan, is kept clean and does cheap daal, veg and rice. Most shops near bus stop also serve omelettes/daal/chai, and sell strong beer.

## ◉ Entertainment

**Leh** *p171, maps p173 and p174*
Ladakhi dancing and singing, below entrance to the palace, by Soma Gompa, 1730 (1 hr), Rs 200.

## ✿ Festivals

**Leh** *p171, maps p173 and p174*
Dates vary depending on the lunar calendar.
**Apr-May** Buddha Purnima marks the Buddha's birth, at full moon.
**Sep** Ladakh Festival. The main events are held in the Leh polo grounds with smaller events in other districts. Usually during the 1st 2 weeks in Sep, there are dances, displays of traditional costumes, handicrafts, Ladakhi plays, archery and polo matches.
**Dec** Celebration of Losar which originated in the 15th century to protect people before going to battle.

**Hemis** *p177*
**Jun** Hemis Tsechu is perhaps the biggest cultural festival in Ladakh. It commemorates the birth of **Guru Padmasambhava** who is believed to have fought local demons to protect the people. Young and old of both sexes join *lamas* in masked dance-dramas, while stalls sell handicrafts A colourful display of Ladakhi Buddhist culture, it attracts large numbers of foreign visitors.

## ◉ Shopping

**Leh** *p171, maps p173 and p174*
Please use your own bags. Plastic bags are not allowed in the bazar as they were finding their way into streams when not piled on unsightly heaps.

In **Dzomsa** you can get water refill, dispose of batteries, get laundry done and there's organic goods available. Also at the **Ecological Shop for Organic Products** you can stock up on local produce including apricot jam, fruit and nuts in season, bottled juice.

**Leh Bazar** is full of shops and market stalls selling curios, clothes and knick-knacks. Tea and *chang* (local barley brew) vessels, knitted carpets with Tibetan designs, Tibetan jewellery, prayer flags, musical bowls and pashminas are all available. Prices are high especially in Kashmiri shops so bargain vigorously. There are tight restrictions on the export of anything over 100 years old. Baggage is checked at the airport partly for this reason. However, even though most items are antique-looking, they are, in fact, fresh from the backstreet workshops.

### Books
**Leh-Ling Bookshop**, near the Post Office, Main Bazar. Good selection, especially on trekking in the region.
**Book Worm**, second-hand books, coffee table books and fiction.

## ◉ What to do

**Leh** *p171, maps p173 and p174*
### Archery
The **Archery Stadium** is nearby where winter competitions attract large crowds; the target is a hanging white clay tablet.

### Meditation
**Mahabodhi Meditation Centre**, Changspa Lane, off Changspa Rd, www.mahabodhi-ladakh.com. Enquire about short courses and yoga classes.

## Polo

Polo, the 'national' sport, is popular in the summer and is played in the polo ground east of the city. The local version which is fast and rough appears to follow no rules! The Polo Club is the highest in the world and worth a visit.

## Tour operators

Women on their own should take special care when arranging a tour with a driver/guide.
**Eco-Adventures**, New Delhi, T011-4772 550, www.theecoadventures.com. Tailor-made and group tours.
**Explore Himalayas**, Main Bazar (opposite SBI), T01982-252727, www.explore himalayas.com. Recommended, normally excellent crew though some reports of inept guides, friendly, good to animals, environment conscious.
**K2**, Hill Top Building, Main Bazar, T01982-253980, www.k2adventureleh.com. Good rates for treks (Markha Valley), very friendly, environment conscious.
**Rimo Expeditions**, Kang-lha Chen Hotel, T01982-253348, www.rimoexpeditions.com. Insightful and informative about the local area, running a whole host of treks, as well as mountain biking, mountaineering, river rafting, cultural tours and family holidays. The best of the lot. Highly recommended.
**Shakti Experiences**, Gurgaon, Delhi, T0124 456 3899, www.shaktihimalaya.com. Sensitively run sustainable tours and personalized treks to remote villages 30 km from Leh in the rugged high mountains of Ladakh. Luxurious but understated.
**Travel the Unknown**, London, UK, www.traveltheunknown.com. Eco-conscious and off-the-beaten track tours, award-winning company, with a couple of regular trips to Ladakh each year.
**Yama Treks**, Leh, www.yamatreks.com. Efficient, run by the very personable Mr Rinchen Namgial; cultural tours as well as treks. Recommended.

## Whitewater rafting and kayaking

Possible on the Tsarap Chu, Indus and Zanskar rivers from mid-Jun; the upper reaches of the former (Grade IV rapids) are suitable for experienced rafters only, though the remaining stretch can be enjoyed by all. Along the Indus: Hemis to Choglamsar (easy, very scenic); Phey-Nimmu (Grade III); Nimmu-Khaltse (professional). Ensure that life jackets and wet suits are provided. Half to full day, including transport and lunch, Rs 1000-1500.

## ⊖ Transport

**Leh** *p171, maps p173 and p174*
**Air** The small airport is 5 km away on Srinagar Rd. It is surrounded by hills on 3 sides and the flight over the mountain ranges is spectacular. Transport to town by taxi is around Rs 200.

Allow 2 hrs for check in. Weather conditions may deteriorate rapidly even in the summer resulting in flight cancellations (especially outside Jul and Aug) so always be prepared for a delay or to take alternative road transport out of Ladakh. Furthermore, the airlines fly quite full planes into Leh but can take fewer passengers out because of the high-altitude take-off. This adds to the difficulty of getting a flight out. **Book your tickets as soon as possible** (several months ahead for Jul and Aug).

Air India, office near Shambhala Hotel, T01982-252076, flies to/from **Delhi**, also Jet Airways, Go Air, Spicejet and JetKonnect. To **Srinagar**, direct on Wed, with Air India.
**Local bus** The Bus Stand is near the cemetery. The vehicles are ramshackle but the fares are low. See under monasteries for details. Enquiries J&KSRTC, T01982-252285.
**Long distance** Leh is connected to Manali via Keylong and to Srinagar, via Kargil, by state highways. Both roads can be seriously affected by landslides, causing long delays. The Leh–Srinagar road is also often blocked by army convoys. **Himachal**

Tourism runs regular Deluxe buses between Manali and Leh, 530 km, usually mid-Jun to end Sep. Book at HPTDC Office, 1st Floor, Fort Rd, T(0)9622-374300, a/c Volvo, leaves alternate days at 0500 from opposite the J&K Bank, Fort Rd, overnight in Keylong (Rs 1500); J&K SRTC run ordinary/deluxe buses (Rs 585/850), gruelling journey departs 0430, booked at bus stand, stop overnight at Keylong. J&K SRTC bus **Kargil**, 230 km, 0430, 10 hrs, Rs 300, **Srinagar** 434 km, 1400, 20 hrs, Rs 92.

**Shared jeeps** or **minibuses** make the journey to **Manali** in 1 day, leaving at between 0000-0200 taking 22-24 hrs, costing about Rs 1500 per seat. Jeeps leave from the Old Bus Station, to **Srinagar** at 1700, 15 hrs (Rs 1400); to **Kargil** at 0700, 8-9 hrs (Rs 650). Book seats a day in advance, worth paying the extra for front seats.

**Warning** If you have already spent some time in the Himalaya, you may be better acclimatized, but a mild headache is common and can be treated with aspirin or paracetamol. Drink plenty of fluids on journeys.

The road to **Manali**, crossing some very high passes, is open mid-Jun or early Jul, until end Sep (depending on the weather) and takes 2 days by bus. Road conditions may be poor in places. Departure from Leh can be early (0400) with overnight stop in Keylong; next day to Manali. Alternatively, camp in Sarchu (10 hrs from Leh), or Jespa; next day 14 hrs to Manali (charge Rs 800-1200 per night in Sarchu). Roadside tents provide food en route during the tourist season; carry snacks, water and a good sleeping bag when planning to camp. Many travellers find the mountain roads extremely frightening and they are comparatively dangerous. Some are cut out of extremely unstable hillsides, usually with nothing between the road's edge and the near-vertical drop below; parts remain rough and pot-holed and during the monsoons, landslides and rivers can make it impassable for 2-3 days. It is also a long and uncomfortable journey, but there is some spectacular scenery.

**Taxi** 4WD between Leh and Manali are expensive but recommended if you want to stop en route to visit monasteries. 2-day trip, about Rs 15,000. Taxis often return empty to Manali (some visitors choose to fly out of Leh) so may agree a reduced fare for the return leg. Officially, Manali (or Srinagar) taxis are allowed to carry their passengers to and from Leh but are not permitted to do local tours, a rule fiercely monitored by the Leh Taxi Operators' Union.

**Tourist taxi and jeep** Ladakh Taxi Operators' Union, 1st Floor at bus stand, T01982-252723, open 0700-1900 daily, with fixed-rate fares, e.g. to Stok for Rs 1200. A day's taxi hire to visit nearby *gompas* can also be arranged through travel agents.

### Alchi *p180*
**Bus** One daily direct bus from **Leh** in summer, 1500, 3 hrs, returns around 0700. **Srinagar**-bound buses stop at **Saspol**; from there it is a 2.5-km walk across the bridge.

## ◉ Directory

**Leh** *p171, maps p173 and p174*
**Banks** J&K Bank, Main Bazar, with ATM; State Bank of India, slow exchange and temperamental ATM, next to tourist office. **Medical services** SNM Hospital, T01982-252014, 0900-1700 is well-equipped (also for advice on mountain sickness), after hours, T01982-253629. During the day, doctors have little time; better at clinics in evenings, get advice from your hotel. **Post** There is a Tourist Post Office on Main Bazar. **Useful contacts** Deputy Commisioner's Office, for Inner Line Permits: T01982-252010. Take passport, copies of visa and personal details pages and 2 photos.

# Contents

198 Index

Footnotes

# Index

**A**

accidents 17
accommodation 12
    price codes 13
air travel 6, 7
Akhand Path 71
Alchi 161, 180
alcohol 14
Amritsar 67
    Golden Temple 69
Anandpur Sahib 62, 66
Andretta 129
Atholi 144
Attargo 91
Aut 94, 95
auto-rickshaws 11

**B**

Babur 63
Bahrmaur 148
Baijnath 128
Bajaura Temple 101
Banganga 152
Banjar 95, 143
Baragarh Peak 103
Baralacha La 143
Baralacha La, Pas 120
Barseni 103
Barseri 89
Basgo 161, 180
Bashleo Pass 143
Baspa Valley 87, 145
Bassi 128
Batal 93, 144
Beas River 93
Bema 184
Bhabha Valley 87, 145
Bhagsu 126
Bhakra-Nangal Dam 93
Bhararighat 93
Bharmaur 148
Biama 184
Bijli Mahadev 101
Bilaspur 93
Bir 128
Bose, Nandalal 33
Brahmaur 148
Brahmavarta 63
Brahmpukar 93
Brandy Nala 120

**C**

car hire 10
Cha Cha La 187
Chail 79
Chaini 95
Chamba 130
Chamba Valley 129
Chandigarh 60

Chandratal 144
Chhalal 102
Chharabra 79, 143
Chhatru 93, 144
Chhota Dhara 93
Chitkul 89
Choglamsar 176
Chokhapani 145
Chos Khor Gompa 90
Chumchar 188
climate 6
Connaught Place, Delhi 37
currency 18
    exchange rates 19
Curzon, Lord 143
customs regulations 17

**D**

Dachigam National Park
    157
Dalai Lama 122, 124
Dalhousie 129
Dal Lake 156
Danes Folly 79
Dankar 91
Daora 93
Darcha 120, 143
Delhi 23-58
    activities 54
    Baha'i Temple 44
    Chandni Chowk 27
    Connaught Place 37
    entertainment 51
    festivals 51
    Gandhi Museum 37
    Gurudwara Bangla Sahib
        39
    Hauz Khas 41
    Hazrat Nizamuddin 40
    history 25
    hotels 46
    Humayun's Tomb 40
    India Gate 33
    Jama Masjid 32
    Jantar Mantar 39
    Lakshmi Narayan
        Mandir 38
    Lodi Gardens 39
    Lotus Temple 44
    markets 53
    Memorial Ghats 39
    National Gallery of
        Modern Art 33
    National Museum 36
    Nehru Memorial
        Museum 36
    New Delhi 33
    nightlife 50
    Old Delhi 27

Parliament House 37
    Qutb Minar Complex 41
    Rashtrapati Bhavan 36
    Red Fort 27
    restaurants 48
    transport 55
Deo Tibba 146
Deskit 183
Dha 184
Dhanchho 148
Dharamkot 126
Dharamshala 122
dharma 63
Dhauladhar 126
Dhungri Village 106
Diskit 188
drinks 14
driving 10
Drokpha 182, 184
drugs 17
dukhang 179
Durga 112

**E**

earthquakes 81
electricity 17
embassies 17
emergencies 17
exchange rate 19

**F**

festivals 15
food 13
fossils 92
Fotu La 161

**G**

Gaggal 142
Gandha La 185
Garden of Nek Chand 62
Gelugpa 177, 179, 187
Gete 146
Ghaghas 93
Ghanahatti 93
Ghayaghi 95
Goindwal 73
Gondhla 117
Gongmaru La 185
Goshiani 96
Gramphoo 93, 117
Granth Sahib, Guru 71
Great Himalayan National
    Park 95
Gulmarg 157
Gyephang 93

**H**

Hadimba Devi Temple 106
Hadsar 148
Hamta Pass 144

Hankar 185
Hazratbal 157
health 17
Hemis 177
Hemis High Altitude
    National Park 186
Hikim 92
Himachal 122
    trekking 143
Hindustan Tibet Road 80
holidays 15
homestays 13
hotels 12
    price codes 13
houseboats 163

**I**

ibex, Siberian 92
Iltutmish Tomb 43
immigration 22

**J**

Jahlma 118
Jallianwala Bagh 72
Jallianwala Bagh massacre
    72
Jalori Pass 95, 143
Jamlu 147
Jammu 150
Jangi 89
Jari 146
Jawalamukhi 128
Jhakhri 81
Jhelum River 163
Jibhi 95
Jispa 120
Jogindernagar 128

**K**

Kafnoo 87, 145
Kalatope 130
Kalka 79
Kalpa 89
Kamelong 92
Kang La 144
Kangra 127
Kangra Valley 126
Kangra Valley Railway 75
Karchham 87
Kareri Lake 126
Kargil 159
Karsha 187
Karu 188
Karzog 184
Kashmir Valley 150
Kasol 102, 147
Katrain 103
kayaking 195
Kaza 92, 146
Keylong 119

Khab 90
Khajjiar 130
Khalsa 63
Khaltse 161, 184
Khardung La 183
Khirganga 103, 147
Khoksar 117
Khurna River 187
Kibber-Gete Wildlife
    Sanctuary 92
Kilar 144
Kinnaur 87, 144
Kinner Kailash 89
Kolong 120
Konze La 186
Kothi 89, 117
Kufri 79
Kullu 100
Kullu Valley 93, 100
    trekking 146
Kungri 91
Kunzum La 93, 145
Kurukshetra 63

L
Lachalung La Pass 120
Ladakh 171
Lahaul 116, 143
Lal Qila 27
Lalung Gompa 91
Lamayuru 161, 182
language 18
Larji Gorge 95
Le Corbusier 61
Leh 114, 171
Lekir (Likir) 161, 180
Lingti Valley 92
Losar 93

M
Malana 146, 147
Manali 103, 104
Manali–Leh road 116
Mandi 93
Manikaran 102
Manimahesh 148
Markha 185
Masrur 128
McLeodganj 126
Mikkim 91
Minamarg 161
Miyar Nullah 144
money 18
Morang 89
Mount Gya 92
Mudh 145, 147
Mulbek 161

N
Naddi Gaon 126
Naggar 104
Nakli La, Pas 120
Nako 90

Nalagarh 80
Naldera 79, 143
Namgyal Monastery 123
Namika La 161
Namlung La 184
Narkanda 80, 143
Nathpa 81
Nimaling 185
Nimmu 161, 179
Norbulingka Institute 124
Nubra Valley 182, 187
Nur Jahan 156
Nyona 182

P
Padum 143, 144, 160
Pahalgam 158
Palampur 128
Panamik 183
Pandoh 95
Pang 120
Pangi 89
Pangi Valley 144
Pangong-Tso 183
Panipat 63
Parvati Valley 101
Pattan Valley 118
Pensi La 160
Peon 94
Phugtal Monastery 187
Phyang 161, 179
Pinjore 62
Pin Valley 91, 145, 147
Pin Valley National Park 92
Pir Panjal 148
polo 195
Pragpur 128
Prashar 94
Prini 108
prohibitions 17
Puga 184
Puh 89
Pulga 103
Purni 187

R
rafting 195
Rajpath 33
Rakh 148
Rampur 143
Rampur Bushahr 80
Rashtrapati Bhavan 36
Ravi River 93
Recong Peo 89
restaurants 13
    price codes 13
Rizong 161
Rohalla Falls 117
Rohtang Pass 117
Rubarung La 187
Ruding 118
Rumjack 187
Rupshu 184

S
Sach Pass 144
safety 20
saffron 89
Sahor 93
Sahoor 93
Samtanling 183
Sangam 92
Sangla 88
sapphire 144
Sarahan 81
Sarchu 120
Saspol 161
Seraj 143
Sethan 107
Shah Jahan 157
Shalaghat 93
Shalimar Bagh 156
Shankaracharya Hill 156
Shansha 118
Shanti Stupa 175
Shargol 161
Shey 176
Shichling 91
Shingo La 143, 187
Shogdu 185
Shrikhand Mahadev peak 81
Shyok Valley 187
Singh, Sobha 129
Singi La 187
skiing 79
Sojha 95
Solang 107
Sonamarg 158
Spiti 90, 145
Spiti River 89
Spituk 161, 179, 184
Srinagar 152
Srinagar Road, monasteries
    178
Srinagar to Leh road 160
Stakna 177
Stok 176
Sumdo 90, 145
Sumdo Chenmo 186
Sutlej River 93
Swaminarayan Akshardham
    45

T
Tabo 90, 146
Taglang La Pass 120
Tandi 118
Tangyar 188
Tapri 87
Tarn Taran 73
Tashigang 92
taxis 11
tea 14
Teh 120
telephone 21
Thangi 145

Thikse 177
Thirot 118
Tiger 183
time 21
tipping 21
Tirthan Sanctuary 95
Tirthan Valley 95
tourist information 21
train travel 8
transport 6-11
travel tips, bus 10
trekking
    Chamba 148
    Himachal Pradesh 143
    Kangra 147
    Kinnaur 143
    Kullu Valley 146
    Ladakh 184
    Lahaul 143
    Parvati Valley 146
    Spiti 143
    Zanskar 186
Trilokinath 119, 148
Triund 126
Tsokar 184
Tso-Moriri 184
Tsuglhakhang 90
Tughluqabad 27

U
Udaipur 119
Udeypur 119, 144, 148
Una 93
Upper Mulling 145
Utse 185

V
vaccinations 18
Vaishno Devi 151
Valley of the Gods 100
Vashisht 106
visas 22

W
Wagah 73
Wakha Gorge 161
Wangtu 87
water, drinking 14

Z
Zangla 187
Zanskar 159
Zingchen Valley 184
Zingzingbar 120

# Titles available in the Footprint *Focus* range

| Latin America | UK RRP | US RRP |
|---|---|---|
| Bahia & Salvador | £7.99 | $11.95 |
| Brazilian Amazon | £7.99 | $11.95 |
| Brazilian Pantanal | £6.99 | $9.95 |
| Buenos Aires & Pampas | £7.99 | $11.95 |
| Cartagena & Caribbean Coast | £7.99 | $11.95 |
| Costa Rica | £8.99 | $12.95 |
| Cuzco, La Paz & Lake Titicaca | £8.99 | $12.95 |
| El Salvador | £5.99 | $8.95 |
| Guadalajara & Pacific Coast | £6.99 | $9.95 |
| Guatemala | £8.99 | $12.95 |
| Guyana, Guyane & Suriname | £5.99 | $8.95 |
| Havana | £6.99 | $9.95 |
| Honduras | £7.99 | $11.95 |
| Nicaragua | £7.99 | $11.95 |
| Northeast Argentina & Uruguay | £8.99 | $12.95 |
| Paraguay | £5.99 | $8.95 |
| Quito & Galápagos Islands | £7.99 | $11.95 |
| Recife & Northeast Brazil | £7.99 | $11.95 |
| Rio de Janeiro | £8.99 | $12.95 |
| São Paulo | £5.99 | $8.95 |
| Uruguay | £6.99 | $9.95 |
| Venezuela | £8.99 | $12.95 |
| Yucatán Peninsula | £6.99 | $9.95 |

| Asia | UK RRP | US RRP |
|---|---|---|
| Angkor Wat | £5.99 | $8.95 |
| Bali & Lombok | £8.99 | $12.95 |
| Chennai & Tamil Nadu | £8.99 | $12.95 |
| Chiang Mai & Northern Thailand | £7.99 | $11.95 |
| Goa | £6.99 | $9.95 |
| Gulf of Thailand | £8.99 | $12.95 |
| Hanoi & Northern Vietnam | £8.99 | $12.95 |
| Ho Chi Minh City & Mekong Delta | £7.99 | $11.95 |
| Java | £7.99 | $11.95 |
| Kerala | £7.99 | $11.95 |
| Kolkata & West Bengal | £5.99 | $8.95 |
| Mumbai & Gujarat | £8.99 | $12.95 |

| Africa & Middle East | UK RRP | US RRP |
|---|---|---|
| Beirut | £6.99 | $9.95 |
| Cairo & Nile Delta | £8.99 | $12.95 |
| Damascus | £5.99 | $8.95 |
| Durban & KwaZulu Natal | £8.99 | $12.95 |
| Fès & Northern Morocco | £8.99 | $12.95 |
| Jerusalem | £8.99 | $12.95 |
| Johannesburg & Kruger National Park | £7.99 | $11.95 |
| Kenya's Beaches | £8.99 | $12.95 |
| Kilimanjaro & Northern Tanzania | £8.99 | $12.95 |
| Luxor to Aswan | £8.99 | $12.95 |
| Nairobi & Rift Valley | £7.99 | $11.95 |
| Red Sea & Sinai | £7.99 | $11.95 |
| Zanzibar & Pemba | £7.99 | $11.95 |

| Europe | UK RRP | US RRP |
|---|---|---|
| Bilbao & Basque Region | £6.99 | $9.95 |
| Brittany West Coast | £7.99 | $11.95 |
| Cádiz & Costa de la Luz | £6.99 | $9.95 |
| Granada & Sierra Nevada | £6.99 | $9.95 |
| Languedoc: Carcassonne to Montpellier | £7.99 | $11.95 |
| Málaga | £5.99 | $8.95 |
| Marseille & Western Provence | £7.99 | $11.95 |
| Orkney & Shetland Islands | £5.99 | $8.95 |
| Santander & Picos de Europa | £7.99 | $11.95 |
| Sardinia: Alghero & the North | £7.99 | $11.95 |
| Sardinia: Cagliari & the South | £7.99 | $11.95 |
| Seville | £5.99 | $8.95 |
| Sicily: Palermo & the Northwest | £7.99 | $11.95 |
| Sicily: Catania & the Southeast | £7.99 | $11.95 |
| Siena & Southern Tuscany | £7.99 | $11.95 |
| Sorrento, Capri & Amalfi Coast | £6.99 | $9.95 |
| Skye & Outer Hebrides | £6.99 | $9.95 |
| Verona & Lake Garda | £7.99 | $11.95 |

| North America | UK RRP | US RRP |
|---|---|---|
| Vancouver & Rockies | £8.99 | $12.95 |

| Australasia | UK RRP | US RRP |
|---|---|---|
| Brisbane & Queensland | £8.99 | $12.95 |
| Perth | £7.99 | $11.95 |

For the latest books, e-books and a wealth of travel information, visit us at: www.footprinttravelguides.com.

**footprint**travelguides.com

Join us on facebook for the latest travel news, product releases, offers and amazing competitions: www.facebook.com/footprintbooks.